Introduction to Environmental Economics

Introduction to Environmental Economics

SECOND EDITION

Professor Nick Hanley
Professor of Economics, University of Stirling

Professor Jason F. Shogren
Stroock Professor of Natural Resource Conservation and
Management, University of Wyoming

Dr Ben White
Professor in the School of Agricultural and Resource Economics,
University of Western Australia

OXFORD
UNIVERSITY PRESS

OXFORD

UNIVERSITY PRESS

Great Clarendon Street, Oxford, OX2 6DP,
United Kingdom

Oxford University Press is a department of the University of Oxford.
It furthers the University's objective of excellence in research, scholarship,
and education by publishing worldwide. Oxford is a registered trade mark of
Oxford University Press in the UK and in certain other countries

© Nick Hanley, Jason F. Shogren, and Ben White 2013

The moral rights of the authors have been asserted

First Edition copyright 2001

Impression: 2

British Library Cataloguing in Publication Data

Data available

Library of Congress Cataloging in Publication Data

Data available

ISBN 978–0–19–956873–4

Printed in Great Britain by
Bell & Bain Ltd, Glasgow

Acknowledgements

The authors thank staff at OUP for all their hard work and encouragement. Nick thanks Mik Czajkowski and Dervla Brennan for help on several chapters, and Jack Pezzey for many discussions. He also thanks the Crawford School, Australian National University, for their hospitality whilst writing the final drafts. Ben would like to thank Michael Burton for his insights into environmental economics and Deborah Swindells for administrative support. Jason thanks his teachers and students over the years for their willingness to share ideas, agreeably and otherwise.

New to this Edition

Building on the success of the first edition, the second edition of an *Introduction to Environmental Economics* features the following updated material:

- Substantial revision of all existing chapters
- Greater focus on environmental policy and management links to policy issues which have recently emerged
- Updating of box sections with recent findings from the literature
- New pedagogical features including tutorial questions and definitions.

PRAISE FOR THE BOOK

'It bases heavily on empirical evidence and also provides an extensive number of examples, which explain well definitions mentioned in the text.'

Leon Vinokur, Queen Mary, University of London

'The writing style is of a high quality and is pitched at the appropriate level for an introduction to Environmental Economics. Economic concepts are introduced using easy-to-understand language and examples.'

Professor Mike Christie, Aberystwyth University

Detailed Contents

List of Boxes

List of Figures

List of Tables

Part I

Economic Tools for the Environment

Introduction: Economics *for* the Environment

Welcome! The title of this chapter is 'Economics *for* the Environment'. Why? Because we believe that economics has an important contribution to make in helping us understand and solve the many environmental problems facing people throughout the world today. People often equate 'economics' with 'financial and commercial', yet economics is as much about Main Street as it is about Wall Street. Economic arguments can often be used to help protect the environment, rather than harm it. In Part I of this book, we set out the principal insights that economics has to offer. Then, in Part II, we take a range of important environmental problems, and show how these insights can improve how people respond to these problems. We believe strongly that an environmental policy that does not address the economic behaviour of consumers and firms is likely to get things badly wrong. Often, economic actors can be induced to take account of their impacts on the environment, by getting prices on environmental goods and services right. Economic and environmental systems are closely interlinked: by not addressing economic insights, we are unlikely to produce cost-effective outcomes for either system.

People are paying more attention to the environmental consequences of economic activity, and to the economic value of the environment. Partly, this is due to greater public awareness of environmental issues such as climate change or the loss of treasured local landscapes. Partly, it is a consequence of the increasing interest of policy-makers to understand the benefits and costs of environmental regulation. People have started to care and know more about environmental degradation and the benefits of ecosystem services. Sustainable development and green growth have become key concepts within many public policy pronouncements, yet the usefulness of these concepts is unclear—whilst predictions of impending doom due to world population increases and climate change continue to circulate. Given our belief that economics has an important, indeed vital, contribution to make in understanding these issues and the trade-offs that lie behind them, we think that a book that tries to get the basic ideas across to a wide audience seems a good idea.

This is the second edition of a book first published in 2001. Since then, public debates over climate change (the evidence for it, and what to do about it) have greatly increased, whilst there has been a growing awareness since the Millennium Ecosystem Assessment of the benefits that ecosystems provide to people. Many countries have greatly expanded their renewable energy capacities, whilst global targets on reducing biodiversity losses have not been achieved. The links between the increasing scale of global economic activity, trade, and environmental quality continue to be debated. We thus felt that there was still a need for an introductory-level textbook that explains the contributions that economics can make to understanding and resolving these problems. In revising the text, we have taken account of both the evolution of environmental issues and the advances in environmental economics since the first edition appeared. We have also tried to take into account feedback from people who have used our textbook, both students and faculty.

In the rest of this chapter, we:

- Discuss the connections between the economy and the environment.
- Review ten key insights from environmental and resource economics that environmental scientists, managers, and politicians ought to be aware of.
- Explain how this book is best used.
- Provide an overview of what happens in the rest of the book.

1.1 The Economy and the Environment

This book explores why economics matters more to environmental and natural resource policy than many people think. To begin with, it is important to say that economics is not just about financial comings and goings within markets: the 'unpriced' or non-market services that the natural environment provides us with are equally its concern. The value of protecting wetlands for their biodiversity, flood defence, and pollution treatment functions is just as much an economic value as this week's production of oil from a Texas oilfield.

Next, people can benefit from a better appreciation of how the economy and the environment are interlinked. The economy operates from inside the environmental system, with conditions in the two systems being simultaneously determined in an evolving, dynamic way. By 'the economy', we mean all the firms that make up industry; households (people) in their twin roles as consumers and suppliers of labour; governments; the institutions that govern interactions between these groups, such as markets; the state of technology; and our stocks of produced capital (such as roads and space stations). By 'the environment', we mean all natural resources found in the biosphere, including land, land cover, and ecosystems (flora and fauna); resource deposits under the land surface; the world's oceans and atmosphere; and the natural climate and nutrient cycles. As Figure 1.1 shows, there are many links between these two systems.

First, the environment provides the economic system with *inputs* of raw material and energy resources, including minerals, metals, food, hydrocarbons, and fibres such as wood and cotton. These resources may be either non-renewable—such as coal or iron ore—or renewable, such as fisheries or forests. Inputs are transformed by the economic system into outputs that consumers demand—wood into paper and oil into petrol, for example.

Second, the economy uses the environment as a *waste sink*. Wastes may originate from either production processes, such as CO_2 from electricity generation; or from consumption activities, for instance, when households put out the garbage for collection and disposal. Wastes come in a number of basic types—solid, air-, or water borne—and the environment has a limited assimilative capacity to absorb and transform some wastes into harmless

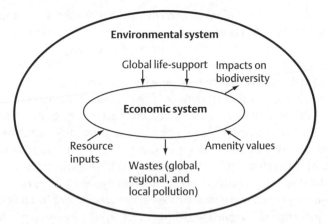

Figure 1.1 Economy–environment interactions.

substances. Pollution is said to occur when emissions exceed assimilative capacity, and produce some undesirable impact.

Third, the environment provides households with a direct source of *amenity*. People derive utility (happiness, satisfaction) from the contemplation of scenic beauty and wildlife, and from hiking and fishing. As Chapter 3 makes clear, these direct utility impacts are both important and relevant from an economics viewpoint.

Finally, the environment provides the economic system with basic life-support services. Since the Millennium Ecosystem Assessment, these services have increasingly been referred to as *ecosystem services*. These include climate regulation, the operation of the water cycle, the regulation of atmospheric composition, and nutrient cycling.

One obvious point is that if the economy increases its demand on the environment with regard to any one of these four service flows, this can impact on the environment's ability to provide other services. For example:

- An increase in the use of the environment as a waste sink due to increased emissions of pollutants may reduce the environment's ability to supply basic life-support by interfering with climate regulation; or may reduce the amenity value of the environment by degrading wildlife populations.

- An increase in demand on the environment for resource inputs may mean a reduction in amenity flows; for example, if quarries are developed in national parks or as logging reduces the area of rainforest.

- We also show a link in Figure 1.1 between the economy and *biodiversity*. This shows that economic activity can affect natural diversity, most notably by taking over habitats (e.g. when a rainforest is turned into a gold mine). Diversity is thought to be an important property of natural systems, especially with regard to their ability to withstand shocks such as drought and fire (this property is sometimes known as *resilience*). Thus, ultimately, reductions in biodiversity can have direct and indirect effects on human well-being.

An important feature of the interdependent economic–environmental system is co-evolution. This means that the way in which the economic subsystem evolves over time depends on the changing conditions of the environmental subsystem, and vice versa. A good illustration of this, in terms of impacts of the changing environment on the evolution of the economy, concerns climate change in Neolithic Scotland. In around 4000 BC, Neolithic farmers settled many parts of the west coast of Scotland, including islands such as Arran. The prosperity of this society may be seen from the large stone monuments they erected. Substantial land-cover alterations occurred, notably the onset of clearing land of trees.[1] However, as the climate became cooler, crop growth rates declined and the land became harder to subsist in. Areas of peat bog began to expand. Settlements became abandoned as people moved east and south: the evolution of economic activity was changed by exogenous alterations in environmental conditions (Whittington and Edwards, 1997).

Environmental systems may change for reasons endogenous to the economic system as well as in response to exogenous factors such as climate change. For instance, in nineteenth-century Egypt, a change to irrigated agriculture in the Nile valley to produce cotton for exporting, away from the system of natural flooding that had been in use since 5000 BC, resulted in the increasing salinity of farmland, and its eventual abandonment. Overexploitation of farmlands in areas as diverse as Mesopotamia, Easter Island, the Indus valley, and the Mayan civilization of Central America caused food production crashes that changed the course of the development of entire societies (Ponting, 1991).

Economic changes also impact on ecosystem evolution. Examples include the following:

- *Introductions of invasive species.* For instance, the introduction of possums from Australia to New Zealand, and earlier introductions of rats and stoats, have changed the types and abundance of flora and fauna there. Zebra mussels invading the Great Lakes of the United States have transformed the basic nature of freshwater ecosystem services.

- *Changes in aquatic ecosystems.* Changes took place as the Industrial Revolution unfolded in nineteenth-century Britain. The resultant increased sulphur deposition via acid rain reduced pH values in lakes and lochs, changing the composition of vertebrate and invertebrate fauna over time.

1.2 Key Insights from Economics of which Environmental Scientists, Environmental Managers, and Politicians Should be Aware

The previous section set out the interactions between the economy and the environment. What do economists have to say about these interactions? In the rest of this book, we will explain the contribution that economics can make to understanding and solving environmental problems. But suppose someone was too busy to read the rest of this book. What, at a minimum, would we wish to leave them with? The following list is one possibility:

1. Economic and environmental systems are determined simultaneously. This means that to fully understand these systems, economics must incorporate the mechanical

---

[1] There were in fact many phases of change in the woodland area up to 2,000 years ago, whilst the exact causes of change are still much debated. See Whittington and Edwards (1997).

underpinnings of the natural sciences, and the natural sciences must incorporate the behavioural underpinnings of economics.

2. The behavioural underpinnings of economics matter for environmental policy. First, people respond to incentives, as do firms. The most important incentives tend to be prices. Second, people make decisions 'at the margin': in other words, they try to balance out the costs and benefits of going one step further. Finally, expect firms and households to usually act in their own best interests. For firms, this typically means maximizing profits and for households it means maximizing their well-being (their *utility*). This implies that we should not be surprised when either behaves strategically: for example, when someone free-rides when asked to make a donation for an environmental good cause, or when a farmer threatens to destroy a wetland in return for a compensation payment not to do so. Institutions need to be designed that take these kinds of responses into account. Recent advances in mainstream economics that take a broader view of the motivations behind human behaviour than the standard model of 'rational choice' have become increasingly important within environmental economics (Shogren and Taylor, 2008).

3. Environmental resources are scarce, and using them in one way has an opportunity cost. By 'scarce', we mean that there are not enough environmental resources around to simultaneously meet every possible demand on them. By 'opportunity cost', we mean the net benefits forgone from the next-best use. For example, suppose that a piece of land has three possible uses, namely agriculture, forestry, and recreation, which have returns of £2,000/ha, £3,000/ha, and £4,000/ha. These activities we will assume to be mutually exclusive, in that the land cannot be used for more than one purpose at the same time. Deciding to use the land for recreation purposes forgoes a return from either agriculture or forestry, and the opportunity cost is the next-best return forgone, namely £3,000/ha. This cost should be taken into account when evaluating the net benefits of using the land for recreation.

4. The free market system can generate the 'wrong' level of environmental quality. Too many environmental bads (e.g. too much pollution) and too few environmental goods (such as beautiful landscapes) will result from the point of view of social optimality. Why should this be?—Because the system of property rights in existence means that no market price exists either to discourage economic agents from polluting or to encourage them to produce environmental benefits. This problem is known in economics as market failure: Chapter 2 investigates this issue in detail, and suggests alternative ways of solving such problems. Another way of thinking about this is to say that the environment is valuable in many ways, but not all of these show up in market values or prices. For example, it is hard for a private landowner to charge for the landscape benefits that his farm 'produces', and no market price exists for many aspects of landscape beauty.

5. However, markets have proved to be the best way of allocating a vast range of resources: Adam Smith's 'invisible hand' still has much to recommend it. Markets are good at coordinating actions and at transmitting information. For many resources, the market system is also good at responding to changes in relative scarcity. For example, the significant hikes in oil prices in the 1970s produced automatic adjustments in supply and demand. Finally, markets allow people the opportunity to trade, which turns out to

be a good way of increasing social welfare on the whole. Markets can also be made to work for the environment: see, for example, the discussion of the idea of tradable pollution permits in Chapter 2.

6. Government intervention does not always make things better, and can make things worse. The Common Agricultural Policy of the European Union (EU) has been frequently criticized as having given farmers an incentive to damage the environment: this might be called 'government failure'. When governments interfere with the free operation of markets, they need to be aware that they are likely to bring about coordination and information problems. Government intervention may well hinder the responsiveness of markets to changes in relative scarcity; for example, if they keep prices at levels other than the market clearing rate (Chapter 2).

7. Environmental protection costs money. Scarcity means that opportunity costs exist for all choices, even those driven by moral imperatives. Protecting endangered species costs money, both directly (e.g. in monitoring) and indirectly (in that land can no longer be used for development). Spending more public money on public transport systems to reduce air pollution may mean that less money is available to spend on schools. What is more, the costs of protecting the environment typically increase at the margin. As emissions from industrial sources are progressively cleaned up, each extra reduction gets more and more expensive to achieve.

8. When managing renewable resources such as fish and forests, choosing the maximum sustainable yield as the best level at which to harvest is rarely optimal. This is because this rule ignores the economic costs and benefits of renewable resource management. Catching at the maximum sustainable yield usually means too many boats chasing too few fish.

9. Whilst economic growth may contribute to current environmental problems, few people would swap their position today with their equivalent 200 years ago, due to the huge increases in real incomes per capita and improvements in life expectancy. It is hard to think of economic growth as a bad thing, but it is something that gives rise to a series of environmental consequences that need to be dealt with.

10. Many of the world's most serious environmental problems are global in nature; however, economics predicts that getting countries to agree to do something about these problems together is going to be tough (Chapter 7). This is because game theory shows us that countries have an incentive to 'free-ride' on the actions of others and so, for example, to avoid signing up for international agreements to cut global pollutant emissions. However, economists can help in designing institutional arrangements to reduce these problems.

1.3 The Rest of this Book: An Overview

We divide the book into two parts. Part I explores some important concepts in economics, and illustrates why they matter for environmental issues. Chapter 2 explores the role of markets in determining the level of environmental quality, what 'market failure' means, and how markets can be used to work for the environment. The practice of placing monetary values on the environment has become controversial, but is an important component of the economist's toolbox: Chapters 3 and 4 deal with this issue, and with the methodology of cost–benefit analysis. Many environmental decision-making problems are characterized by high levels of risk and uncertainty, so Chapter 5 introduces economic approaches to these issues. Sustainable development and green growth are fashionable buzzwords in environmental and development debates at present: Chapter 6 investigates what economics has to contribute to this debate, and to understanding the relationship between growth and indicators of environmental quality. In Chapter 7, game theory techniques are introduced as a useful tool to help understand situations in which people behave strategically, be they countries arguing over climate change conventions or fishermen competing over harvests. Finally, Chapter 8 lays out some basic economics of the debate over free trade: Does free trade always increase people's well-being? Can trade restrictions be justified on environmental grounds?

In Part II, we explore how economics can help us understand the causes of a series of important environmental problems and, more importantly, provide more environmental protection at lower cost. The issues studied are:

- Climate change
- Forests and forest loss
- Water pollution
- Biodiversity loss
- Energy policy

These chapters are brief considerations of these important and complex issues, so we only have space to highlight how economics can be useful in thinking about our impacts on the natural world. Yet the material in Part II does show (we hope!) the richness of analysis that economics can bring to these problems.

1.4 Using this Book for Teaching and Learning

This book is aimed at a wide audience. Little economics background is assumed, and the use of mathematical explanations is downplayed as much as possible. The book is suitable for introductory courses in environmental and natural resource economics, both for economics students and non-economists. It should also be suitable for undergraduate- and MSc-level interdisciplinary courses in which many students lack a background in economics.

Instructors will see that we do not follow a traditional path in explaining the subject: for example, there is no chapter on the economics of renewable resources *per se*, nor on the economics of the mine. The key ideas may all be found either in Part I (e.g. in Chapter 7 on game theory, for renewables) or in the case studies in Part II (e.g. in the energy chapter for non-renewables and the forest chapter for forestry economics). We recognize that there are costs to presenting things this way, but we feel these are outweighed by the benefits: an initial introduction to important economic concepts; and then a look at important environmental issues, which draws on these concepts and develops others. At the end of each chapter, we include a list of suggested questions for use in tutorials or seminars, and a glossary of key terms. References are provided at the end of each chapter, rather than being collected together at the end of the book.

References and Additional Readings

Ponting, C. (1991). *A Green History of the World* (London: Penguin).

Shogren, J., and Taylor, L. (2008). 'On behavioral–environmental economics', *Review of Environmental Economics and Policy* 2(1): 26–44.

Whittington, G., and Edwards, K. (1997). 'Climate change', in K. Edwards and I. Ralston (eds.), *Scotland: Environment and Archaeology, 8000 BC–AD 1000* (Chichester: Wiley).

2 Markets and the Environment

We all use markets every day. Markets allow us to trade—buying and selling goods allows us to create economic value. We appreciate the choices and opportunities that markets provide to us, because we like choice and the freedom to choose. But what is a *market* to an economist? To non-economists, a market is a tangible place in which to spend money; such as a neighbourhood mall or a village market in France, or a global website on which you buy and sell apples or armchairs. But to economists, the idea of a market is more conceptual—they see the market as a way to create value through the voluntary exchange of goods and services regulated by competition.

Economists champion the marketplace as the most useful way to organize economic activity. Markets arise spontaneously because people can create value in trade. Markets create wealth through voluntary exchange of scarce resources, in which prices guide how people decide to trade. Wealth is created when resources move from low-value to high-value uses. Markets *create* value—the benefits exceed the costs—rather than just *redistributing* wealth between people.

Markets are powerful for another reason than just trade. Markets send signals; they are a channel of communication. Many scientists dedicated to protecting the environment believe that markets are the most effective tool humans have 'discovered' to organize and coordinate the diffuse set of information spread throughout society; for example, information on what people want, how much of the good is in supply, given drought or rainy conditions. Markets use prices to communicate scarcity—as defined by both the laws of nature and the laws of humanity. Prices send signals to coordinate decentralized economic decisions. Markets succeed when prices define the trade-offs we face such that resources are allocated to their highest-valued use in society.

But markets fail too. Markets fail when prices send bad information about the true nature of scarcity, or when markets fail to exist at all because they are too costly to construct. For example, we suffer from over-pollution or overdevelopment when a market price is too low to communicate our preferences for environmental protection. Prices might misstate the economic value of a reduction in health risk from an environmental threat, or prices might not even exist to signal the value. Left alone, a market might produce too few or too many goods or services. A wedge is driven between what people want as individuals and what society wants as a collective.

The protection of endangered species on private land is a classic example of market failure. By one estimate, about half of the listed endangered species in the United States have 80 per cent of their habitat on private land. The challenge is that the benefits of the protection of endangered species extend to everyone—the entire world—but the costs of protection fall on private landowners. Since the market price of private land does not capture the social benefits of species protection, landowners have more incentive to protect their own private investment (e.g. their capacity to produce cattle) than to protect endangered species. The market fails when private decisions generate a less-protected habitat than society desires.

But even when markets fail, they can be the cornerstone of the solution. Rather than turning to more government regulation or stakeholder-participation processes, society can fix existing markets or create new markets to manage our environment and natural resources; for example, when we create markets in rights to emit pollution. Since a market is a tool, its precision depends on how society defines the rules to regulate its behaviour; that is, property rights, liability, and information. People who dislike the prices that a market produces have to rethink the connection between price signals and market rules. We can work together to change these rules. We should view markets as having the potential to work for us, not against us.

This chapter explores the nature of markets, market failure, and market redemption. We discuss the power of markets, and why economists continue to promote markets despite their flaws. We examine how markets can fail the environment due to externalities, public goods, common property, thresholds, and hidden information. We end by exploring how we can use elements of markets to correct market failure, or policy failure due to government subsidies.

2.1 The Power of Markets

A market serves society by creating value through free exchange. Markets use prices to communicate the wants and limits of a diffuse and diverse society so as to bring about coordinated economic decisions efficiently. The power of a market system rests in the decentralized process of decision-making and exchange. No omnipotent central planner is needed to allocate resources. Rather, market prices ration resources to those who value them the most, and in doing so under certain conditions, people are swept along by Adam Smith's 'invisible hand' to achieve what is best for society as a whole. Self-interest is the driving power, and competition the regulator of that power—together, they work to improve the lives of common people.

A key idea behind the power of markets and free exchange is *comparative advantage*. One person has a comparative advantage over another person in one good relative to another good if that person's relative *efficiency* in the production of the first good is greater than that of the other person. Alternatively, a person has a comparative advantage if his or her opportunity cost is less than that of the other person. The *opportunity cost* is the economic cost as measured by what we have to give up to do something else.

Absolute advantage does not translate into comparative advantage. Everyone, skilled or unskilled, has a comparative advantage at something, because opportunity costs are lower for some people for different activities. Markets and trade benefit everyone in society because they allow people to specialize in activities in which they have a comparative advantage, and then trade for what they want to consume (for an extension of this idea to the benefit of trade between nations, see Chapter 8). A market succeeds when it allows for the *efficient* allocation of resources. Efficiency gains exist in an economy if it is possible to trade goods and services such that at least one person is better off and no one else is worse off. This is called *Pareto efficiency*—the inability to reallocate resources without making at least one person worse off.

For example, should you shovel your own snow? No, not necessarily. If you follow the idea of opportunity cost and comparative advantage, it might be to your and to society's advantage to use the market and hire someone to shovel your snow. Everyone has a comparative advantage at something, based on his or her relative opportunity cost. Suppose you can shovel snow better than the next person, but it might be that your opportunity costs are too great. Say you could remove the snow in two hours; but in those two hours you could have written a new essay on Napoleon's wild youth and earned $5,000 selling it to a blog on historical French leadership. In contrast, your teenage neighbour could do the job in four hours at $10 per hour, so it would cost you $40 to remove the snow. The teenager's opportunity cost is that he or she would have to give up gaming on the PlayStation for four hours —which we assume he or she values at less than $40. Both you and the teenager gain from the trade: you write the essay and get paid, the teenager shovels your snow and gets paid, and society is better off since you both gained—it is a Pareto-efficient trade. Box 2.1 illustrates the idea of gains from trade, by means of an example.

What is the key to a successful market? Most economists agree that well-defined property rights are the key. A well-defined property rights system represents a set of entitlements that define the owners' privileges and obligations for use of a resource or asset. A well-defined property rights system is based on four characteristics:

- *Comprehensive*—all resources are either privately or collectively owned, and all entitlements are defined, well known, and enforced.

- *Exclusive*—all benefits and costs from use of a resource accrue to the owner(s), and only to the owner(s), either directly or by sale to others. This applies to both private and common-property resources.

- *Transferable*—property rights should be transferable from one owner to another through a voluntary exchange. The owner has an incentive to conserve the resource beyond the time during which he or she expects to make use of it.

- *Secure*—property rights to resources should be secure from involuntary seizure or encroachment by other people, firms, and governments. Security provides the owner with an incentive to improve and preserve a resource while it is in his or her control, rather than exploit the assets.

These four conditions represent an ideal scenario in which gains from trade are created and captured by people who trade. The idea of a complete set of markets does not reflect reality, however; rather, the notion of *complete markets* represents a theoretical benchmark against which economists can judge the effectiveness of different plans to organize economic activity. This orthodoxy of maximization and equilibrium to capture the interactions of intelligent self-interested people is a necessary fiction rather than literal truth.

Markets also force people to make a distinction between rhetoric and action in the context of environmental assets. We all have opinions. Markets help separate those opinions we

BOX 2.1 Market Equilibrium and the Gains from Trade

Consider the following market. Suppose that a market exists for a classic Ansel Adams photo of the Grand Tetons National Park, with eight buyers and eight sellers. Each buyer has his or her maximum willingness to pay (WTP) for one photo; each seller has his or her minimum willingness to accept compensation (WTA) for one photo:

Buyer ID	WTP	Seller ID	WTA
B1	$300	S1	250
B2	$200	S2	350
B3	$50	S3	150
B4	$500	S4	450
B5	$300	S5	250
B6	$250	S6	100
B7	$400	S7	200
B8	$100	S8	100

Using the WTP and WTA data, we can graph the market demand and supply curves, and then calculate the equilibrium price and quantity, and the total gains from trade. First, we can rank-order the buyers from highest to lowest WTP, and draw them as a set of downward steps. This is the market demand curve. Now we rank-order the sellers from lowest to highest WTA, and graph them as a set of upward steps. This is the market supply curve. When market demand intersects market supply, we find the market equilibrium—the market clearing price and quantity sold. In this example, then, the equilibrium market price equals $250 and the equilibrium quantity is 4 or 5.

How do economists measure the gains from trade? We have defined the total gain from trade as the sum of two measures of welfare—the *consumer surplus* and the *producer surplus*. The consumer surplus (CS) represents the gains to each buyer, and is represented as the difference between each buyer's WTP and the market price:

$$CS = (\$500 - 250) + (\$400 - 250) + (\$300 - 250) + (\$300 - 250) + (\$250 - 250) = \$500.$$

For example, buyer 7 was willing to pay $400, but since the market set the price at $250, that is all he had to pay; his consumer surplus equals $150 (= $400–250). The consumer surplus represents his gain from exchange. If we add up each buyer's consumer surplus we have measured the total benefits to all the consumers in this market.

Similarly, the producer surplus (PS) represents what the sellers gain from this market. Here the producer surplus is the difference between the market price and each seller's WTA:

$$PS = (\$250 - 100) + (\$250 - 100) + (\$250 - 150) + (\$250 - 200) + (\$250 - 250) = \$450.$$

For example, seller 6 was willing to accept $100 to sell, but since the market set the price at $250, her producer surplus equals $150 (= $250 – 100). Again, if we add up each seller's producer surplus, we have measured the total benefits to all the producers.

Finally, the total gains from trade in this market equal the sum of the consumer and the producer surplus, which in our example is $950 = ($500 + 450). This is represented by the shaded area between the demand and supply curves. Both the low-cost sellers and the high-value buyers gain in this market. The market is *efficient* because it has helped move low-valued resources to high-valued uses (for more details, Krugman and Wells, 2008).

are willing to back up with real economic commitments from those we are not. The discipline provided by the market forces people to relate their choices to the choices of others and to the consequences of these choices.

People tend to overstate their real willingness to pay or to co-operate—say, to protect threatened tree frogs or critical wetlands—when asked a hypothetical survey question. Good intentions are just that; but markets do not sustain cheap talk. Markets force us to decide how to use our scarce resources for development or conservation, or some combination of the two.

2.2 Market Failure

Market failure is a reality that we must confront. *Market failure* exists when resources do not attain their highest social value. For environmental goods and natural resources, markets fail when benefits and costs cannot be allocated with precision across and within nations and generations. Sometimes, the needed conditions of well-defined property rights do not hold up for environmental goods. Markets fail when private self-interested actions could still be improved on relative to collective goals.

Market failure comes about when people cannot define property rights clearly. Markets fail when we cannot transfer rights; when we cannot exclude others from using the good; or when we cannot protect our rights to use the good. Under these conditions, free exchange does not lead to a socially desirable outcome, because private actions provide too many 'bads', such as pollution, or too few goods, such as open space. Since everyone 'owns' the right to clean air and biodiversity, nobody owns the right. This makes it a challenge for a market to operate effectively. The market system is said to be 'incomplete', and we have the problem of 'missing markets'.

For example, most societies do not currently have well-defined rights to produce or consume pig odour (i.e. the smell of manure) from a large-scale pig-farming enterprise. Those up- or downwind cannot buy or sell tickets for fragrant air. The pig farm upwind cannot sell fresh air; those downwind cannot buy fresh air. Since the farm does not bear the downwind costs, it can ignore these costs. With incomplete markets, the pig farmer lacks a motivating economic incentive to control emissions or to switch to less-polluting practices. Similarly, if no legal or institutional basis exists, people who use polluted river water cannot receive compensation from upstream farmers whose sediments, pesticides, or fertilizers impose downstream costs in the form of contaminated drinking water, poor fishing, or reduced recreational opportunities. Farmers can impose 'external costs' on these other users of the river.

A market can fail for several reasons. Economists use a taxonomy to help identify and categorize the different types of market failure. Understanding how and why a market fails is the first step to correcting the problem. We examine four types of market failure for environmental resources—*externalities, public goods, open-access common property*, and *hidden information*. Some overlap exists between these types of market failure, whilst there are other types of market failure—such as market power or monopoly—that we do not discuss here.

Externalities. Externalities are the classic type of market failure for environmental problems. Pollution is an externality when a person or firm does not bear all the costs or receive all the benefits of his or her actions. An externality can arise when the market price or cost of production excludes its social impact, cost, or benefit. If you look around, you can see externalities everywhere. Think of how your actions affect other's well-being, for better or worse, and how you do not pay or receive compensation for the extra costs or benefits. The market fails because the market is *missing*—no exchange institution exists in which people pay others for extra benefits or receive compensation for extra costs (see also Box 2.2).

BOX 2.2 An Example of an Externality: Air Pollution in Ecuador

Failing to put the correct 'price' on using the environment can lead to too much environmental degradation. Factory owners who decide to increase output face no cost for any resultant increase in pollution. This suggests that they have no economic incentive to cut down on emissions, and then society has too much pollution. Another example is the air pollution arising from driving to work. When people drive to work, they pay no immediate price for the pollution coming from their cars.

Jurado and Southgate (1999) explore these factory and automobile externalities in a study of air quality in Quito, the capital of Ecuador. Quito lies high up in an Andean mountain valley, which exacerbates its air quality problem. The table below shows that the major sources of pollutants are vehicles and factories. Neither factory nor vehicle owners face any immediate economic price for the pollution for which they are responsible.

	Total suspended particulates (TSP)	Sulphur dioxide (SO_2)	Nitrous oxides (NO_x)
Vehicles	1,069	659	5,298
Factories	7,170	18,707	5,023

These levels of air pollution exceed the maximum recommended levels set by the World Health Organization (WHO). The concentrations of TSP in 1991 averaged 149.9 g/m^3, compared with the WHO standard of 60 g/m^3.

The authors estimated the economic costs of air pollution as measured by the impact on human health. Pneumonia and other respiratory ailments are the leading cause of death in all age groups in the city, and are exacerbated by the high TSP levels. The study used statistical relationships between TSP levels and three standard measures of ill-health: restricted activity days, work days lost, and excess mortality.

The predicted increases in ill-health from pollution were valued in economic terms using several approaches, including the value of working time, and the cost of illness (e.g. hospital resources used up in treating patients; see rows 2 and 3 of the table below). Extra deaths were valued as the discounted value of lifetime earnings, a somewhat dated approach. This yields a value of $16,887 per avoided death, which then gives the values in row 4 of the table.

	Annual costs to citizens of Quito (US$)
Restricted activity day costs (given 3,433,000 restricted days)	$14,418,600
Working days lost costs (given 1,765,000 working days lost)	$12,708,000
Excess mortality costs, as per study (given 94 extra deaths per year)	$1,587,378
Excess mortality costs, revised	$12,220,000

We have used 'value of statistical life' estimates based on how much people are willing to pay for risk reductions (for details, see Chapter 5). The value of the reduced risk is increased by an order of magnitude in row 4. These new estimates are based on the figure of $130,000 per avoided death from Fankhauser et al. (1998) for developing countries. Whatever the values used, the message is clear: externalities due to private air pollution decisions impose social costs on the citizens of Quito.

For instance, driving your car around town creates numerous externalities. The exhaust contributes to air pollution, driving at rush hour adds to congestion, road rage increases the risk to others and yourself, and the beautiful racing flames painted on the side add to cultural pride. No explicit markets exist to exchange the good for the bad. You live with it. But from an efficiency viewpoint, in which society is trying to get the most out of its limited resources, the lack of a market leads to too many exhaust fumes, too much congestion, too much road rage, and so on.

Consider another example of a negative externality, or external cost, in a local environment. The village of Centennial sits at the base of the Snowy Range Mountains. Not many people live in Centennial, and development of new houses is slow. The houses and yurts (originally, a Central Asian dwelling type) that exist sit below the ridgeline, so they do not stick out as people look towards the horizon. Citizens of Centennial and people driving through enjoy the wide-open space that the current development promotes. But suppose that a newcomer called Riley moves into the valley and wants to build a new house on his private property. This property sits on a prominent ridge, a 'hogback', and the proposed three-storey house is to be built on top of the ridge, visible to everyone in the valley.

Suppose that Ole lives below the ridge and has an undisturbed view of Centennial valley and the mountains beyond. If Riley, the newcomer, builds his house on the ridge, Ole's view of the wide open spaces in Centennial valley will disappear. Riley's actions reduce Ole's well-being. But Riley does not have to pay compensation to Ole or anyone else, since no one owns the right to the vista. Riley's private decision to build his house on his own land does not account for the losses suffered by the rest of the community who valued the open space—a wedge is driven between the private and socially optimal allocation of resources.

Figure 2.1 illustrates this example. Riley accounts for his own marginal benefits and costs, and chooses to develop his house at level H'. If he had accounted for the social costs of lost open space suffered by Ole and the rest of the community, Riley would have developed at level H^*—a smaller house built below the ridge. Since $H' > H^*$, the market is said to have failed to allocate resources efficiently—there is too much housing on the ridge in Centennial valley.

This example involves a loss of aesthetics; other externalities affect matters of life and death. Many externalities increase the risks to human life and limb. Toxic wastes that leach into drinking water are an example; urban air pollution due to transportation, which curtails the activities of young children, is another. All actions that alter the health risk to others in which no compensation is paid or received create externalities that are left unattended by the market.

These examples of pollution reflect a direct externality—you breathe or drink polluted air or water and there is a direct impact on your health. But over the past century tracking the direct effects of an externality has become more complicated, as humanity has developed new technologies to separate itself from the whims of nature. In many cases, it is less obvious to determine the cause and potential effects: the effects are less direct and more roundabout. The idea of *ecosystem externalities* captures these indirect impacts. An action affects an environmental system at one obvious point, at which no harm seems to be done. But the action is working its way through the system, and can show up somewhere else as an unexpected and unwelcome surprise. For example, citizens who kill predators in order to protect

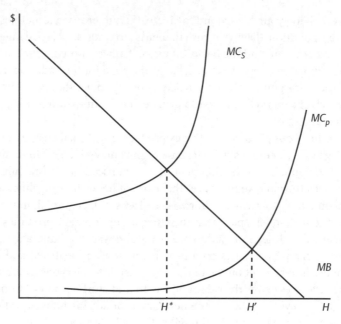

Figure 2.1 Marginal benefits and marginal costs: private and social.

children and domestic animals can generate large rodent infestations that affect crops and sanity. DDT does not kill birds but, rather, it thins the shells of their eggs.

Ecosystem externalities highlight the fact that the economist cannot presume that the cause and effect of production and consumption decisions are obvious; and that even though there is no effect 'under the streetlamp', there might be an unanticipated effect somewhere else (Finnoff and Tschirhart, 2008). Economists have to work with natural scientists in the life sciences to better anticipate the potential for indirect externalities, feedbacks between the economic and ecological systems, and the subsequent unintended and unpleasant surprises.

Public goods. Public goods are a second form of market failure. A public good exists when a person cannot be excluded from its benefits or costs—*non-excludability*; and when one person's consumption of the good does not reduce its availability to anyone else—*non-rival consumption.* Together, non-excludability and non-rival consumption are what separates a public good from a private good, which is excludable and rival in consumption.

Economists make use of the terms *pure* and *impure* public goods. The difference is that a pure public good is both non-excludable and non-rival; whereas an impure public good might be either non-excludable or non-rival, but not both. Climate-change protection, the ozone layer, and biodiversity are examples of pure public goods in which the benefits accrue to all those around the globe. Common-property and club goods such as rivers, local parks, and lakes are impure public goods because the benefits can be excluded from non-members of the group that owns the resource. We focus first on pure public goods, and then turn to common property in the next section.

Non-exclusion depends on the physical characteristics of the good and the property rights regime. Climate-change protection is the most obvious form of public good in the environment. No nation can be excluded from the benefits of the emission reduction efforts of another nation. Biodiversity preservation is another example of a public good. No person can be excluded from the public benefits created from a stable ecosystem created by preserving species. For wildlife viewing, unless the species exist on private reserves, it is difficult to exclude potential beneficiaries from enjoying the prospect of seeing them. If people derive value from the existence of a species, exclusion is impossible. This holds for many environmental resources—if air quality in a city improves, nobody who lives in or visits the city can be excluded from the benefits. Other environmental resources are excludable in consumption. For example, market prices control recreational access to downhill skiing at a resort.

Non-rivalry depends on the characteristics of the good. Non-rivalry means that the benefits gained from the resource are independent of the number of other people who wish to use it. Better air quality, for instance, increases one person's well-being, no matter how many other citizens there are. If an endangered species is protected, the number of people affected does not reduce the benefits to each person. Some environmental resources do not possess this property. If designating a wilderness area as a recreational resource protects it from future development and yet also increases its profile, then the presence of more people implies more congestion and fewer benefits per trip for many visitors. Many people visiting Yellowstone National Park, for example, feel that congestion is a 'bad': too many people, too little solitude.

What is the relevance of these properties for the socially optimal provision of public goods and market failure? Let's revisit the Centennial open space issue as a public goods problem. Open spaces are a public good if defined as an aesthetic available to all people in the same amount—my visual consumption of open space does not reduce your access, nor reduce the amount of open space. The potential problem with using the market to provide this public good voluntarily is *free-riding*—since he or she cannot be excluded from the same amount of the good, each person has an incentive to let someone else provide the public good. Everyone has an incentive to free-ride off the efforts of others.

Free-riding can lead to the well-known case of the *prisoner's dilemma*, also called the *social trap* or the *tragedy of the commons* (for more details, see Box 2.3 and Chapter 7). The dilemma exists when people find that individual incentives lead them to the worst outcome possible—for themselves and society. The idea is compelling: a person looks out for his or her own self-interest and knows that other people are doing the same. Given the incentives, he or she cannot avoid the worst outcome, because the private incentives always push the person towards the non-cooperative outcome. In public good terms, this means that a person knows he or she should not free-ride, because it is better to be a good citizen. Yet the incentives still exist to free-ride. If he does not free-ride but everyone else does, he ends up in the worst position.

In reality, people do contribute to the provision of some public good voluntarily. Whether people contribute to the public good is not the question. The question is whether they voluntarily contribute 'enough'—do people pay enough to create the social optimal level of the public good? If so, a decentralized market approach has succeeded in allocating a public good. If not, by definition the market fails. The market fails because people have undersupplied the social optimal level of the public good, or oversupplied a public 'bad' such as pollution. Free-riding can be partial or complete; the market might fail by a little or a lot. But

BOX 2.3 The Tragedy of the Commons

Biologist Garrett Hardin coined the phrase 'the tragedy of the commons' in the journal *Science* in 1968. The word 'tragedy' meant a 'remorseless working of things'. Hardin was concerned with unchecked global population growth, which he saw as unsustainable for common property. His example of a pasture open to all graziers to let their cattle roam over leads to overgrazing. Each grazier gets the full benefit of adding one more animal to the common (the profit per beast). But as cattle numbers rise, overgrazing occurs, which then causes everyone to lose. Each person rushes headlong down a path that leads to social ruin, destroying the idea of Adam Smith's beneficial invisible hand. This tragedy gets serious, Hardin argues, as population rises, since rising population equates to more people wanting to graze their animals.

Hardin's analysis has been praised, criticized, and extended. We now know that overgrazing of common areas is not new—it happened in ancient Mayan civilization and ancient Egypt. We also know that the price of the good produced on the commons matters more to the rate of exploitation than Hardin thought. We also know that many commons throughout the world are regulated by rules set by those who have access to the area.

Yet Hardin's message is powerful. We can find many examples of open-access resources damaged by overuse. An example is a study of common grazing areas in the Northern Isles off the Scottish coast. On Shetland, common grazings seem to suffer higher levels of environmental damage than comparable privately owned areas.

technically, the market still fails. Market failure occurs with voluntarily public good provision when people contribute any amount less than their true benefits for the good.

Consider the incentives to free-ride on open space provision. Suppose that Ole and the citizens of Centennial are considering pooling their resources and using the market to buy out Riley, to stop him from building his new mansion on the hogback. Since no one can be excluded from the potential benefits of open space, the marginal benefit to society from one more unit of visibility equals the summed marginal benefits from each person who gains enjoyment from the view. Marginal social benefits reflect how society values each extra unit of the public good. The 'optimal level' of the public good is the level that maximizes the net benefits to society. The optimal level is determined by comparing the marginal social benefits to the marginal social cost to provide one more unit of the good. The public good should be provided up to the point at which the marginal social benefits equal the marginal social costs. This optimal level is called the *Lindahl equilibrium*, named after the Swedish economist who first identified it.

If the market fails to generate the optimal level of the public good, how can society attain the optimal level? One possibility is to build a club: everyone who benefits from the good gets together to provide the good, and the benefits of this provision are then restricted to those people belonging to the club. This seems attractive since the beneficiaries of the good pay for it, and government is not forced to intervene. Organizations such as the Royal Society for the Protection of Birds (RSPB) in the United Kingdom and the Sierra Club in the USA, are partial examples of this. The RSPB buys and safeguards nature reserves using funds generated by club members.

But while club members get reduced fees for entry to sites, non-members also benefit from environmental preservation. The non-excludability of benefits means that fewer nature reserves would be provided than optimal if their provision was left to the RSPB.

What is more, club financing is likely to be less than optimal, in that people do not have to join and pay, even though they know they will benefit anyway. The strategic incentive to free-ride still exists.

Common property. Common property, or the *commons*, can be managed in many ways depending on how property rights are defined and enforced. Open-access commons exist when people cannot be excluded from accessing a resource, such that one person's use rivals another's use. If a person's use reduces the total available to all, everyone has an incentive to capture the benefits before someone else gets them. This open-access free-for-all leads to inefficient use of the resource. The moratorium on fishing for cod and witch flounder off the Grand Banks in the North Atlantic is a prime example. By inefficiency, we mean that the fishers harvest to the point at which the marginal costs exceed the marginal revenue (i.e. the market price) of harvesting. Overuse implies that the market price has failed to signal the true scarcity of the asset. Since a fish caught by one fisher is one fewer fish for all others to catch, fishers have no private incentive to account for the scarcity value of the resource. They expend too much effort and end up overharvesting the fish stock relative to what is economically efficient and potentially biologically inefficient. Again, we return to this problem in Chapter 7.

What happens in open-access commons? Each fisher has an incentive to catch as many fish as possible before someone else catches the same fish. He has no incentive to value the scarcity of the fish, because if he does not catch them, someone else will. His decision to let the fish be is not respected by others, because they have as much right to the fish as he does. He starts expending effort and in doing so his effort is such that his marginal costs end up exceeding his marginal revenue. This violates the standard efficiency condition that says that net benefits are maximized when marginal revenue equals marginal costs.

Why? Efficiency is breached because each fisher imposes an external cost on all the other fishers. This external cost arises because each time a fish is caught, it makes it more costly for everyone else to catch the next one. This is like a variant of the infamous 90–10 rule of diminishing returns to effort—you get 90 per cent of the fish with 10 per cent of the effort, but catching the remaining 10 per cent takes 90 per cent of the effort because they are harder to find.

When do the fishers stop their effort in open access? A fisher stops when his marginal costs equal the average revenue, or when his economic profits are zero. In this case, even though net profits to fishers are zero, the net social value is negative, because the scarcity value of the fish has been ignored in the free-for-all. In this case, each fisher does not earn the economic rent that would reflect the scarcity value of the fish to society.

Open access is the classic case of a 'tragedy of the commons'. Since everyone has access, all have the rights to the resource and scarcity value is ignored. But the reality is that most commons have a property-right scheme, either formal or informal, that works to allocate resources in a more efficient manner. There are numerous documented examples of self-governing commons in which people work as a collective unit and respect the scarcity value of the resource. These groups succeed when they establish common-property rights that include sharing rules, exclusion principles, and enforcement and punishment schemes (see Ostrom's classic 1990 book of examples of alternative management schemes for common property).

Market failure need not always occur with the commons. People have defined—and continue to define—rules to capture the scarcity value of a resource shared by many people. Be aware that market failure is associated with the commons in situations in which people use the term 'the commons' or the 'global commons' when they mean a global or regional public good that is both non-rival and non-excludable. Pure public goods are much more of a challenge to handle because of the need for a larger coalition of affected parties. We expand on this in Chapter 9, on the economics of climate change.

Hidden information. Market failure occurs when people cannot observe either the actions or types of other people. *Moral hazard* confounds market operations because one person cannot observe the hidden actions of others. *Adverse selection* frustrates markets because a person cannot observe the hidden type of a person (e.g. whether a farmer has high or low opportunity costs for increasing biodiversity on his or her land) or the hidden quality of some good or service (e.g. whether or not a loaf of bread is organic). Both types of hidden information slow the creation of markets that could be used to allocate resources to more efficient use, such as the reduction of environmental risk.

Moral hazard implies that a regulator cannot perfectly monitor pollution abatement, and a firm could shirk on pollution control. The firm has an incentive to shirk if it bears all the control costs in return for a fraction of the benefits. The result is again too much pollution relative to the efficient level. Also, moral hazard can lead to an inefficient 'pooling' of environmental risk, a topic that we take up in Chapter 5.

Environmental risks are part of life, and it would be better to find markets to allow those who are less willing to bear risk to sell the risk to those who are willing to buy it. But moral hazard reduces the ability to reallocate risk among different economic agents. When the private market cannot monitor actions, an insurer withdraws from the pollution liability market because insurance affects the individual's incentives to take precautions.

Given that accidental spills or storage of pollution can create potential financial liabilities (e.g. clean-up costs, medical expenses), a firm would like to pay to pass these risks on to a less risk-averse agent such as an insurer. But since there is a trade-off between risk-bearing and incentives, the market for pollution liability insurance is incomplete, as insurers reduce the information rents of the better-informed individual. The market produces an inefficient allocation of risk.

Adverse selection affects the environment too. One key recommendation of environmental policy is sustainable production of products. These products should be produced using methods that protect the environment. The challenge facing these sustainable products is that these products are more expensive and demand a higher market price. But if buyers cannot be guaranteed that they are getting their 'sustainability' bang for their buck, they will not buy them. Reporting that a product is sustainable is not enough for many consumers—they need a warranty or label.

If a consumer cannot distinguish the sustainable product from a similar product produced using standard practices, he has no incentive to pay the price premium. Why should he or she pay more than average when he or she cannot distinguish high-quality from low-quality products? The problem is that if the buyers disappear, the sellers have to withdraw from the market. The sellers with an above-average quality product who cannot get a price premium have no incentive to stay in the market, because they could do better investing elsewhere with greater returns. And if enough buyers who are willing to pay a high price disappear, the sellers disappear too, and the market collapses. Preventing this collapse requires a voluntary approach to certification (e.g. the AB scheme in France, or the Soil Association scheme in the UK) or a government-sponsored certification scheme.

2.3 Markets for the Environment

Market failure can create environmental problems. But even if markets fail, we can still use the ideas behind markets to address the problems that might exist. We do not need to turn to command-and-control government intervention or collaborative stakeholder processes. Rather, people can rewrite the rules to create new markets to address the failings of existing markets. They can use market-based policy as a substitute for technocratic or stakeholder processes, which have their own successes and failures (see Box 2.4).

Think about other kinds of real issues—such as financial assets, for instance—in which we are much less willing to delegate decision-making authority to the government or stakeholders. That people have been creating and using markets to manage many assets for the past three centuries signals their power. For example, the relative stakes per percentage risk are larger in financial assets than in risks from environmental dilemmas. But we do not ask the

---

BOX 2.4 Government Intervention Failure: The Common Agricultural Policy

In this chapter, we are discussing how market failure can lead to undesirable consequences for the environment. Governments have a case for some level of intervention to do something about it. Sometimes, however, government intervention can make things worse for the environment. A good recent historical example of this is the Common Agricultural Policy of the European Union, known as the CAP.

Through a complex system of import levies, export subsidies, and intervention buying, the CAP offered farmers throughout the EU higher prices for their outputs than the free market would generate. The official reasons given were to support farm incomes, stabilize crop prices, and increase self-sufficiency rates for major food products. Casting aside the dubious economic arguments that could be made in support of these goals, let us focus instead on what the implications were for the environment. Farmers responded to higher prices by increasing output, both by cultivating more land and increasing the intensity of production on all farmland. Coupled with technological progress, this policy altered the countryside, especially in a country such as the United Kingdom, where farmland accounts for about 80 per cent of the total land area. The most important impacts on farming historically are as follows:

- The removal of hedgerows, the ploughing of field margins, and the loss of farm woodlands
- Replacement of permanent pasture with temporary pastures and arable
- Land drainage
- Significant increases in the use of pesticides, herbicides, and fertilizers

The effects of these changes in farm practices on wildlife and landscape were extensive.
Figures from the Nature Conservancy Council published in 1983 showed, for example:

- A 50–60 per cent loss in lowland heaths since 1949
- A 95 per cent loss in herb-rich flower meadows
- An 80 per cent loss in chalk grasslands of high ecological value

The CAP has since been reformed, with the removal of many aspects of direct commodity price support and the introduction of a range of agri-environmental schemes that offer farmers payments to undertake actions likely to produce environmental benefits, such as reducing grazing pressures or cutting fertilizer or pesticide application rates. For an analysis of the effects of agricultural land use on one indicator of biodiversity—birds—see Dallimer et al. (2009).

government to dictate the price of stocks and bonds. We ask the government to help establish, monitor, and enforce the trading rules of the market, but not the market price itself.

We now consider three ways to create new markets to address market failure associated with the environment. A market has a supply side and a demand side, which together produce quantity exchange at a market price that reflects the value of the asset. Working from this basic construction, we consider three options. First, we can assign property rights for environmental assets and let people negotiate over the price and quantity of the good. Second, we can work through regulators to set a market price per unit of the environmental asset and let people decide how much of the asset they want to buy. Third, we can use regulators to set the quantity of the asset that can be bought and let the people decide what price they are willing to pay for the fixed quantity. Let us consider each in turn.

Assign property rights and bargain over price and quantity. In 1960, economist Ronald Coase argued that we can create new markets for non-market goods such as the environment as long as we are willing to remove institutional constraints to assigning well-defined property rights. Coase noted that two parties have an incentive to negotiate an economically efficient and mutually advantageous solution to a dispute provided that one party is given unilateral property rights to the asset in question. The key point for efficiency is that property rights are assigned, not to whom they are assigned (that is an equity issue). The outcome is the same—an efficient allocation of resources. This is the Coase theorem as traditionally defined. The theorem only holds if transaction costs are low and legal entitlements can be exchanged and enforced. The transaction costs are the price paid to organize the economic activity, including information, negotiation, writing and enforcing contracts, specifying property rights, and changing institutional designs.

Consider our open space example. Riley and Ole disagree about the amount of open space in Centennial valley. Riley owns the right to build his house on the hogback and Ole owns his own land below. All the citizens own the right to the view of the Centennial valley and ridge around the Snowy Range Mountains. But again, the rub is that if everyone owns the right to the view, no one owns the right.

One solution to the conflict is for the government to intervene and restrict Riley's development, or to tell Ole to live with it. This command-and-control approach allows a third party to select the winner and loser(s). In contrast, the citizens or government could work with the community to create a dispute resolution process in which everyone could sit down at the bargaining table, and try to come to some agreement. This would require the stakeholders to agree to some solution. It would promote collaboration, and by avoiding polarization it would produce creative solutions with political momentum. This could support local leadership and collaborative efforts to help Riley and the others enhance the environment and achieve economic productivity—or it could collapse into a bitter confrontation, with no resolution.

Alternatively, we could promote a Coasean solution that would create a market for open space by assigning property rights to either Riley or Ole. First, suppose that a third party assigns the property rights to Ole. Ole now has the right to keep the open spaces as he sees fit. This means that he could choose to keep the open spaces to his liking, and have the legal power to ask Riley to build a house that would not disturb the open spaces. This would make Ole the supplier of development, and he would have to decide how much open space to surrender to development under a specific price schedule. Ole's supply schedule of development space reflects his marginal costs from development, which increases as development increases: the more development, the greater loss of well-being as measured by more marginal costs.

Riley would now have to come to Ole to buy the use of open space for development. Riley would have to decide how much open space he would demand for a specific price. His demand schedule for development space would reflect his marginal benefits from development, which are assumed to be decreasing in development—more development implies lower marginal benefits. The market for development space would clear at the market price at which all the space demanded would equal all supplied. Both Ole and Riley would benefit from the trade: Ole would earn benefits pay through receiving a price for open space that exceeded his opportunity cost; Riley would benefit from paying for space that is less than his benefits for developing. The market leads to an efficient outcome—the marginal benefits from development equal the marginal costs.

Now suppose instead that the third party assigned the property rights to Riley. The roles are reversed—Riley has the right to use up open space as he sees fit; Ole has the right to try to buy open space. The power of the Coase theorem is that the outcome would be the same as before—same market price, same market quantity, same efficiency result. The economic efficiency is the same. Note, however, that the distribution of wealth differs. Now Riley receives the payment from Ole. Whether this is preferable to Ole receiving the wealth is a question of ethics.

What happens is that we redefine Ole and Riley's schedules to reflect the new property-right structure. Ole's supply curve for development now becomes his demand curve for open space. Ole now demands open space—different levels for specific prices. Riley's demand curve for development now becomes his supply curve for open space. He chooses to sell different amounts of open space at specific prices.

The market for open space would again clear at the identical market price at which all the space demanded would equal all supplied. Ole and Riley would capture the same benefit from the trade: Ole would earn benefits by paying a price for open space that was less than his opportunity cost of development; Riley benefits from selling open space at a price that exceeds his costs for forgoing developing. Again the market is efficient—the marginal benefits from open-space preservation equal the marginal costs. The smaller the number of people involved in the dispute, the more likely the Coase theorem is to work. More people increase the transaction costs necessary to come to an agreement, and make the market less efficient. It is also hard to identify responsible parties in some cases, and people have more incentive to free-ride in larger groups. In the case of larger numbers, we can still use the market. Now, we can set either the price or the quantity traded, which will allow the market to work.

Set the price of social damage—Pigovian taxes or green taxes. For over a century, economists have promoted the idea that we can adjust market prices to fix environmental dilemmas. We create new economic incentives in the market by altering the relative price of pollution or an otherwise unpriced environmental asset. The economist Alfred Pigou suggested in the early twentieth century that an effective solution to pollution problems is to add a tax on to the market price. This tax, now called a *Pigovian tax* or a *green tax*, would be set to equal the external cost, or marginal damage, suffered by those affected by the pollution.

In principle, society can alter a person's choices by imposing a green tax. The person continues to produce and pay the tax as long as the marginal benefits he or she receives from the output exceed the tax. Once the green tax exceeds the marginal benefits, he or she cuts off production. Ideally, if the green tax is set such that it reflects the equilibrium level of marginal damage, the person voluntarily selects the level of output that is the social optimum.

For Riley and Ole, a regulator could set the green tax at the equilibrium level of Ole's marginal damage suffered from the loss of open space. Now Riley would develop the space up to the point at which the tax exceeded his marginal benefits, and then he would stop. This would result in the same level of development as the Coasean solution.

Economists have debated the idea of whether a *double dividend* exists with green taxes. A double dividend exists: (i) when a green tax reduces the amount of pollution emitted; and (ii) when the revenues raised by the taxes are used to offset other distortionary taxes, such as income or capital gains taxes. A distortionary tax is a charge on activities that society wants to promote rather than discourage, such as working and investing. If we can use green taxes to reduce pollution and then use the extra revenue to reduce income taxes, society has two hits with one shot.

Unfortunately, if you compare it to the optimal benchmark, the double dividend story has a twist. We know that environmental protection benefits society. But this protection also raises prices and the overall cost of living, which cuts into a person's wages. Environmental protection is like a second labour tax added on to the already distortionary income tax. Now, our worker has even more reason to decrease his labour supply, which is an additional cost to society—less labour, less wealth created. The open question remains whether the environmental benefits of the green tax offset the losses from the decreased labour supply. The double dividend moral is this: correcting one mistake can make a second even worse.

In addition, green taxes have historically been set to raise small amounts of revenue, not induce big changes in behaviour. Taxes have been set too low to induce people to increase significantly either pollution abatement or environmental protection (Hanley et al., 2007). This reality is in part affected by the lack of information required to successfully implement an incentive to approach some social goal. Setting an efficient green tax requires information on the marginal costs and benefits schedules. We also need information on the environmental fate and transport systems and the monetary value of risks to life and limb. The information required to find this marginal damage function is not free, as had been presumed in the original green tax models.

An important extension to the idea of an optimal green tax was suggested by Baumol and Oates four decades ago. They showed that if society wants to achieve a given target level of emissions reduction, a tax on emissions could be the lowest-cost way of achieving this reduction, compared with a command-and-control approach such as design standards (the government tells firms how to control pollution) or a performance standard (the government tells them how much pollution they can emit). To understand the Baumol and Oates approach, we introduce the idea of a *marginal abatement cost* curve, or *MAC*.

Abatement costs are the costs of reducing emissions. Polluters can reduce emissions by several alternative means:

- installing 'end-of-pipe' treatment plants;
- changing their production processes—for example, by using cleaner inputs or recycling waste; and
- reducing output.

We assume that polluters know the range of options, and that they always choose the lowest-cost means. This may vary as emissions are reduced. A useful way of thinking about how abatement costs vary with the level of emission reduction is shown in Figure 2.2(a). This shows a *MAC* for a firm, the Jones Company, for reducing emissions by installing end-of-pipe treatment. The graph is read right to left, since this shows falling emissions. As can be seen, the *MAC* rises as the firm progressively cuts back on its emissions.

What does this mean?—That as emissions fall, the additional cost of reducing emissions increases still further: in other words, that the marginal abatement costs are rising. This rising *MAC* curve is an almost-universal empirical finding. Marginal abatement costs 'take off' at a 75 per cent cut, since end-of-pipe technology cannot cut emissions by more than this. The area under the *MAC* curve at any point gives the total abatement cost (e.g. area 'a' shows the total abatement cost of going from 100 per cent emissions to 75 per cent emissions). Figure 2.2(b) shows the *MAC* curve for the firm defined across all emission reduction options; this is now flatter past the 75 per cent reduction level, as the firm can choose to use other methods, such as changing its inputs. The curve takes off at extreme levels of emission reduction (95%), as emission reductions become costly at high levels of pollutant removal.

Another important empirical finding in the literature is that *MAC* curves can vary across firms for the same pollutant. For example, for Biological Oxygen demand (BOD) discharges into the Forth Estuary in Scotland, the actual abatement costs varied by as much as 2,500 times per kilogram of BOD removed. This may be due to firms that emit the same pollutant having different production processes and plant; having different levels of managerial skills; or being located in different areas (e.g. facing different transportation costs for bringing in cleaner inputs).

In Figure 2.2(a), we show the *MAC* curves for Jones PLC and another firm (Bloggs) that both emit BOD into a river. Jones has higher abatement costs than Bloggs, since it operates a different production process. Assume for simplicity that, in the absence of spending any money on pollution control, both firms discharge the same level of emissions, which we show as e^0 in the figure, equal to 10,000 tonnes/BOD/week each. The total unregulated discharge is 20,000 tonnes/week.[1] Figure 2.2(b) shows the aggregate *MAC* curve, which is just the horizontal summation of the *MAC* curves of Jones and Bloggs, referred to as MAC_I. Suppose that a control authority, the Environmental Protection Agency (EPA), wants to get an overall reduction of 10,000 tonnes/week. How could it use economic incentives to achieve this cut, and what might the outcomes be?

Suppose that the EPA sets a tax of *t* on every unit of emissions from Jones. This means that if Jones emits level of emissions e', it pays $(e' \cdot t)$ in taxes. What should the managers of Jones do? Imagine that they are emitting at e^0. The best they can do is to reduce emissions to e^t, since above e^t the marginal benefits of cutting emissions are greater than the marginal costs ($t > MAC$); whereas below e^t the marginal benefits of increasing emissions (savings in abatement costs, measured by *MAC*) are greater than the marginal costs (increased tax payments of *t* per unit). Setting emissions equal to e^t is the firm's best response: it implies an equilibrium of

$$t = MAC.$$

---

[1] In practice, it is unlikely that firms would engage in *zero levels of* pollution control in the absence of regulation, since some control might result from changes in operations motivated by cost saving, such as the recycling of waste streams.

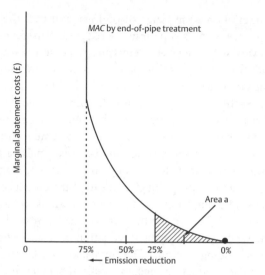

Figure 2.2a A *MAC* for the Jones Company, for reducing emissions by installing end-of-pipe treatment.

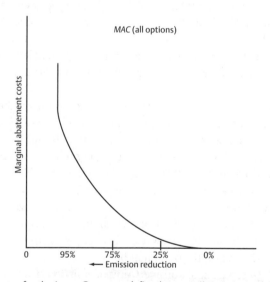

Figure 2.2b The *MAC* curve for the Jones Company defined across all emission reduction options.

At e^t, the firm pays tax revenues equal to area 'b' and, relative to the pre-tax position, has increased abatement spending by area 'a'. How does the control authority know what tax rate to set? Suppose that it knows the marginal abatement cost schedule MAC_1 from Figure 2.3. The target level of aggregate emissions is shown at E^*, equal to 10,000 tonnes of BOD. At this emission level, the aggregate *MAC* schedule has a value of t. This is the correct level at which to set the tax to achieve the target reduction.

But what if the EPA does not have this information? Information, or the lack of the needed information, is a likely scenario in reality. The EPA has to guess the tax rate and observe firms' reactions. If it sets the tax rate too high, the firms cut emissions by too much and the target is overshot;[2] if the tax rate is set too low, the opposite occurs; emission

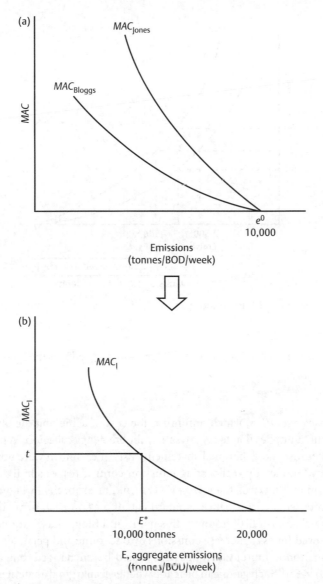

Figure 2.3 From firm's emissions to aggregate emissions.

reductions are undersupplied. The EPA iterates on to the correct tax rate. Firms dislike this approach, however, since the future tax rate is uncertain, which makes planning for investment more difficult.

The main attraction of taxes over regulation can now be explained. Under a tax, and as already shown, each firm's best response is to adjust its emissions so that we get

$$t = MAC$$

---

[2] While it might seem odd to talk about achieving too much pollution control, remember that each extra reduction in pollution that we aim for imposes a cost on society.

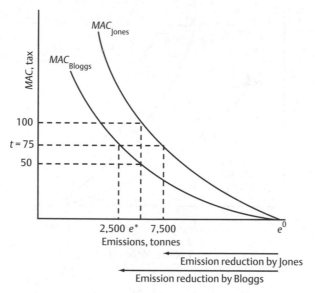

Figure 2.4 Pollution taxes as the least-cost solution.

for each firm. This means that for Jones and Bloggs, the tax produces the following outcome:

$$t = MAC_{Jones} = MAC_{Bloggs}.$$

This is the *least-cost solution*, which minimizes the cost of achieving the target reduction. That is important: it implies that taxes can satisfy the efficiency criterion. Why is it the least-cost solution? Because if the marginal abatement costs of each firm were not equal, society could always save money by reallocating emission control responsibility away from the higher-*MAC* firm and towards the lower-*MAC* firm. For example, in Figure 2.4, suppose that the EPA imposed a performance standard equal to e^* on each firm. This means that Jones has marginal costs of £100/tonne at this point, and Bloggs has marginal costs of £50/tonne. If we allowed Jones to increase emissions by one tonne and persuaded Bloggs to cut emissions by one tonne more, total emissions would be unchanged, but we would have saved $(100 − 50) = £50$. Such gains can be made whenever marginal abatement costs are not equal. But how could Bloggs be persuaded to cut emissions by more than Jones?—By setting the tax of $t = 75$. This gives the desired reduction in emissions (Jones emits 7,500 and Bloggs 2,500, so that new emissions are 10,000 tonnes), but at the lowest cost, since the tax results in marginal abatement costs being equalized.

The least-cost property of pollution taxes (also known as the static efficiency property) is their most important attribute, and it was first set down by Baumol and Oates in 1971 (see their 1988 book). Pollution taxes have one other major advantage. Since each unit of emissions now costs the firm money in tax payments, firms have more incentive to invest in cleaner, greener technology than under regulation. This is known as the 'dynamic efficiency' property of taxes, and has been argued by some to be their most important feature in the long run. What are the problems with pollution taxes as a policy solution?

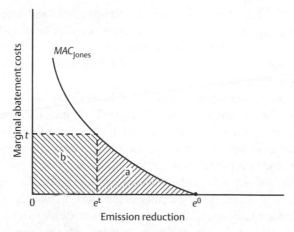

Figure 2.5 The impact of a water pollution tax.

- When pollutants are non-uniformly mixed, then a single tax rate is not efficient. This happens because the tax is levied on emissions rather than on their environmental impact. Firms that cause more damage per unit of emissions should be taxed at a higher rate than firms that cause lower per-unit-of-emission damage. At the limit, correcting this problem involves a unique tax rate for each firm. More pragmatically, suggestions have been made for banded tax rates to try to control for non-uniform mixing to at least some degree.

- Taxes minimize the total abatement costs of hitting the target from society's point of view. But taxes can be more expensive than regulation for firms themselves. This is because firms pay for both abatement and the pollution tax on their remaining emissions. This tax payment could be greater than the abatement costs, and can result in the total financial burden of taxes (areas 'a' + 'b' in Figure 2.5) exceeding that under regulation. This aspect of pollution taxes has, unsurprisingly, resulted in industry lobbying against their wider use.

- The EPA has insufficient information with which to set the tax rate correctly. Additionally, these taxes have to be updated based on new information; for example, as firms' abatement costs change. This makes the uncertainty problem more serious, since it means that the EPA has to keep on re-guessing what the tax rate should be.

Set the quantity of social damages—tradable pollution permit systems, or cap-and-trade. An alternative to a fixed tax is a fixed quantity of pollution that can be traded in a market. Pollution permit markets work by assigning the property rights to pollute to firms, governments, and people (see Gayer, 2008). These rights create and add value to something that was otherwise a free good; for example, clean air or water. This tradable permits, or cap-and-trade, system was first introduced by Professors Thomas Crocker and J. Dales in the mid-1960s. The idea was controversial then because many people did not think that we should 'put a price' on nature. Today, many environmental groups promote the idea of cap-and-trade as the most cost-effective way to protect nature.

Tradable permits focus on the quantity side of the market equation. A regulator selects a fixed quantity of pollution or development, and then sets the number of permits available for trade accordingly. These permits are then allocated to firms and people in the affected area. People then buy and sell these permits on the open market. People who keep pollution or development below their allotted permit level can sell or lease their surplus permits. People who exceed their allocation must buy permits from those who either produce less or find less-polluting technologies.

What makes a tradable permit system effective? Economists have identified the conditions under which such a system is more likely to work. Permits must be well defined and scarce, so that their value can be estimated accurately. Free trade should dominate the permit market. Government intervention, bottlenecks, and transaction costs that limit the scope of trading should be minimal. Less friction increases the odds that people who value the permits the most will buy or keep them. Permits should be 'bankable', such that people have the flexibility to save and spend permits as the market conditions fluctuate. People should be allowed to keep any profits they earn from the trade of permits. The penalties for violating a permit must exceed the permit price, to help make sure people play by the rules.

Again consider the case of Riley and Ole. With a tradable permit system, the regulator selects the amount of ridge development allowable in the valley: development quotas are selected at the socially efficient level, in which marginal benefits equal marginal cost. The regulator allocates permits to the Centennial community based on some predetermined rule—perhaps the number of acres or years spent in the valley. The permits are then free to be traded. If Riley wants to develop open space by building on the ridgeline, he can buy more development permits on the open market. In theory, the equilibrium permit price equates the marginal costs to the marginal benefits of development. Again, the efficient outcome is achieved.

To see how this works, consider our example of a pollution tax. The EPA faced a situation in which two firms emitted a total of 20,000 tonnes of BOD per week, whereas the target level of emissions was only 10,000 tonnes. Instead of imposing a tax, the EPA could have created 10,000 emission permits and allowed firms to trade them between themselves. Because it would be illegal to emit beyond one's permit holding, the target emissions reduction would be reached: with 10,000 permits available, 10,000 tonnes of BOD could be legally discharged in total.

What advantages do tradable permit systems possess? In Figure 2.6, the *MAC* curves for Jones and Bloggs are shown again. Suppose that each firm is given 5,000 permits. Both must cut emissions because their unregulated level is 10,000 tonnes, but by how much? Imagine that, at first, neither firm is willing to trade permits. At an emission level of 5,000 tonnes, Jones faces marginal costs of 100, and so could save this amount if it could increase its emissions by one tonne. That would involve buying a permit from Bloggs, who would have to be willing to sell. Bloggs might sell provided that the permit price was greater than its cost of reducing emissions. The cost to Bloggs of this sale is 50 (its marginal abatement cost at this level of emission): the minimum Bloggs would take is less than the most Jones will offer—a deal can be done. Both Jones and Bloggs gain from this trade. If the permit was to change hands for a price of £80, both would be better off. If all such gains from trade can be captured, we expect trading to continue until the *MAC*s are equalized across sources in a competitive market for permits. This idea of trading until we 'equalize *MAC*s' is a necessary condition for the cost-minimizing outcome: tradable permits, like taxes, can offer a least-cost way of controlling pollution.

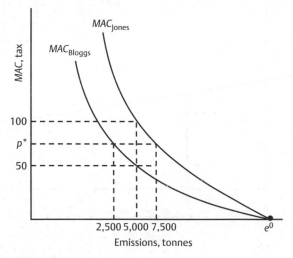

Figure 2.6 Tradable permits as the least-cost solution.

Another way of thinking about trading permits is to consider how a firm would react if offered permits for sale at some fixed price, such as p^* in Figure 2.7(a). Jones would choose to buy e^* permits at this price, which necessitates a cut in emissions from e^0 to e^*. Why? Because if Jones were to buy more permits, they would have spent more on permits, at the margin, than it would cost to abate. If they were to buy less than e^*, they would have spent too little on permits given the cost of abatement. The optimal amount to purchase is the level at which marginal costs intersects with marginal benefits, e^*: Jones should purchase permits until the price exceeds the benefits. If the permit price were to increase, the firm would choose to buy less, and would have to spend more on emissions control (e.g. at p^{**}). If the price fell, they would buy more permits and spend less on pollution control. The firm's MAC curve is its demand curve for permits.

Where does this permit price come from? One way to think about this is as the interaction of supply and demand in the permit market. Supply is determined by the number of permits available in total, and that is determined by the EPA when it sets the maximum desired level of emissions, E^* in Figure 2.7(b). The supply curve S is vertical at this point, since no more permits are available from the EPA, irrespective of the price. MAC_I is the aggregate marginal abatement cost curve: its shows the market demand for permits. At E^*, supply and demand are equal at price p^*, and this is the market clearing permit price. If all firms behave as Jones, in a multi-firm market with many dischargers (firms a, b, c, ...), we end up with the situation that

$$MAC(a) = MAC(b) = MAC(c) = ...p^*,$$

which is the same efficient outcome as with a tax.

In practice, permit trading can take place in two ways. First, the EPA may decide to launch the permit market by auctioning permits. All firms bid for permits from a single seller. Once firms have acquired their initial holding, they can trade with each other as their circumstances change or as firms enter and leave the industry/area. In this case, the permit price depends on the bargains that firms strike with each other.

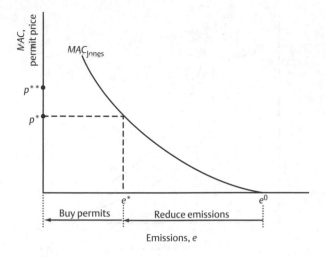

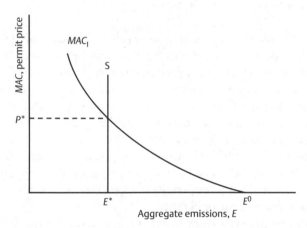

Figure 2.7 Prices in the permit market (a) individual (b) aggregate.

Second, the EPA could give permits away, a practice known as 'grandfathering'. All trades will be inter-firm, unless environmental groups buy permits and then withhold them from the market (to reduce the maximum legal level of emissions). Firms prefer grandfathering to auctioning, since the financial burden is less on average. As with taxes, this financial burden has two parts: the resource costs of pollution abatement, and payments (net of receipts) for permits.

We have seen that permits can generate a least-cost, efficient means of controlling pollution. So what is the catch?

- Transaction costs imply that fewer trades take place than needed to realize all potential abatement cost-savings. The transaction costs are the costs associated with finding potential buyers/sellers, and with negotiating subsequent trades. Evidence from the sulphur-trading programme in the USA suggests that these can be a high percentage of the gains from trade.

- If few firms participate in the permit market, they are less likely to behave competitively. For example, a large, powerful permit seller may withhold some permits from the market to keep their price high. This kind of behaviour, by both buyers and/or sellers, may result in a loss of permit market efficiency, but this depends on the precise circumstances.

- When pollutants are non-uniformly mixed, allowing permits to trade at a one-for-one rate may result in local violations in water quality standards. Imagine that two firms are thinking of trading. In Figure 2.8, firm A is a potential buyer from firm B. Because A is located upstream of B, each unit of A's emissions does more harm than each unit from B. If A buys 100 permits from B, total emissions remain constant, but environmental damage rises, especially in the zone immediately downstream of A. This situation arises in water pollution control, and several solutions have been proposed. One is zonal trading—here, a zone rule would prohibit trades between A and B, and would allow trades between A and another firm, C. But the more trade is restricted in this way, the lower is the cost-saving potential. Another idea is to use trading rules, which would restrict the rate at which A and B can trade. Suppose that A's emissions are twice as harmful per unit as B's in terms of average water quality. The regulator could impose an exchange rate of 0.5/1 per trade between the two. Under this scheme, exchange rates are calculated for all firms on the river, which is possible given current water quality models. In reality, however, one of the largest actual Tradable Pollution Permit (TPP) systems in use, sulphur trading in the USA, does not address the fact that SO_2 is a non-uniformly mixed pollutant, and allows emission-based trades to go ahead at a one-for-one rate.

- Existing firms may use permits as a barrier to entry, to keep out new firms who want to set up.

None of these criticisms means that *all* of the cost-saving potential of TPPs is lost. We would expect some cost savings if a change were to be made from regulation to trading. Relative to pollution taxes, TPPs possess some advantages too. Most importantly, the EPA does not need to know the firms' *MAC* curves to set the system up. All it does is decide how many permits to issue, and what restrictions—if any—to place on trade, and then police the system. Firms may also prefer trading to pollution taxes if permits are allocated free of charge (grandfathered) rather than auctioned. Financial burdens are lower than with an

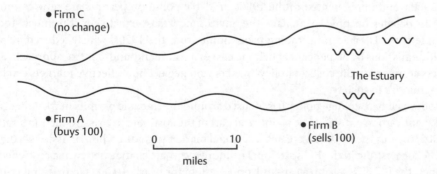

Figure 2.8 Permit trading in an estuary.

BOX 2.5 Trading Pollution Permits: What's the Evidence?

Up until the introduction of the European Union's carbon cap-and-trade scheme, the USA had the most extensive experience of using tradable permit markets to control pollution. The initial moves towards use of TPPs came in the 1970s, due to conflicts between achieving national targets for clean air and allowing economic growth in industrialized states that were in violation of these national targets. Policy initiatives such as offsets, netting, and banking were brought together under the Emissions Trading Program in 1986. This allowed for limited permit trading in 'emission credits' for seven pollutants in 247 control regions across the USA.

In 1992, amendments to the Clean Air Act paved the way for a nationwide cap-and-trade system for sulphur dioxide emissions from power stations. The aim was to reduce total emissions to 50 per cent of existing levels. The market began in 1995. Some 110 of the largest power stations were allocated permits based on historical emissions, and then allowed to trade. Even though SO_2 is a non-uniformly mixed pollutant, permits traded at a one-for-one rate. In 2000, 800 additional power stations were to be brought into the scheme.

Evidence suggests that the pollution permit markets have performed well. First, total emissions fell by more than the target level in phase 1, as firms banked permits for future use. The market in permits grew steadily, and permits prices fell from an initial high of around $1,000/tonne to around $100/tonne. The increasing volume of trading, which reduced transaction costs, and falling abatement costs caused this price fall. This last factor was due to suppliers of abatement equipment cutting their prices, since firms now had an alternative (buying permits), and by reductions in the price of low-sulphur coal due to deregulation.

Overall, the cost savings of the sulphur trading programme have been estimated at up to 50 per cent of what the costs would had been if regulation had been employed instead. This implies a saving to the US economy of nearly $1 billion per year (Carlson et al., 2000). Finally, the total costs of the scheme seem to be less than the benefits, which include the economic value of avoided damage to human health, ecosystems, and recreational activities. Tradable permits have provided good value for the money.

emission tax system. TPP mechanisms also do not need updating if firms' abatement costs shift, since this changes the demand for permits: actual emissions cannot rise above the maximum permitted (see also Box 2.5).

Whether tradable permit markets can flourish as a tool to manage environmental and health dilemmas will be determined over time. Conceived in the 1960s, tested in the 1970s and 1980s, and implemented in the 1990s, tradable pollution permits are now commonplace in debates on how to manage the environment cost-effectively. The most studied example is the US acid rain trading programme from the 1990s, which reduced sulphur dioxide emissions by 50 per cent at half the cost of a command-and-control approach. Such success stories raise the costs to policy-makers who neglect how effective markets can be at managing risk to society.

Modern climate change policy has focused around the tradable permits market that is the market for carbon emissions, as an integral part of the cost-effective risk reduction strategy. In 2005, the European Union created a regional market to trade carbon emissions—the EU ETS. A cornerstone in the EU's attempts to address climate change policy in a cost-effective manner, the EU ETS sets up a cap-and-trade system for nearly 10,000 factories, oil refineries, electricity utilities, and more. The ETS market allows buyers the flexibility to find low-cost carbon emissions from around the world. Estimates suggest that a well-functioning market would cut the costs of reaching the Kyoto targets by between 50–80 per cent (see Chapter 9). The main criticism is that the EU ETS caps were set in too loose a fashion in Phases I and II to induce a significant reduction in carbon emissions. The counter-argument is that Phases I and II helped the EU define how the system would work—better emissions data, better monitoring, and creating a positive price on carbon emissions. Phase III begins in 2013, with the stated goal of reducing carbon emissions in the EU by 21 per cent from 2005 levels (see Parker, 2010).

Summary

Over millennia, humans increased their life expectancy by a few years. About 200 years ago, something changed, and since then Western culture has witnessed a thirty-year increase in our longevity. Economists do not see this as a coincidence. In 1776, Adam Smith published his classic work *The Wealth of Nations*, which explained the power of the market to create wealth through trade. Economists argue that understanding how markets collect, codify, and disseminate diffuse information has helped to create the social order to improve the quality and length of life in our modern world for many people.

In this chapter, we have examined how markets can work against and for the environment and natural resources. Markets are a process of discovery. Markets allow us to create wealth, which in turn allows us to create more health. And even when one market fails, a new market can be constructed to manage the environment. Markets do not substitute for good environmental policy; rather, they can be a good tool to promote more protection for less wealth. Markets can make good environmental policy better by allowing for the flexibility to protect valuable resources cost-effectively. Remember: markets work for us, and not the other way around. Identifying if and how markets can be created or corrected is a major task for all of us who are interested in providing more environmental protection at less cost.

Tutorial Questions

2.1 Define Pareto efficiency.

2.2 Explain the four conditions that must hold for the existence of a well-defined property rights system, and address why all four matter.

2.3 Why do economists promote the idea of creating markets for environmental protection?

2.4 What is a public good and why are public goods considered a market failure?

2.5 Explain the idea behind the phrase the 'tragedy of the commons'.

2.6 Explain why moral hazard and adverse selection are market failures?

2.7 How can government help solve the problems of hidden information?

2.8 Explain how Pigovian taxes work to control pollution.

2.9 How do tradable pollution permits work in theory and in practice?

References and Additional Readings

Arrow, K. (1969). 'The organization of economic activity: issues pertinent to the choice of market versus nonmarket allocation', *The Analysis and Evaluation of Public Expenditures: The PPB System* (Washington, DC: Joint Economic Committee, 91st Congress): 47–64.

Baumol, W., and Oates, W. (1988). *The Theory of Environmental Policy*, 2nd edn. (Cambridge: Cambridge University Press).

Carlson, C., Burtraw, D., Cropper, M., and Palmer, K. (2000). 'Sulfur dioxide control by electric utilities: What are the gains from trade?' *Journal of Political Economy* 108: 1292–326.

Coase, R. (1960). 'The problem of social cost', *Journal of Law and Economics* 3: 1–44.

Cornes, R., and Sandler, T. (1996). *The Theory of Externalities, Public Goods, and Club Goods*, 2nd edn. (Cambridge: Cambridge University Press).

Crocker, T. (1966). 'The structure of atmospheric pollution control systems', in H. Wolozing (ed.), *The Economics of Air Pollution* (New York: W.W. Norton): 61–86.

Dales, J. (1968). *Pollution, Property, and Prices* (Toronto: University of Toronto Press).

Dallimer, M., Acs, S., Hanley, N., Wilson, P., Gaston, K., and Armsworth, P. (2009). 'What explains property-level variation in avian diversity? An inter-disciplinary approach', *Journal of Applied Ecology* 46: 647–56.

Fankhauser, S., Tol, R.S.J., and Pearce, D.W. (1998). 'Extensions and alternatives to climate change impact valuation: on the critique of IPCC Working Group III's impact estimates', *Environment and Development Economics* 3: 59–81.

Finnoff, D., and Tschirhart, J. (2008). 'Linking dynamic ecological and economic general equilibrium models', *Resource and Energy Economics* 30(2): 91–114.

Gayer, T. (2008). 'Pollution permits', in S. Durlauf and L. Blume (eds.), *The New Palgrave Dictionary of Economics*, 2nd edn. (New York: W.W. Norton). http://www.dictionaryofeconomics.com/dictionary.

Gordon, S. (1954). 'The economic theory of a common property resource: the fishery', *Journal of Political Economy* 62: 124–42.

Hanley, N., Shogren, J., and White, B. (2007). *Environmental Economics in Theory and Practice*, 2nd edn. (London: Palgrave Macmillan).

Hardin, G. (1968). 'The tragedy of the commons', *Science* 162: 1243–8.

Jurado, J., and Southgate, D. (1999). 'Dealing with air-pollution in Latin America: the case of Quito, Ecuador', *Environment and Development Economics* 4(3): 375–89.

Krugman, P., and Wells, R. (2008). *Microeconomics* (New York: Worth).

Ledyard, J. (2008). 'Market failure', in S. Durlauf and L. Blume (eds.), *The New Palgrave Dictionary of Economics*, 2nd edn. (New York: W.W. Norton). http://www.dictionaryofeconomics.com/dictionary.

Ostrom, E. (1990). *Governing the Commons* (Cambridge: Cambridge University Press).

Parker, L. (2010). *Climate Change and the EU Emissions Trading Scheme (ETS): Looking to 2020* (Washington, DC: Congressional Research Service). http://www.crs.gov.

Platteau, J-P. (2008). 'Common property resources', in S. Durlauf and L. Blume (eds.), *The New Palgrave Dictionary of Economics*, 2nd edn. (New York: W.W. Norton). http://www.dictionaryofeconomics.com/dictionary.

Samuelson, P. (1954). 'The pure theory of public expenditure', *Review of Economics and Statistics* 36: 387–9.

Sandmo, A. (2008). 'Pigouvian taxes', in S. Durlauf and L. Blume (eds.), *The New Palgrave Dictionary of Economics*, 2nd edn. (New York: W.W. Norton). http://www.dictionaryofeconomics.com/dictionary.

Schoeb, R. (2006). 'The double dividend hypothesis of environmental taxes: a survey', in H. Folmer and T. Tietenberg (eds.), *The International Yearbook of Environmental and Resources Economics 2005/2006* (Cheltenham: Edward Elgar): 223–79.

Stavins, R. (2003). 'Experience with market-based environmental policy instruments', in K. Mäler and J. Vincent (eds.), *The Handbook of Environmental Economics* (Amsterdam: North-Holland/Elsevier Science).

Weitzman, M. (1974). 'Prices vs. quantities', *Quarterly Journal of Economics* 41: 477–91.

3 Valuing the Environment: Concepts

In this chapter, we are going to consider:

- What 'economic value' means.
- In what ways the environment has economic value.
- How economic values might be measured.
- How measures of the economic value of the environment can help society make better decisions, particularly through cost–benefit analysis.

In the next chapter, empirical methods for measuring environmental values will be explained.

3.1 What Does Economic Value Mean?

Economics is often described as the study of how to allocate limited resources in the face of unlimited wants. The fact that resources are scarce means that using up resources in one way prevents us from using them in another way. The cost of these forgone uses is called an *opportunity cost*, defined as the best alternative use forgone. This concept is very relevant to the environment: using a river for waste disposal has an opportunity cost of lost recreation and wildlife benefits. Designating a mountain area as a national park means that we forgo mineral extraction opportunities. In other words, deciding to use the environment in one way entails a sacrifice, namely the benefits we could have gained by using it in another other way. Environmental policy may also imply non-environmental sacrifices: for example, the decision to impose an energy tax to reduce carbon dioxide emissions may mean that poor households forgo significant consumption possibilities (Sterner, 2011). However, if society decides to go ahead with the tax, then a judgement must have been made, either explicitly or implicitly, that the benefits of reduced emissions are 'worth it', in the sense that they justify the costs.

The idea that the value of something is dependent on what we are willing to give up to have it is a key economic principle. But how should we express what is being given up? In the preceding example, poor households could be giving up a significant proportion of their consumption goods. In the case of preserving a mountain area from mineral extraction, the profits from extraction could also have funded a wide variety of forms of consumption. One approach, therefore, is to take the most general measure of what is being sacrificed, namely *income*. The simplest way to see this is by considering an example. Suppose that poor households were asked whether they would support a local tax on petrol and diesel fuel used by cars and lorries, with the objective of improving air quality in their city. One way of putting this question would be to ask if their willingness to pay (to give up income) for the air quality improvement was higher than the cost to them of the tax.

An important point to note here is that a *change* in environmental quality is being valued, not the *total* environment. Economic value really only has any meaning when it is defined over a change; that is, when it is measured with regard to more or less of a good or service being provided. The change could be 'marginal', in the sense of a relatively small change in the amount or level of environmental service (e.g. a 5% reduction in current ambient particulate levels in a city), or 'non-marginal', such as the total loss of a forest or the draining of a wetland. Willingness to pay (WTP)—or, more exactly, *maximum* willingness to pay—would, in this case, measure the benefits to people of a beneficial change in environmental quality. For instance, for a prospective increase in air quality, the WTP is the most income that an individual would give up to have the improvement in air quality. The logic here revolves around rationality: no one would be willing to give up more for a change than it is worth to them, in whatever way they were to derive value (utility) from this change. An objection that could be made is that if WTP is used as a measure of value to an individual, then this measure depends not just on their preferences (how much they dislike air pollution, relative to their likes or dislikes of other things) but also on their income. A rich household, with the same preferences, could clearly afford to pay more than a poor household. Economic values based on WTP would therefore always be biased in favour of the rich. Economists usually answer 'Yes, that's right. But willingness to pay is a pretty useless concept unless backed up by ability to pay. At the level of the economy as a whole, we clearly cannot give up more than we actually have or expect to earn.' Economic value, as measured by WTP, is thus a function of the existing income distribution, and may change as this distribution changes. If preferences differ, then people with similar amounts of income will be willing to pay different amounts for the same change in environmental quality. For example, if Joe is more concerned about urban air pollution problems because his kids suffer from asthma, but Josephine has no kids, then if their incomes are equal, Joe's WTP for a given improvement in air quality may well be higher than Josephine's.

To recap, given that resources are scarce, using them in one way implies an opportunity cost. The value of a particular resource use can be measured in terms of the sacrifice that people are willing to make to have it. At the most general level, this sacrifice is in terms of income, so therefore WTP makes sense as a measure of economic value to the individual. However, we have to accept that this measure is sensitive to changes in the distribution of income.

An alternative measure of economic value exists, based on the same principles of scarcity. This involves asking what compensation an individual would accept to give something up. This is a very familiar idea in everyday life. For example, the value you place on your favourite guitar is equal to the *minimum* you would accept to go without it (to sell it), which we can call your minimum 'willingness to accept compensation' (WTA). For workers, the value of their working time is measurable by the minimum hourly wage they would accept to work. This compensation-for-loss concept of value can also be extended to environmental resources. The value you place on your garden could be estimated by the minimum compensation you would accept to sell it to your neighbour. Similarly, the value of peace and quiet could be thought of as the minimum compensation you would demand to agree to a new airport runway being constructed near to your house.

The question of whether we use WTP or WTA as the basis for valuation matters. According to a famous paper by Robert Willig (1976), the differences between WTP and WTA for most goods should be small, and should depend on the relationship between income and demand, and on how much of a person's income is spent on the good. However, experimental findings in economics have revealed quite large differences between WTP and WTA that seem to violate this finding. Competing explanations have emerged for this disparity. The first, based on work by Michael Hanemann (1991), shows that the difference is explicable in terms of how close a substitute exists for a commodity. For example, if we were to compare WTP with WTA for tickets for two ice hockey games, one of which was also being televised live, we might expect the difference between WTP and WTA to be smaller for the game that people could watch live on TV instead of only being able to watch it live at the stadium. If there are no close substitutes, then we could expect quite large differences between WTP and WTA, whereas if close substitutes exist, then WTP and WTA should not be that different. The second explanation is rooted in behavioural psychology, in the concept of loss aversion. This concept suggests that people systematically value what they already have more highly than that which they could acquire, so that losses are always valued more highly than equivalent gains. Experimental economics has also shown that differences between WTP and WTA can be much reduced as people gain experience in trading in a good, although such experience can be hard to gain for many environmental goods. This relates to a third possible explanation for the disparity, namely that people are unsure about their preferences (Loomes et al., 2003).

It seems likely, therefore, that important choices will often have to be made by economists between measuring WTP or WTA. Such choices can be based around the concept of property rights. If people have a moral, legal, or assumed right to a good, we would ask them about their WTA for a reduction in that good, not their WTP to prevent this reduction. If, instead, people have no right to an increase in a good, then it is reasonable to ask for their WTP for an increase, rather than their WTA to forgo such an increase.

To summarize, if an increase in an environmental good is being valued, we can try to measure either what people's maximum WTP is to have this increase, or what their minimum WTA is to forgo this increase. If a reduction in the same good is being valued, we can try to uncover either their maximum WTP to prevent such a reduction, or their minimum WTA to tolerate it. Either approach allows a monetary value to be placed on an environmental gain or loss, which is an estimate of the underlying utility gain or loss for an individual.

But how might WTP vary for that person for different amounts of an environmental good being offered? Imagine an experiment in which an individual is asked about his or her maximum WTP for a succession of increases in an environmental good. For one such person, Gavin, we might get results such as are shown in Figure 3.1(a). As the quantity of the

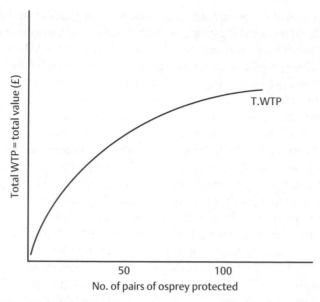

Figure 3.1(a) WTP for wildlife protection.

good rises (as an example, we might consider pairs of ospreys protected in Scotland), Gavin's total WTP increases: for example, he is willing to pay more to protect 100 pairs than for fifty pairs, since, as a birdwatcher, his utility is higher for 100 pairs than for fifty. Note that as the number of pairs 'offered' continues to increase, his total WTP (the total value to him of ospreys) increases at a decreasing rate. Transforming Figure 3.1(a) into a marginal WTP curve—by measuring the increase in total WTP as the number of pairs, Q, rises—we get Figure 3.1(b), which shows marginal WTP decreasing but always positive[1] (no satiation is setting in, so that utility always goes up as consumption rises). Marginal WTP declines as Q rises due to diminishing marginal utility. Figure 3.1(c) shows Gavin's marginal WTP curve, which we now term a marginal value curve, MV^G, since it indeed shows the value at the margin to him of increasing numbers of ospreys. His friend Kitty is also a birdwatcher, who likes ospreys even more: her marginal value curve, MV^K, thus lies above Gavin's at every point (we assume, for simplicity, that Gavin and Kitty have equal incomes). Drawing MV curves as smooth and continuously decreasing is a theoretical assumption that makes the analysis easier, but that may not be borne out in reality. However, the assumption of declining marginal utility does seem to be well supported by a large amount of evidence from economic research.

Figure 3.2 shows the derivation of WTP and WTA for an individual who is offered an increase in environmental quality from Q_0 to Q_1. This diagram shows utility as being a function of two things: environmental quality, Q, and income, Y. The curves U_0 and U_1 are *indifference curves*. These have the property that along a given indifference curve, utility is constant. Indifference curves are shaped the way they are drawn as we assume diminishing

---

[1] Marginal WTP for any value of Q, say Q*, is equal to the slope of the total WTP curve at Q*. It is the partial derivative of total WTP with respect to Q, evaluated at Q*.

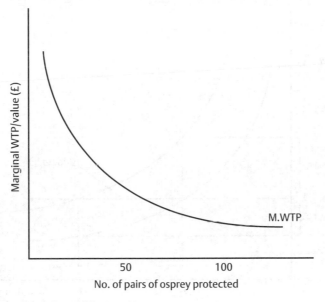

Figure 3.1(b) Marginal WTP for wildlife protection.

marginal utility, as in Figures 3.1: as we move along a particular indifference curve, the additional amount of one good we are willing to give up to have more and more of another good is falling, since the extra utility from having more of something declines as we consume more and more of that thing. The further an indifference curve is away from the origin, the higher is the level of utility, thus U_1 is greater than U_0. We start at point a, with an income of y and an environmental quality of Q_0. Now suppose that the environmental

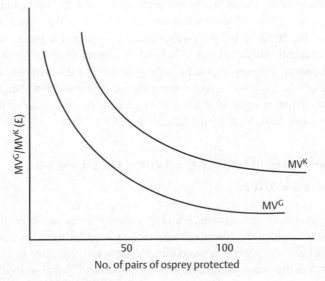

Figure 3.1(c) Marginal WTP for two people.

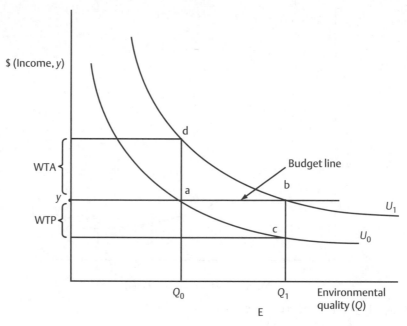

Figure 3.2 Indifference curves and the value of an increase in environmental quality.

Note: Environmental quality increases from Q_0 to Q_1. This increases consumer utility from U_0 to U_1 along their fixed budget line, moving the consumer from point a to point b. This also implies that consumers have a maximum willingness to pay of WTP. Alternatively, they would be willing to accept compensation of WTA to forgo an improvement in environmental benefits. Note that WTA is greater than WTP.

quality increases to Q_1. With the same income, the individual moves to point b, on a higher indifference curve. They are thus better off. What is their maximum WTP for this increase in environmental quality? This is the most income they could give up from point a and still have utility equal to U_0. We can see that this amount is the vertical distance labelled WTP in the figure; that is, the distance (bc). This diagram can also be used to work out the minimum compensation that this individual would have to be offered to forgo the improvement in environmental quality. Starting at point b, if income rises by the amount shown as WTA, this keeps the individual at utility level U_1, even when the environmental quality stays at Q_0. Thus the difference (da) is equal to WTA. Notice that, given the way in which the diagram is drawn, WTP is less than WTA for the same change in Q.

3.2 In What Sense Does the Environment Have Economic Value?

In Chapter 1, we saw how environmental and economic systems are interlinked. Figure 1.1 shows that the environment provides four services to the economy: (i) as a source of energy and material resources (inputs) to production; (ii) as a waste sink; (iii) as a direct source of amenity; and (iv) as the provider of other local, regional, and global support services, such as nutrient cycling and climate regulation. Services (i), (ii), and (iv) can be grouped together

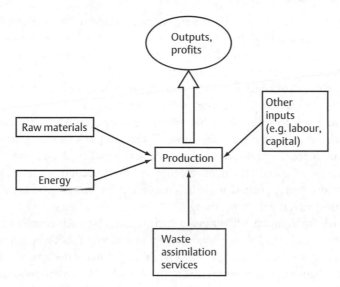

Figure 3.3 Indirect environmental values.

as they both provide inputs to the production process, of raw materials, energy, nutrients, and waste disposal services. Climate change may also impact on production; for example, in agriculture. Figure 3.3 shows these inputs, combined with other inputs such as labour and capital, producing goods and services for sale in markets. For example, inputs of bauxite, energy, and waste assimilation capabilities allow the production of aluminium. One monetary value of each unit of output is its price. The value of a *change* in the level of environmental and resource inputs to the production of any good might thus be approximated by the value of the change in profits due to this change in environmental service flows or inputs. The values of the environment in roles (i) or (ii) or (iv) above can thus be partly determined as the change in the value of profits for a change in the value of environmental inputs: in other words, if bauxite inputs are reduced by one tonne, what is the value of the associated profit decrease? For waste assimilation services, essentially the same question could again be asked: What is the loss in profits associated with a unit reduction in emissions? This marginal productivity approach for determining environmental values is essentially no different from the approach used to determine the value of other inputs to production, such as labour and capital. Let us call these types of environmental values *indirect benefits*, since the environment is valued indirectly through its role in the production process.

For amenity values, we need to consider more direct impacts of the environment on utility. We can speak of environmental 'goods' as those environmental inputs of which the individual prefers more to less (e.g. landscape quality, good air quality). Environmental 'bads' would then be those environmental inputs that decrease utility as they increase: for example, noise or water pollution. Clearly, some environmental goods and bads are mirror images of each other; for example, river water quality (a good) and river water pollution (a bad). The economic value of any environmental good can be thought of as the increase in utility if that environmental input is increased by a given amount; or the reduction in utility if the quantity and/or quality of that good is decreased. Similarly, for an environmental bad, we are interested in the amount by which utility increases if the environmental bad is reduced. Ideally, we would seek to measure the marginal utility of changes in environmental goods (and bads), this being the change in utility for a one-unit increase in the good expressed in terms of WTP or WTA. These types of environmental values could be called *direct* benefits, since their effect on utility is direct, rather than indirectly through their role in the production of consumption goods and services.

An important point to note here is that the environment can thus have economic value, in terms of both indirect and direct values, even if it has no market value or price. For example, many of the environmental goods, such as landscape quality, clean air, and wildlife, may have a zero market price and yet will most certainly have an economic value, provided that at least one person derives positive utility from them. Therefore, economic values and market prices are *not* generally the same thing.

There is no reason to suppose that a given environmental good is equally valuable to everyone (economists refer to this as *preference heterogeneity*). It is to be expected that the marginal utility of the good (that is, the change in utility when the level of the good itself changes by a small amount) will vary across individuals, whilst some individuals may derive no utility at all from some environmental resources. For example, if Joe is completely uninterested in birdwatching, then an increase in his local population of curlews may well have zero value to him. If his neighbour Jane is a keen ornithologist, then her marginal utility for this same increase may be very high. This means that these two people would have different WTP amounts for a given change in bird populations.

As shown in Figure 1.1, the economic process benefits from the many support services provided by the natural environment, such as global climate regulation, the maintenance of a global atmospheric chemistry suitable for sustaining life, the stratospheric ozone layer, and local nutrient and hydrological cycles. It is possible to think about the value of preventing changes in these services. For example, the value of preventing further changes in the global climate through enhanced warming could be measured by looking at the costs (and benefits) that would result from a given change in greenhouse gas emissions. Chapter 9 considers this in detail. As another example, reductions in the stratospheric ozone layer could be valued by estimating the economic costs of an increased incidence of skin cancer.

A recent way of thinking about these links between the environment and the economy is the idea of *ecosystem services*. This conceptualization of the value of conserving or enhancing ecosystems is most associated with the Millennium Ecosystem Assessment.[2] More recently, the National Ecosystem Assessment (NEA) exercise in the United Kingdom[3] has shown the links between the state of different ecosystems (in the UK) and the economic values that flow from the services generated by these ecosystems (see the UK NEA). In this world view, ecosystems are thought of as capital assets (Barbier, 2009) generating a flow of valuable services (economic goods). The conservation of ecosystems can then be described as investment, since it enables the flow of ecosystem services and their associated goods to be protected into the future. Ecosystems depreciate when their ability to supply people with useful services is reduced; for example, if a wetland is drained, or a coastal mangrove forest converted into a shrimp farm.

[2] See http://www.millenniumassessment.org/en/index.aspx.
[3] See http://uknea.unep-wcmc.org.

Following from the Millennium Ecosystem Assessment, ecosystem services are often categorized into four groups:

- Provisioning services, such as the production of food supplies
- Regulating services, such as the maintenance of a good water quality
- Support services, such as the provision of habitat for mammals and birds
- Cultural services, such as the values associated with landscapes

Table 3.1 shows an illustrative categorization of some ecosystem service flows for one ecosystem (moorlands and heaths) in the United Kingdom, from the UK's National Ecosystem Assessment. Actual or predicted changes in any of these service flows can then be expressed in terms of economic costs or benefits by multiplying the actual or predicted change in ecosystem service by the marginal economic value (e.g. from market prices, or from some other source). For instance, if degradation of moorland leads to a net loss of carbon, these tonnes of lost carbon could be valued using the CO_2 permit price from the European Emissions Trading Scheme, since this is one measure of the value of each tonne of carbon sequestered. If moorland loss also means a decline in water quality downstream

Table 3.1 Some of the ecosystem service flows from moorlands and heaths

Provisioning services	Food provision—livestock and crops:
	• Livestock products from sheep and some beef cattle
	Food provision—deer and game birds:
	• Wild harvest products, including venison and grouse meat
	Fibre from sheep wool
	Traditional lifestyle products, including honey and whisky
	Peat extraction for fuel and horticultural use
	Freshwater provision for domestic and industrial use
	Alternative energy provision:
	• Opportunity for wind energy schemes
	• Generation of water flows for hydro-energy in freshwater habitats
Regulating services	Climate regulation:
	• Carbon storage; maintenance of plant and soil C stores
	• Carbon sequestration potential
	Natural hazard regulation:
	• Potential for flood risk mitigation
	• Opportunities for wildfire risk mitigation
	Pollution mitigation:
	• Interception and retention of airborne pollutants by plants and soil
	• Regulation of particulate matter and pH buffering
	• Dilution by water from uplands of pollutants in downstream locations
	Disease regulation:
	• Disease transmission through ticks
	• Disease regulation of waterborne bacteria (e.g. *Cryptosporidia*)

Source: Van der Wal et al. (2011).

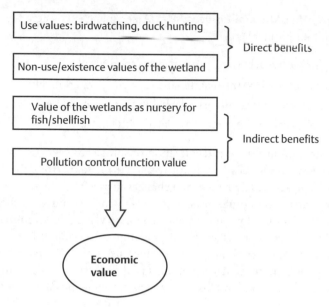

Figure 3.4 The economic value of a wetland.

in the catchment, then this could be valued by looking at the additional costs to water companies of cleaning up the water prior to supplying it to customers. If moorlands are replaced by forests, then lost sheep production could be valued using the market price of lambs.

This idea of 'valuing ecosystem services' can be related to a further categorization system of environmental benefits that has become popular in the literature (Pearce and Turner, 1989). Take, as an example, the preservation of a wetland that is important to birds, but that also functions as a nursery for fish/shellfish and as a natural pollution control plant. How might the *total economic value* of this wetland be described (Figure 3.4)?

Consider first what we have called direct benefits; that is, direct sources of utility. Some of those who benefit from the wetland in this way may participate in activities that make the wetland valuable to them, such as birdwatching or duck hunting. Such benefits are often known as *use values*, since they require actual participation to enjoy them. Use values may be consumptive (hunting) or non-consumptive (birdwatching). However, people other than those who actually visit the wetland may derive benefits, in terms of the utility they get from just knowing that the wetland is preserved. These types of benefit have become known as *non-use* or *existence values*. They may be motivated by selfish reasons, or by altruism, either for other members of the current generation, or for future generations. Existence values may be particularly high for unique, irreplaceable natural assets, such as the Grand Canyon in the United States or Kakadu National Park in Australia.

The sum of use and existence values gives the total direct benefits of preserving the wetland. The wetland's role as a nursery for fish and shellfish could be evaluated by estimating biological models of the contribution that the wetland makes to fish/shellfish populations, and then by looking at the economic (commercial) value of these species. Changes in these

Table 3.2 Values provided by tropical coastal and marine ecosystems

Direct values	Indirect values	Existence and bequest values
Fishing:	Nutrient retention and cycling:	Cultural heritage:
• Aquaculture	• Flood control	• Resources for future generations
• Transport	• Storm protection	• Existence of charismatic species
• Wild resources	• Habitat for species	• Existence of wild places
• Water supply	• Shoreline stabilization	
• Recreation		
• Genetic material		

Source: Adapted from Heal et al. (2005).

economic values, in terms of gains/losses in consumers' surplus[4] and producers' profits from some change in the wetland, could be calculated. Finally, the wetland's pollution control function could be valued either by using the value of avoided pollution damages (say, from sedimentation of coral reef fisheries, or from nutrient enrichment), or the pollution control costs that would have to be incurred to replace the role currently being played by the wetland. The sum of avoided pollution and/or pollution control costs, plus the value of commercial fisheries, would give the indirect benefits of preserving the wetland. Adding the wetland's direct and indirect benefits gives its total economic value. Table 3.2 shows an illustration of a similar breakdown of benefits for tropical coastal ecosystems, such as a mangrove wetland (note that this employs a somewhat different categorization of benefits than we have used).

3.3 Why Place Economic Values on the Environment?

Economic estimates of the value of changes in environmental and resource quality may be useful in a number of contexts. The main use that we review here is cost–benefit analysis (CBA; also called benefit–cost analysis in the USA), although only a brief explanation of this method is provided (for more details, see Hanley and Barbier, 2009). Other uses of environmental values are noted at the end of this section.

3.3.1 Cost–benefit analysis

Economists have long been intrigued by the problem of how to decide whether one outcome is better than another from society's point of view (see Box 3.1). Ideally, we would like to find decision-making rules that give consistent outcomes; outcomes that are the same when applied in the same circumstances. We would also like to find a method that is democratic, in some sense, and practical; and that can be shown to be consistent with economic theory. Welfare economics developed out of the search for such a method. Cost–benefit analysis developed from welfare economics as a practical application of a decision-making rule that

[4] As Chapter 2 explains, the consumers' surplus is the difference between the most you are willing to pay for something and the price you actually pay. In a market-traded good, it is the area underneath the demand curve but above the equilibrium price.

BOX 3.1 What Role Should CBA Play in the Policy Process?

One of the earliest uses of cost–benefit analysis in public policy appraisal was in the assessment of water resource projects such as new dams or flood control investments in the USA. The 1936 Flood Control Act stated that the federal government should undertake public investments in flood alleviation if 'the benefits to whomsoever they may accrue are in excess of the estimated costs'. As Banzhaf (2009) explains, this eventually resulted in fierce debate amongst economists in the USA as to the proper role of CBA in the policy appraisal process. Essentially, the argument was between those who viewed the philosophical and theoretical structures of CBA to be robust enough for the outcome of a CBA to be viewed as actually determining whether a particular project should go ahead (this group was associated particularly with a think tank called Resources for the Future, which is still in existence today) and those who were sufficiently uneasy about the principle of making interpersonal utility comparisons in dollar terms to conclude that CBA should only inform the decision-making process. This latter group, most identified with Harvard University's Water Program, felt that political or 'expert' judgement should always be decisive, and that the role of the CBA analyst was no more than to make clear the trade-offs involved in deciding whether or not to proceed with a project. Moreover, the Harvard team viewed CBA as focusing too closely on a single objective—economic efficiency—in contrast to the multiple objectives of public policy.

These arguments over the correct role of CBA within the public policy process, and of the advantages and disadvantages of CBA relative to other project and policy appraisal methods, have continued ever since. However, CBA emerges as a remarkably robust institution, perhaps because of its apparent simplicity of approach: add up the benefits to society of a particular project and compare these with the costs. This still makes sense to a lot of economists and policy analysts as a way of thinking about decisions.

could be used to decide between different policy options or projects in terms of their net contribution to social well-being. CBA consists of identifying the impacts of a project or policy, valuing these impacts in terms of their effects on social well-being, and then comparing the good effects (benefits) with the bad effects (costs). Costs and benefits are expressed in monetary terms to allow comparison. The links with welfare economics come in terms of how benefits and costs are measured (e.g. using the principles of WTP and opportunity costs), and with the basis on which the difference between benefits and costs can be viewed as a proxy for the underlying change in net social welfare. This basis is often referred to as the *Kaldor–Hicks compensation test*. This asks: Could the gainers (those who benefit from a project) compensate the losers, and still be better off? Acceptance of this principle as the basis for evaluating contributions to social well-being in turn requires us to accept that: (i) all relevant benefits and costs can be expressed in the same units; and (ii) benefits and costs can be compared with each other, so that any cost (loss) can always be compensated by some offsetting benefit (gain). Clearly, not all would agree with these statements (see, e.g., Aldred, 2006).

3.3.1.1 The stages of a CBA

(1) Project/policy definition

This involves setting out exactly what is being analysed; whose welfare is being considered; and over what time period. In terms of 'whose welfare', the usual answer is that it is national well-being that is considered, although defining the 'relevant population' is often a difficult issue. For instance, if a new dam in Indonesia would threaten an internationally rare habitat, should the costs to foreign conservationists be counted?

(2) Identify physical impacts of the policy/project

Any project/policy has implications for resource allocation: for example, labour used to build access roads to a new hydroelectric dam; additional electricity production; land used up in the creation of the reservoir; or less pollution being generated from a coal-fired power station that can now be closed early. The next stage of a CBA is to identify these outcomes in physical magnitudes. Frequently, these changes in resource allocation will not be known with certainty—For example, how many tonnes of pollution will be displaced? Once physical impacts have been identified and quantified, it is then necessary to ask which of them are relevant to the CBA. Essentially, anything that impacts on the quantity or quality of resources, or on their price, may be said to be relevant, if these impacts can be traced back to a link to the well-being of the relevant population. Since we specify relevant impacts in terms of utility impacts, it is not necessary to restrict attention to market-valued impacts, since non-market value changes (such as an improvement in air quality) are relevant if they affect people's utility.

(3) Valuing impacts

One important feature of CBA is that all relevant effects are expressed in monetary values, so that they can then be aggregated. The general principle of monetary valuation in CBA is to value impacts in terms of their marginal social cost or marginal social benefit. Here, 'social' means 'evaluated with regard to the economy as a whole'. But where are these marginal social benefits and costs derived from? Under certain conditions, this information is contained in market prices, as Chapter 2 explains. Market prices contain information on both the value to consumers of a particular product (say, electricity) being supplied, and the costs to producers of supplying it. The market wage rate, similarly, shows both the value of labour to employers and the value of leisure to workers. Assuming that the impacts of the project are not large enough to actually change these prices, then market prices are a good first approximation to the values of benefits and costs. But markets often 'fail', as Chapter 2 shows. Moreover, for some environmental goods such as biodiversity and river water quality, no market at all exists from which a price can be observed. In this case, methods described in Chapter 4, and based on the principles of valuation outlined earlier in this chapter, will need to be employed.

(4) Discounting of cost and benefit flows

Once all relevant cost and benefit flows that can be expressed in monetary amounts have been so expressed, it is necessary to convert them all into *present value* (PV) terms. This necessity arises out of the time value of money, or time preference. To take a simple example, suppose that an individual is asked to choose between receiving £100 today and receiving that same £100 in one year's time. The more immediate sum might be preferred due to impatience (I want to spend the money right now). Alternatively, I may not want to spend the money for a year, but if I have it now, I can invest it in a bank at an interest rate of, say, 10 per cent and have $£100 \times (1 + i) = £110$ in one year's time, where i is the rate of interest. Benefits are more highly valued the sooner they are received. Similarly, a sum of money to be paid out, or any kind of cost, seems less onerous the further away in time we have to bear it. A bill of £1 million to repackage hazardous wastes seems preferable if paid in 100 years time rather than in 10 years time. This is nothing to do with inflation, but more to do with the expectation that we might expect to be better off in the future. Box 3.2 gives an example

BOX 3.2 An Illustrative CBA

Consider a project to support the construction of a new renewable energy source. A plan is proposed to build a small-scale wind farm in a scenic area. The initial construction costs are estimated to be £750,000. Following start-up, annual maintenance costs of £5,000 are expected throughout the 15-year lifespan of the plant. At the end of this 15-year period, the wind farm will need to be dismantled and the site restored, at an expected cost of £35,000. Every year after the initial construction year, the site will produce electricity with a market value of £150,000, which for now we take to be a constant flow in real terms (we will ignore the effects of inflation here). Objectors have protested about the visual impact of the windmills, and so the government has commissioned a contingent valuation study of local residents. The results suggest that the mean annual compensation demanded by locals is £25 per household: 2,000 households are thought to be affected (this mean is calculated across both those against the project and those in favour).

It is easy to set up a basic CBA of this project. The initial ('year zero') construction costs are not discounted, as they occur at the start of the project. Maintenance costs are then discounted each year using the relevant discount factor, for a discount rate of 6 per cent. Annual environmental costs of (£25 × 2,000) are also discounted over the 15 years of the project; and are assumed to stop when the site is restored at a cost of £35,000 in year 15. This year-15 cost also needs to be discounted. Annual benefits of £150,000 get discounted each year; you can see how the present value of this fixed amount falls each year as we move forward in time. The following table shows all workings:

Year	Discount factor at 6% discount rate, $(1.06)^{-t}$	Benefits (£)	Present value of benefits (£)	Costs (£)	Present value of costs (£)
0	1		0	750,000	750,000
1	0.9433	150,000	141,495	55,000	51,881
2	0.8899	150,000	133,485	55,000	48,944
3	0.8396	150,000	125,940	55,000	46,178
4	0.7921	150,000	118,815	55,000	43,565
5	0.7472	150,000	112,080	55,000	41,096
6	0.7049	150,000	105,735	55,000	38,769
7	0.6650	150,000	99,750	55,000	36,575
8	0.6274	150,000	94,110	55,000	34,507
9	0.5918	150,000	88,770	55,000	32,549
10	0.5583	150,000	83,745	55,000	30,706
11	0.5267	150,000	79,005	55,000	28,968
12	0.4969	150,000	74,535	55,000	27,329
13	0.4688	150,000	70,320	55,000	25,784
14	0.4423	150,000	66,345	55,000	24,326
15	0.4172			35,000	14,602
Total discounted benefits/costs			1,394,130		1,275,779

As we can see, the total present value of costs is £1,275 million, whilst the total present value of benefits is £1,394 million. Thus the net present value of the project is positive, at £118,351, which passes the CBA test at the 6 per cent discount rate. Note how little the site renovation cost of £35,000 amounts to in present-value terms: less than half its future value.

BOX 3.3 Discounting and the Discount Rate

Discounting means placing a lower value on benefits and costs the further away in time they occur. Why might this make sense? Two main reasons have been given for discounting. These revolve around:

- the productivity of capital, and
- preferences.

These motivate two possible choices for the discount rate to be used in public-sector policy and project appraisal:

- The social opportunity cost of capital, *r*, and
- The rate of social time preference, *s*.

Economies grow over time for many reasons, but an important one is that by building up the stock of capital, an economy increases its potential output. The act of investing in a new factory is expected to generate a flow of returns over time to the owner of that capital, in terms of annual sales of goods produced. Across the entire economy, invested capital generates a positive rate of return, meaning that the value of consumption goods in year $t + 1$ that could be produced should all of the resources of an economy be invested in year t will be greater than the maximum value of consumption goods that could be produced in year t. However, capital is scarce: investing £1 million in a new factory means that we cannot invest the same £1 million in another scheme. Choosing to invest in a particular scheme thus involves an opportunity cost, which is the return on capital forgone from some other use (in particular, from its most profitable alternative). Across the economy as a whole, we could rank investment projects in terms of their rates of return. These rates of return show the net benefits from investing resources rather than consuming. At the margin, this is known as the opportunity cost of capital, which can be used to measure the *social opportunity cost of capital*, *r*.

The other motivation for discounting is that 'pure time preference'—the desire for benefits to come sooner rather than later—is a fundamental feature of human desires. Various motivations have been suggested for time preference: impatience; the fact that we might not be around in the future to collect on benefits; that future benefits are less certain than present-day benefits; and that we might expect to be richer in the future, and thus will regard each extra pound of income as less valuable than we do today. An important distinction is between a discount rate that applies to individual well-being and that which might be applied to collective well-being. We could refer to the former as being a reflection of individual time preference and the latter as a reflection of the *rate of social time preference*, *s*.

For more detailed discussion of the discount rate and of alternative approaches to discounting, see Hanley and Barbier (2009: ch. 7).

of discounting of benefits and costs, whilst Box 3.3 discusses the concept of discount rates in more detail.

How is this time effect taken into account, and how are cost and benefit flows made comparable regardless of when they occur? The answer is that all cost and benefit flows are *discounted*, using a discount rate that is here assumed to be a market rate of interest, *i*. The present value (*PV*) of a cost or benefit (*X*) received in time *t* is then calculated as follows:

$$PV(X_t) = X_t \left[(1 + i)^{-t} \right]. \tag{3.1}$$

The expression in square brackets in equation (3.1) is known as a discount factor. Discount factors have the property that they always lie between 0 and +1. The further away in time a cost or benefit occurs (the higher the value of t), the lower is the discount factor. The higher the discount rate i for a given t, the lower is the discount factor, since a higher discount rate means a greater preference for things now rather than later.

(5) Applying the net present value test

The main purpose of CBA is to help select projects and policies that are efficient in terms of their use of resources. The criterion applied is the *net present value (NPV)* test, which is how the Kaldor–Hicks compensation principle is implemented. This test simply asks whether the sum of discounted gains exceeds the sum of discounted losses. If so, the project can be said to represent an efficient shift in resource allocation, given the data used in the CBA. The *NPV* of a project is thus as follows:

$$NPV = \sum B_t (1 + i)^{-t} - \sum C_t (1 + i)^{-t}, \tag{3.2}$$

where the summations (indicated by the 'Σ' symbols) run from $t = 0$ (the first year of the project) to $t = T$ (the last year of the project). Note that no costs or benefits before year 0 are counted. The criterion for project acceptance is as follows: accept if $NPV > 0$ (i.e. is positive). Any project passing the *NPV* test is deemed to be an improvement in social welfare.

(6) Sensitivity analysis

The *NPV* test described above tells us about the relative efficiency of a given project, given the data input to the calculations. If this data changes, then clearly the results of the *NPV* test will change too. But why should data change? The main reason concerns uncertainty. In many cases in which CBA is used, the analyst must make predictions concerning future physical flows (e.g. the quantity of electricity produced per year) and future relative values (e.g. the wholesale price of electricity). None of these predictions can be made with perfect foresight. When environmental impacts are involved, this uncertainty may be even more widespread; for example, if a policy to reduce global greenhouse gas emissions is planned, then the impacts of this in terms of avoided damage may be subject to a wide range of predictions. Therefore, an essential final stage of any CBA is to conduct a sensitivity analysis. This means recalculating the *NPV* when the values of certain key parameters are changed.

3.3.1.2 Why is CBA useful?

In one very important sense, the practice of CBA addresses what might be called the fundamental economic problem: how to allocate scarce resources in the face of unlimited wants. Resources are scarce because the sum total of demands on them exceeds their availability, and using up scarce resources in one way imposes an opportunity cost on society in that we cannot use those same resources for some other purpose. For example, a proposal in 2007 to expand irrigated agriculture on the Canterbury Plains in New Zealand suggested diverting water from two rivers to a newly constructed reservoir that would then be used to supply irrigation schemes for dairy farmers. However, if land is used up to create a reservoir, that same land cannot also be used for sheep farming. If water is taken from a river to supply a reservoir and then to irrigate dairy farms, that same water is not available in the river to maintain in-stream ecological quality, or to support water-based recreation such as kayaking.

Society might find it useful, in determining whether to allow such schemes, to know whether the economic benefits of irrigated dairy farming were bigger or smaller than the costs of reservoir construction, lost sheep farming output, losses in river ecological quality and losses in kayaking opportunities.

CBA is a decision-aiding tool that conveys this manner of useful information to decision-makers. Not only does CBA allow a comparison of the benefits and costs of particular actions, reflecting therein the scarcity of resources, but it also allows for ordinary people's *preferences* to be included in government decision-making. Economic values in a CBA depend partly on what people like (their preferences), what they are prepared to give up to have more of what they like (their WTP), and what they can afford to pay (their budget constraints). In a sense, CBA is an exercise in economic democracy, since every citizen gets an economic vote in terms of his or her WTP. CBA is also a formal way of setting out the impacts of a project or policy over time, of organizing debate over an issue, and of identifying who enjoys the gains and who suffers the losses from such undertakings. It is also, as Arrow et al. (1998) have noted, a good way of ensuring consistency and perhaps transparency in public-sector decision-making.

3.3.1.3 Uses of environmental CBA

One way in which CBA can be useful is as part of the *policy appraisal* process. Worldwide, much of the funding for environmental valuation studies has come from government departments and agencies with responsibilities for environmental policy design and implementation (e.g. in the United Kingdom, with the Forestry Commission and the Environment Agency); or with responsibility for policies that impact on the environment (e.g. roads policy). Within the European Union, CBA is an important aspect of implementing the Water Framework Directive and the REACH directive on chemicals registration. Within both the UK and the USA, CBA is also a part of the process by which the costs to the economy of new government regulations—for example, the costs of setting stricter targets for recycling of waste (garbage)—are regularly assessed.

Much early work on CBA was carried out in a *project appraisal* context. A good early example is its use in assessing the development of hydroelectric power in the USA (see Box 3.4 and Krutilla and Fisher, 1985). CBA is also used by public forest authorities in the UK in assessing the net benefits of alternative forest management regimes, and in the appraisal of major transport projects, such as new rail lines. The World Bank also has a long history of using CBA in project appraisal. Many governments worldwide have official guidelines on how CBA should be applied to the appraisal of public-sector projects (see, e.g., http://www.hm-treasury.gov.uk/data_greenbook_index.htm, which describes the procedures followed in the UK for both policy and project appraisal).

3.3.2 Other uses of environmental valuation

3.3.2.1 Setting environmental taxes

Environmental valuation has been used in the UK for setting eco-taxes; for example, with regard to the landfill tax and the tax on quarrying. Valuation has been used in both justifying

> **BOX 3.4 An Example of Cost–benefit Analysis of Hydropower Regulation**
>
> Kotchen et al. (2006) carry out a CBA of the re-licensing of two hydroelectric dams in Michigan. The policy context involves a move to reduce the environmental impacts of hydropower operations, by changing how rivers are managed. The changes investigated by Kotchen et al. involve managing releases from dams and reservoirs in a way that more closely parallels natural fluctuations in water levels, rather than timing releases to coincide with maximum electricity demands. This change imposes costs in terms of lost electricity output on hydro operators at peak periods, which must be compensated for with more expensive output from other sources—here, from fossil fuel-powered generation. The gain is an environmental one—in this case, an increase of about 270,000 salmon per year emigrating from the Manistee River to Lake Michigan. Due to the mix of fossil fuel power supplied to the grid, there is also an environmental gain from reduced net air pollution, since the peak-period demands are met from less polluting natural gas-powered generation rather than the more polluting coal sources.
>
> The costs to producers of the change in operations is given by the differences in marginal costs per kilowatt hour (kWh) between hydro-derived and fossil fuel-derived electricity. This implies that the annual costs for the two dams rise by about $310,000. For air pollution, the authors consider five pollutants, including NO_x, CO_2, and SO_2. Changes in air pollution between the two water management regimes are then converted into dollars using estimates from the literature of marginal damage costs, reporting a range of possible values. Finally, changes in migrating salmon numbers are converted into changes in predicted catches for recreational anglers, and then valued using travel cost-derived estimates of the value of recreational fishing (see Chapter 4).
>
> The conclusion of the study is that the benefits of changing the way in which the river system is managed for hydropower produces benefits that are larger than costs. Annual losses in electricity output imply costs in the range of $219,132–$402,094, with a best guess of $310,612. Annual benefits from emission reductions are in the range $67,756–$246,680, whilst gains in recreational fishing are worth $301,900–$1,068,600, with a most likely estimate of $738,400. The authors conclude that 'the benefits exceed the costs of the switch ... even ignoring the air quality benefits entirely, the best estimate of recreational fishing benefits exceeds the upper bound of producer costs'. In this case then, changing how water resources are managed to reduce adverse environmental impacts seems to pass the cost–benefit test.

a tax and determining its level. However, the application of an estimate of the average external cost at the current level of activity does not constitute the Pigovian tax that it is made out to be, since this would typically measure the marginal external cost at the optimal level of externality. Here, the crucial issue would appear to be to know how marginal damages vary with the level of the externality-causing activity.

3.3.2.2 Environmental damage claims

Under the CERLA and Oil Pollution Acts in the USA, firms that cause accidental environmental damages can be sued in the courts by states and by the Federal government to recover the monetary value of such damage. The most famous such incident to date has been the *Exxon Valdez* oil spill in 1989; another example was the accident involving the oil tanker *American Trader* in February 1990, which spilled up to 400,000 gallons of crude oil into the Pacific Ocean off the coast of California (Dunford, 1999). The State of California sued the 'responsible parties' for damages. Interestingly, in this case, the two parties produced alternative sets of estimates of these damages, which resulted in the main from the temporary closure of a number of beaches. The State of California's experts estimated the value of a lost day's recreation on the beach to be around $15 per visit; unsurprisingly, the defendants' economists came up with a lower value of $4–8 per visit. Arguments also raged about how many visits were lost.

3.3.2.3 National accounting

In Chapter 6, we will discuss the issue of making 'green' adjustments to national accounting figures such as gross national product, as a way of producing a better measure of welfare and an indicator of sustainability. Governments can use environmental valuation in calculating such green adjustments to the national accounts; for example, to take account of changes in the level of pollution between this year and the previous year, or to value changes in water quality in a nation's rivers.

Summary

Changes in the quantity or quality of environmental resources have economic value if they have an impact on utility. We can base our measures of these values upon either the most that people are willing to give up to acquire some (desirable) change or the least they are willing to accept to forgo it (for an undesirable change, then we can use either the most people are willing to pay to prevent it, or the lowest compensation they would accept to put up with it). Governments can and have made extensive use of environmental valuation in a number of contexts, particularly cost–benefit analysis in the context of policy and project appraisal. Other uses also exist, including the settling of environmental damage claims and the calculation of green tax rates.

Tutorial Questions

3.1 Why do economists use WTP as a measure of the value someone places on an environmental good or ecosystem service?

3.2 What determines how WTP for a particular change in environmental quality (e.g. a fall in air pollution) may vary across people?

3.3 Several studies have shown that WTP differs substantially from WTA for a given change in environmental quality. Why might this be? Does it matter, from a policy analysis viewpoint?

3.4 What is meant by the economic value of an ecosystem service? How could changes in pressures on an ecosystem (such as an estuary or a forest) produce a change in ecosystem service values? What would we need to know to be able to estimate the monetary value of such a change?

3.5 Explain how you would undertake a cost–benefit analysis of a planned new nuclear power station. Why might the choice of discount rate be particularly crucial to the net present value calculation in this instance? How could uncertainty over (i) the future price of electricity and (ii) future waste storage costs be included in this analysis?

3.6 What are the advantages and problems of applying cost–benefit analysis to environmental policy decisions?

References and Additional Readings

Aldred, J. (2006). 'Incommensurability and monetary valuation', *Land Economics* 82(2): 141–61.

Arrow, K., Cropper, M., Eads, G., Hahn, R., Lave, L., Noll, R., Portney, P., Russell, M., Schmalensee, R., Smith, V.K., and Stavins, R. (1998). 'Is there a role for benefit–cost analysis in environmental, health and safety regulation?' *Environment and Development Economics* 2: 196–201.

Banzhaf, H.S. (2009). 'Objective or multi-objective? Two historically competing visions for benefit cost analysis', *Land Economics* 85(1): 3–23.

Barbier, E.B. (2009). 'Ecosystems as natural assets', *Foundations and Trends in Microeconomics* 4(8): 611–81.

Dunford, R. (1999). 'The American Oil Trader spill', *AERE Newsletter* (May): 12–20.

Hanemann, M. (1991). 'Willingness to pay and willingness to accept: how much can they differ?' *American Economic Review* 81: 635–47.

Hanley, N., and Barbier, E.B. (2009). *Pricing Nature: Cost-Benefit Analysis and Environmental Policy Appraisal* (Cheltenham: Edward Elgar).

Heal, G.M., Barbier, E.B., Boyle, K.J., Covich, A.P., Gloss, S.P., Hershner, C.H., Hoehn, J.P., Pringle, C.M., Polasky, S., Segerson, K., and Shrader-Frechette, K. (2005). *Valuing Ecosystem Services: Toward Better Environmental Decision Making*

(Washington, DC: The National Academies Press).

Kotchen, M., Moore, M., Lupi, F., and Rutherford, E. (2006). 'Environmental constraints on hydropower: an *ex post* benefit cost analysis of dam re-licensing', *Land Economics* 82(3): 384–403.

Krutilla, J.V., and Fisher, A.C. (1985). *The Economics of Natural Environments* (Washington, DC: Resources for the Future).

Loomes, G., Starmer, C., and Sudgen, R. (2003). 'Do anomalies disappear in repeated markets?' *Economic Journal* 113 (March): C153–66.

Pearce, D.W., and Turner, R.K. (1989). *Economics of Natural Resources and the Environment* (London: Harvester Wheatsheaf).

Sterner, T. (2011). *Fuel Taxes and the Poor* (Washington, DC: Resources for the Future).

Van der Wal, R., Bonn, A., Monteith, D., Reed, M., Blackstock, K.L., Hanley, N., Thompson, D., Evans, M., Alonso, I., Allott, T., Armitage, H., Beharry, N., Glass, J., Johnson, S., McMorrow, J., Ross, L., Pakeman, R.J., Perry, S., and Tinch, D. (2011). 'Mountains, moorlands and heaths', in *The UK National Ecosystem Assessment Technical Report* (Cambridge: UNEP-WCMC): 106–59.

Willig, R. (1976). 'Consumers surplus without apology', *American Economic Review* 66: 589–97.

4 Valuing the Environment: Methods

In this chapter, we are going to consider different approaches to estimating the economic values for environmental change that were explained in Chapter 3. These methods include:

- Stated-preference approaches, such as contingent valuation and choice experiments.
- Revealed-preference approaches, such as travel-cost models and hedonic pricing.
- Production-function approaches, which value the environment as an input.

We will also consider the problem of 'benefits transfer'. For more detail on all of the methods outlined in this chapter, see Hanley and Barbier (2009); or for a more technical treatment, see Freeman (2003) or Haab and McConnell (2002).

4.1 An Overview of the Methods

How do we empirically estimate economic values for non-market environmental goods? Whilst most of the methods used are aimed at measuring the public's willingness to pay (WTP) for changes in the natural environment, some are directed instead at evaluating the contribution the environment makes as an input to the production of goods and services, which are themselves sources of utility. Directly or indirectly then, all environmental values are traced back to effects on utility. There are many ways of categorizing environmental valuation methods: one useful way is to place methods into the following groups:

1. Stated-preference methods.
2. Revealed-preference methods.
3. Production-function approaches.

Stated- and revealed-preference methods focus on direct impacts of the environment on utility. Production-function approaches focus on the environment as an input. Valuing changes in ecosystem service flows can involve the use of all of these approaches.

4.2 **Stated-preference Approaches**

These include the following:

- Contingent valuation
- Choice experiments

These methods have the common feature that they are all based on surveys in which the public (or some specific subset of the public, such as users of some recreational resource such as a national park) is directly questioned about its WTP or willingness to accept compensation (WTA) for *hypothetical* changes in environmental quality. The contingent valuation method (CVM) is the older and more developed method, but choice experiments are now a fast-developing technique.

4.2.1 **Contingent valuation**

Contingent valuation originated in the early 1960s, but did not become widely used until the mid-1970s. The publication of Mitchell and Carson's book *Using Surveys to Value Public Goods* in 1989 was an important milestone in the development of the method, and by 1995, Richard Carson had identified over 2,000 published CVM studies. CVM has been applied in many settings all over the world, often to help answer important questions of public policy design. In principle, the method is very simple. Given that the absence of prices for many environmental goods is due to the absence of a market, CVM asks respondents how they would behave *if* such a market existed. For example, a CVM survey could ask:

> Suppose the only way of improving water quality in your local river was for all residents to agree to pay a surcharge on their taxes. If you were asked to pay an additional $25 per year, would you agree in order to have these water quality improvements go ahead?

Respondents are drawn from a random sample of the relevant population, which might in different settings comprise the general public, local residents, or visitors to a recreation area. The important point about CVM is that respondents are asked to reveal what they would be willing to pay (or willing to accept as compensation) for a clearly specified hypothetical increase or decrease in environmental quality.

There are several main design features of a CVM questionnaire:

- People must be given a reason why they might be asked to pay for something that they currently do not see themselves as paying for. For example, if the purpose of the CVM was to estimate the benefits of an improvement in river quality, respondents might be told that extra local tax revenues would be needed to finance an investment in better sewage treatment. They must also think that their responses are in some way *consequential*—for instance, that they will be used to help inform a decision.

- A *bid vehicle* must be used that is both credible and uncontroversial. The bid vehicle is the means by which respondents pay in the hypothetical market (local taxes, in the above example). Bid vehicles must be credible in the sense that respondents feel that they could be applied in practice. For example, if the value of a large wilderness area with many access points was being studied, the specification of an entrance fee as a bid vehicle would not be credible if people thought it would be impossible to enforce, or if it would be too politically unpopular to imagine it being introduced.

- Respondents should be given adequate, unbiased information on the environmental good and its hypothetical market, in order to let them make an informed judgement.

- A decision has to be made on how to ask the WTP/WTA question. This can be done using an open-ended format ('What is the most you would be willing to pay?'), through payment cards where respondents are shown a series of amounts and are asked to indicate their maximum WTP/minimum WTA from amongst these amounts; and dichotomous choice formats, where respondents are asked to say whether they would be willing to pay—or willing to accept as compensation—a specific amount, known as the bid price. This bid price is then varied across individuals, which yields yes/no responses to different amounts. A refinement of the dichotomous choice approach is to ask those people who say 'no' to the first amount offered if they would be willing to pay a lower bid, and to ask those who said 'yes' to the first amount offered if they would be willing to pay a higher amount. This is known as double-bounded dichotomous choice. All of these alternatives have advantages and disadvantages, but most researchers now avoid the use of open-ended formats.

- 'Protest bids' should be identified. When respondents are asked how much they would be willing to pay, a proportion will likely give a zero response. For some people, this is because they do not value the good, in that it does not impact on their utility. If I am asked my WTP to protect a wildlife species that I don't care about, then I place zero value on it and, accordingly, will state a zero WTP. I may also say that I would not be willing to pay anything because I cannot afford it. Both types of response are referred to as 'genuine zeros'. But I might bid zero, even if I care about the species, because I am protesting about being asked the question in this way, or because I do not find the hypothetical market to be credible. Similarly, respondents who are asked their minimum WTA to allow a local woodland to be felled may state a zero amount because they feel that no amount of monetary compensation would make up for the loss of the wood: this is another form of protest bid. Protest bidders are usually separated out from genuine zeros and positive bidders before analysis progresses.

- Many surveys include debriefing questions, which seek to analyse how well respondents understood the survey questions, what exactly they thought they were paying for/being compensated for, how credible they found the survey, how sure they are about their responses, and whether the survey had changed their opinions on the issue at hand.

Given all these issues, CVM studies start by undertaking focus group sessions, in which different scenarios, bid vehicles, information sets, and question formats can be tested out by the researcher in small groups before surveying begins. Surveys may be carried out by mail, telephone, Internet, or face-to-face interviews. Once a sufficient sample has been collected, mean or median WTP/WTA is calculated from the sample, using the individual responses (once protest bidders have been excluded). This sample average can then be aggregated into a population mean/median. A *bid curve* analysis is usually undertaken, whereby WTP responses are related, using regression analysis, to variables thought likely to influence them, such as education, experience with the good, and income. The purpose of doing this would be to: (i) see how much of the variation in WTP across the sample could be explained (and therefore how much is unexplained); and (ii) whether the signs on the variables of interest are in accord with such a priori expectations as we have: for example, income would be expected to be positively related with WTP, in that higher-income levels should, on average—and other things being held equal—imply higher WTP amounts (Jacobsen and Hanley, 2009). For some CVM designs, notably dichotomous choice versions, bid curves must be estimated in order to calculate mean WTP.

The fact that CVM has become so widely used implies that it has some advantages as a method. Principal amongst these are the following:

1. It is a very generalizable method, in that it can be applied in an extremely wide range of situations, from the benefits of preserving global biodiversity to the benefits of improving a city's air quality or protecting a local wetland.

2. It is capable of measuring both use and non-use values. Non-use (existence) values have been found to be very important in many cases. CVM questionnaires can also be designed so that the researcher gains some insight into *why* people value a given environmental good, and how this valuation changes when, for example, uncertainty surrounding the supply of the good changes.

However, CVM has also attracted much criticism. In general, this has focused on three issues. First, CVM measures what people say they would do, which may be different from what they would actually do. Stated WTP could be greater or less than actual, true WTP for a number of reasons. If respondents think that their answer may influence how much they would actually get charged, they may free-ride by understating their WTP. On the other hand, if respondents believe that their answer is not linked to what they would actually be charged, but is linked to how likely the environmental change is to happen, then they may overstate their WTP for an environmental change, which increases their utility. Testing for such *hypothetical market bias* is clearly a little difficult for many environmental goods, since it is the absence of markets for such goods (and thus of market prices) that encourages us to use CVM in the first place. Nevertheless, experiments can be set up that compare real and hypothetical payments. Murphy et al. (2005) found that across a number of studies, hypothetical WTP was on average 2.6 times greater than actual WTP. The issue of 'calibrating' CVM responses has thus attracted much attention. Research has found that the extent to which hypothetical WTP over- or understates actual WTP depends on the type of environmental good being studied and the design of the CVM exercise itself—in particular, on how the payment question is asked, and on how 'consequential' people think that their responses are. Other researchers have found that filtering CVM responses in terms of how sure respondents are of their WTP statements can help reduce hypothetical market bias (Poe et al., 2002).

Another criticism of CVM is that it produces estimates of WTP that are insensitive to the amount of the environmental good being bid for: the 'scoping' problem. One reason for people saying they would pay roughly the same to protect one lake in Ontario from acidification as they would pay to protect all lakes in Ontario is that their stated WTP is actually a symbolic number motivated by a feel-good factor referred to as 'warm glow'. Attention has thus focused on the results of scope tests, which measure WTP for different quantities of the same good (Heberlein et al., 2005). For example, different subsamples of a population could be asked their WTP to protect 100, 500, or 1,000 hectares of forests from felling, and statistical tests performed to see whether WTP was indeed sensitive to the area of forest protected.

Third, CVM results have been criticized as being dependent on the information they provide to respondents, and of asking respondents to undertake a task that they are not up to. In many cases, the population of interest may be quite uninformed about the environmental resource that is being studied: we would not expect people to be able to give a WTP figure for a function of an ecosystem that they do not understand. For example, suppose that a policy of protecting the population of an obscure species is being evaluated. We wish to know the value people place on this species, yet we expect that many folks will never even have heard of it before. To successfully implement the survey, researchers will need to inform respondents about the species, the threats to it, and what can be done to avert these threats. Yet this changes their knowledge in the process of undertaking the survey: thus by implementing a CVM survey, we are possibly changing the preferences that we wish to measure (MacMillan et al., 2006). Different types and amounts of information may significantly affect stated WTP. The question that CVM must answer, then, is 'How much information is enough, and what should it cover?'

4.?? The choice experiment method

The choice experiment method[1] adopts a particular view on how the demand for the environmental goods is best pictured, known as the *characteristics theory of value*. This states

---

BOX 4.1 Valuing Heritage Sites: Stonehenge

In many countries, the landscape that we see now has been formed by a tremendous mixture of human and natural influences. For example, semi-natural habitats such as hay meadows and heather moorland are the product of a particular type of farming regime, combined with environmental conditions that make such habitats viable. The built environment is also part of the landscape, and historical remains are very important in this context. One of the most famous archaeological sites in Europe is Stonehenge, on Salisbury Plain in England, a World Heritage Site. Stonehenge, as its name implies, is a henge monument (circle and surrounding ditch) made of stones, in this case massive Sarcen stones. It dates from 5,000 to 3,500 years ago.

In the late 1990s, the quality of the site for visitors was increasingly impaired by the proximity of a noisy and busy road, the A303. Accordingly, English Heritage, who manage the site jointly with the National Trust, proposed the construction of a covered tunnel for the A303 in the area around the site, which would essentially hide all of the passing traffic and greatly reduce noise levels. The cost of this project was estimated at £125 million: but was it worth it? To answer this question, a contingent valuation study was commissioned. Mourato and Maddison (2000) designed a survey whereby visitors and the general public were asked their WTP in higher taxes for the road tunnel project. The general public were included in order to capture non-use values. The most conservative estimate of benefits showed them to be worth £150 million; that is, more than the cost of the tunnel.

---

[1] Sometimes referred to as 'choice modelling' or, less commonly, as 'conjoint analysis'.

that the value of, say, a forest, is best explained in terms of the characteristics or *attributes* of that forest. Different forests are actually different 'bundles' of attributes, and it is these bundles that people value. Moreover, the value of any particular forest then can be broken down into the values of each attribute of that forest. Using observations of people's choices between different bundles of attributes, the researcher can infer: (i) which attributes significantly influence their choices, (ii) assuming that price or cost is included as one attribute, what they are willing to pay for an increase in any other attribute; and (iii) what they would be willing to pay for a policy that changed several attributes simultaneously. The choice experiment (CE) method is becoming increasingly popular as a tool for estimating and indeed investigating environmental values. Policy-makers have seen a powerful set of advantages for the CE method, in terms of being able to measure benefits for a wide range of policy changes. Birol and Koundouri (2008) give several examples of the use of the method in the policy process. For a very useful guide to the CE method, see Henscher et al. (2005).

In the choice experiment method, the researcher first of all identifies the main attributes that are relevant for describing the environmental good in question. This is done using focus groups, and by finding out from policy-makers and administrators which aspects of the environmental good are likely to be affected by a policy action. For a river, the attributes might be in-stream ecological quality, flow rates, and the condition of the river banks. For a national park management problem, the attributes could be provision of guided walks, set-aside of conservation areas, traffic management, and management of agricultural areas. If the researcher wants to use the CE to measure economic values, then a price or cost attribute must also be included. For river quality, it could be local water and sewerage rates; for a national park, it could be a tourist tax. The researcher needs to be sure that the selected attributes are: (i) likely to be relevant in terms of the preferences of the population to be surveyed; and (ii) likely to be amenable to change by environmental managers.

Different bundles of these attributes are then combined using experimental design principles. Bundles are often arranged in pairs, and respondents asked to choose between them and some status quo alternative, in what is known as a 'choice set'. Typically, each individual might answer between four and eight choice sets. For example, a study by Morrison et al. (2002) looked at the benefits of protecting wetlands in Australia. Each respondent was asked to choose most preferred alternatives amongst pairs of different wetland management options, such as the choice set shown in Table 4.1 (this has been adapted a little from the original). Respondents were asked: *Which option would you prefer that the government went ahead with?—A, B, or C?*

Table 4.1 Choice experiment for valuing Australian wetlands

	Management option A	Management option B	Management option C (status quo: no change on present)
Wetland area conserved (ha)	1,000	800	700
Bird species conserved (number)	40	30	25
Farm jobs protected	15	16	20
Cost per household in terms of increase in local taxes over next 5 years ($)	30	15	0

A choice experiment questionnaire would be designed, piloted, and implemented just like a contingent valuation study, as described in the previous section. Similar requirements exist for the description of the hypothetical market.

Once questionnaires have been completed, the researcher now has data on which options individuals chose (option A, option B, the status quo), and she can relate these choices to the levels that the attributes took in these options. In this way, choices can be statistically related to attribute levels, including price. The usual statistical model employed is known as the conditional logit model. This means that we can write down the probability that an individual i chose a particular option A like this:

$$P_i(choose\ A) = \frac{\exp(\mu V_{iA})}{\sum_j \exp(\mu V_{iJ})}, \tag{4.1}$$

where V is the 'observable' part of utility, μ is a 'scale parameter' that shows the variance of the errors in the choice model, and J are all the other options that the individual could have chosen instead of A. A typical assumption is that V is a linear function of the attributes of the good (and thus of the choice alternatives):

$$V = \alpha + \beta_1 X_1 + \beta_2 X_2 + \ldots \beta_n X_n + \beta_c C. \tag{4.2}$$

For each attribute $X_1, X_2, \ldots$, the model estimates a value β that shows the effect on utility of a change in the level of each attribute. Thus β_1 shows the effect on utility of a change in attribute X_1. The model also estimates a parameter β_c, which is the effect of a change (increase or decrease) in the price or cost of the option on the likelihood of choosing that option. Software packages such as Stata and Limdep can be used for this kind of estimation. It is interesting to know the β values, since now we know how much utility goes up or down when the attributes increase or decrease (albeit moderated by the scale parameter). These values tell us whether people prefer an increase or a decrease in each attribute; we can also see, by looking at the *prob* or *t*-statistic values from the computer output, whether or not these attributes are statistically significant.

The final steps in a choice experiment are to calculate WTP estimates, based on the β values already discussed. The β values show the effect on *utility* of changes in the attributes, but for cost–benefit analysis we need measures of WTP. For a marginal change in an attribute, this WTP value is given by, for attribute X_1:

$$IP_{x1} = \beta_{x1}/\beta_c. \tag{4.3}$$

This value for any attribute (other than price!) is called the *implicit price* (*IP*, in equation (4.3)). For instance, in Table 4.1 one of the attributes was the number of bird species conserved. Dividing the β value for this attribute by the β value for the tax increase would show the (average) WTP of people in the sample to increase the number of bird species conserved by one. However, often we wish to value multiple changes in attributes. For instance, a new policy on wetlands conservation could alter the area conserved (labelled A below), the numbers of bird species conserved (labelled B), and the provision of recreational trails, labelled R.

The price for this would be an increase in local taxes, which are attribute c. The average WTP for this suite of changes in attributes can be calculated using the following equations:

$$CS = -\frac{1}{\beta_c}(V_1 - V_0),\tag{4.4}$$

$$V_o = \alpha + \beta_A A_0 + \beta_B B_0 + \beta_R R_0,\tag{4.5}$$

$$V_1 = \alpha + \beta_A A_1 + \beta_B B_1 + \beta_R R_1.\tag{4.6}$$

This might look at bit complicated but is actually very easy, and can be calculated using a spreadsheet once you have got your estimates from the choice model in equation (4.1). Equation (4.4) says that the compensating surplus (CS) from an improvement in wetlands conservation—that is, the average person's WTP for this package of changes—is given by the difference between their (measurable) utility before the improvement goes ahead, given by V_0, and their measurable utility after the change, V_1, converted into monetary units using the coefficient on the tax or price attribute, β_c. In turn, utility in the 'before' and 'after' cases is given by the levels of the attributes in each case (so A_0, B_0, and R_0 in the 'before' case, and A_1, B_1, and R_1 in the 'after' case), multiplied by the attribute coefficients, and including the term α. This was the constant in equation (4.2), and it is usually referred to as the *alternative specific constant*. It shows the utility that people get simply from either staying in the status quo or leaving it (depending on whether it is positive or negative), independently of the values taken by the attributes. By fixing the status quo utility and varying the levels of the attributes, compensating surplus figures can be produced for as many combinations of attributes and levels as the design makes possible; that is, for a wide range of policy outcomes.

4.2.2.1 Problems with the choice experiment method

Accommodating variation in preferences across people. The standard approach to choice experiments, which was described above, has one important feature that is worthy of comment. This is that if we use a conditional logit model to represent the choices that people make, then we are effectively assuming that each person in the sample places the same value on each attribute used in the design. In other words, we effectively assume that the marginal utility for Joe if attribute X_1 is increased—β_1—is the same as the marginal utility for Jane; and that the marginal utility for Joe of an increase in attribute X_2, β_2, is the same as that for Jane. This is because we only estimate one value for β_1 and one value for β_2 in equation (4.2). However, we might expect that people will care about the same attribute to differing degrees. Choice experiment practitioners have thus looked for alternative ways of modelling such *preference heterogeneity*. For an example of different approaches to solving this problem, see Birol et al. (2006).

　　Issues with experimental design. Designing a choice experiment is almost an art form! Decisions must be taken on a great number of issues:

1. What attributes to include.
2. How to describe them to respondents.
3. What levels are to be used for each attribute.

4. What price or cost term will be used.

5. How the attributes and levels are combined in choice sets.

6. How many choice sets respondents can deal with.

7. How many choice options are included in each choice set.

The overall success of the choice experiment in terms of what it tells us about people's choices and values depends on these steps. Many papers exist that investigate these issues, mostly in non-environmental applications of the method (e.g. in a transport, marketing, and health context): lessons learnt can be found in choice experiment textbooks such as Henscher et al. (2005).

Hypothetical market bias. Another parallel between choice experiments and contingent valuation is the possibility that responses in a hypothetical market setting will tell us little about how respondents would behave in a real market. This issue has been addressed in a couple of ways within the CE literature, comparing real with hypothetical responses in terms of (i) how well hypothetical choices predict real choices and (ii) how close predicted WTP from hypothetical choices is to real WTP in an actual market. Of course, the same problem faces the CE practitioner as faces the CVM analyst—that for most environmental goods, we cannot observe 'real' market prices! However, some findings exist that compare real with hypothetical choices. Evidence is presented by List et al. (2006), who compared actual with hypothetical scenarios for two choice experiments. They argue that two tests are of interest—whether a hypothetical choice experiment overstates the extent to which people would actually pay for, say, wetland conservation and the differences, if any, in the marginal values of the attributes used in the choice experiment between 'real' and 'hypothetical' choices. They found statistically significant differences between hypothetical and real WTP, but not between the marginal values of attributes. Ready et al. (2010) also study this problem—their findings are discussed in Box 4.2.

4.3 Revealed-preference Approaches

In revealed-preference (RP) approaches, the analyst tries to infer the value that people place on environmental goods from their behaviour in markets for related goods. A major difference between RP and stated-preference approaches is thus that with RP methods we make use of people's *actual* behaviour, rather than their intentions. Two principal RP approaches will be discussed here: the hedonic pricing method and travel-cost models.

4.3.1 The hedonic pricing method

The hedonic pricing method (HPM) has its basis in the same characteristics theory of value as choice experiments. In other words, people are pictured as valuing goods in terms of the bundles of attributes that these possess. For a house, these attributes might include the number of bedrooms, the age of the house, the size of garden, and whether it has a garage. These could all be a particular property's site characteristics, S_i. Also important to buyers and sellers will be the locational aspects of the house, such as how far it is from major

BOX 4.2 Hypothetical Bias in Choice Experiments

As the main text indicates, one worry in the choice experiment method is the extent to which estimates of WTP produced by this approach suffer from a hypothetical market bias. Ready et al. (2010) investigate this issue by carrying out a choice experiment with both hypothetical and real payments. Their application is concerned with the extent to which people's uncertainty about how they value an environmental good can help explain the degree of hypothetical market bias.

A choice experiment was conducted using students from Penn State University as the subjects. The good being valued was a rescue programme for injured wild animals called Centre Wildlife Care (CWC). The payment vehicle was donations to the CWC, which is funded entirely from donations. The attributes in the design were:

- Whether care was focused on mammals, birds, or turtles

- Whether the animal was common or rare

- Whether the animal could be returned to the wild, after care

If respondents chose the 'no donation' option, then they were told that animals would need to be turned away, since funds did not permit their rehabilitation. After making each of four choices, respondents were asked how certain they were about each choice. Two types of experiment were run, depending on whether the donations were purely hypothetical or were for real (in other words, respondents had to hand over the money that they said they would donate at the end of the session).

Some 249 surveys were completed. Mean WTP for hypothetical payments was around $5, and mean WTP with real payments was around $1.70. However, the results also showed that respondents who gave hypothetical responses that were significantly different from their real behaviour tended to state higher levels of uncertainty over their choices. This suggests that asking people how sure they are about choices, and then filtering out those who are rather unsure, would be one way of reducing hypothetical market bias in choice experiments. Calibrating responses by reclassifying people who chose a payment option in the hypothetical scenario with a level of stated uncertainty greater than a given threshold value produces the result that mean WTP with hypothetical payments is insignificantly different from mean WTP with real payments (calibrated hypothetical WTP = $1.71; real WTP = $1.68).

employment areas, how good the local school is, and how good its public transport links are. Call these the neighbourhood characteristics, N_i. Finally, the environmental characteristics (E_i) may also be an important determinant of house prices: for example, these could include noise levels, air quality, scenic views, and proximity to landfill sites (see, e.g., Eshet et al., 2007).

The basic assumption of the HPM is that people's valuation of environmental attributes can be inferred from the amount they are willing to pay for these attributes through the housing market. For example, other things being equal, a house in a quieter part of town may sell for more than a similar house in a noisier part of town. If I value peace and quiet, then I may be willing to pay this premium, whilst sellers will know this when advertising their house. For the buyer, the highest premium he or she would be willing to pay for any environmental attribute would indicate the maximum value that he or she places on it. If these premia could be identified from market transactions, then this would thus tell us something about the value of those environmental attributes (such as noise) that can be linked to house prices.

The HPM thus proceeds by collecting data on (most usually) house prices from sales records,[2] along with data on E_i, N_i, and S_i. A regression analysis can then be carried out to estimate the equation:

$$P_i = f(E_{il} \ldots E_{im}, N_{il} \ldots N_{in}, S_{il} \ldots S_{iq}),$$ (4.7)

where there are m environmental attributes, n neighbourhood attributes, and q site attributes, and where P_i is the price of the ith house. For those attributes that turn out to have a statistically significant effect on house prices, the 'implicit price' (that is, the price premium) can be calculated. This might tell us, for example, that a 1 per cent improvement in air-quality levels increases house prices by 0.2 per cent on average: this could then be used to work out the implied WTP in money for this air-quality improvement. In this manner, money values can be placed on environmental attributes that are linked to house prices. In Figure 4.1, we show the kind of relationship that one might find in the data: as the level of air pollution falls, and so air quality rises, house prices go up, other things being equal. In other words, to 'buy' an improvement in local air quality from E_1 to E_2, the house-buyer has to spend an additional amount equal to ΔP.

The HPM has been widely used to study the implicit prices of changes in air quality, noise, and proximity to waste sites. An excellent survey of much of this work can be found in Taylor (2003). A number of drawbacks can be identified with the technique, as follows:

- Many environmental goods are not linked to housing markets. For these goods, the HPM will not work. Even for those goods that are so linked, the method provides only an indication of partial value. For example, air-quality improvements may benefit visitors and commuters to a city, as well as those who own a house there, but only house-owners' values get picked up by the method.

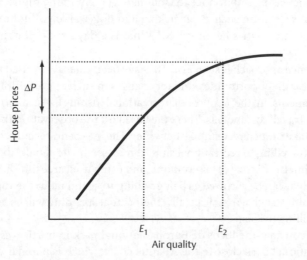

Figure 4.1 The value in the housing market of an improvement in air quality.

[2] Information on property rents can also be used.

- The method assumes that the housing market is in equilibrium in a rather special sense: that, for every attribute, house-buyers are able to locate a house that allows them to equate their marginal value for each environmental attribute with the marginal cost (implicit price) of these attributes.

- Essentially, we must assume that all buyers and sellers are well informed about how environmental attributes vary spatially across the area being studied.

- House purchases are investments, in the sense that people make them for a relatively long period of time, often in the anticipation of capital gains. Their maximum WTP for a house depends not just on current levels of environmental attributes, but also on expectations of changes in the levels of these attributes over the time during which they expect to own the house.

- A property market may be segmented into a set of sub-markets, each with its own hedonic price functions, facing the researcher with the difficult task of discovering what this segmentation looks like.

Box 4.3 shows an example of the HPM applied to valuing noise reductions.

4.3.2 **Travel-cost models**

Models of this kind are amongst the oldest environmental valuation techniques. They originated in the United States, in the context of the planning and management of outdoor recreation in national parks. Informal outdoor recreation is clearly a source of utility for many people, and such recreation often takes place in areas managed or regulated by governments. Activities such as hill-walking, kayaking, angling, climbing, cross-country skiing, and rock climbing have all increased in terms of participation in the last 50 years, and seem certain to be of increasing importance to land management in the future, along with more informal types of recreation such as picnicking and dog-walking. But how could the economic value of such activities be measured? What is a day's rock climbing 'worth' to the climber?

Stated-preference approaches such as CVM have been intensively used to estimate WTP for outdoor recreation opportunities, and for changes in such opportunities (e.g. for water-quality improvements in the context of recreational fishing). An alternative approach, though, is to use travel-cost models. These are based on the observation that expenditure is necessary to partake in such recreational activities. These expenditures include the time and money spent in travelling to recreational sites (it may seem odd to talk about time spent as an expenditure, but time is scarce for everyone, and using up scarce time has an opportunity cost). An individual can be pictured as being willing to spend up to the value in utility that they get from making such a trip. Typically, their actual spending will be less than the most they would be willing to spend.

For example, consider the Picos de Europa national park in north-west Spain. This is a mountainous national park close to the Atlantic coast, which is popular with walkers and nature-lovers. Suppose that we want to estimate the value of informal recreation in this area. Visitors would be irrational if they were to spend more in visiting the park than the utility that they derive from their visit. For any individual, the total cost of visiting (time

BOX 4.3 Hedonic Price Measures of Noise Externalities

Urban noise is a persistent and growing problem for millions of people. Measures are taken to reduce noise, but these impose costs on society. It is therefore of interest to enquire whether the benefits of noise reduction strategies justify their costs. Day et al. (2007) use the hedonic price method to estimate the benefits of reducing urban noise levels in Birmingham, UK. This research was used to inform the UK Department for Transport's assessment methods for transport system investments. Data was collected on 10,848 house sales during 1997 and on-the-site attributes of each house sold (e.g. total floor area). Using a geographic information system, variables were constructed to measure the walking time to different amenities and disamenities (e.g. landfill sites), and local school quality. Digital noise maps were then used to summarize each property's exposure to road, railway, and aircraft noise. Further neighbourhood variables were assembled to measure household wealth, ethnic minorities, age, and the number of households with children.

Eight different market segments were identified in the data, based on income, property size, the ethnicity of district, and the number of children. For each of these segments, a separate hedonic price model was estimated. Road noise was found to significantly affect house prices in around half of all segments, although aircraft noise only had a significant effect in two out of eight segments. They are then able to generate the following results for 1 decibel (dB) increases in road and rail noise above a baseline of 56 dB:

Change in road noise	Annual benefits, in £1,997 per annum mean value and (95% confidence interval)
From 55 to 56 dB	31 (24–52)
From 60 to 61 dB	43 (33–75)
From 65 to 66 dB	55 (41–99)
From 70 to 71 dB	67 (49–123)

Change in rail noise	Annual benefits, in £1,997 per annum mean value and (95% confidence interval)
From 55 to 56 dB	83 (43–461)
From 60 to 61 dB	94 (49–519)
From 65 to 66 dB	106 (55–580)
From 70 to 71 dB	117 (61–654)

Notice that the costs of increases in railway noise are higher than those of equivalent increases in road noise. Also, the economic costs of a 1 dB increase are higher the greater the baseline is from which this increase occurs. This paper is a very good illustration of how complex hedonic price modelling can be.

plus distance) will almost certainly be less than the maximum they would be willing to spend, which is equal to the value that they place on a trip to the park. They thus enjoy a consumers' surplus from visiting, equal to the difference between the most they would pay (per trip) and what they actually pay. By observing the relationship between visits and travel costs, it might thus be possible to infer the value (consumers' surplus) that recreationalists enjoy.

A simple travel-cost analysis would proceed as follows. Visitors to the national park would be surveyed, and asked how far they had travelled to make this visit, and how often in the last

12 months they had visited the site. They might also be asked how many other similar sites they had visited in the area, and about their income, recreational experiences, and family size. In Figure 4.2(a), we show a possible relationship between the number of visits that individuals make to the park (V_i) and the costs to them per visit (C_i), where the C_i are the costs of driving to the park from their home. For example, visitor V_1 faces a cost per trip of €25 and makes only two trips per year, whilst visitor V_2 faces a cost of €12 per trip and makes six trips. If responses from, say, 1,000 visitors were collected, then this would probably allow us to estimate such a curve with reasonable precision. The curve in Figure 4.2(a) is really a demand curve for the site since it shows, at any price, how many trips are taken. Since the area under a demand curve shows total value, we can measure the area under travel-cost curves and use these to measure total value, or, more usually, consumers' surplus per visit.

We show visually how this could be done in Figure 4.2(b). Imagine that we select one individual (Begoña) from the sample. Begoña currently faces a travel cost of €18 per visit, and makes three trips per year, shown as V^*. However, the value she places on each visit is more than €18, so currently she enjoys a consumers' surplus. Using the average relationship between visits and travel costs in Figure 4.2(a), it is possible to see what would happen to the number of trips that Begoña would make if the cost to her was increased; for example, if a hypothetical admission fee to the park were introduced. At an admission fee of A_1, her trips fall to V_1; whilst at a higher admission fee of A_2, they fall further, to V_2. By repeating this exercise, we could trace out the function shown originating at V^* and passing through the points (A_1, V_1) and (A_2, V_2). The area under this curve and above the horizontal line originating at A_0 (the current cost she actually faces) is the consumers' surplus she enjoys from making $V^* = 3$ trips per year.

In practice, it is not necessary to trace out the kind of curve shown in Figure 4.2(b) to calculate consumers' surplus, since it can be calculated mathematically from the equation relating actual trips to actual visits. This might be estimated as follows:

$$\ln(V_i) = a - bC_i + \varepsilon, \qquad (4.8)$$

where $\ln(V_i)$ is the log of visits per year per person, and ε is an error term. This simple version of the travel-cost model has a number of drawbacks, which we now investigate.

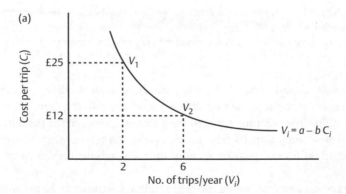

Figure 4.2(a) The relationship between visits and travel costs.

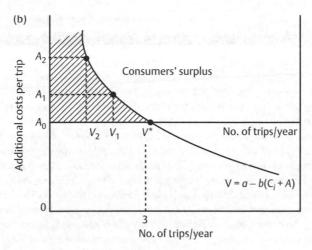

Figure 4.2(b) A derivation of consumers' surplus from the visit–cost relationship.

Substitute sites. The simple travel-cost model discussed so far was presented in terms of predicting visits at one single site. Suppose, however, that there are many similar sites within reach of at least part of our sample of visitors. Clearly, the more alternatives an individual has, the less likely he or she is to visit the site that is being modelled. Moreover, we might want to estimate demand across a set of sites, which all differ in some respects from each other (e.g. fishing rivers with different expected catches, or different types of fish or accessibility). Two approaches may be noted. Most simply, if we are still interested in modelling demand for one site, we could allow for the influence of other sites by including the costs of trips to these other sites in the travel-cost equation. However, this approach suffers from the fact that the alternative sites may be quite different from the site we are interested in respects other than just travel costs. A better approach has been to more explicitly model site choice using random utility models. These adapt a probabilistic approach, and predict the probability that an individual will visit a given site out of a list of alternative sites, as a function of the attributes of this site relative to those of the alternatives: for example, which river(s) a person will choose to visit out of all salmon rivers in Ireland. Random utility models can be combined with *count models*, which estimate the number of trips that a person will make to all sites of this general type—all salmon-fishing streams in Ireland—in a year (Martinez-Espineira and Amoako-Tuffour, 2008). For an example of random utility and count models in use, see Johnstone and Markandya (2006). Box 4.4 shows an example of a random utility travel-cost model of whitewater kayaking.

The value of travel time. What is the monetary value of leisure time? Above, we argued that since time is scarce, then using it up in travelling to a recreational site has an opportunity cost. But what is this equal to? This depends very much on individual circumstances. Imagine the case of a self-employed carpenter who likes to go fishing. Every hour he spends fishing is one less hour spent working. In this case, the value of his leisure time is equal to his hourly earnings in work or, more generally, to the wage rate. For people who are giving up working opportunities in order to pursue leisure at the margin, then their wage rate

BOX 4.4 Using the Travel-cost Model to Value Outdoor Recreation

Whitewater kayaking is an invigorating sport, which is typically unpriced in that access to rivers is free. However, kayakers incur travel costs in getting to access points, and these costs enable a travel-cost analysis to be undertaken. Moreover, the fact that kayakers can usually choose between several different rivers, with differing site qualities and differing travel costs from their homes, means that a random utility site choice travel-cost model is particularly appropriate.

Stephen Hynes and co-authors (2009) questioned 279 kayakers in Ireland about their recreational behaviour. For each person, trips in the last 12 months to eleven different rivers were recorded. Each person then rated each river in terms of a number of attributes that described their kayaking experiences. These attributes included average quality of parking at the site, average crowding, the quality of the kayaking site as measured by the star rating system used in the Irish Whitewater Guidebook, water quality, scenic quality, and travel time from home. A travel-cost measure was constructed for each respondent for each river. People were asked to rate their levels of skill and experience as a kayaker, and these variables were used to estimate separate travel-cost models for different skill levels, on the grounds that highly skilled kayakers might have different preferences for site attributes than those just beginning with the sport. The following table shows the results from the random utility travel-cost models, comparing a generic (all observations) model with two skills-based models—dummy variables were included for each site apart from the most visited:

Variable	All kayakers	Skill level 1[a]	Skill level 2[a]	RUM with skill interaction dummies
Travel cost	−0.069	−0.099	−0.059	−0.092
	(17.93)**	(14.15)**	(11.74)**	(1531)**
Quality of parking	−0.145	−0.089	−0.22	−0.063
	(2.04)*	−0.71	(2.16)*	−0.57
Crowding	0.153	0.172	0.129	014
	(2.19)*	−1.51	−1.39	−1.34
Star quality of the white-water site	0.351	0.163	0.488	−0.214
	(2.32)**	−0.82	(2.86)**	−1.36
Water quality	0.142	−0.241	0.397	0.042
	−1.39	−1.45	(2.87)**	−0.32
Scenic quality	0.285	0.492	0.107	0.199
	(2.99)**	(3.22)**	−0.84	−1.55
Availability of information on water levels	−0.08	−0.311	0.178	−0.067
	−0.92	(2.19)*	−1.52	−0.57
Advanced skill*Travel cost				0.028
				(4.22)**
Advanced skill*Quality of parking				−0.198
				−1.47
Advanced skill*Crowding				0.046
				−0.35
Advanced skill*Quality of the whitewater site				0.984
				(5.84)**

BOX 4.4

Variable	All kayakers	Skill level 1[a]	Skill level 2[a]	RUM with skill interaction dummies
Advanced skill*Water quality				0.137
				−0.95
Advanced skill*Scenic quality				0.127
				−0.88
Advanced skill*Availability of information on water levels				0.068
				−0.5
Clifden Play Hole	−0.905	0.304	−1.643	−0.737
	(2.47)*	−0.54	(3.18)**	(1.97)*
Curragower Wave on the Shannon	−1.413	−1.141	−1.586	−1.333
	(5.34)**	(2.89)*	(4.10)**	(4.94)**
The Boyle	−1.772	−1.586	−1.864	−1.715
	(5.93)**	(3.51)**	(4.41)**	(5.63)**
The Roughty	−1.641	−1.707	−1.397	−1.432
	(4.10)**	(2.67)**	(2.51)*	(3.10)**
The Clare Glens	−3.387	−4.224	−2.734	−3.243
	(8.63)**	(6.72)**	(4.99)**	(0.08)**
The Annamoe	−2.076	−1.787	−2.105	−1.888
	(6.25)**	(3.58)**	(4.47)**	(5.59)**
The Barrow	−2.914	−2.408	−3.115	−2.806
	(9.27)**	(5.18)**	(7.07)**	(8.86)**
The Dargle	−5.011	−6.195	−4.303	−4.935
	(12.33)**	(8.96)**	(7.87)**	(11.90)**
The Inny	−1.769	−0.892	−2.393	−1.684
	(6.04)**	(2.07)*	(5.70)**	(5.70)**
The Boluisce (Spiddle)	−2.344	−1.437	−2.899	−2.257
	(6.96)**	(2.81)**	(6.06)**	(6.57)**

Notes: Absolute value of z statistics in parentheses; * significant at 5%; ** significant at 1%. Models CL1, CL2, and CL3 have log likelihood values of −913.95, −358.22, and −447.78, respectively.
[a] Skill level 1 refers to kayakers who have basic and intermediate proficiency level kayak handling skills. Skill level 2 refers to kayakers who have advanced proficiency level kayak handling skills.

These results were then used to calculate how consumers' surplus per trip would change if the attributes of rivers were to change, or if access to certain rivers was curtailed. This showed that allowing for differences in the preferences of kayakers according to their skill levels made for differences in consumers' surplus estimates. For instance, loss of access to one river (the Roughty) where a hydroelectric scheme had been proposed would impose a cost of €5.97 per kayaker per trip in a model where no account was taken of different skill levels, and €7.72 per trip where skill level variations are included. Kayakers incur these losses in utility since loss of access to this popular river reduces their available choice set.

measures the value of their leisure time. However, for many people, this is not a good description of the situation. For example, unemployed workers, parents staying at home, and retired people do not give up work for leisure at the margin. This is also true for the majority of workers, who tend to be on fixed-hours contracts. For example, if Fanny is a schoolteacher, then she is unlikely to be giving up earnings (at the margin) during her holidays in order to go fishing. In such cases, where people are not making marginal wage/leisure choices, it is harder to know how to value leisure time.

Most research in this area has used either stated- or revealed-preference approaches to estimate leisure time values in contexts where people choose between faster, more expensive routes and slower, cheaper ones. These studies reveal that leisure time values are positively related, on the whole, to income, so that some fraction of the wage for an individual is a reasonable guess as to the monetary value of their leisure time. However, the valuation of leisure time is still an inexact science. This is problematic for models of the travel-cost type, since consumer surplus estimates for recreation have been shown to depend on which value for leisure time is used (Hynes et al., 2009).

Use values versus non-use values. Finally, it should be obvious that since the travel-cost approach infers values from expenditure, those who make no such expenditures have no inferred valuation for the good. If all values were use values, this would not be such a problem. However, if there are non-use values associated with an environmental resource such as a national park, then travel-cost approaches cannot pick up such values, since they can accrue to people who do not visit the site.

4.4 Production-function Approaches

In production-function approaches, the environment is typically valued as an input to the production of some market-valued good or service (Barbier, 2007). Changes in the quality or quantity of an environmental resource are valued by estimating the implications of this for outputs and prices of market goods/services, usually in terms of changes in consumers' surplus and producers' profits. This class of methods includes *dose–response models*, which are used to study the impacts of pollution on market-valued outputs (e.g. the effects of increases in low-level ozone on agricultural crops). More recent terminology discusses 'ecosystem service valuation' models, but the basic approach is similar.

To take a simple example, consider the role that coastal wetlands play in fisheries. Wetlands provide important nursery areas for fish and shellfish, including crabs. Ellis and Fisher (1987) modelled the case of wetlands off the gulf coast of Florida. Human effort (in terms of numbers of traps set) and wetland acreage were found to jointly determine the output of blue crabs. Having identified this production function, the authors then found the profit-maximizing levels of effort for different levels of wetland acreage. It was then possible to see the effects on welfare, measured as changes in consumer and producer surplus, of reductions in wetland area. A similar analysis was conducted by Barbier and Strand (1998), who study the link between conserving mangrove forest in coastal areas in the Gulf of Campeche, Mexico, and shrimp fishing. Mangroves act as a nursery for shrimp. As mangroves are lost due to conversion to aquaculture or hotel developments, shrimp population dynamics are impacted: an economic model of the fishery thus needs to be considered to

Table 4.2 Costs of mangrove losses in Thailand, 1996–2004

Basis for calculation	Economic costs of mangrove loss in terms of impacts on coastal fishery (US$)
Static model: annual welfare loss	99,004
Static model: net present value over the whole period, discount rate = 10%	570,167
Dynamic model, net present value, discount rate = 10%	1,980,128

Source: Barbier (2007).

estimate the change in producers' surplus from lost biomass production. Barbier and Strand calculate the economic cost of each kilometre squared of mangroves lost, in terms of lost profits to shrimp fishers, of $86,345–$153,300 per year. Barbier (2007) also calculates the costs to consumers and fishers from historic losses of mangroves in Thailand over the period 1996–2004. These are shown in Table 4.2.

Table 4.2 shows that, for an annual average loss rate of 18 km², the annual costs measured from a static model of the fishery are nearly $100,000. Over the 9 years within which data for mangrove losses exist, this translates into a net present value of losses of $570,167 at a 10 per cent discount rate. However, the static model does not take into account the impacts of the loss in mangroves on the dynamics of the fish populations, and the responses of fishers. Once these dynamic effects are allowed for, losses become much greater. Coastal wetlands could also have value as an input to storm and flood protection, by acting as a natural barrier. If so, then additional values for protecting coastal wetlands exist, in terms of the expected avoided property and human life costs from flooding and storms.

The economic values of the environment as an input to production are also studied in the context of dose–response models. These have been very widely used in the literature, mainly to study the effects of air pollutants on agricultural crops and forests. Polluting emissions from a variety of sources are modelled in terms of their fate in the environment. For example, for SO_2, this might involve being blown from one country to another and then falling as acid rain. This constitutes the 'dose' of pollution, to which a physical response occurs. This physical response (e.g. crop damage, buildings damage, fisheries impacts) is estimated using models produced by natural scientists. An economic response to such damage can then occur; for example, if farmers decide to grow less pollution-sensitive crops. Finally, the net effects on output, consumers' surplus, and producers' profits are evaluated, along with other elements of damage costs (e.g. the costs of restoring old buildings damaged by acid rain).

More recently, economists have considered the costs of climate change in terms of such models. Here, climate is an 'input' to the production of agricultural crops. For example, work by Bateman et al. (2010) for the United Kingdom suggests that wheat production is significantly related to a number of climate variables, including growing season temperatures and rainfall. This statistical model is used to simulate the effects of a 1 degree rise in mean temperatures on wheat production and the market value of outputs. The model allows us to see how the response is highly variable across the UK—wheat yields rise in some areas and fall in others, as farmers switch to more profitable activities. Figure 4.3 shows this predicted spatial variation in output, and how this would be valued using market prices for

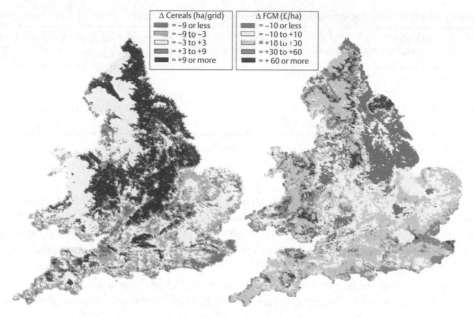

Figure 4.3 Predicted changes in agricultural outputs and market values for a 1 degree rise in mean temperatures in the UK.
Source: Bateman et al. (2010).

inputs and outputs (although this would not reflect changes in net social benefits, since there are externalities associated with agricultural production).

The above examples of valuing the environment as an input relate closely to the idea of valuing ecosystem services, which was discussed in Chapter 3. When these ecosystem services result in outputs valued by the market, then production-function methods are appropriate for valuing changes in such services. But stated- and revealed-preference methods also have a role to play here. Table 4.3 summarizes the range of methods that economists might use to value ecosystem services for the conservation of moorlands.

4.5 Benefits Transfer

Benefit transfer (BT) is the practice of extrapolating existing information on the non-market value of goods or services (Brouwer, 2000). Typically, the practice involves predicting WTP values for an environmental quality or access change at one site (location), based on data collected using either stated- or revealed-preference methods at another, similar site. For example, we may want to predict the value of improvements in water quality on the River Trent in England, based on stated-preference data for the River Tyne (another river in England). Adjustments are often made for differences between the environmental characteristics of the site to which values are to be transferred (known as the 'policy site') and those of the site at which the original data was collected, known as the 'study site'. Differences in

Table 4.3 Valuing ecosystem service flows in moorlands

Ecosystem service	Possible change in this service	Appropriate valuation methods
Carbon sequestration	Net change in carbon flux due to change in land management	Market prices for CO_2 from carbon markets
Informal recreation: birdwatching	Fall or rise due to loss of moorland to forests	Travel-cost models
Landscape quality	Change due to change in frequency of heather burning for grouse shooting; loss of landscape features due to wind farm construction	Stated-preference approaches (contingent valuation or choice experiments)
Water quality	Decrease in water quality due to loss of peat	Production-function approach: additional costs to water supply companies lower down the catchment
Water storage	Decrease in water supply due to forest planting	Production-function approach: costs of measures taken to augment supplies from other sources

some of the socio-economic characteristics of the affected population between the study and policy sites are also allowed for (Morrison et al., 2002).

The aim of BT techniques is to provide decision makers with a monetary valuation of environmental goods and services in a cost-effective and timely manner, since original valuation studies are both expensive and time-consuming. Demands for environmental valuation estimates are rising in the policy community in both Europe and the USA. In Europe, this is partly being driven by the introduction of the Water Framework Directive, which requires benefit–cost analysis of water-quality improvements throughout the European Union, and by the greater emphasis on the application of cost–benefit principles to environmental policy design in the EU. Papers investigating the use and accuracy of BT have become increasingly frequent. Applications of BT include Rozan (2004) on improved air quality in France and Germany, Muthke and Holm-Mueller (2004) on national and international transfers of water-quality improvement benefits, Jiang et al. (2005) on coastal land management, and Colombo and Hanley (2008) on agricultural landscapes.

Two main approaches have been followed in the literature. The first is the transfer of mean WTP values from the policy site to the study site. The transfer of unadjusted mean values has been criticized, since it does not take into account any possible differences between either the populations or the goods at the policy and study site. Because of that, an alternative adjusted mean value approach has developed, which adjusts the mean WTP of the study site to account for differences in the environmental characteristics of the policy site and/or for differences in the socio-economic characteristics of the affected population between the two sites. In the case of the adjusted value transfer, the WTPs are adjusted using data on the socio-economic and environmental characteristics of the policy site, before the comparison takes place. Such adjustments are, to a varying degree, somewhat *ad hoc*.

The second approach to BT is benefit function transfer, where the entire demand function (or choice equation, in a CE setting) estimated at the study site is transferred to the policy site. WTP values at the policy site are predicted using independent variables (such as household income) collected from secondary data at the policy site and parameter values estimated from the study site. In the benefit function transfer, the regression parameters of the study site and the environmental and population characteristics of the policy site are used to test the following equation:

$$\text{predicted WTP } (\beta^s, X^p) = \text{WTP}^p, \tag{4.9}$$

where the predicted WTP (β^s, X^p) is the WTP at the policy site estimated using the parameters of the benefit function of the study site (β^s) and the X values (site attributes, socio-economic characteristics, etc.) of the policy site, and WTP^p is the WTP at the policy site. When several study site data sets are available, a further approach is to use a meta-regression analysis. Here, the analyst is concerned with understanding the influence of methodological and study-specific factors on WTP. Data can be pooled across study sites to produce a BT model for predicting policy site values. Which of these benefits transfer testing approaches is preferable is still open to debate. Economists are still refining how benefits transfer is best carried out, and how to test its accuracy.

Tutorial Questions

4.1 What are the main differences between stated- and revealed-preference methods of environmental valuation?

4.2 List the three main problem areas of contingent valuation as you see it; and explain how researchers could try to minimize the impacts of these problems on estimates of environmental benefits that they have been asked to produce.

4.3 Explain how you would undertake (i) a choice experiment and (ii) a travel-cost study of the benefits of improved management of a national park. What information could such studies generate that would be useful for national park managers?

4.4 What is 'benefits transfer', and how and when should it be undertaken? How accurate could we expect such transferred valued to be?

4.5 What degree of reliance can we place on estimates of environmental value derived from the methods described in this chapter? Are some methods more robust or more valid than others?

4.6 Explain how you would estimate the change in ecosystem service values from a decision to conserve an area of coastal mangrove wetlands, rather than allowing a new harbour development to proceed.

4.7 What role does the discount rate play in environmental valuation?

References and Additional Readings

Barbier, E.B. (2007). 'Valuing ecosystem services as productive inputs', *Economic Policy* 22: 177–229.

—— and Strand, I. (1998). 'Valuing mangrove–fishery linkages: a case study', *Environment and Resource Economics* 12(2): 151–66.

Bateman, I.J., Mace, G.M., Fezzi, C., Atkinson, G., and Turner, R.K. (2010). 'Economic Analysis for Ecosystem Service Assessments', Working Paper EDM 10-10, CSERGE.

Birol, E., Karousakis, K., and Koundouri, P. (2006). 'Using choice experiment to account for preference heterogeneity in wetland attributes: the case of Cheimaditita wetland in Greece', *Ecological Economics* 60: 145–56.

Birol, E., and Koundouri, P. (2008). *Choice Experiments Informing Environmental Policy* (Cheltenham: Edward Elgar).

Brouwer, R. (2000). 'Environmental value transfer: state of the art and future prospects', *Ecological Economics* 32(1): 137–52.

Colombo, S., and Hanley, N. (2008). 'How can we reduce the errors from benefits transfer? An investigation using the choice experiment method', *Land Economics* 84(1): 128–47.

Day, B., Bateman, I., and Lake, I. (2007). 'Beyond implicit prices: recovering theoretically consistent and transferable values for noise avoidance from a hedonic price model', *Environmental and Resource Economics* 37: 211–32.

Ellis, G., and Fisher, A. (1987). 'Valuing the environment as an input', *Journal of Environmental Management* 25: 149–56.

Eshet, T., Baron, M.G., Shechter, M., and Ayalon, O. (2007). 'Measuring externalities of waste transfer stations in Israel using hedonic pricing', *Waste Management* 27: 614–25.

Freeman, A.M. (2003). *The Measurement of Environmental and Resource Values* (Washington, DC: Resources for the Future).

Haab, T., and McConnell, K. (2002). *Valuing Environmental and Natural Resources* (Cheltenham: Edward Elgar).

Hanley, N., and Barbier, E.B. (2009). *Pricing Nature: Cost–Benefit Analysis and Environmental Policy* (Cheltenham: Edward Elgar).

Heberlein, T.A., Wilson, M.A., Bishop, R.C., and Schaeffer, N.C. (2005). 'Rethinking the scope test as a criterion for validity in contingent valuation', *Journal of Environmental Economics and Management* 50(1): 1–22.

Hensher, D., Rose, J., and Greene, W. (2005). *Applied Choice Analysis: A Primer* (Cambridge: Cambridge University Press).

Hynes, S., Hanley, N., and O'Donoghue, C. (2009). 'Alternative treatments of the cost of time in recreational demand models: an application to whitewater kayaking in Ireland', *Journal of Environmental Management* 90(2): 1014–21.

Jacobsen, J.B., and Hanley, N. (2009). 'Are there income effects on global willingness to pay for biodiversity conservation?' *Environmental and Resource Economics* 43: 137–60.

Jiang, Y., Swallow, S.K., and McGonagle, M.P. (2005). 'Context-sensitive benefit transfer using stated choice models: specification and convergent validity for policy analysis'. *Environmental and Resource Economics* 31: 477–99.

Johnstone, C., and Markandya, A. (2006). 'Valuing river characteristics using combined site choice and participation models', *Journal of Environmental Management* 80(3): 237–47.

List, J., Sinha, P., and Taylor, M. (2006). 'Using choice experiments to value non-market goods and services: evidence from field experiments', *Advances in Economic Analysis and Policy* 6(2): 1–37.

MacMillan, D., Hanley, N., and Lienhoop, N. (2006). 'Contingent valuation: environmental polling or preference engine?' *Ecological Economics* 60(1): 299–307.

Martinez-Espineira, R., and Amoako-Tuffour, J. (2008). 'Recreation demand analysis: an application to Gros Morne National Park', *Journal of Environmental Management* 88: 1320–32.

Mitchell, R., and Carson, R. (1989). *Using Surveys to Value Public Goods: The Contingent Valuation Method* (Washington, DC: Resources for the Future).

Morrison, M., Bennett, J., Blamey, R., and Louviere, R. (2002). 'Choice modelling and tests of benefits transfer', *American Journal of Agricultural Economics* 84(1): 161–70.

Mourato, S., and Maddison, D. (2000). 'Valuing different road options for Stonehenge', in S. Navrud and R. Ready (eds.), *Valuing Cultural Heritage* (Cheltenham: Edward Elgar).

Murphy, J., Allen, P., Stevens, T., and Weatherhead, D. (2005). 'A meta-analysis of hypothetical bias in stated preference valuation' *Environmental and Resource Economics* 30(3): 313–25.

Muthke, T., and Holm-Mueller, K. (2004). 'National and international benefit transfer testing with a rigorous test procedure', *Environmental and Resource Economics* 29: 323–36.

Poe, G.L., Clark, J., Rondeau, D., and Schulze, W.D. (2002). 'Provision point mechanisms and field validity tests of contingent valuation', *Environmental and Resource Economics* 23: 105–31.

Ready, R., Champ, P., and Lawton, J. (2010). 'Hypothetical bias in a stated choice experiment', *Land Economics* 86(2): 363–82.

Rozan, A. (2004). 'Benefit transfer: a comparison of WTP for air quality between France and Germany', *Environmental and Resource Economics* 29: 295–306.

Taylor, L. (2003). 'The hedonic method', in P. Champ, K. Boyle, and T. Brown (eds.), *A Primer on Non-Market Valuation* (Dordrecht: Kluwer).

5 Environmental Risk and Behaviour

Environmental protection is like a risky lottery. We invest in protection, but what we really are doing is creating a new lottery. This new lottery exists because environmental policy rarely changes the world so that people are 100 per cent safe from risks to their health, or risks to the environment. Rather, we make environmental policy to reduce the current risk in favour of a new lower level of risk—a new lottery with better odds of good health and a clean environment. When thinking about environmental policy and economics, it makes sense to take the time to better understand how people and policy-makers make decisions under risk and uncertainty, both in theory and in practice.

In theory, policy-as-lottery implies that people think simultaneously about the probabilities and consequences that define the risks to human and environmental health. People know that risks exist in their daily lives—they think about how to invest resources to reduce risks to their heath (e.g. water filters, seat belts, sunscreen, and so on). We think about cost-effective environmental policy that reduces risks to health by suggesting ways to 'fix' market failures. Advice about policies that create new markets or market-like incentives rests on a model that presumes that people facing new incentives will act with purpose and make consistent choices that take into account the consequences of their choices. This model is called *rational choice theory*—people are assumed to make consistent decisions that are in their own best interests within the context of market exchange.

Using rational choice theory to help guide environmental policy makes sense if people make, or act as if they make, consistent and systematic choices when thinking about risk. In practice, however, people struggle with decision-making under risk; instead, we use simple rules and heuristics to make choices. Over the past half century, many empirical studies have documented how rational choice might, in some circumstances, be a poor guide for how people react to environmental risk (see Kahneman, 2011). People make choices that are inconsistent—risk-averse people take a gamble to avoid a loss, we resist change, we overestimate small risks, we think in discrete bundles, we value today more than the future but we are inconsistent, we care about others even in an economic context, and our good intentions can be tainted by money. We also know that the context of choice matters: who gives us the information, social and cultural norms, the default choice and status quo reference point, what draws our attention—uniqueness, access, simplicity—how we are subconsciously primed to make certain choices, emotional responses to goods and information, the degree of commitment to overcome bounded willpower, and ego/self-image (see Metcalfe and Dolan, 2012).

This 'anomalous behaviour' and context-dependent choice arises in many private and public decisions, and serves to undercut the underpinning of rational environmental economics and policy (see Shogren and Taylor, 2008). *Behavioural economics* is the field of research that attempts to explain systematic deviations from rational choice. Behavioural economists apply psychological insight to help reshape economic principles more towards observed behaviour. By 'reshape', we mean adding more humanity to rational choice theory. The end goal is to make environmental policy more efficient by better matching incentives and behaviour (see Thaler and Sunstein, 2008).

In environmental policy, the classic example of energy efficiency illustrates how 'behavioural anomalies' can affect behaviour. An 'energy paradox' is said to exist when people buy less energy conservation than predicted by a present-value calculation given, say, a tax on carbon. Behavioural anomalies that could explain this result include people discounting the future too highly, people who have trouble calculating expected fuel savings, people who focus too intensely on the status quo, and people who rely on heuristic decision-making strategies rather than optimizing net benefits. But all these ideas have rarely been tested within the same experimental design. They are a collection of ideas, in which the policy-maker does not know which effect, if any, dominates choices of energy conservation, and why this particular effect is the key (see Gillingham et al., 2009). Policy options in such cases are limited to more education, information, and standard setting. If people are not responding rationally to pricing changes, green taxes will not have the intended consequences, either in efficiency or distribution of burden (Brekke and Johansson-Stenman, 2008).

In this chapter, we explore environmental risk and behaviour, in theory and in practice. We examine how people behave in response to current levels of risk to human and environmental health, and how we respond to changes in this risk—privately and publicly. By risk, we mean the combination of two elements—the *chance* that a bad event might happen, and the *consequences* that are realized if a bad event does occur. Although actions to improve our lives are not intended to create risk to others and ourselves, we do generate pollution and accidents do happen. Cars pollute. Oil spills. Technology fails. How and when these things happen define the lotteries that we create in a modern economy. Our actions generate rewards—new medicines, new transportation, new communication systems, and new risks; for example, Chernobyl, or Fukushima Daiichi. Today, many observers fear that our choices have put humanity at greater risk due to biodiversity loss and climate change.

Since we cannot achieve a zero-risk society, we make trade-offs based on risks and rewards. For instance, few would pay the necessary price to reduce transportation risks to zero. We could set the speed limit at 10 miles/16 kilometres per hour for all roads and highways. No one would ever die from an automobile accident. But we will never see such a rule. The costs per life saved from driving slow are too expensive—people trade off risk for higher speed limits. We make similar risk–reward trade-offs in our jobs, recreation, and lifestyles. Understanding the nature of health, safety, and environmental risk, how people behave towards risk, and how to identify effective strategies to manage risk is essential for better public policy towards the environment.

5.1 Rational Behaviour under Risk

We begin by defining the rational choice model of decision-making under risk. Assessing risks depends on how people react to the risks that they face. Since the Renaissance, economists and others have been developing a systematic theory of risk and behaviour. As people gained an understanding of how to use trade to increase value, they began to address how to master risks connected to both finances and health. More trade meant more wealth and more risk. Trading partners separated by oceans had an incentive to understand how to manage and control risk. As trade routes turned into world wars and global stock and bond swaps, the gains from risk assessment and management as practical arts increased. Those who had an appreciation of the behavioural underpinnings of risk had a better chance of winning real and metaphorical battles. This holds for environmental risk too.

To follow the intellectual history of understanding how people behave under risk, consider three gambles:

- Gamble X is a certain payment to you of $30—a sure bet.
- Gamble Y is a coin flip in which you win $100 with a heads, and lose $100 with a tails.
- Gamble Z is a roll of a dice in which you win $2,000 if a 1 is rolled; win $1,000 with a 2; win $500 with a 3; lose $0 with a 4; lose $1,000 with a 5; and lose $2,000 with a 6.

Which would you choose? Early theorists speculating on how people make choices under risk first argued that people would prefer the gamble with the highest expected value—the probability weighted average of all possible outcomes of the gamble:

$$\text{Expected value} = (\text{probability of outcome 1}) \times (\$ \text{ of outcome 1})$$
$$+ (\text{probability of outcome 2}) \times (\$ \text{ of outcome 2})$$
$$+ (\text{probability of outcome n}) \times (\$ \text{ of outcome } n)$$

In our case:

- Gamble X: 100 per cent chance of $30 = *$30 expected value.*
- Gamble Y: 50 per cent chance of $100 + 50 per cent chance of –$100 = *$0 expected value.*
- Gamble Z: [1/6] chance of $2,000 + [1/6] chance of $1,000 + [1/6] chance of $500 + [1/6] chance of $0 + [1/6] chance of –$1,000 + [1/6] chance of –$2,000 = *$83.33 expected value.*

Gamble Z has the highest expected value. But we observe that many people take gamble X instead. The old adage that a bird in the hand is worth two in the bush reflects the prudent strategy to go for the sure thing.

But why does the gamble with the lower expected value attract so many people? In the eighteenth century, Nicholas Bernoulli created the St Petersburg paradox to show why. Suppose that you are offered the following proposition. You can buy into a gamble on a fair coin toss. If a head comes up on the first flip, you earn $2; if it takes two flips to uncover a head, you earn

$4; if it takes three flips, you earn $8; four flips, $16; five, $32; six, $64; seven, $128; and so on. What is the maximum you would be willing to pay to buy into this gamble?

Everyone would answer with an amount lower than infinity. But infinity is the expected value of this gamble:

$$\text{Expected value} = [1/2] \text{ chance of } \$2 + [1/4] \text{ chance of } \$4 + [1/8] \text{ chance of } \$8 + \cdots$$
$$= \$1 + \$1 + \$1 + \$1 + \$1 + \cdots$$
$$= \text{infinity}.$$

Should you have been willing to pay more? No. Why? One reason is because the variance of the gamble is also infinite. Variance is considered synonymous with risk because it reflects the potential volatility of the outcome. The variance reflects the distribution around the expected value. More variance implies more chance that bad states—low pay-off outcomes — will be realized.

Nicholas' cousin Daniel Bernoulli offered a reason why people pay less than infinity for a gamble with infinite variance: a gain of $2,000 is not worth twice as much as one of $1,000. People have diminishing marginal returns to wealth. This means that even though you prefer more money to less, the last dollar you earn gives you less satisfaction than the first dollar earned. His key insight is that a person's 'utility' (the degree of satisfaction in possessing wealth) resulting from a small increase in wealth will be inversely proportionate to his current wealth.

Figure 5.1 illustrates the idea of diminishing marginal returns. Increased wealth increases total utility at a decreasing rate, which is why the utility function is curved. Gambles with high variance are less attractive—your gain from an extra dollar added to your wealth is smaller than your loss from an extra dollar taken away. One example of a useful utility function with this property is

$$u(w) = \text{square root(wealth)} \quad \text{or} \quad u(w) = \sqrt{w}.$$

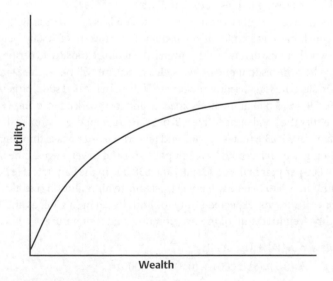

Figure 5.1 Diminishing marginal returns.

For instance, wealth of $10,000 creates a utility level of 100, while wealth of $1,000,000 creates a utility level of 1,000, so that a hundredfold increase in wealth increases a person's utility by tenfold. When a person acts in this way, we say he or she is *risk-averse*. A risk-averse person is more likely to take a certain pay-off over a fair bet—a gamble in which the expected value is zero; for example, 50:50 odds to win or lose $1,000. Our person is *risk-loving* if he or she prefers a fair bet to a certain pay-off equalling the expected value of the gamble. He is *risk-neutral* if he is indifferent between a gamble and certain pay-off equalling the expected value of the gamble.

Bernoulli's insight was formalized into a rational choice framework called *expected utility theory* (EU). Since its introduction in the 1940s by the mathematician John von Neumann and the economist Oscar Morgenstern, EU theory has been the most successful model of how people make decisions under risk. The formal theory of expected utility reflects the idea that people make choices about risk based on their *beliefs* about the probability that good and bad events will be realized, the *consequences* of good and bad events, and the *utility* or *satisfaction* a person gets from the consequence that is realized.

Consider our three gambles from an expected utility perspective. Assume that a person has an initial wealth of, say $2,001, and a square root–style utility function:

- Gamble X: 100 per cent chance of $\sqrt{\$2,031}$ = 45.1 *expected utility*.
- Gamble Y: 50 per cent chance of $\sqrt{\$2,101}$ + 50 per cent chance of $\sqrt{\$1,901}$ = 44.7 *expected utility*.
- Gamble Z: [1/6] chance of $\sqrt{\$4,001}$ + [1/6] chance of $\sqrt{\$3,001}$ + [1/6] chance of $\sqrt{\$2,501}$ + [1/6] chance of $\sqrt{\$2,001}$ + [1/6] chance of $\sqrt{\$1,001}$ + [1/6] chance of $\sqrt{\$1}$ = 40.9 *expected utility*.

On the basis of expected utility, the person should prefer gamble X to either Y or Z: 45.1 > 44.7 > 40.9. This is the insight of expected utility theory—expected values and expected utility do not rank alternative gambles in the same way.

Now consider an example of environmental risk. Travis is a carpenter who lives and works in Las Vegas, which has elevated levels of air pollution. He earns $50,000 per year. But he is uncertain as to whether he will stay healthy given his ongoing exposure to ozone and particulate matter. Suppose he believes that one of two states of nature will be realized—a good and bad state. In the good state, he stays healthy and earns $50,000. In the bad state, he gets sick and earns $35,000 (= $50,000 – $15,000 in medical expenses and lost work). Let π and $(1 - \pi)$ represent his beliefs that either the good or bad state will be realized. Suppose he thinks that the odds that he will stay healthy are 70:30; that is, $\pi = 0.7$ and $(1 - \pi) = 0.3$. Travis is thinking about moving to Baggs, Wyoming, which has both lower air pollution and lower wages. If he moves to Baggs, he can earn $40,000 per year in the good state, and $38,000 in the bad state. He believes his odds of staying healthy are 90:10 that he will not get sick due to air pollution (i.e. π' and $(1 - \pi')$).

We can now write Travis' expected utility for both living in Las Vegas and living in Baggs as the probability-weighted sum of the two potential states of nature:

$$\text{EU(Las Vegas)} = \pi(w) + (1 - \pi)u(w - D)$$
$$= (0.7)u(\$50,000) + (0.3)u(\$35,000)$$
$$= 0.7\sqrt{\$50,000} + 0.3\sqrt{\$35,000}$$
$$= 213;$$

$$\begin{aligned}
\text{EU(Baggs)} &= \pi'(w) + (1 - \pi')u(w - D) \\
&= (0.9)u(\$40,000) + (0.1)u(\$38,000) \\
&= 0.7\sqrt{\$40,000} + 0.3\sqrt{\$40,000} \\
&= 200.
\end{aligned}$$

With these odds and earnings, Travis' expected utility is greater in Las Vegas even though the odds of getting ill are greater, as 213 > 200. He is willing to trade off the greater health risk for the higher earnings. This is common in many jobs in which workers take greater risk for more pay.

Now suppose that his odds of staying healthy in Las Vegas drop to, say 50:50, holding everything else constant. Now his expected utility from staying in Vegas falls to 205. But he still prefers Las Vegas to Baggs, since 205 > 200. Travis would think about leaving Las Vegas if the odds changed to 30:70, at which point his expected utility would drop to 198. Now Baggs would be the more attractive option, as 200 > 198. For sure, numerous factors influence our decision on where to live, in addition to simply wages and the changes of getting sick, such as school quality, crime, and recreation opportunities. We would have to adapt the expected utility framework to account for these factors as well. This is more complicated, but doable—as we saw in Section 4.3.1.

The next step in understanding rational choices within the expected utility model is to account for a person's ability to *influence* the risk that he or she confronts, either privately or collectively, through alternative risk reduction investments. Travis is not as helpless against the risk as the model suggests. He has more options than moving to Baggs. He can purchase market insurance against illness. He can invest in different risk-reduction strategies to change the odds of suffering from some illness due to the air pollution. He can buy an air filter for his home, or he can eat better and exercise more. His actions can reduce the likelihood that the bad state will occur or reduce the severity of the bad state if realized, or do both. We refer to actions to reduce the likelihood of illness as *self-protection* or *mitigation*; and to actions to reduce the severity of a realized outcome as *self-insurance* or *adaptation*.

Travis' problem is now more complicated. He selects the level of self-protection and self-insurance that balances the extra gains he gets from lower odds of illness and less severity with the costs of protecting and insuring himself:

$$\text{EU(Las Vegas} \mid \text{risk reduction)} = \pi(z)u(w - z - x) + (1 - \pi(z))u(w - D(x) - z - x),$$

where $\pi(z)$ is the probability of the good state, which depends on his level of self-protection, z; and $D(x)$ is the severity of illness, which depends on his level of self-insurance, x. Including the private ability to reduce risk is helpful in order to understand choice under environmental risk, because these actions link risk assessment with risk management. One must account for these actions to measure risk accurately and to manage risk effectively (Shogren and Crocker, 1999).

Although risk assessment has amassed a useful record of estimating potential threats to humans and nature, one problem permeates the risk assessment literature—the under-emphasis on how people adapt to the risk that they face or have created. Over the past decade, scientists have acknowledged that environmental risk is endogenous. People can influence many of the risks they confront. Examples abound. People move or reduce physical activities when air pollution becomes intolerable. They buy bottled water if they fear that their drinking water is polluted, and they apply sunscreen to protect their skin from UV radiation. A person can invest in a water filter, move, buy a membership to a health club, jog, or eat food low in fat and high in fibre—each choice alters his or her risk to health and welfare. How a person invests resources to increase the likelihood that good things happen and bad things does not depend on both his or her attitudes towards risk and his or her ability to reduce risk.

Cases exist in which people have little time to react to protect themselves, such as the Chernobyl nuclear accident in the former USSR. While it can be argued that we can redefine the problem so that risk is independent of human action, this approach is self-defeating. Consider a situation in which bacterial groundwater contamination threatens a household's drinking water. The probability of illness among household members can be altered if they boil the water. An analyst could define the situation as independent of the household's actions by focusing on groundwater contamination, over which the household probably has no control. But this definition is economically irrelevant if the question has to do with the household's response to the risks from groundwater contamination. The household is concerned about the likelihood of illness and the realized severity, and it is able to exercise some control over those events. The household's risk is endogenous because by expending its valuable resources, it influences probability and severity.

People substitute private actions for collectively supplied safety programmes: the use of stronger building materials to reduce the damage from tornadoes, storms, and earthquakes; more thorough weeding and crop storage in response to the prospect of drought; sandbagging and evacuation in anticipation of floods; and improved nutrition and exercise regimens to cope with health threats. At the policy level, these private risk-reduction choices can affect the success of collective regulations that promote safety. The use of car seat belts reduces both the probability and the severity of injury, but their mandatory installation cannot guarantee that passengers will choose to wear them. Highway speed limits are also effective at reducing fatalities, when drivers observe them. At work, rules promoting personal protective gear (e.g. hard hats) suffer from the same problem: they protect those workers who wear them. In each case, individual decisions influence both the probability and the magnitude of harm.

Endogenous risk implies that observed risks are functions of both natural science parameters and an individual's self-protection decisions. Given the relative marginal effectiveness of alternative self-protection efforts, how people make decisions about risk differs across individuals and situations, even though the natural phenomena that trigger these efforts apply equally to everyone. Assessing risk levels according to natural science parameters only can be misleading. Relative prices, incomes, and other economic and social parameters that influence any person's self-protection decisions affect risk. Just as good public policy-based economics requires an understanding of the physical and natural phenomena that underpin choices, good public policy-based natural science requires an understanding of the economic phenomena that affect risk. Accounting for private decisions can increase the precision of risk assessment. Failure to acknowledge the depths of private choice in environmental risk will result in less environmental protection at a greater cost.

5.2 **Behavioural Economics and Risk**

We now consider how the rational choice model matches up with actual behaviour. To illustrate, think how hazardous material conjures up images of a sanitized storage facility or an abandoned toxic waste dump-site. The two images induce different perceptions of risk to public health. Yet such a range of risk perceptions exists among people. Determining whether an environmental risk needs to be regulated depends on how people are willing to trade off risks for the benefits that flow from risk-generating activities. People's willingness to surrender benefits for reduced risk represents the value that they place on risk reduction. Estimating this value for risk reduction is a critical component of risk–benefit analysis used in policy-making on environmental risk.

This value of reduced risk depends on human behaviour—how people perceive risk and their *preference* towards risk. People who are wary of risks are likely to value risk reduction more than those who live to take risks. This statement seems straightforward enough, and the logic behind it guides most economists who address environmental risk. Those at most risk, who are most afraid of risk, and/or who have the most income should value risk reduction the most.

Economists who work with risk use the expected utility framework, which presumes that people have well-defined preferences for risk and can form rational perceptions of risk. The working presumption is that people have a solid foundation that drives their choices, such that when they confront a risk, new or old, they are able to evaluate the odds and consequences in a systematic and consistent way. A person's stated value for risk reduction is based on a logical foundation of choice from which we can judge the overall economic efficiency of some policy decision. Without well-grounded preferences and perceptions, a crack exists in the foundation of the rational theory of choice on which the economist's risk–benefit analysis rests (Hanley and Shogren, 2005).

Such cracks do exist. Psychologists and some economists have documented numerous exceptions to the idea of a rational theory of choice (see Daniel Kahneman's 2011 book *Thinking, Fast and Slow*). These behavioural researchers have shown how people use rules of thumb, or heuristics, to simplify their reasoning about risk. Using these rules, people react to risk in broader patterns than predicted by expected utility theory. This suggests that the standard model used to guide risk–benefit decisions is 'too thin', and does not predict systematic aspects of behaviour under risk that are observed in many situations. The evidence suggests that risk preference and perceptions seem to be influenced by the context of choice (see Box 5.1).

People who make judgements about risk use heuristics that the popular expected utility framework fails to capture. There is a long list of behavioural anomalies and paradoxes that have been uncovered by cognitive researchers. One bias in judgement is when people overestimate low-probability risks and underestimate high-probability risks. Figure 5.2 illustrates the bias. The 45-degree line represents the case in which the general public's subjective risk equals objective risk as defined by expert opinion. The flatter dashed line reflects the evidence from different experiments and surveys examining how people rank the threats posed by different risks. People seem to inflate low risks over which they have little to no control (e.g. nuclear power) and deflate high risks that they can control to some degree (e.g. driving to work). They tend to worry more about how and where a risk arises than its magnitude; for

BOX 5.1 The Allais Paradox

Several techniques have been used to construct counter-examples to expected utility theory. The most common method involves obtaining an individual's response to a pair of choices designed to give inconsistent answers. Allais (1953) provided the first counter-example with the following two pairs of choices:

		10% chance of $5 million
A: 100% chance of $1 million	vs.	B: 89% chance of $1 million
		1% chance of $0

and

C: 10% chance of $5 million	vs.	D: 11% chance of $1 million
90% chance of $0		89% chance of $0

If the person maximizes expected utility, he must either prefer the pair (A, D) or the pair (B, C). However, Allais and numerous other variations have observed that the modal number, and the majority, of people prefer (A, C) (Machina, 1987). This suggests that expected utility theory is too thin a theory of choice under risk—people are making systematic choices that are not captured by the theory.

example, synthetic versus natural carcinogens. This poor calibration between experts' objective opinions and the laypersons' perceptions can lead to constraints on choice, for example, over whether or not to include nuclear power in a country's energy portfolio.

Some risks are more acceptable than others. People who accept the risk of smoking or driving without seat belts may not accept the risk associated with nearby treatment, stor-

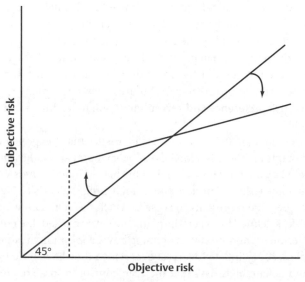

Figure 5.2 Objective and subjective risk perception.

age, and disposal of hazardous material. Voluntary risks that people think they can control are more acceptable than involuntary risks that they believe are outside their control. Technologies that inhibit the sense that this risk is 'voluntary'—for example, nuclear power—are less acceptable.

The perception gap raises a potential dilemma for the regulation. Suppose experts argue that the risks from a certain product are unacceptable, while many people perceive the opposite. Does the policy-maker ban the product or allow people to use their own discretion? The 1997 beef-on-the-bone ban in the United Kingdom in the wake of 'mad cow disease' (bovine spongiform encephalopathy, BSE), was a good example of not leaving the decision to people. The policy-maker's dilemma is to balance the trade-off between preserving individual freedom of choice and maintaining public safety. The policy-maker may be tempted to step in and regulate the risk in the best interests of society. Such paternalistic action, however, conflicts with societies committed to consumer sovereignty—the assumption that a person is best able to judge what is in his or her own best self-interest.

Risk perception examines laypersons' perceptions of risky technologies, and the determinants of their relative acceptability. The majority of risk acceptance research has been in the area of public perception of low-probability/high-consequence technology such as nuclear power. Laypersons will not accept risk if the hazard is perceived as uncontrollable, regardless of expert opinion. For example, in the 1980s, laypersons perceived nuclear power as the number one risk to public safety, while experts ranked it twentieth—below the risk of a household accident. Regardless of expert opinion, during the late 1970s and the 1980s, Swedish citizens perceived the nuclear power risk as unacceptable, and policy-makers agreed to phase out the entire industry within three decades. Today, the citizens of Japan are reconsidering the future of nuclear power given the tsunami and the Fukushima nuclear disaster.

Another risk perception effect is when people judge a risk by its familiarity with other risks they have confronted. They base their decisions on how well what they know represents the new event. This tendency to stick with their prejudices can cause people to discount risks with novel characteristics. One person underestimates the risk of radon because it is an odourless and colourless gas; another person overreacts to the risk for the same reason. Occasions exist when people fear the worst even when they have both good and bad information, because we recall bad events first. People have alarmist reactions to well-publicized risks to health or the environment.

People attach more weight to small losses than huge opportunities. We tend to dislike losses more than we like the equivalent gains. This 'loss-aversion' idea suggests that people treat perceived gains and losses differently. We seek out risk when gambles involve loss; but we avoid risk for the equivalent gambles that involve gains. This evidence suggests that rather than thinking about overall wealth, people seem to judge the value of gains and losses from a status quo—a reference point. They judge risk by what they have experienced and how it affects their current standing. The context in this case is the status quo. A person's value for risk reduction will then depend on the reference point, and on the nature of the gains and losses of the lottery (Tversky and Kahneman, 1981).

In addition, how the risk is 'framed' affects choice in ways that are not predicted by expected utility. If a person has well-formed preferences and values, a choice between two options should be independent of how they are represented or described. But again, psychologists show how choice and values can be systematically influenced by different ways of framing an identical problem The importance of framing effects can be illustrated using with a famous example. Answer the following three questions:

Q.1: Which of the following options do you prefer?

    A. A 100 per cent chance to win $30.

    B. An 80 per cent chance to win $45.

Q.2: This is a two-stage game. In the first stage, there is a 75 per cent chance that the game will end with no prize and a 25 per cent chance to move to the second stage. If you reach the second stage, you have a choice between:

    C. A 100 per cent chance to win $30.

    D. An 80 per cent chance to win $45.

Your choice must be made before the game starts. Please indicate the option you prefer.

Q.3: Which of the following options do you prefer?

    E. A 25 per cent chance to win $30.

    F. A 20 per cent chance to win $45.

Questions 2 and 3 are identical in odds and rewards, and should produce identical choices from a person. But, instead, people treat Q.1 and Q.2 the same, not Q.2 and Q.3. People prefer option C in Q.2 and option A in Q.1, while they prefer option E in Q.3. This is the so-called 'certainty effect'—an option framed as a sure thing appears as attractive as a certain option. This suggests that framing matters to risk policy. Regulators should pay as much attention to *how* they provide the information as to *what* information they provide. People also place varying levels of trust in information on environmental risk according to the source.

Many risks associated with the environment are hard to measure—the exact odds and consequences are 'ambiguous'—they cover a range of possibilities. Most people are averse to such ambiguity in risk. Ambiguity implies that the probabilities of bad events are uncertain—the odds of a bad event might range between 1 and 10 per cent. Ambiguous risks dominate many decisions that people must make; for example, with regard to investments, health care, exercise, and food. And while the expected utility model assumes that people handle ambiguous risk, consider the following example. Suppose you had the choice between choosing a ball from an urn with a known number of coloured balls and an urn with an unknown number of coloured balls, in a pay-off situation. Most people prefer to draw from the urn with the known distribution, even if the expected pay-off is lower. This is called the Ellsberg paradox. Even in experiments using professionals who deal with risk every day—such as actuaries, business executives, and life insurance executives—people are averse to ambiguous risk.

Finally, people find it a challenge to translate their preferences for risk into dollar values when thinking about risky situations. Frequently, they 'reverse their preferences'—that is, they rank gamble A over B, but state a higher dollar value for gamble B than A. That is, they prefer gamble A to B, but they assign a higher selling price to B than to A. To understand better, answer the following questions:

Q.3: Which gamble do you prefer, A or B?

  Gamble A: 35/36 chances to win $4.

             1/36 chance to lose $1.

  Gamble B: 11/36 chances to win $16.

             25/36 chances to lose $1.50.

Q.4: Suppose that you own both gambles. What is your selling price for:

  Gamble A: $_____

  Gamble B: $ _____

Decision theory based on expected utility requires that you be consistent—the gamble you select (either A or B) should also be the gamble you put the highest selling price on. But many people say they prefer gamble A to B, and then assign a higher dollar value to gamble B than A. If you did so, you can add your name to the long list of people who 'reversed their preferences'.

The logical inconsistency is this: suppose that you preferred A to B, and valued A at $2 and B at $8. Now if your statements are a true indication of your preferences, we can turn you into a 'money pump' in three easy steps: (1) sell you B for $8, (2) ask you to switch B for A because, after all, you preferred A to B, and then (3) buy A back from you for $2. Now you have neither gamble, and a $6 hole in your pocket (–$6 = $2 – $8). If you prefer more money to less, this is not good. Your choices should be consistent, which is what expected utility presumes. But the preference reversal phenomenon has been duplicated in numerous settings, including with real gamblers in Las Vegas and economists retesting the work of psychologists (also see Box 5.2 on inconsistent preferences over time; i.e. hyperbolic discounting).

In conclusion, behaviour towards risk matters to environmental policy because if people's stated values for risk reduction are inconsistent with their underlying preferences, or if the set preferences are a fantasy, society has less information to use to judge the relative net benefits of one environmental policy over another. If values are context-specific so that they change with the policy, then we cannot compare two policies using risk–benefit analysis, because it would be like comparing apples and oranges. If the values always depend on the context, economists can question standard risk–benefit analysis or cost–benefit analysis to guide policy. They cannot rely on the foundation of welfare economics to define a consistent ranking of environmental policy based on our statements of how much we prefer reductions in risk.

5.3 Valuing Risks to Life and Limb

We now examine how people value a reduction in risks to human and environmental health, for both private and collective strategies. We focus on rational risk reductions, recognizing the caveats that arise from the behavioural issues that we just discussed. Constrained budgets and increased fiscal accountability prevent a policy-maker from reducing all risk to all individuals. Deciding which risks to reduce, and by how much, requires evaluation of

BOX 5.2 Hyperbolic Discounting

People make economic decisions every day about what goods to purchase, when to purchase them, and how much money to allocate to current consumption or save for future consumption. When making these intertemporal choices, people implicitly discount possible future events to compare them to current benefits. The standard economic model suggests that dynamically consistent behaviour based on this implicit discounting assumes that people have a constant marginal rate of time preference, or a discount rate, when determining the current value of future streams of benefits. While the correct size of the discount rate to use in cost–benefit analysis has been discussed at length in the literature—including issues such as the social rate of discount versus producer and consumer rates, the social discount rate versus the social rate of time preference, tax-induced distortions, intertemporal investment decisions, and imperfect markets—under each of these scenarios, the form of the discount rate is assumed constant for cost–benefit analysis. Cost–benefit analysis uses constant discounting to determine present values.

But empirical evidence now suggests that people do not use a constant discount rate when taking actions that affect the future. Evidence suggests that people are less patient in the near term, implying higher discount rates relative to the discount rates they use for actions in the far distant future; here, people seem more patient with lower discount rates. This behaviour is typically called *hyperbolic discounting*. Hyperbolic discounting implies that people make inconstant choices and plans over time; for example, 'I will fix the water pipe … tomorrow.' We believe that whatever we are doing later will not be as important as what we are doing right now (see Thaler and Benartzi, 2004). Such time-inconsistent plans help to explain such behavioural regularities as self-control, addiction, low savings rates, and procrastination.

The evidence has led to a great deal of new research, as well as disagreement, on the role of hyperbolic discounting in economic analysis. Most of this work on hyperbolic discounting looks for evidence to either support or reject the use of the method, whether it is the choice of the correct discount rate or the correct discount model. Relatively few attempts have been made to assess how hyperbolic discounting can affect the outcomes of environmental and resource policy. Two exceptions are Settle and Shogren (2004) and Hepburn et al. (2010). Shogren and Settle examine how hyperbolic discounting affects behaviour within a bio-economic model of a fishery in Yellowstone National Park, Yellowstone Lake, Wyoming. They find that hyperbolic discounting increases the size of the net policy efficiency gains compared with constant discounting using the same initial discount rate. In addition, they estimate that hyperbolic and constant discounting can yield the same gains, but the results lead to different time frames for the policy. Hepburn et al. (2010) examine a fisheries model given hyperbolic discounting. They model a scenario that allows a social planner to either commit to a time-consistent policy or re-evaluate the policy in the future. The planner's lack of self-control causes him to change policy in the future, which leads to the collapse of the resource stock.

In sum, most people discount the near term at higher rates than they do the far distant future. This hyperbolic discounting can lead to various forms of non-constant dynamic choices, such as procrastination and a lack of self-control. Time-inconsistent choices can lead to too little investment in current savings and too little concern about current stocks of natural resources and ecosystem services.

each new or revised regulation. Comparability of value across all sectors of the economy requires that policy-makers rank regulatory alternatives in terms of a common unit. Arguably, the most common denominator is money, or monetary equivalence. Rational risk valuation systematically evaluates each regulation by estimating the monetary value—both benefits and costs—of a reduction in risk.

Valuing the costs and benefits of reduced risk is challenging. Measuring the cost of controlling risk is relatively straightforward; measuring the benefits means monetizing lower risks to life and limb Measuring the benefits of fewer death and injuries is difficult, because life and limb are typically not bought and sold on the auction block. These goods enter markets indirectly.

Valuing risk reductions requires that we place a value on death and illness. These efforts give rise to the loaded term 'the value of statistical life', or VSL—the idea of a monetary value of life or, more correctly, the value of reduced mortality risk. Ethical and moral beliefs force a person to baulk at the idea. But our everyday choices and the trade-offs that we make implicitly generate a value on life; it is another matter whether we explicitly quantify the VSL. Whenever a policy change is enacted or whenever the status quo remains, life and limb are implicitly valued. Economists take it to the next step by measuring how people will trade off goods and services for a risk reduction in the change of sudden death or injury.

Economists value a rational reduction in risk as follows:

The economic value of a small risk reduction =
[WTP for a small change in risk]/[the small change in risk].

A person's value for a risk reduction equals his or her maximum willingness to pay (WTP) to increase the chances to stay healthy, conditional of his or her previous private actions to reduce risk. For example, suppose that a person was willing to pay $6 to reduce the risk of death to 1 life in 1,000,000 from 4 lives in 1,000,000—a 3 in 1 million risk reduction. The value of life is then $2,000,000 (= $6/(3/1,000,000)). If the person was willing to pay $0.60, the implied value of life would be $200,000.

This WTP is called the *option price*. The option price is the maximum that a person is willing to pay that keeps him or her indifferent between the gamble and the next-best alternative. Consider Travis again and his decision to move to Baggs. Suppose that regulators are thinking about a policy that would reduce air pollution so as to increase the odds of being healthy in Las Vegas to 90:10. The maximum option price, *OP*, that Travis would pay for this risk reduction is the amount that would make him indifferent between the status quo and staying and leaving Las Vegas for Baggs:

$$(0.9)u(\$50,000 - OP) + (0.1)u(\$35,000 - OP) = (0.7)u(\$50,000) + (0.3)u(\$35,000);$$

$$0.9\sqrt{(\$50,000 - OP)} + 0.1\sqrt{(\$35,000 - OP)} = 0.7\sqrt{(\$50,000} + 0.3\sqrt{(\$35,000} = 213;$$

$$0.9\sqrt{(\$50,000 - \$3,000)} + 0.1\sqrt{(\$35,000 - \$3,000)} = 213.$$

In this case, Travis would be willing to pay at most $3,000 to reduce the risk of illness in Las Vegas.

Alternatively, we could ask him to reveal his minimum willingness to accept compensation (WTA), *C*, to forgo the potential risk reduction:

$$(0.7)u(\$50,000 + C) + (0.3)u(\$35,000 + C) = (0.9)u(\$50,000) + (0.1)u(\$35,000)$$
$$= 220;$$

$$0.7\sqrt{\$50,000 + C} + 0.3\sqrt{\$35,000 + C} = 0.9\sqrt{\$50,000} + 0.1\sqrt{\$35,000};$$

$$0.7\sqrt{\$50,000 + 3,1000} + 0.3\sqrt{\$35,000 + 3,1000} = 220.$$

Travis would take at a minimum $3,100 to forgo the proposed risk reduction policy.

How do economists measure the value of risk reduction? The literature on risk valuation has developed two general approaches to measuring the economic benefits of reduced risk: the human capital and WTP approaches:

- *The human capital approach.* This values risk reductions by examining a person's lifetime earnings and activities. The value of a risk reduction is the gain in future earnings and consumption. The value of saving a life is calculated as what the individual contributes to society through the net present value of future earnings and consumption. The human capital approach has an advantage in that it is actuarial; it uses full age-specific accounting to evaluate risk reductions. The major drawback of the approach is that it lacks justification based on traditional economic theory. We are measuring {price and quantity} rather than preferences and welfare.

- *The WTP approach.* Most economists prefer to measure the value of risk reductions assuming that they are capturing a person's underlying preferences for trading of risk and reward. The WTP approach is based on traditional economic theory. Here, a person values a risk reduction if it leads to higher satisfaction. The welfare change is measured by the maximum that he would be willing to pay to reduce risk, or the minimum compensation he would be willing to accept for an increase in risk. Economists use this willingness to pay or accept to infer the implied value of life and limb. Four empirical approaches are used to determine the WTP for risk reduction: revealed preferences, stated preferences, experimental auctions, and averting behaviour. These are comparable with the general valuation methods described in Chapters 3 and 4.

1. *Revealed preferences/wage–risk trade-offs.* Wage–risk trade-offs are based on the theory of hedonic prices. Hedonic price theory captures the idea that a person's wage rate depends on skill, education, occupation, location, environment of work, and job safety or risk. A worker will accept a higher wage for more risk, holding all other job attributes constant—the greater the risk, the higher the wages. And a worker selects his job to equate the incremental WTP for each attribute to the incremental contribution of each attribute to the wage rate. The value of risk reduction is the incremental WTP for the attribute 'job safety'. Workers then compare their risk–wage trade-offs to the rate at which the market is willing to trade risk for wages. The market equilibrium between workers and employers then determines the risk premium—the extra compensation for risky jobs. The wage–risk trade-off is determined, other job attributes held constant. Recent reviews of wage–risk studies set the average value of a statistical life at around $7 million (2008 dollars). These values have been challenged. Critics question the presumptions that workers know all the risks in the job, and can change jobs without cost. Also they point out the weak correlation between job safety and environmental hazards. They also stress that hedonic models consider a segment of the population—people with a job; children and seniors are underrepresented.

2. *Stated preferences.* As we saw in Chapter 4, stated preference methods (e.g. contingent valuation) ask people directly how much they would be willing to pay to reduce risk

through a survey or interview. The approach constructs a hypothetical market, in which a person buys or sells safety. The method attempts to reveal a person's WTP for a risk reduction. The challenge is to make these hypothetical markets realistic and relevant to people. The biggest complaint is that a person answers a hypothetical question that does not enforce his or her actual budget constraint.

3. *Experimental auctions.* Experimental auction markets are a recent approach to directly value reductions in risk. Experimental auctions use the laboratory to sell real goods to real people within a stylized setting. Laboratory experiments can isolate and control how different auctions and market settings affect values in a setting of replication and repetition. Experiments with repeated market experience provide a well-defined incentive structure that allows a person to learn that the honest revelation of his or her true preferences is his or her best strategy. Using demand revealing auctions (e.g. the second-price, sealed-bid auction mechanism), subjects will participate in an auction market that allows for learning as participants realize the actual monetary consequences of their bidding. The non-hypothetical auctions with repeated market experience can help improve the precision of risk valuation. For example, work in experimental markets has elicited the *ex ante* WTP for safer food. These experiments used real money, real food, repeated opportunities to participate in the auction market, and full information on the probability and severity of disease resulting from the food-borne pathogens. The value of statistical life implied by bidding behaviour in laboratory work exceeds—by an order of magnitude—the value estimated in other valuation methods, ranging from $2 million to $70 million (see Box 5.3).

4. *Self-protection/averting behaviour.* The averting behaviour method estimates WTP for risk based on what people pay to protect their families and themselves. People reveal their preferences for lower risk through the market for self-protection, such as smoke detectors, seat belts, medicine, bottled water, and water filters. People use these private markets to reduce risk themselves. This self-protection raises an important issue in the value of life and limb. The value of life or limb is defined as the cost of an unidentified single death or injury weighted by a probability of death or injury that is uniform across people. The WTP approach captures this cost by revealing the unobserved preferences for risk reduction. But here is the rub. These estimates contain more than just unobserved preferences—they capture preferences for risk reduction conditional on each person's unobserved ability to reduce risk privately.

Consider an example. Suppose that people have identical preferences for risk reduction from contaminated drinking water, but that they differ in their ability to access private risk reduction markets. And now say that each person is asked to reveal his or her value for a collective programme to reduce risk. Each person's value for this collective risk reduction is conditional on his or her private actions. Following the standard procedures to value life, one might assume that people with a low value for collective risk reduction would be willing to tolerate greater risk. But it just might be that they have access to effective private risk reduction and have reduced the risk themselves.

Why does this matter? This matters because the statistical value of life used in benefit–cost estimates is biased upwards because it has not addressed these private actions. To see this, consider the value of life used by the US Environmental Protection Agency (EPA).

> **BOX 5.3 Valuing Reduced Risk from Food-borne Pathogens in the Laboratory**
>
> The World Health Organization has estimated that one in three people around the world get sick from food-borne illness every year. What is the economic value of reducing the risks from food-borne pathogens? Almost two decades ago, Hayes et al. (1995) designed a set of experimental auctions to explore this question. They constructed an experimental auction to elicit both the option price and compensation measures of value for five different food-borne pathogens. They used additional treatments to evaluate how subjects respond to changes in the risk of illness for a given pathogen, *Salmonella*, and to explore if pathogen-specific values act as surrogate measures of general food safety preferences. All experiments used real money, real food, repeated opportunities to participate in the auction market, and full information on the probability and severity of the food-borne pathogen. The design used a classic second-price auction. The auction is 'incentive compatible'—a bidder's weakly dominant strategy is to bid his or her true preferences for risk reduction.
>
> Four results emerged from their experiments. First, people underestimated the objective risk of food-borne pathogens. Second, values across food-borne pathogens were not robust to changes in the relative probabilities and severity, suggesting that people were placing more weight on their own prior perceptions than on new information on the odds of illness. Third, marginal willingness to pay an option price decreased as risk increases, again suggesting that the people weighted their prior beliefs more than new information. Fourth, they found support for the theory that values for specific pathogens might act as surrogates for general food-safety preferences.
>
> Overall, the results suggest that the average subject in our experimental environment was willing to pay approximately $0.70 per meal for safer food. The *Salmonella* treatments under alternative risk levels indicate that the average person would pay about $0.30 per meal to reduce the risk of food-borne pathogens by a fraction of ten. At the time of the auctions, if these values were to be transferred to the US population, the value of food safety would have been at least three times the largest available estimates.

Today, the US EPA uses a value of statistical life (VSL) of about $7 million. This value is generated from the mid-point estimate of different valuation exercises. A prominent example is the US EPA's application of the VSL to justify the 2000 diesel sulphur rule. Here, the VSL accounted for nearly 90 per cent of the estimated annual total benefits from improved air quality, at $62.6 billion out of $70.4 billion.

The VSL estimate depends in part on the private ability to reduce risk. To apply a fixed VSL to other risk reduction policies assumes that people in another context have the same private risk reduction opportunities. Whether this assumption holds for all markets is not obvious. Why should the market for the private reduction of water risk be identical to the market for toxic air risk? By focusing on collective risk reduction, the statistical life approach can bias the value of risk reduction, which can lead to inefficient levels of environmental degradation. Allowing a person to reveal whether he or she would prefer to reduce risk privately or collectively, or both, will elicit a more exact measure of the value of risk reduction.

The value of reduced risk depends on the WTP and the change in risk. If we do not account for people starting from different baselines due to their personal ability to access private markets, the value will be biased. Consider two kinsmen, Riley and Ole, who are identical in every way except for their unobserved skill or access to private risk reduction markets. Suppose that they are asked to state their WTP for a collective policy that will increase the odds of a gamble from 50:50 to a 100 per cent chance that the good state of the world will be realized.

Riley says he will pay nothing for the change in risk, and Ole says he'll pay $100. The traditional estimate of the value of this risk reduction is

Value of risk reduction without private action = 1/2[$0/0.5] + 1/2[$100/0.5] = $100.

But this presumes that Riley and Ole face the same baseline and the same change in risk, 50:50, even though their unobserved skill or market access differs. Let Riley have high skill or access, such that his real odds are 90:10 of a good outcome prior to the collective policy, such that he is paying for a real change in risk that equals 0.1 = 1.00 − 0.9; whereas Ole has low skill or access and his real odds are 10:90. Ole is paying $100 for a 0.9 change in risk: 1.0 − 0.1. The value of risk reduction conditional on private risk reduction is then

Value of risk reduction with private action = 1/2[$0/0.1] + 1/2[$100/0.9] = $56.

The value of risk reduction is lower than the traditional measure if one accounts for private actions changing the baseline risk. If the WTP amounts were reversed such that Riley paid $100 and Ole paid nothing, the new value would exceed the traditional measure:

Value of risk reduction with private action = 1/2[$100/0.1] + 1/2[$0/0.9] = $500.

This example is less likely to be observed, however, since low skill and low risk aversion are more likely to be correlated. Private actions affect the baseline risk, and this alters the value of risk reduction of the average person.

5.4 Regulating Risk

Managing and regulating risk in society requires regulators to integrate assessment, psychology, economics, and political factors. Risk-management policies are complicated by numerous factors: scientific complexity and uncertainty, political and economic pressure from special interest groups, financial abilities to clean up disposal sites, jurisdictional disputes, unresolved liability, and variations in local, state, and federal policy goals. Successful strategies to manage risk should address which risks we want to confront now and in the future, how we will control these risks in a cost-effective manner, and how we balance who faces what risk.

Consider several ways in which to select the risks we choose to face. A common first reaction is to want to set a target of *zero risk* to society. Regulation in the United States—such as the Delaney Clause of the Food, Drug, and Cosmetic Act, which prohibited the presence of any known carcinogen as a food additive in processed food—is a zero-risk regulation. As science becomes better at measuring small amounts of trace chemicals that are potential carcinogens, the zero-risk approach is restrictive. If almost everything is feared to cause cancer of some form, what can we eliminate? The costs of hitting a zero-risk target become prohibitive. Some actions and activities can be so risky that society should ban their use—zero risk because they are gone from society.

The next wave is for society to set an acceptable risk target that can be reached using current or new technology. *Technology-based standards* are a centralized process of setting permissible levels of contamination or building codes. People or firms who ignore these standards would be punished in civil or criminal court. Examples include uniform limits on total emissions per day or year, the emission per tonne of input used in a production process, and the type of equipment used in production, such that it is the best available control technology. One argument advanced by proponents of technology standards is that technology-based engineering decisions that construct a uniform threshold of acceptable risk have to be measured; costs and benefits are left unmeasured. But uniform standards are likely to be inefficient, as we saw in Chapter 2.

A third wave is to promote cost-effective risk reduction. Dollars now enter into the picture. Costs matter. *Cost-effectiveness* allows regulators to set a target and then asks that people be allowed to find the most cost-effective path to achieve the target. The idea is to take the public's preferences and perceptions of risk into consideration. This can be accomplished through open meetings in which regulators and the public set health and safety targets. Cost-effectiveness attempts to find the least costly method to achieve the goals. One advantage of cost-effectiveness is that it does not have to measure the benefits of the target. The method maximizes lives saved given a fixed budget in which assumptions on values are built into the model.

If we want to consider trade-offs involved in risk management but still not measure costs or benefits, regulators can address *risk–risk trade-offs*, or *comparative risk analysis*. Risk–risk analysis compares how we trade off one risk for another. For example, an energy policy that would switch to more nuclear power and less coal power would shift the nature of risk to radiation rather than climate change. A shift to more hydropower would shift the risk towards more protection of endangered species. The framework requires estimation of the trade-off between consumer health risks and substances that offer a direct health benefit. The health benefits of drugs, exercise, and diet, for example, fit into this framework. The benefit of the risk–risk framework is that regulators can convert health outcomes into fatality risk equivalents, which might allow more meaningful comparisons than a risk–dollar trade-off.

Finally, policy-makers can use cost–benefit analyses, as we saw in the previous chapter. Here, we ask for dollar measures of both costs and benefits, and a direct comparison of the trade-off between risk and dollar benefits. As we discussed, economists have devoted considerable effort to determining the value of reduced risk. Cost–benefit analysis can be used as a tool to measure the economic efficiency of a regulation. Cost–benefit analysis attempts to measure the costs associated with the risk regulation and the subsequent welfare benefits from a risk reduction. The costs of differing policy alternatives are then compared with their benefits to determine if, and to what extent, the risk will be reduced. The goal of cost–benefit analysis is to maximize economic efficiency and make the resulting risk reductions as large as possible.

There are many controversial aspects to cost–benefit analysis. The value of risks to life must be addressed in a policy context. The appropriate discount rate remains a question. Exponential discount rates place less weight on the future. We must address equity and distributional questions: Whose risk will be reduced and who will pay? An equity criterion spreads out the costs and benefits of risk based on some subjective measures, to weigh who gets what for which price. Risk can be distributed equally among the population; or it can be progressively or regressively distributed based on, say, wealth.

Environmental risk to children is a prime example of questions over whose risk we should be reducing. Evidence suggests that children face disproportionate health risks from environmental hazards. These unbalanced risks stem from several fundamental differences in the physiologies and activities of children and adults. As children develop, their digestive, nerve, and immune systems are more susceptible to toxic pollutants and other environmental hazards. Children eat, drink, and breathe more for their weight, and spend more time outside, exposing themselves to greater amounts of contamination and pollution for their weight than adults. They also face potential exposures over their entire lifetime. They are also less able to recognize and to protect themselves. All of this suggests that children require special attention when dealing with environmental risk.

On the basis of this argument, many politicians promote policies that explicitly aim to protect children from environmental risks. In the USA, the federal government has been tasked with safeguarding children from environmental threats through more policy, better research coordination, and more federal regulatory analysis. All US federal agencies now make the protection of children a high priority when implementing their statutory responsibilities and fulfilling their overall missions. Agencies promulgating major regulations that may have a disproportionate impact on children must now evaluate how regulation could affect children's risk, and then explain why the planned regulation is preferable to alternative actions that might have more cost and less risk.

This forces agencies to ratchet up their regulatory standards, with a corresponding increase in the costs and burden of regulation. The pressure to raise standards across the board may generate criticism from industry and other groups who argue that analysis of impacts on children can lead to costly decisions; in other words, Superfund clean-ups based on exposure of children to toxins, and analytical flaws in the public health data supporting recent Clean Air Act proposals on ozone and particulate matter. The additional burden may further delay the regulatory process, and add resource demands to agencies confronting tight budgetary constraints.

Regulators have many tools at their disposal to reduce risk, either to adults or children. They can impose mandates, liability rules, pollution taxes, and subsidies, create new markets, and use informed consent through risk communication. We have discussed taxes and markets previously. Consider risk communication strategies.

The major benefit of risk communication and informed consent is that people are allowed to make informed choices based on preferences towards risk rather than uniform government bans or regulation. The risk manager must be sure that the information that consumers have will result in more accurate private decisions regarding risk. But the language of the hazard warnings seems to maximize political interests rather than advancing the primary objective of informing consumers and enabling them to make better decisions. By ignoring fundamental economic and psychological concepts of decision-making under risk, warnings will not convey the information necessary for consumers to make sound choices regarding risks and precautions.

But the regulators and the public must also be aware that risks can be regulated by being transformed and transferred elsewhere. Transferable risk implies that people protect themselves by transferring the risk through space, to another location, or through time, to another generation. Most environmental programmes do not reduce environmental risks by cutting the mass of materials used or causing them to accumulate in the economy. People select a technology that transfers a risk that creates conflict and induces strategic behaviour. Some nations and states reduce their air pollution by building tall stacks such that the winds carry the emissions to those downwind. Some local governments ban toxin storage within their jurisdictions, thereby shifting the problems elsewhere. Effective risk management should address the question of transferability.

We now examine how behavioural economics might affect how we design policy to address market failure and environmental policy. As we discussed, if their rationality and willpower are bounded, people do not always react as predicted. One idea for incentives for people with self-control problems and temptation is for the person to choose from a smaller rather than a larger menu of actions for protection. This smaller-is-better finding also appears to exist for US and Canadian smokers, who act as if they are happier with higher cigarette taxes. Few such examples of applying behavioural economics to incentives exist in the environmental economics literature. If a person is altruistic towards others, then the existence of altruism itself is insufficient to generate a lower Pigovian tax. But if people behave as if they are 'addicted to' the good generating the negative environmental impact, an optimal environmental tax should exceed the standard Pigovian tax.

In the case of environmental issues, there is also scope for incorporating inputs from behavioural economics to maximize the policy goals. In recent research, some of the environmental and ecological economists have used the alternative models of rationality in their analyses related to environmental policy. Kallbekken et al. (2011) examine behavioural economics and Pigovian taxation in the laboratory. They consider how aversion to paying taxes affects the framing and functioning of the classic Pigovian tax. Two results emerge. First, people were not confused about the nature of Pigovian taxation; they understood how these taxes work and why society might need them—they just did not like the 't-word', tax. Second, reframing the tax as a 'fee' increased support, especially when revenues were earmarked for the environmental problem. A targeted rebate that reduced inequalities in the distribution of wealth was also preferred by the subjects, which supports the behavioural economics notion of 'inequality aversion'.

Another example is Banerjee and Shogren's (2012) model of environmental protection given the existence of *social preferences*. The authors consider how to design incentives when a firm has some non-monetary reason to protect the environment. Consider a concrete piece of reality to help think about the relevance of the theory. People have social preferences to help out even though it is privately costly to them; for example, a landowner who protects endangered species on his land even if it reduces his land rents. Some people have social preferences to protect the environment without having to pay. Paying them to protect nature might be counterproductive. Money 'crowds out' their willingness to do the good deed. Behavioural economists have argued that monetary rewards weaken intrinsic motivation; their terms are dramatic—the *hidden cost of reward*, the *over-justification effect*, or the *corruption effect*. Here, monetary rewards reduce the ability to indulge altruistic feelings; or cause others to doubt our true motive for doing a good deed. If the crowding out effect holds, monetary reward decreases effort—the exact opposite of what economics would predict. For example, in case of forest habitat preservation in Finland, private property owners with a positive attitude towards environmental protection actually claim less monetary transfer (Mantymaa et al., 2009).

In contrast, other people do not have strong social preferences for the environment. They are unwilling to pick up the tab to protect a public good. But it is difficult to identify, by observing people's behaviour, why they contribute to a social project—whether this is due to intrinsic motivation or sociality—as people care about reputation too. These folks might want to protect the environment to 'buy' a good reputation. A good reputation might be useful to attract new customers, gain better access to capital or credit markets, entice new property buyers, and so on. Offering up monetary rewards to these folks could be counter-productive if they wish to avoid being viewed as 'greedy' rather than generous.

The regulator's dilemma is that she does not know which person is which—social preferences or reputation buyer. How does she design a mechanism given that she knows both types exist, but that she does not know who is who. She does not want to chase away the person with social preferences by crowding out that person's incentives to do the right thing; she does not want to reward the reputation seeker by paying out extra money that could be spent elsewhere. The open question is whether she can design a mechanism that specifies a menu of monetary transfer-to-effort that gets the best out of both types of people. First, the social firm receives less transfer than is optimal and thereby under-invests in effort (relative to the full information case). In contrast, the reputation-driven firm receives the optimal level of monetary reward and expends optimal effort. Second, the social firm earns no information rents; but the reputation-driven firm earns negative information rents. The reputation-driven firm pays out money; it 'buys' a reputation for environmental protection.

Summary

People affect nature, and nature affects people. Together, people interacting with nature create risks to human and environmental health. More understanding is needed on how we create risk, how we behave towards risk—rationally or otherwise, how we trade off risk and rewards, and how we can design incentives to induce people to reduce risks to human and environmental health. Understanding economic behaviour under risk can help make our decisions to control risk more effective—reducing more risk for more people and for nature. Knowing how to assess risk accurately, whether people make risky choices with reason or at random, what people are willing to pay to reduce risk, and what options exist to control risk can help us make better decisions on how to save lives and protect nature at less cost.

Tutorial Questions

5.1 Is a zero-risk society possible?

5.2 Explain the pros and cons of using rational choice theory to help think about how to manage risks to human and environmental health.

5.3 How might private self-protection and self-insurance affect the demand for governmental reduction in risks to life and limb?

5.4 How does expected utility differ from expected values? Why does this difference matter for policy?

5.5 If people reverse their preferences for risky events, should the government incorporate or ignore their behaviour when making public policy?

5.6 Explain how one might measure the value of statistical life.

References and Additional Readings

Allais, M. (1953). 'Le comportement de l'homme rationnel devant le risque: critique des postulats et axiomes de l'ecole Americaine', *Econometrica* 21: 503–46.

Banerjee, P., and Shogren, J. (2012). 'Material interests, moral reputation, and crowding out species protection on private land', *Journal of Environmental Economics and Management* 63: 137–49.

Baron, R. (2008). *Thinking and Deciding* (Cambridge: Cambridge University Press).

Brekke, K., and Johansson-Stenman, O. (2008). 'The behavioural economics of climate change', *Oxford Review of Economic Policy* 24(2): 280–97.

Cameron, T.A. (2010). 'Euthanizing the value of a statistical life', *Review of Environmental Economics and Policy* 4: 161–78.

Ehrlich, I., and Becker, G.S. (1972). 'Market insurance, self-insurance and self-protection', *Journal of Political Economy* 80: 623–48.

Gillingham, K., Newell, R., and Palmer, K. (2009). 'Energy efficiency economics and policy', NBER Working Paper No. 15031.

Hanley, N., and Shogren, J. (2005). 'Is cost–benefit analysis anomaly-proof?' *Environmental and Resource Economics* 32(1): 13–34.

Hayes, D., Shogren, J., Shin, S., and Kliebenstein, J. (1995). 'Valuing food safety in experimental auction markets', *American Journal of Agricultural Economics* 77: 40–53.

Hepburn, C., Duncan, S., and Papachristodoulou, A. (2010). 'Behavioural economics, hyperbolic discounting, and environmental policy', *Environmental and Resource Economics* 46: 189–206.

Kahneman, D. (2011). *Thinking, Fast and Slow* (New York: Farrar, Straus, and Giroux).

Kahneman, D., and Tversky, A. (eds.) (2000). *Choices, Values, and Frames* (Cambridge: Cambridge University Press).

Kallbekken, S., Kroll, S., and Cherry, T. (2011). 'Do you not like Pigou, or do you not understand him? Tax aversion and revenue recycling in the lab', *Journal of Environmental Economics and Management* 62: 53–64.

Machina, M. (1987). 'Choice under uncertainty: problems solved and unsolved', *Journal of Economic Perspectives* 1: 121–54.

Mantymaa, E., Juutinen, A., Monkkonen, M., and Svento, R. (2009). 'Participation and compensation claims in voluntary forest conservation: a case of privately owned forests in Finland', *Forest Policy and Economics* 11: 498–507.

Metcalfe, R., and Dolan, P. (2012). 'Behavioural economics and its implications for transport', *Journal of Transport Geography* (in press).

Settle, C., and Shogren, J. (2004). 'Hyperbolic discounting and time inconsistency in a native–exotic species conflict', *Resource and Energy Economics* 26: 255–74.

Shogren, J. F., and Crocker, T. (1999). 'Risk and its consequences', *Journal of Environmental Economics and Management* 37: 44–51.

——and Taylor, L. (2008). 'On behavioral–environmental economics', *Review of Environmental Economics and Policy* 2: 26–44.

Thaler, R., and Benartzi, S. (2004). 'Save More Tomorrow™: using behavioral economics to increase employee savings', *Journal of Political Economy* 112: S164–87.

Thaler, R., and Sunstein, C. (2008). *Nudge: Improving Decisions about Health, Wealth, and Happiness* (New Haven, CT: Yale University Press).

Tversky, A., and Kahneman, D. (1981). 'The framing of decisions and the psychology of choice', *Science* 211: 453–8.

Viscusi, W.K. (2009). 'The devaluation of life', *Regulation & Governance* 3: 103–27.

Economic Growth, the Environment, and Sustainable Development

This chapter discusses the concepts of economic growth and sustainable development. Section 6.1 outlines what we mean by growth, a general understanding of how economies grow, and the differences between growth and development. In Section 6.2 we review the history of economic thinking about the links between growth and the environment. One controversial aspect of the debate is whether an economy can grow its way out of environmental problems, and this is covered in Section 6.3. Most debates on the links between growth and the environment are now undertaken in the context of the idea of 'sustainable development'. Section 6.4 explains how economists view this concept. The chapter closes with a review of different economic indicators of sustainability (Section 6.5).[1]

6.1 Economic Growth and Development

Governments worldwide are concerned with *economic growth* as a measure of a country's performance, both in absolute terms (how fast are we growing?) and in relative terms (are we growing faster than our neighbours?). Newspapers and television often report actual growth figures and predictions of future growth. But growth in what? Why does it occur? Are 'growth' and 'development' the same thing? This section addresses these questions, before turning to the relationship between growth and the environment.

Economic growth is commonly understood to reflect an increase in people's living standards over time. What we want is an indicator of how well we are doing as a society. This is a hard question to answer. Economists have developed the idea of *gross national product*, or GNP, a Nobel Prize–winning idea. GNP is a monetary measure of the total value of output of a country in any time period. GNP is also a measure of national incomes to all factors of production involved in economic activity (land, labour, and capital), and of total spending (consumption plus gross investment). GNP is often expressed in per capita terms, to allow for the

---

[1] We are grateful to one reviewer for pointing out that, as part of the Convention of Biological Diversity Aichi targets (2011), countries are now required to develop national green accounting measures, which might well include the kinds of economic indicator of sustainability described here.

Table 6.1 The ranking of global economies by GDP in purchasing power parity (PPP) terms, 2008

Ranking	Country	Economy (millions of international dollars)
(a) Top twenty		
1	United States	14,093,310
2	China	7,909,261
3	Japan	4,358,472
4	India	3,358,871
5	Germany	2,904,557
6	Russian Federation	2,260,202
7	United Kingdom	2,178,205
8	France	2,121,724
9	Brazil	1,978,139
10	Italy	1,871,709
11	Mexico	1,549,490
12	Spain	1,442,936
13	Republic of Korea	1,344,360
14	Canada	1,301,737
15	Turkey	991,715
16	Indonesia	907,955
17	Australia	831,220
18	Islamic Republic of Iran	778,779
19	Netherlands	673,634
20	Poland	658,611
(b) Countries ranked from 140th to 160th		
140	Rwanda	9,985
141	Mongolia	9,396
142	Malta	8,649
143	Montenegro	8,330
144	Mauritania	6,021
145	Swaziland	5,754
146	Togo	5,361
147	Sierra Leone	4,350
148	Suriname	3,812
149	Fiji	3,678
150	Bhutan	3,268
151	Central African Republic	3,216
152	Lesotho	3,205
153	Eritrea	3,161
154	Burundi	3,093
155	Guyana	2,339
156	The Gambia	2,263
157	Belize	2,172
158	Seychelles	1,860
159	Antigua and Barbuda	1,817
160	Djibouti	1,816

Note: 'Purchasing power parity' means that the data have been adjusted to take into account the different prices in the countries in the table—each dollar of PPP is supposed to buy the same 'basket' of goods.

Source: World Bank Development Indicators database, 2010.

Table 6.2 Per capita gross national income (GNI) for ten highest-ranked and ten lowest-ranked countries, 2008

Rank	Country	GNI per capita (US$)
Ten richest countries on GNI per capita terms		
1	Lichtenstein	97,990
2	Norway	87,340
3	Channel Islands	68,610
4	Luxembourg	69,390
5	Denmark	58,800
6	Switzerland	55,510
7	Sweden	50,910
8	Ireland	49,770
9	Netherlands	49,340
10	Kuwait	43,930
Ten poorest countries on GNI per capita terms		
200	Guinea	350
201	Niger	330
202	Sierra Leone	320
203	Eritrea	300
204	Ethiopia	280
205	Malawi	280
206	Guinea-Bissau	250
207	Liberia	170
208	Democratic Republic of the Congo	150
209	Burundi	140

effects of changes in population. If real per capita GNP is rising, it is usual to say that a country is experiencing economic growth. Tables 6.1 and 6.2 show gross domestic product (closely related to GNP) and gross national income (the income measure of GNP) per capita for the world in 2008. GNP is a measure of living standards in the sense that it measures the size of the 'economic cake' to be divided amongst the inhabitants of a country; that is, the amount of total income to be divided up. Looking at Table 6.2 in particular, which focuses on per-person measures, it is striking how the ten poorest countries in the world on this measure are all from Africa, whilst the 'ten richest' list is dominated by countries from Northern Europe, along with a Middle Eastern oil economy—incidentally, the United States comes after Kuwait in terms of the ranking by GNI per capita. In terms of absolute gross domestic product (GDP) levels, the USA is the world's biggest economy, followed by China.

Economic growth is measured as the change in GDP or GNP over a time period such as a year. Table 6.3 shows rates of economic growth for four countries: Vietnam, Turkey, Brazil, and Malawi. Table 6.3 also illustrates the effects of population change on how much growth benefits the 'average citizen' for Malawi, China and Peru: Malawi looks to have grown appreciably over the 10 years to 2008 (3%), but because of a high population growth, its per capita GDP only rose by 0.1 per cent on average over the decade. China, on the other hand, has had a rate of growth of more than 9 per cent in both absolute GDP and GDP per capita. Rising GNP per capita would not necessarily mean that absolutely everyone is better

Table 6.3 Economic growth rates for a selection of countries

	1988–98 (mean)	1998 2008 (mean)	2008 only
Vietnam	8.0	7.4	6.2
Turkey	4.3	4.7	0.9
Brazil	2.3	3.3	5.1
Malawi	3.5	3.0	9.7

	Malawi	China	Peru
Rate of growth of GDP, 1998–2008	3%	9.9%	5%
Rate of growth of GDP per capita, 1998–2008	0.1%	9.2%	3.6%

off, since some could lose or stand still, whilst others gain more than average. GNP tells us nothing of changes in the income distribution. However, rising real GNP might be claimed to show that, on average, people were getting better off over time. Lower growth rates have a big opportunity cost over time, since high rates of GNP growth can imply very big increases in the absolute level of real GNP over time. Compound growth tells us that an economy growing at 10 per cent per annum could double its GNP in 7 years. A country that cannot maintain growth rates falls further and further behind its competitors.

Many critics complain that GNP is an inadequate measure of well-being, as Box 6.1 shows. However, despite these criticisms, nations still use increases in real GNP per capita to measure their economic performance over time. But how can GNP increase over time? In other words, what is the theory behind economic growth?

BOX 6.1 Is GNP a Good Measure of Well-being?

Since the end of the Second World War, countries around the world have measured and compared their levels of well-being using gross national product, following guidelines laid out in the System of National Accounts. This seems sensible, since GNP measures our income as a country, as well as the value of what we are producing. If population is changing, or we wish to compare GNP across different countries, then we can divide GNP by population to get GNP per capita, which shows how much income, on average, each person in a country has. GNP has also been promoted as an indicator of national well-being, or welfare. Another measure of economic performance from the System of National Accounts is net national product (NNP): this is defined as GNP minus depreciation (wearing out) of the stock of manufactured capital during the year.

However, GNP has been widely criticized as a measure of well-being. Some of the main criticisms are as follows:

- The effects of the economy on the environment are not well measured by GNP. For example, if there was a major oil spill in a country and a great deal of money had to be spent to clean it up, then GNP could rise (since the pollution clean-up industry increases its output) even if people feel worse off as a result.

- A closely related point is that changes in our natural resource stocks do not show up in GNP; for example, if farming generates high levels of soil erosion so that the productive stocks of soil in a country are significantly depleted.

- Although GNP measures the size of the economic pie, it does not tell us how fairly it is divided up. GNP per capita could be increasing but income inequalities could worsen.

6.1.1 **Why do economies grow?**

Economic growth over the long term is due to increases in potential output, rather than short-term fluctuations. What causes potential output to rise? Two factors are important: growth in the resources that can be devoted to production, and changes in the productivity of these resources.

Increasing resources. If a country experiences an increase in its resource base, then GNP can increase. This resource base includes capital, labour, land, energy, and material resources. Labour supplies can rise with population growth or migration, although this might not mean that GNP per capita is increasing, even though aggregate GNP is. Land resources can increase if a country exploits overseas colonies, or converts marginal land to more profitable uses. Energy and material resources can increase through new discoveries, such as oil or gas deposits. Technological progress can also drive down the costs of exploiting natural resources, and thus make more of the physical resource stock profitable to exploit. This increases the economic reserves of that resource. Capital stocks also rise over time. Indeed, capital accumulation was one of the earliest explanations for economic growth put forward by the Classical economists and by Marx. Capital accumulates over time through the process of investment. The productivity of capital means that positive net investment (i.e. gross investment minus depreciation) can occur even with constant consumption. Capital productivity means that each £1 of resources invested in capital will generate more than £1 in consumption goods over time.

Productivity growth. As people learn more through education and training, the productivity of all of the resources used in economic activity increases. For example, the average productivity of miners in terms of tonnes of coal extracted per worker per annum, and the average productivity of agricultural land in terms of yields per hectare, have both risen steadily over time. The more a country invests in its workers, through education and training, the faster we expect growth to be. Education pays by increasing the stock of human capital through increasing the skills of the workforce. Human productivity can also increase through learning-by-doing. A famous example of this refers to steelworkers in Horndal, Sweden in the 1800s, who despite no changes in the machinery they worked with, or in the size of the workforce, managed to increase output by 2 per cent per year, just through becoming more experienced at their jobs (Begg et al., 1987). Produced capital can also become more productive, with the embodiment of knowledge in new designs of machinery. This source of growth is endogenous in the sense that the greater the amount of resources devoted to research and development activities, the greater will be the rate of technological innovation (other things being equal).

6.1.2 **Growth versus development**

Growth, as measured by rising GNP per capita, is not usually assumed to be the same as 'development'. This is because development is interpreted much more broadly (see, e.g., the UN *Human Development Report*); and because of the limitations of GNP as a measure of well-being referred to in Box 6.1. For an economy to be experiencing development, as distinct from growth, we might expect to see a whole series of indicators improving over time. These might include:

Table 6.4 Human Development Index scores, 2007 data

Rank on HDI	Country	HDI score	GDP per capita in PPP
1	Norway	0.97	53,433
2	Australia	0.97	34,923
3	Iceland	0.96	35,742
4	Canada	0.96	35,812
5	Ireland	0.96	44,613
157	Uganda	0.51	1,059
158	Nigeria	0.51	1,969
159	Togo	0.49	788
160	Malawi	0.49	761
161	Benin	0.49	1,312

Source: Human Development Report (2009).

- GNP per capita—this is still important
- A reduction in income inequality
- An improvement in adult literacy rates
- A reduction in infant mortality
- Reductions in morbidity (illness) and mortality (death) rates amongst adults
- An improvement in a range of environmental indicators

These indicators are both monetary and non-monetary. The *human development indicator* (HDI) was introduced by the United Nations (UN) in 1990 (UNDP, 1990) and is published annually. A set of three indicators was chosen to represent aspects of development for a nation. These comprise GDP, a measure of education levels, and a measure of life expectancy. In Table 6.4, HDI rankings are compared with ranking in terms of GDP per capita. As may be seen, there is a strong correlation between the two for these countries over these years. This is because income is a very major determinant of the other measures of well-being incorporated in the HDI. Countries that do well in terms of GDP per capita also tend to do well in terms of the HDI. However, *both* the HDI and GNP measures omit any direct account of environmental degradation.

6.2 Predictions from the Past

Above, we reviewed the main reasons why GNP per capita can grow over time, and thus why economic growth occurs. But for how long can growth continue? Does continual economic growth come with a health warning? One of the biggest intellectual debates throughout the history of economics has been concerned with these questions, and part of this debate has been the nature of the relationship between the economic system and the environment. The earliest economists, known as the Classical School, worried about the interaction of these two systems. Thomas Malthus (1766–1834) set out to formalize the implications for people's standard of living of exponential population growth coupled with linear growth in food output from farming. In Malthus' view (1798), rising living standards were causing the birth rate to rise. Eventually, food demand would outstrip food supply, and war, disease, or famine would occur. The population would then crash, before restarting its exponential growth once food production per head had recovered. It is not surprising, given this picture, that economics became known as the dismal science, since the only equilibrium situation was one of subsistence wages. Malthus' model was overly simplistic, since it ignored many of the factors that we now see as important, such as technological progress. His predictions have not come true in general, but they had a great influence on later thinkers, including Darwin and Keynes.

David Ricardo's work (1772–1823) led to a similar long-run gloomy prediction as that of Malthus, although at a more general level. Ricardo (1817) made use of the concept of diminishing marginal returns: as wages rose above subsistence levels and population increased, the rise in food demand caused agriculture to expand on to land of lower and lower productive quality. Since food prices would have to rise to cover the increasing costs of producing on less and less fertile land, those farmers growing on the most fertile land would earn a profit, or rent, as the difference between price and production cost. The distributional implications were profound: as food prices rose, workers got poorer and poorer, whilst landlords earned higher and higher rents. Ricardo and Malthus thus put forward two different explanations for increasing scarcity. For Malthus, the problem was that we have a fixed amount of natural resources (land) but increasing demands on those resources. For Ricardo, the most important fact was that as demand for food rose, the average productivity of land fell and the cost of producing food rose. These two views, of absolute and relative scarcity, are now referred to as *Malthusian* and *Ricardian* scarcity, respectively.

Ricardo's work is still very important; for example, in current work on understanding the movements of cultivation frontiers in developing countries (see Chapter 10), and the impacts of climate change on agriculture (Seo et al., 2009). However, his gloomy predictions did not come true due to productivity improvements and the development of colonialism, which effectively greatly increased the productive land base of European countries such as the United Kingdom and Germany, as well as expanding trade opportunities. Increasing use of fossil fuels meant that transportation became faster and cheaper, which also greatly expanded world trade (Common, 1988).

Two other early economists have also shaped our thinking about environmental and natural resources. These are John Stuart Mill (1806–73) and W. Stanley Jevons (1835–82). Mill's *Principles of Political Economy*, published in 1857, is now viewed as the climax of Classical economics. Mill makes clear that economic growth is a race between diminishing marginal returns and technological progress: technological progress drives down production costs as increasing Ricardian scarcity drives them up. Economic growth, through capital accumulation, results in higher living standards. Mill saw natural resources as productive (land for food, mines for coal) *and* as a direct source of utility in itself. He also suggested that economies would eventually evolve into a steady state, where growth ceased. In this steady state, Mill saw it as important that we do not completely devastate the environment in the pursuit of growth:

> Nor is there much satisfaction in contemplating the world with nothing left to the spontaneous action of nature: with every rood of land brought into cultivation and . . . every flowery waste

ploughed up . . . If the earth must lose that great portion of its pleasantness . . . for the mere purpose of enabling it to support a larger population . . . then I hope (they) will content to be stationary long before necessity compels them to it.

(Mill, 1857; quoted in Common, 1988)

Jevons is usually credited as being one of the first neoclassical economists, in that he helped introduce the marginal analysis that enabled economics to become systematic and rigorous in its approach to formulating how markets worked and the action of Adam Smith's 'invisible hand'. Jevons was also concerned about the implications of limited non-renewable resource inputs for economic growth. Coal was the most important natural resource powering the British Industrial Revolution from the early eighteenth century onwards (Warde, 2007). As more and more coal was dug up, both Jevons and Mill worried that it would become more expensive to extract, since mines would have to be dug deeper and deeper, increasing labour costs per ton. This is an application of the law of diminishing returns to resource deposits, and is an example of the concept of Ricardian scarcity. Jevons indeed viewed limited resource stocks as a great threat to British development, as his work *The Coal Question* (1865) made clear.

The idea that perpetual economic growth was neither inevitable nor desirable was thus first introduced to economics by Mill in 1857. This idea was reinvigorated within economics in the 1970s by writers such as Mishan and Daly, particularly in the latter's book *Steady State Economics*. This view, along with those of ecologists such as Holling, Erhlich, and Odum, was influential in the development of the paradigm of ecological economics in the late 1980s and 1990s. The links between economic growth and the environment, and the concept of *sustainable development*, have been a crucial part of this paradigm. Mainstream economics has become increasingly interested in links between economic growth and measures of personal well-being; for instance, in the question as to whether rising real incomes necessarily result in increasing 'happiness', as measured by survey questions. One finding that emerges from this new literature is that increases in absolute incomes do not seem to matter as much as changes in relative income (Blanchflower and Oswald, 2004), although this is not true for households below certain thresholds (in other words, rising absolute incomes always makes very poor households happier). A good review of the income–happiness relationship can be found in Clark et al. (2008). In developed countries, there seems to be a relationship between 'happiness' and local environmental quality. For example, air pollution has been found to have a direct negative effect on individuals' subjective well-being in different countries and using different data sets (see Levinson, 2009; Ferreira and Moro, 2010).

6.3 Growth and the Environment: The Environmental Kuznets Curve

Can economies grow their way out of environmental problems? What are the links between economic growth and environmental quality? One concept that has been much used to address this question is the *environmental Kuznets curve* (EKC). This was named after Simon Kuznets, who in 1955 hypothesized an inverted-U-shaped relationship between the equality of income distribution and income levels. A similar relationship has been claimed to exist between income levels and environmental quality by proponents of the EKC hypothesis. This relationship was first identified empirically by Grossman and Krueger (1995).

Indeed, the relationship between economic growth and environmental quality has been the focus of much work historically. For example, the 'limits to growth' school (Meadows et al., 1972) argued strongly that this relationship is negative, in that economic growth is, by definition, bad for the environment as it leads to more resource use and more pollution. The EKC hypothesis suggests otherwise. In the EKC literature, growth is usually measured as the change in income (GNP) per capita. Environmental quality is commonly measured by individual pollutant emission levels, ambient air quality or water quality. Most empirical EKCs are estimated for a single pollutant. The EKC hypothesis states that as per capita incomes grow, environmental impacts rise, hit a maximum, and then decline. This implies an 'inverted-U' shape, as shown in Figure 6.1.

Two parts of the curve can be identified, before and after a turning point at Y^*. Up to Y^* pollution is rising, and environmental quality is falling. What gives rise to this pattern? Economic growth is argued to result in *rising* pollution since:

- Economic growth results in an increasing use of resources, which also gives rise to an increase in waste. This is known as a 'scale effect'.

- If a country starts from an early development stage as an agricultural economy, then industrialization also leads to an increase in emissions as manufacturing takes over from agriculture as the dominant economic activity. In other words, growth is associated with a change in the structure of an economy that results in more pollution.

After Y^*, though, emissions *fall*. Why?

- There may be an increasing demand for environmental quality as incomes go up. This leads to an increase in government protection of the environment, and increasing green consumerism.

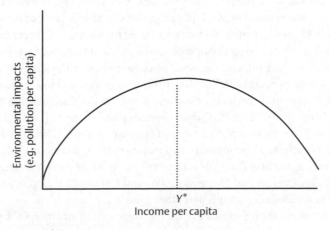

Figure 6.1 The environmental Kuznets curve.

- Technological improvements over time make production per unit of output cleaner (a 'technique effect'), whilst economies of scale in pollution abatement might also kick in (Andreoni and Levinson, 2001).

- Further changes in the structure of the economy occur, such as moves from manufacturing to service-sector or high-tech industries.

- Increasing scarcity of 'environmental quality' drives up its relative price, and this means that less is 'consumed' and more is preserved—although the non-market nature of many environmental goods means that this pressure fails to translate into appropriate market signals. Another way of thinking about this is to say that as pollution increases, marginal damage costs rise, which increases the incentive for society to take actions to reduce pollution (McConnell, 1997).

What evidence exists to support the EKC theory? Empirical evidence *for* the EKC has been found in a number of studies, mainly for local and regional pollutants. These include those looking at SO_2, urban emissions of particulates, and hazardous waste sites. The level of income per capita where the 'turning point' is reached (Y^* in Figure 6.1) varies across these studies. For example, Grossman and Krueger (1995) found a turning point for SO_2 and particulates at \$4,000–\$6,000/year GNP/capita, when using air-quality data from around the world. Markandya et al. (2006) looked at data on SO_2 and growth from 1870 for twelve European countries: they found a turning point in most (eight out of twelve) cases. They also found that the EKC has shifted over time, mostly in the direction of a lower turning point. Others, though, find empirical evidence *against* the EKC hypothesis. This seems often to be the case for CO_2 and other global/long-term pollutants, as well as for energy use and solid waste. For example, Cole et al. (1997) found no EKC for traffic, nitrates, or methane. Other researchers have found that the turning point is very high relative to current mean incomes. Richmond and Kaufmann (2006) found no turning point for CO_2 in non-OECD countries, and Dijkgraff and Vollerbergh (2005) cast doubt on the likelihood of rising GDP leading to falling CO_2 emissions even in OECD economies. Box 6.2 gives some further evidence on CO_2.

Why are there differences in these empirical findings? These could be due to three factors. First, there is the nature of the pollutants studied. EKCs seem more likely to exist for local and regional pollutants (such as SO_2 and particulates) and less likely to exist for global pollutants such as CO_2. Second, other factors also drive emission levels. These factors have been found to include trade (the degree of protection); political freedom (e.g. such as measured by an index of civil liberties); and the effect of economic growth (scale of economy), independently of income per capita. Political corruption and rent-seeking can also co-determine the level of pollution and the level of income at which the EKC reaches a turning point (Lopez and Mitra, 2000). Third, for some countries and some pollutants, we are not rich enough yet to be 'over the hump'. We can also imagine that much EKC analysis has trouble separating out the effects on pollution of two factors that work concurrently: that economic growth is occurring, but also that time is passing—itself leading to pollution-reducing technological advance. Deacon and Norman (2006) and Carson (2010) give a good discussion and overview of the evidence on this and other points.

To conclude, we might imagine a debate between a critic of the EKC hypothesis and a supporter going something like the following:

BOX 6.2 Testing the Environmental Kuznets Curve

The standard view on why an EKC might exist is that income growth initially drives up pollution, but that factors related to continued income growth (such as rising demand for environmental quality) contribute to a subsequent reduction of pollution at higher income levels. This relationship is typically tested using 'panel data'; that is, data where we study both the variation in pollution and income across different countries, but also across time. However, time itself may be related to pollution. For example, as time passes, technology improves, which might result in cleaner production techniques. How can we be sure what is driving the patterns contained in the data?

Vollerbergh et al. (2009) examine this question for both CO_2 and SO_2. As they say: '… separating the correlation between pollution and income from the correlation between pollution and time is difficult because income is (also) correlated with time'. The authors use data on pollution and income from OECD countries between 1960 and 2000. Performing a 'traditional' analysis of the data, controlling for the effects of time passing and for unobserved country-specific effects, they find a strong U-shape relationship between per capita income and per capita SO_2 emissions, with a turning point at around about the mean income level for the sample. Similar results are also found for CO_2.

However, they also find that their results are very sensitive to modelling assumptions, which is unsatisfactory. By imposing the weakest set of restrictions on their models, they are able to show that rising income always has the effect of *increasing* emissions of both SO_2 and CO_2—reductions in either which appear to be due to income rising further are in fact more likely to be due to time effects; and that this time effect is stronger for SO_2 than for CO_2. They attribute these time effects to technological advance and changes in the structure of OECD economies—for example, due to the decline in iron and steel manufacturing.

Critic: 'Although total incomes can rise with economic growth, incomes per capita might not rise if population is growing faster. Population changes are a very important part of environmental pressures.'

Supporter: 'Ah, but higher levels of income usually result in a slowing down of population growth rates.'

Critic: 'Not all technological change reduces environmental degradation; for example, new "exotic" pollutants may be introduced.'

Supporter: 'Yes, but for certain "classic" pollutants such as SO_2, the trends are good.'

Critic: 'The empirical evidence is that whilst demand for environmental quality goes up as people get richer, it does not rise as quickly as the demand for other goods. So consumer pressures will not moderate emissions.'

Supporter: 'That is a potential problem, although faster growth will give us more resources to counter these problems. We need to keep an eye on things, and intervene where necessary.'

Critic: 'At the world level, there are awkward problems over whose environmental quality and whose income we are measuring. Also at world level, the fact that the UK has got cleaner is partly because we have imported "dirty" products from elsewhere (e.g. coal-mining): but *someone* has to do it!'

Supporter: 'Yes, but trade is good, so we don't want to restrict it on environmental grounds. Trade restrictions only end up hurting people more in the long run.'

Critic: 'The world has a limited carrying capacity and thresholds for total global emissions: once these thresholds/capacities are breached, environmental *impacts* must increase, and perhaps exponentially. Such dynamic "surprises" mean that the EKC is a poor policy guide.'

Supporter: 'Well, that means we should act with care and not rely on the EKC to sort our environmental problems out. We need government to intervene where market failures persist, or where critical environmental limits are being approached.'

Critic: 'Where environmental effects are irreversible, what if we reach the turning point after these have been triggered?'

Supporter: 'That is one of the difficult cases I referred to above.'

And so on. To conclude, the EKC hypothesis is an interesting empirical phenomenon that we can observe for some pollutants, although it is difficult to separate out the effects of income growth from other factors that might have caused pollution levels to change. However, we should not rely on it as a guide for how we manage the environmental impacts of growth: we would also be unwise to rely on economic growth to solve our environmental problems on its own, since solving them typically requires a revision of property rights or a correction of prices. In a sense, economic growth is both the cause of and cure for environmental problems: growth increases our demands on the environment, but growth also gives us the time and money to do something about its undesirable side-effects. In other words, even with economic growth, market failures still remain.

6.4 Broadening the Issue: The Economics of Sustainable Development

6.4.1 Definitions of sustainable development

'Sustainable development' is now a popular phrase. But what exactly does it mean? That is a difficult question to answer, since sustainable development (SD from now on) means different things to different people. People place varying emphasis on the different aspects of SD; for example, in terms of poverty alleviation compared to environmental management. The best-known definition is the one given by the UN's Bruntland Commission in 1987: 'development that meets the needs of present generations without compromising the ability of future generations to meet their own needs'. Another definition was offered by the Norwegian economist Ger Asheim: 'A requirement to our generation to manage the resource base such that the average quality of life we ensure ourselves can potentially be shared by all future generations.' As Atkinson et al. (2007) note, interest in the concept of SD is drawn from a 'broad church', which implies that many, possibly conflicting, objectives are brought together under this heading. However, a common feature of many definitions is that SD is primarily concerned with fairness over time. SD is thus principally an equity, rather than efficiency issue.

Economists' views on what constitutes a sustainable development path for an economy over time may be divided into two broad groups. The first (the *outcome approach*) is concerned with how the economic process affects well-being directly. Such ends-based definitions of SD include non-declining utility per capita and non-declining consumption per capita. Within a neoclassical model of growth, it is possible to investigate whether such a sustainable time-path exists. A typical finding is that: (i) optimal economic growth implies that consumption will fall at some point in the future, due to discounting; (ii) that there is therefore a trade-off between what is optimal and what is sustainable; and (iii) that there are many possible sustainable development paths, one of which will give higher *sustainable* consumption over time (Pezzey and Withagen, 1998).

The second approach (*the opportunity approach*) to an economic definition of SD asks us to consider the means that are available to society to generate well-being or consumption: its resources. 'Resources' consist of physical stocks and the technology that we use to exploit them. Economists have thought about SD from this viewpoint in terms of capital (Ruta and Hamilton, 2007). Four forms of capital may be distinguished:

1. *Produced capital, Kp.* This is the 'capital' with which most economics students are familiar. It is comprised of the results of past production, as the excess of output over consumption. Kp includes machinery, roads, bridges, phone networks, satellites, and so on, and may be used up in the production of consumption goods and services. This depreciation needs to be offset with new investment, or else the stock of Kp will decline.

2. *Human capital, Kh.* This includes all skills and knowledge embodied within people. The stock of Kh can also depreciate (e.g. if unemployed people lose their skills), and can be added to through training and education.

3. *Social capital, Ks.* This has been defined as social networks that facilitate mutually beneficial collective action (Sanginga et al., 2007). For example, co-operative groups that manage common-access resources can agree to implement rules for utilizing such resources (which might include grazing lands, or coastal fisheries) for mutual, long-term benefits. Social capital can also be viewed as including some measure of the quality of a country's institutions: for example, the degree of corruption, political openness, or the quality of justice. Box 6.3 discusses the measurement of social capital, and how changes in social capital can be related to changes in environmental quality.

4. *Natural capital, Kn.* This comprises all gifts of nature, and so includes renewable and non-renewable energy and material resources; clean air and water; nutrient and carbon cycles; and biodiversity. Natural capital can clearly be depreciated when, for example, a non-renewable resource such as oil is used up, when a species dies out, or when the global stock of atmospheric carbon increases. Investments in Kn would include forest replanting, cutting emissions of greenhouse gases, and restocking of fisheries. Economic work on sustainable development typically proceeds from the assumption that the natural capital stock can be aggregated (added together) in monetary units. In this way, we would add the dollar value of forest stocks to the dollar value of agricultural land to the dollar value of oil reserves. Things become more difficult in practice when we also want to include monetary values of the stock of biodiversity, or carbon sinks. Conceptually, however, we can think of 'shadow' prices existing for all forms of natural capital, which can be used to add together the different elements of this stock. Such shadow prices would indicate how much better off society would be if the stock of any capital asset was increased by one unit.

BOX 6.3 Social Capital and the EKC

We defined social capital as 'shared norms, trust and social networks' that help people respond co-operatively and collectively. A long-standing argument in economics is that, other things being equal, high levels of social capital lead to greater well-being, since social capital allows people to respond better to shocks, and since the quality of institutions (e.g. lack of corruption) is related to how much wasteful effort is expended in avoiding regulation, committing crimes, or gaining rents (Knack and Keefer, 1997). Some authors have also argued that communities with higher levels of social capital manage environmental resources (particularly common-property resources) in a better way than areas with low social capital.

Paudel and Schafer (2009) construct a measure of social capital for parishes in Louisiana, USA, and relate this index to measures of water quality. Their hypothesis is that variations in water quality over space and over time will be related to variations in social capital. The social capital index is constructed from data on membership of civic associations per 10,000 persons over the period from 1988 to 1997. A panel data model is used to explore the relationship between three measures of water quality (nitrate levels, phosphate levels, and dissolved oxygen), social capital, and population density. The authors found no significant relationship between social capital (as measured) and either phosphate or dissolved oxygen levels. However, they found a significant quadratic relationship between social capital and nitrate pollution. Interestingly, this showed that higher pollution is associated with lower levels of social capital, but also with the highest levels of social capital. Pollution was lowest when social capital was at intermediate levels (i.e. neither high nor low). So, on the basis of this study, the shape of the EKC for social capital and pollution is the opposite of that proposed between income and pollution.

Table 6.5 shows World Bank estimates of the relative importance of different forms of capital to a country's overall wealth (the value of its total capital stocks), divided into produced capital, natural capital, and 'intangible capital'—which includes both human and social capital as defined above. As can be seen, natural capital is relatively more important in low-income countries as a proportion of total wealth. The share of produced capital is roughly the same in low-, middle-, and high-income countries. This suggests that the process of economic growth involves the transformation of natural capital into human and social capital.

Thinking about a nation's total capital stock, two different opportunity-based definitions of sustainability exist. The first, which has become known as *weak sustainability*, requires the total capital stock K, where K = {Kn + Kh + Kp + Ks}, to be non-declining.

Table 6.5 Shares of capital in total wealth, 2000

	Natural capital share (%)	Produced capital share (%)	Intangible capital share (%)
Low-income countries	26	16	59
Middle-income countries	13	19	68
High-income countries	2	17	80
World	4	18	78

Note: 'Intangible' includes human and social capital.
Source: World Bank (2006).

This permits natural capital to be run down (through extracting oil stocks, say) so long as human, social, or produced capital are increased sufficiently to offset this loss. This view clearly presumes that we can aggregate the different capital stocks in the same units and that they are substitutes for each other (Markandya and Pedroso-Galinato, 2007). The Hartwick rule and the genuine savings measure, both discussed below, rely on this view of sustainable development. An alternative view has been to maintain that SD requires us to keep the stock of Kn as non-declining. This might be either in monetary or in physical terms (Neumayer, 2009). This view has been called *strong sustainability*, and derives primarily from the view that reductions in Kn cannot be substituted for by increases in other forms of capita (van den Bergh, 2007). A somewhat different position is taken by those who focus on *critical natural capital* only. Critical natural capital is the subset of Kn that is either (i) essential for human survival and/or (ii) not substitutable for by increases in either other forms of capital. An example might be certain aspects of biodiversity. Modern schools of thought on sustainability thus revolve around the ease with which natural capital can be replaced by other forms of capital, in terms of both its direct contribution to well-being and its role in supporting the production of goods and services (Neumayer, 2009). It turns out to very difficult to establish empirically what this 'ease of substitutability' might be.

Sustainable development therefore appears to have two distinct economic meanings. In the outcome approach, it means that consumption or utility does not decline over time. In the opportunity approach, it means we pass on to future generations at least as much capital as we have, so that they have no less a chance than us of achieving certain levels of well-being. In fact, these two approaches can be thought of as two sides of the same coin. Capital can be interpreted as wealth, which in turn is defined as the present value of future consumption or utility flows. Maintaining capital is thus key to maintaining the flow of well-being into the future.

6.4.2 Sustainability rules?

A powerful myth in economics is that of the 'free market', since all markets operate under some kind of rules imposed by governments. These rules may be introduced for a wide variety of reasons, such as protecting the environment, supporting producer incomes, or keeping down prices to consumers. But what kind of interventions by governments might be beneficial in the case of sustainability?

We have already noted that the optimal time-path of consumption is unlikely to be sustainable, since consumption eventually falls. This path comes about through the maximization of the present value (i.e. discounted sum over time) of future consumption. To generalize, if the market system results in efficient outcomes through utility and profit-maximization, then it is unlikely to result in a sustainable outcome. With regard to natural capital stock-based definitions of SD, we have already shown (Chapter 2) how the market system tends to lead to the overuse of environmental resources; this will mean Kn falling over time in terms of its physical stocks, whilst the lack of a market value for many environmental resources and service flows means that this increasing scarcity is not corrected for, even at the level of efficiency, by the market. Market forces might conceivably lead to enough offsetting investment in other forms of capital even if Kn was falling over time, so that weak sustainability might be achieved even if strong sustainability was not. But what rules could the government impose on markets if we wanted to ensure a sustainable pattern of development? Two possibilities exist, dependent on whether one takes a weak or strong view of sustainability.

6.4.2.1 The Hartwick rule

In work closely related to the idea of weak sustainability, although it precedes it historically, John Hartwick showed that an economy dependent on a non-renewable resource as one input to production could have constant (and therefore non-declining) consumption level over time provided that it followed a simple rule: to reinvest all rents (the difference between price and marginal cost) from exploiting the non-renewable resource in produced capital. This 'zero net investment' rule can be shown to result in non-declining consumption under a range of circumstances (Hartwick, 1977, 1997; Hamilton and Withagen, 2007). The Hartwick rule is in fact the basis for the genuine savings measure of SD discussed in the next section. If we adopt a broader notion of capital, then the rents could equally well be invested in human, social, or natural capital.

Two problems exist with the rule. First, it assumes that utility depends on consumption only, and that the environment is only important as a source of inputs to production. If the state of the environment is a direct determinant of utility, then the rule does hold *utility* constant even if consumption is not falling—although it is possible to amend the rule to allow for this (d'Autume and Schubert, 2008). Second, the rule only works if the various forms of capital are good enough substitutes for each other. We have already mentioned that this may not be true. However, the rule does suggest that countries which do not reinvest sufficient of the rents from natural resource exploitation may be doing so at the expense of future well-being: Box 6.4 gives some examples of what these losses might be.

6.4.2.2 Rules based on the natural capital stock: the safe minimum standard

The 'strong sustainability' view is that SD requires a non-declining stock of natural capital, somehow defined. It is clear that this could be a very restrictive rule for a country to impose on itself. If no trade-offs are allowed between different components of Kn (wetlands, forests, etc.), then no economic action that depleted the stock of any component could be allowed, no matter how large the economic benefits. A way around the potentially high forgone benefits that this implies is the idea of *shadow projects* (Pearce et al., 1990). This would require any action that reduces the stock of, say, wetlands, to be offset by a physical project that generates an offsetting replacement (by creating a new wetland). Costing in such a replacement would be an essential part of cost–benefit analysis. However, considerable practical and theoretical difficulties exist here: for example, if a 500-year-old oak forest is threatened with destruction by a development project, does a newly planted oak forest of equivalent size provide an acceptable offset? What if the new wood is planted on an area of heathland? Now the area of heathland has decreased, so an offset must be created for this. Finally, for many environmental effects, no physical substitute exists (e.g. if a unique national park is threatened). Does this imply that no development is allowed that threatens unique assets?

One answer to these sorts of question is provided by the concept of the *safe minimum standard* (SMS). The SMS is usually thought of as a means of assessing a proposed change

BOX 6.4 The Costs of Not Following the Hartwick Rule

As explained in the text, the Hartwick rule states that a country can maintain non-declining consumption over time if it reinvests rents from non-renewable resource extraction (calculated as the volume of annual production, valued using the difference between price and marginal cost) in other forms of capital. This allows the total value of the capital stock to be maintained in terms of its ability to generate future well-being. An exercise in the World Bank's *Where is the Wealth of Nations?* report discusses how much richer a range of countries would be in 2000 if they had followed the Hartwick rule over the period from 1970 to 2000. The test of 'how much richer?' involves comparing the measured (estimated) capital stock in 2000 with calculations of what the capital stock would have been had each country followed the Hartwick rule.

In the Hartwick rule scenario, it is assumed that all resource rents were reinvested in produced capital: investment is set equal to this amount in each year over the period from 1970 to 2000. The resources covered are oil, gas, coal, bauxite, copper, gold, iron, lead, nickel, phosphate, silver, and zinc. The table below gives results for a small selection of countries: 'resource-dependent' countries, where resource rents add up to more than 5 per cent of GDP; and others. For the resource-dependent countries, such as Bolivia, Algeria, and Nigeria, we see that the actual capital stock in 2000 is much lower than it could have been had these countries followed the Hartwick rule. No countries with resource rents higher than 15 per cent of GDP have followed the Hartwick rule—all are now poorer in 2000 than they could have been had they followed this rule. Countries such as Chile and Mexico seem to have roughly followed the rule, since the difference in the capital stock between the two scenarios is very small. However, there are some countries, in which GDP does not depend heavily on resource rents, where the actual capital stock in 2000 was higher than it would have been under the rule—Brazil, for example. Such countries seem to have invested more in their productive capital than the Hartwick rule would suggest. However, even for these countries, the report points out that the quality of investments may be just as important as the quantity:

(1) Country	(2) Capital stock in 2000, $billion (1995 dollars)	(3) Percentage increase in capital stock in 2000 with Hartwick rule, compared to column (2)	(4) Resource dependence (resource rents as % of GDP)
Nigeria	53	359	33
Algeria	195	51	23
Bolivia	14	116	13
Jamaica	13	40	6
Chile	151	−3	9
Mexico	975	−1	8
Brazil	1,750	−59	2
China	2,899	−62	11

Source: Adapted from World Bank (2006: 58–9).

that threatens wildlife or its habitats. It involves first identifying the minimum viable population or habitat size for a population, or the minimum required stock of some other natural asset, or the minimum flow of some ecosystem service. Management alternatives for safeguarding this minimum are then identified, and cost estimates made of these actions. If a proposed development threatens the SMS, then decision-makers are presumed to rule against it, unless the social opportunity costs of so doing are judged to be too high. These costs should include the costs of future development benefits forgone. For example, Berrens et al. (1998) describe the means by which an SMS for endangered fish populations in the Colorado River is identified, and the costs of the management actions needed to defend these SMS values estimated. In this case, this involved costing restrictions on water abstraction and hydroelectric power station operation in order to maintain minimum in-stream flows.

The SMS is attractive as a mechanism that protects important elements of the natural capital stock. It has also been put forward as a way of preventing ecosystems or biodiversity from being pushed past thresholds involving irreversible costs to society—for example, for ocean acidification (falling pH levels in sea water as CO_2 levels increase). The most obvious problem with the SMS principle is the difficulty of identifying how society should decide whether the cost of defending the SMS is 'too high'. This might be through a referendum or a decision-maker judgement, although Berrens et al. (1998) suggest that if costs in terms of lost output lie within the range of historical fluctuations, then the SMS should be automatically safeguarded. Other problems with the SMS include extending the concept to elements of Kn other than wildlife populations and their habitats; and the difficulty in identifying safe minimum population/habitat sizes (which might well change over time). The approach also involves reversing the normal burden of proof in development cases, placing this on the developer rather than the conservationist to show that SMS-type constraints are not being violated by a proposal, such as developing a new mining site in Madagascar; or that the costs of not proceeding with the development are in some sense 'too big' to justify forgoing the new mine (Randall, 2007). The SMS is very much a quantity constraint, imposed on economic activity in the name of sustainability to safeguard a subset of the stock of natural capital: yet it does not address the dilemma of whether it is the value or physical quantity of natural capital that we should be sustaining, nor the implications of imposing such a rule on future well-being.

Recently, Rockström et al. (2009) have suggested the concept of a *safe operating space* for the planet, a series of thresholds for important ecosystem processes, which the authors maintain should be viewed as levels that should not be exceeded (see Figure 6.2). They identify key levels for 'control variables' (such as CO_2 levels) that can be related to each threshold. What they refer to as 'planetary boundaries' are then levels for each control variable that are a 'safe distance' from each threshold. The argument is that these boundaries should be thought of as constraints that can be related to economic activity—for example, in terms of maximum allowable levels of greenhouse gas emissions, or maximum allowable rates of habitat loss. This seems similar in spirit to the idea of safe minimum standards discussed above, although it is interesting that the authors do not suggest that any consideration of the costs of staying within these boundaries is appropriate. The idea of a safe operating space for the global economy also reminds us of the idea of environmental 'limits to growth', which was a popular notion in the 1970s.

6.5 Measuring 'Sustainability'

At the Earth Summit in Rio in 1992, the world's nations agreed to set about producing annual statistics on the sustainability of their economies. This resulted in the production

PLANETARY BOUNDARIES

Earth-system process	Parameters	Proposed boundary	Current status	Pre-industrial value
Climate change	(i) Atmospheric carbon dioxide concentration (parts per million by volume)	350	387	280
	(ii) Change in radiative forcing (watts per metre squared)	1	1.5	0
Rate of biodiversity loss	Extinction rate (number of species per million species per year)	10	>100	0.1–1
Nitrogen cycle (part of a boundary with the phosphorus cycle)	Amount of N_2 removed from the atmosphere for human use (millions of tonnes per year)	35	121	0
Phosphorus cycle (part of a boundary with the nitrogen cycle)	Quantity of P flowing into the oceans (millions of tonnes per year)	11	8.5–9.5	–1
Stratospheric ozone depletion	Concentration of ozone (Dobson unit)	276	283	290
Ocean acidification	Global mean saturation state of aragonite in surface sea water	2.75	2.90	3.44
Global freshwater use	Consumption of freshwater by humans (km^3 per year)	4,000	2,600	415
Change in land use	Percentage of global land cover converted to cropland	15	11.7	Low
Atmospheric aerosol loading	Overall particulate concentration in the atomosphere, on a regional basis	To be determined		
Chemical pollution	For example, amount emitted to, or concentration of persistent organic pollutants, plastics, endocrine disrupters, heavy metals and nuclear waste in, the global environment, or the effects on ecosystem and functioning of earth system thereof	To be determined		

Figure 6.2 Critical thresholds and planetary boundaries.
Source: Rockström et al. (2009).

of a very large set of proposals for *indicators* of SD; for example, by the UN (1995, 2003). Given that SD is such a broad concept, it is unlikely that any one measure would tell us all we want to know about the sustainability of the economic–environmental system. Also, given the complexity of this system and the uncertainties that pervade its interactions, it is probably better to talk of indicators of system performance, rather than exact measures. Indicators of sustainability have been developed from a number of different disciplinary perspectives, including economics, ecology, politics, and sociology. We now discuss two put forward by economists: green net national product and genuine savings. For an interesting discussion of the available indicators, and how these relate to the concepts of wealth, substitutability between types of capital, and the prices used to value capital changes, see Heal (2012).

6.5.1 **Green net national product**

An extensive literature has emerged on whether the System of National Accounts can be transformed to produce both a better welfare measure and a possible indicator of SD. GNP has traditionally been thought of as a welfare measure, and as a measure of national income. By relating this to the idea of 'income' put forward by Sir John Hicks in 1930, some authors have sought to produce an indicator of SD. Hicks' view on income was that it represented that portion of the value of output that could be consumed in any year without reducing one's wealth (i.e. the potential for future consumption). This clearly has resonances with some definitions of SD. In this sense, then, an adjusted national income figure would tell us the maximum level of consumption that was sustainable in any year, in the sense that it leaves enough of a residual to be invested, which preserves the national capital stock or national wealth (here, wealth is interpreted as the discounted value of future consumption). If adjusted GNP were rising, then an economy would have the potential of higher sustainable consumption levels; as such, a rising 'green' GNP would be an indicator of sustainability.

Why, though, is it necessary to adjust the conventional national accounts? Partly this is because, as noted in Box 6.1, these accounts omit many of the inputs that the environment provides to the economy, since they are unpriced by the market. When a country depletes its natural capital, this is typically ignored in the national accounts, even though depreciation of man-made capital is allowed for (to convert from GNP to *net* national product, NNP). Calculating *green net national product* involves correcting for these omissions, and for other changes that impact on well-being, such as changes in pollution.

The approach draws theoretically on Weitzman (1976). The main intention is: (i) to include the depreciation of *natural* capital just as conventional NNP allows for changes in produced capital; and (ii) to include the value of changes in environmental quality that impact directly on people's utility. Greening the national accounts could thus involve adjustments such as the following:

- For non-renewable resources, deduct from NNP an amount equal to the value of annual production (less discoveries) multiplied by the difference between price and marginal costs.
- For renewable resources, annual production is first deducted from annual growth. This amount is then valued using the same (price-marginal cost) term.
- For pollution, deduct an amount equal to the change in the emissions of each pollutant multiplied by its marginal damage costs.
- For changes in biodiversity and landscape quality, adjust NNP by an amount showing people's willingness to pay (WTP) for these changes, since this has direct impacts on utility.

Ignoring this last correction as being hard to do, this would then give us a green NNP measure equal to the following:

$$\text{green } NNP = NNP - (p_1 - mc_1)\Delta NR - (p_2 - mc_2)\Delta R - v(\Delta S), \tag{6.1}$$

where p_1 and mc_1 are the price and marginal cost of non-renewable resources, and ΔNR is the change in the stock of non-renewables; p_2 and mc_2 are the price and marginal cost of renewables, and ΔR the change in their stock; and v is the marginal damage cost for pollution emissions S. In practice, one would have to aggregate over many different non-renewable and renewable resource types, and over many pollutants. If green NNP is rising over time, then development is judged to be sustainable.

There is certainly disagreement among economists as to exactly how these and similar adjustments should be made. It is also true that for the adjustments to be correct, the price and marginal cost values used should be 'correct'. For example, some have argued that the prices should be those that result from a competitive, dynamically optimal use of resources; others that the prices should be those that would hold along a sustainable path. Well-known problems of property rights mean that using market prices to undertake green adjustments

---

BOX 6.5 Green Net National Product and Genuine Savings for Scotland

Pezzey et al. (2006) construct measures of green NNP and genuine savings for Scotland over the period from 1992 to 1999. The main environmental adjustments to the national accounts which they make are as follows:

- Estimates of pollution emissions over time for NO_x, PM10, SO_2, CO_2, CO, and CH_4 based on sectoral emission intensities are costed using estimates of marginal damage costs from a range of studies.

- Natural capital changes are valued using estimates of prices and marginal costs to value changes in stocks of forestry, ocean fisheries, coal, aggregates, and oil.

- The value of environmental amenities in each year is included in green NNP using used hectares enrolled in agri-environmental schemes, valued using WTP/ha figures taken from the literature.

In addition, they adjust both GS and green NNP for estimates of technological progress, and resource price changes for oil—giving rise to the use of the term 'augmented' in the paper's title.

Scotland is not a highly resource-dependent economy, so the effects of these adjustments on 'standard' measures of economic well-being—such as NNP—are not large. Both GS and green NNP show Scotland to be sustainable over the time period in question, as the following diagram shows:

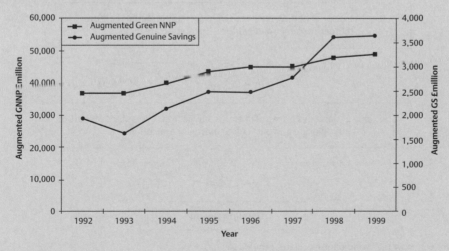

Source: Pezzey et al. (2006).

Genuine savings is positive in all years, and green NNP is rising over time.

will mean that the former is unlikely to be true, especially for fisheries, whereas the latter will almost certainly not be the case. There is also dispute amongst economists about whether green NNP can indeed be used as a sustainability indicator. Box 6.5 shows example calculations from Pezzey et al. (2006) for Scotland.

6.5.2 Genuine savings

An alternative economic indicator of SD is the *genuine savings* concept, put forward by Pearce and Atkinson (1993). Genuine savings (GS) compares reinvestment in an economy

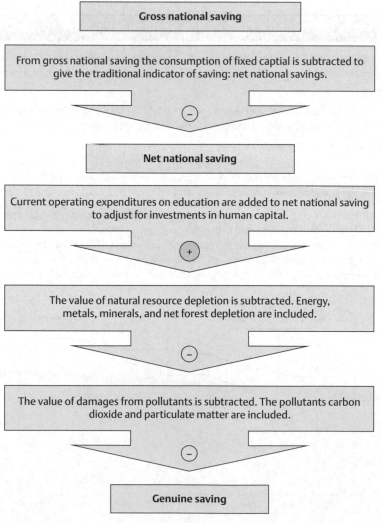

Figure 6.3 How the World Bank calculates genuine savings.
Source: World Bank (2006).

with depreciation of all forms of capital. In this way, GS measures the value of the net change, over a period, of all forms of capital in an economy. If we restrict capital to just natural and produced capital, then GS is often shown as being equal to the following:

$$GS = S - \Delta p - \Delta n, \tag{6.2}$$

where GS is genuine savings, S is total (aggregate) savings, Δp is depreciation of produced capital, and Δn is depreciation of natural capital. This natural capital depreciation is calculated in the same manner as the environmental adjustments to NNP noted in equation (6.1), in that it includes the same components (e.g. reductions in oil reserves) valued in the same way (multiplying the change in the stock by the rent). Alternatively, we could simply work out the annual change in each type of capital, and add these together. To be more complete, we would wish to add changes in the stock of human capital, Kh, to equation (6.2). The World Bank (2006) do this by adding national expenditure on education to equation (6.2); they also include changes in certain pollution damages, as shown in Figure 6.3 (although some economists would argue that pollution damage costs should show up in green NNP, not in GS, since direct impacts on utility from pollution would impact on the well-being measure that NNP is supposed to be, whereas GS shows changes in the aggregate capital stock).

The genuine savings measure tests for weak sustainability; that is, it assumes that natural capital and man-made capital are perfect substitutes for each other. A negative GS indicates unsustainable development, since it implies that a country is running down its total capital (perhaps in order to fund current consumption at the expense of future consumption). It is also an empirical test for whether a country is, on average, following the Hartwick rule. Table 6.6 shows estimates of GS for a range of countries, whilst Box 6.5 shows GS calculations for Scotland. Note that there are many empirical conceptual and empirical problems with calculating GS across countries or over time. These include what value to use for the cost of carbon emissions, and how to measure the effects of technological progress on a country's wealth.

Table 6.6 Genuine savings estimates for a range of countries, 2000 (all figures are as percentages of gross national income)

	Gross national savings	CFC	Education investments	Energy depl.	Mineral depl.	Net forest depl.	PM damage	CO_2 damage	Genuine savings
New Zealand	17.7	10.9	6.9	1.3	0.1	0.0	0.0	0.4	+11.8
Nicaragua	17.3	9.1	3.7	0	0.1	0.9	0	0.6	+10.3
Niger	2.6	6.7	2.3	0	0	4.1	0.4	0.4	−6.7
Nigeria	25.7	8.4	0.9	50.8	0	0	0.8	0.6	−33.9
Norway	36.9	16.2	6.1	8.0	0	0	0.1	0.2	+18.5
Pakistan	19.9	7.8	2.3	3.1	0	0.8	1.0	0.9	+8.6
Poland	18.8	11.0	6.3	0.5	0.1	0.0	0.7	1.1	+11.7
Saudi Arabia	29.4	10	7.2	51	0	0	1.0	1.2	−26.5

Notes: CFC, depreciation of produced capital; 'depl.', depletion of energy and mineral reserves and of forest stocks; PM, particulate matter (PM10).

Source: World Bank (2006).

Genuine savings and green NNP are closely linked to each other, since they are both derived from the same underlying theory. GS is an easier measure to calculate, since it omits direct impacts of environmental changes on utility. Asheim and Weitzman (2001) show a theoretical link between GS and utility. However, GS seems to have emerged as a more popular indicator than green NNP, possibly because its direct link to changes in a nation's assets is more intuitively appealing as a measure of sustainability. However, the ability of GS to predict changes in future well-being over the long run is so far untested.

6.5.3 Other sustainability indicators

As mentioned above, indicators of sustainable development have been developed by many disciplines, including ecology. These include ecological footprints, human appropriation of net primary productivity, and the index of sustainable economic welfare (for more details, see Bohringer and Jochem, 2007; Erb et al., 2009).

Summary

This chapter has been concerned with the implications for the environment of economic growth, and the extent to which this growth causes undesirable feedbacks for people's well-being. These questions have been of interest to economists ever since Adam Smith. The debate over the links between economic growth, environmental quality, and quality of life are now largely conducted under the heading of sustainable development. We reviewed how economists have interpreted this often-nebulous concept, and saw how economic indicators of weak sustainability can be calculated. Whilst the economic inter-pretation of sustainability is only one amongst many, it is at least fairly rigorous. It also recognizes that people's abilities (reflected in human capital) are as important to securing sustainable development as safeguarding the environment and investing in a nation's produced assets.

Tutorial Questions

6.1 What do we mean by economic growth? Why do economies grow? In principle, what are the main implications of such growth for the environment?

6.2 What did the early, Classical economists such as Ricardo and Mill have to say about the links between economic growth and natural resources? Why did economics become known as the 'dismal science'?

6.3 What are the theoretical explanations for the environmental Kuznets curve, and why is empirical evidence on the existence of such a relationship so mixed?

6.4 Explain the main differences between weak and strong sustainability, and why these matter for government policy on sustainable development.

6.5 What economic indicators of weak sustainability exist, and how much do we know about the robustness of these indicators in practice *or* in theory?

References and Additional Readings

Andreoni, J., and Levinson, A. (2001). 'The simple analytics of the environmental Kuznets curve', *Journal of Public Economics* 80: 269–86.

Asheim, G., and Weitzman, M. (2001). 'Does NNP growth indicate welfare improvement?' *Economics Letters* 73: 233–9.

Atkinson, G., Dietz, S., and Neumayer, E. (2007). *Handbook of Sustainable Development* (Cheltenham: Edward Elgar).

Begg, D., Fischer, S., and Dorbusch, R. (1987). *Economics*, 2nd edn (London: McGraw-Hill).

Berrens, R., Brookshire, D., McKee, M., and Schmidt, C. (1998). 'Implementing the safe minimum standard', *Land Economics* 74: 147–61.

Blanchflower, D.G., and Oswald, A.J. (2004). 'Well-being over time in Britain and the USA', *Journal of Public Economics* 88: 1359–86.

Bohringer, C., and Jochem, P. (2007). 'Measuring the immeasurable: a survey of sustainability indices', *Ecological Economics* 63: 1–8.

Carson, R. (2010). 'The environmental Kuznets curve: seeking empirical regularity and theoretical structure', *Review of Environmental Economics and Policy* 4(1): 3–23.

Clark, A.E., Frijters, P., and Shields, M.A. (2008). 'Relative income, happiness and utility: an explanation for the Easterlin paradox and other puzzles', *Journal of Economic Literature* 46(1): 95–144.

Cole, M., Rayner, A., and Bates, J. (1997). 'The environmental Kuznets curve: an empirical analysis', *Environment and Development Economics* 2: 401–16.

Common, M.S. (1988). *Environmental and Resource Economics: An Introduction* (London: Longman).

d'Autume, A., and Schubert, K. (2008). 'Hartwick's rule and the maximin paths when the exhaustible resource has an amenity value', *Journal of Environmental Economics and Management* 56(3): 260–74.

Deacon, R., and Norman, C. (2006). 'The environmental Kuznets curve and how countries behave', *Land Economics* 82(2): 291–315.

Dijkgraff, E., and Vollerbergh, H.R. (2005). 'A test for parameter homogeneity in CO_2 panel EKC estimates', *Environmental and Resource Economics* 32(2): 229–39.

Easterlin, R.A. (1973). 'Does money buy happiness?' *The Public Interest* 30: 3–10.

Erb, K.-H., Krausmann, F., Gaube, V., Gingrich, S., Bondeau, A., Fischer-Kowalski, M., and Haberl, H. (2009). 'Analysing the global human appropriation of net primary production', *Ecological Economics* 69: 250–9.

Ferreira, S., and Moro, M. (2010). 'On the use of subjective well-being data for environmental valuation', *Environmental and Resource Economics* 46(3): 249.

Gowdy, J., and McDaniel, C. (1999). 'The physical destruction of Nauru: an example of weak sustainability', *Land Economics* 75(2): 333–8.

Grossman, G., and Krueger, A. (1995). 'Economic growth and the environment', *Quarterly Journal of Economics* 110(2): 353–77.

Hamilton, K., and Withagen, C. (2007). 'Savings growth and the path of utility', *Canadian Journal of Economics* 40(2): 703–13.

Hartwick, J.M. (1977). 'Intergenerational equity and the investing of rents from exhaustible resources', *American Economic Review* 67(5): 972–4.

——(1997). 'National wealth, constant consumption and sustainable development', in H. Folmer and T. Tietenberg (eds.), *The International Yearbook of Environmental and Resource Economics* (Cheltenham: Edward Elgar).

Heal, G. (2012). 'Reflections: defining and measuring sustainability', *Review of Environmental Economics and Policy* 6(1): 147–63.

Jevons, W. S. (1865). *The Coal Question* (reprinted 1965 New York: A.M. Kelly).

Knack, S., and Keefer, P. (1997). 'Does social capital have an economic payoff?' *Quarterly Journal of Economics* 112: 1251–88.

Levinson, A. (2009). 'Valuing public goods using happiness data: the case of air quality', NBER Working Paper No. 15156.

Lopez, R., and Mitra, S. (2000). 'Corruption, pollution and the Environmental Kuznets Curve', *Journal of Environmental Economics and Management* 40: 137–50.

McConnell, K.E. (1997). 'Income and the demand for environmental quality', *Environment and Development Economics* 2: 383–99.

Markandya, A., and Pedroso-Galinato, S. (2007). 'How substituteable is natural capital?' *Environmental and Resource Economics* 37: 297–312.

Markandya, A., Golub, A., and Pedrosa-Gallinato, S. (2006). 'Empirical analysis of national income and SO$_2$ emissions in selected European countries', *Environmental and Resource Economics* 35: 221–57.

Malthus, T. (1798). *An Essay on the Principles of Population* (reprinted 1970 London: Penguin).

Meadows, D., Meadows, D., Randers, J., and Behrens, W. (1972). *The Limits to Growth* (New York: Universe Books).

Mill, J.S. (1857). *Principles of Political Economy* (London: J.W. Parker).

Neumayer, E.. (2009). *Weak versus Strong Sustainability* (Cheltenham: Edward Elgar).

Paudel, K., and Schafer, M. (2009). 'The environmental Kuznets curve under a new framework: the role of social capital in water pollution', *Environmental and Resource Economics* 42(2): 265–78.

Pearce, D., and Atkinson, G. (1993). 'Capital theory and the measurement of sustainable development: an indicator of weak sustainability', *Ecological Economics* 8(2): 103–8.

Pearce, D.W., Makandya, A., and Barbier, E. (1990). *Sustainable Development* (Cheltenham: Edward Elgar).

Pezzey, J.C.V., Hanley, N., Turner, K., and Tinch, D. (2006). 'Augmented sustainability tests for Scotland', *Ecological Economics* 57(1): 60–74.

—— and Withagen, C.A. (1998). 'The rise, fall and sustainability of capital-resource economies', *Scandinavian Journal of Economics* 100(2): 513–27.

Randall, A. (2007). 'Benefit cost analysis and a safe minimum standard', in G. Atkinson, S. Dietz, and E. Neumayer (eds.), *Handbook of Sustainable Development* (Cheltenham: Edward Elgar).

Ricardo, D. (1817). *The Principles of Political Economy* (reprinted 1926 London: Everyman).

Richmond, A., and Kaufmann, R. (2006). 'Is there a turning point in the relationship between income and energy use and/or carbon emissions?' *Ecological Economics* 56: 176–89.

Rockström, J., Steffen, W., Noone, K., Persson, A., Chapin, F.S. III, Lambin, E.F., Lenton, T.M., Scheffer, M., Folke, C., Schellnhuber, H.J., Nykvist, B., de Wit, C.A., Hughes, T., van der Leeuw, S., Rodhe, H., Sorlin, S., Snyder, P.K., Costanza, R.,

Svedin, U., Falkenmark, M., Karlberg, L., Corell, R.W., Fabry, V.J., Hansen, J., Walker, B., Liverman, D., Richardson, K., Crutzen, P., and Foley, J A (2009). 'A safe operating space for humanity', *Nature* 461(7263): 472–5.

Ruta, G., and Hamilton, K. (2007). 'The capital approach to sustainability', in G. Atkinson, S. Dietz, and E. Neumayer (eds.), *Handbook of Sustainable Development* (Cheltenham: Edward Elgar).

Sanginga, P., Kamugisha, R., and Martin, A. (2007). 'The dynamics of social capital and conflict management in multiple resource regimes', *Ecology and Society* 12(1).

Seo, S.N., Mendelsohn, R., Dinar, A., Hassan, R., and Krurkulasuriya, P. (2009). 'A Ricardian analysis of the distribution of climate change impacts on agriculture in Africa', *Environmental and Resource Economics* 43: 313–32.

UN (United Nations) (1995). *Indicators of Sustainable Development* (New York: UN Commission for Sustainable Development).

—— (2003). *Integrated Environmental and Economic Accounting* (New York: United Nations).

van den Bergh, J. (2007). 'Sustainable development in ecological economics', in S. Dietz and E. Neumayer (eds.), *Handbook of Sustainable Development* (Cheltenham: Edward Elgar).

Vollerbergh, H., Melenberg, B., and Dijkgraaf, E. (2009). 'Identifying reduced-form relations with panel data: the case of pollution and income', *Journal of Environmental Economics and Management* 58: 27–42.

UNDP (United Nations Development Program) (1990). *Human Development Report: Concept and Measurement of Human Development* (New York: UNDP).

—— (2009). *Human Development Report* (New York: UNDP).

Warde, P. (2007). *Energy Consumption in England and Wales, 1560–2000* (Rome: Consiglio Nazionale delle Ricerche).

Weitzman, M. (1976). 'On the welfare significance of national product in a dynamic economy', *Quarterly Journal of Economics* 90: 156–62.

World Bank (2006). *Where is the Wealth of Nations?* (Washington, DC: World Bank).

Strategic Interactions and the Environment

Many of the world's major environmental and natural resource management problems arise from interactions between economic agents. Examples include negotiations between countries about reducing greenhouse gases and marine fisheries where fishers compete with each other over fish stocks for profits. These types of interactions are recognized by economists and mathematicians as problems in game theory. Game theory can be applied to games such as chess and poker, but it can also be applied to make sense of the 'games' that governments, individuals, households, and firms 'play' that affect the environment.

This chapter:

- Introduces game theory.
- Discusses an important game called the prisoner's dilemma.
- Applies the basic model to fishery management.
- Considers how co-operation may emerge through institutions over time.
- Gives an analysis of the formation of alliances using co-operative game theory.
- Analyses a transboundary pollution problem.

7.1 Introduction

At local, international, and global levels, interactions between individuals, firms, and governments over environment goods and bads and natural resources involve strategic choices. Like chess players, the 'players' in environmental and natural resource 'games' develop strategies to counter their opponents' strategies. To start to understand these interactions requires a theory of strategic interaction between decision-makers. In 1944, a mathematician, John von Neumann, and an economist, Oskar Morgenstern, introduced game theory to economics. Their approach concerned players who take choices in response to or in anticipation of what others decide to do. Their models have revolutionized the analysis of strategic interactions between decision-makers from both normative (i.e. what decision-makers *should* do) and positive (what decision-makers *actually* do) perspectives (for an introductory review, see Dixit et al., 2009).

BOX 7.1 Cod Wars

In 1972 Iceland unilaterally extended its Exclusive Economic Zone (EEZ) beyond its territorial waters, in an attempt to exclude British trawlers and reduce overfishing. It policed its newly introduced catch quotas through the Icelandic Coastguard cutting the trawl lines of UK vessels. The UK responded by sending in naval vessels to protect the fishing fleet. The dispute ended in 1976 after Iceland threatened to close a major NATO base in retaliation for Britain's deployment of naval vessels within the disputed zone. The British government backed down, and agreed that after 1 December 1976, British vessels would not fish within the zone.

The interaction between the players (the UK and Icelandic governments) involves a set of strategies: Iceland plays 'send coastguard boats', to which the UK government responds with 'send the navy to protect trawlers'. Finally, Iceland plays its trump card, 'close NATO base', to which the UK responds 'concede'. What is driving these responses? The pay-offs are the economic gains to the UK of access to the fishery, whilst the pay-offs to Iceland are increasing the economic gains from a larger share of a better-managed fishery. In the final play, Iceland switches strategies, and in the threat to close a NATO base finds an action that would impose costs on the UK that exceed the losses in profitability of the UK fishing industry from access to the Icelandic EEZ. In this game, the two players interact repeatedly and the strategies evolve through time.

Economists have applied game theory to environmental and natural resource allocation problems. In one of the first applications, Levhari and Mirman (1980) analyse interactions between two countries sharing a fish stock, a so-called 'fish war' (see Box 7.1). The 'war' is waged through fisheries policies where fishery regulators decide to be more or less conservationist in their setting of fishing quotas depending on how conservationist they expect other countries to be. Countries impose an externality on each other by reducing the fish stock and thus making fish more expensive to catch. Another early application of game theory in environmental economics was by Maler (1989), who considers international negotiations to reduce the level of acid rain. When countries negotiate over the total levels of SO_2 emissions to be permitted, there is a strategic interaction in which countries benefit from co-operation (since acid rain has impacts in 'receiving' countries as well as in 'emitter' countries), but a mechanism has to be found to encourage those countries responsible for the externality to agree to a reduction in SO_2. Maler also found that a cost-effective solution to reducing European emissions would result in some countries incurring a net loss, and the countries with a net benefit paying them compensation. A third example is Agenda 21, agreed at the Rio de Janeiro Earth Summit in 1992 and recently renegotiated in Nagoya in 2010, which aims to protect biodiversity (Barrett, 1994a; Normile, 2010). Biodiversity represents a global public good, but the countries that benefit most from conservation may be the richer developed nations, while the less-developed tropical countries that host much of global biodiversity bear the opportunity costs of conservation through lost marine, agricultural, and forestry output. The issue is how an agreement can be reached that provides an incentive for these biodiversity host countries to reduce the rate of biodiversity loss.

Game theory has been applied to analyse national environmental problems; for instance, the strategic interaction between producers over a common-property resource such as common land grazing (Mesterton-Gibbons, 2000) and the interaction between regulators and the firms regulated in pollution control (Batabayal, 1995). The key element of all of these problems—both domestic and global—is that the actions of one decision-maker affect the welfare of others. All these problems are the subject matter of game theory.

7.2 Game Theory

7.2.1 Basic concepts

The elements of game theory are as follows. A decision-maker (player) has preferences over a set of outcomes, and these preferences determine the choices made, but the outcomes depend upon the choices made by the other players in the game. Game theory has developed two distinct approaches to analysing such problems. *Non-cooperative* game theory concerns how players choose strategies, whilst *co-operative* game theory concerns how players choose to form alliances. Non-cooperative game theory can be further classified into *static* and *dynamic* games, where static games have only one turn (one shot) and dynamic games have a number of turns through time. Dynamic games can be further subdivided into repeated games, where the same game is repeated, and more complex dynamic games, where the actual game itself changes through time.

Information, or the lack of it, determines how the game is played: games of *imperfect information* are those where the players are uncertain about the outcome of a combination of choices. For instance, in the fishing problem, uncertainty about the fish stock and harvest means that the profit is uncertain. Games of *incomplete information* are where players are uncertain about the preferences of other players. For instance, a regulator may be uncertain about the cost to a firm of complying with pollution regulation, and therefore be uncertain about an appropriate level of monitoring (Russell, 1990). Modern game theory makes use of advanced mathematics, and a general analysis is beyond the scope of this book. Fortunately, some simple models—for example, the prisoner's dilemma—offer insights into a wide range of environmental problems.

7.2.2 The prisoner's dilemma

The prisoner's dilemma is an important concept in environmental and resource economics. The original game, called the prisoner's dilemma by A.W. Tucker in 1950, has the following form. Two prisoners, Fred and George, have been caught with stolen goods and are suspected of burglary, but there is insufficient evidence to convict them unless one of them confesses. The police can convict both of them of the lesser offence of possessing stolen goods without further evidence. They are interrogated in separate rooms. The prisoners expect the following outcomes: if they both confess and agree to testify they both get 2 years in prison; if neither confesses they will both get a 6-month sentence; if one confesses, he will go free, while the other will get the maximum sentence of 5 years. The 'pay-offs' (measured as years in jail) from this situation are represented in the *strategic form* of the game given in Table 7.1. In each of the four cells, the pay-off to George is given first and the pay-off to Fred second.

Table 7.1 The prisoner's dilemma, strategic form

		Fred	
		Confess	Deny
George	Confess	2 years, 2 years	Free, 5 years
	Deny	5 years, free	6 months, 6 months

How might this game be played? George considers his options: if Fred denies burglary, then his best response is to confess, and go free, whilst if Fred confesses, then George's best response is still to confess. Therefore, George concludes that his best strategy is to confess, as it gives the best outcome whether Fred confesses or denies. We say that 'confess' is a *dominant strategy* and that the strategy 'deny' is *dominated*. Fred, following a similar line of reasoning, decides to confess as well.

This game has been of interest to game theorists and economists because in equilibrium both players are rational in the way in which they select their dominant strategy, but the resulting equilibrium outcome gives lower pay-offs to both players than they could have achieved had they both selected their dominated strategies; namely, 'deny'. Thus, if Fred and George had made a binding pact not to confess, before they were arrested, both players would be better off compared with the dominant strategies. Co-operation requires either trust or some other mechanism that enforces a co-operative outcome. This is the essence of the prisoner's dilemmas that arise in environmental economics: an optimal solution is often rejected because of distrust or a lack of co-operation between players. Examples of prisoner's dilemmas from natural resources and environmental economics include the following:

- Countries that impose an acid rain problem on each other would both be better off collectively if they could agree to curtail sulphur dioxide emissions. Without agreement, it is individually rational for a country to only account for its national external costs instead of international external costs—that is, for the damages it imposes on others as well as itself.

- Countries are reluctant to sign global agreements to cut greenhouse gases, since the actions of others to reduce emissions deliver benefits to non-signatories and signatories alike.

- Urban dwellers who suffer from congested roads and air pollution would be collectively better off if they used their cars less, but it may still be rational for individuals to not change their pattern of car use.

- Sheep farmers sharing common grazing land degrade the land by overstocking because they cannot agree to binding reductions in stocking rates.

- Fishers, who share a common-property marine fishery, overfish because they cannot devise a way of sharing the benefits of conservation.

How does the dilemma arise? In the acid rain example, the lack of property rights concerns air quality: neither country has a right to control international air quality, even though it may be in their interests to agree on improvement. Similarly, collective action to limit car use is often beneficial, but there is a public good aspect to this (see Chapter 2): good air quality is a pure public good, since it is non-rival and non-excludable. Thus, there is little incentive for an individual to voluntarily limit his or her car use unless he or she could be sure that everyone else would do the same. Fisheries and common land grazing are overexploited because they are either common property (shared by a group of owners), or open access, owned by all (again, see Chapter 2). The problem is conventionally seen as one of an absence of, or shared rights over, a resource where each firm imposes an externality on other firms who share the resource. We now consider the last of these examples in more detail and give a brief introduction to fishery economics.

7.2.3 **Common property—the fisher's dilemma**

Currently, many of the world's major marine fisheries are in a state of either full exploitation or depletion (FAO, 2008: 7). The terms 'full exploitation' and 'depletion' are defined in relation to the maximum catch that is possible without depleting the fish stock, termed the *maximum sustainable yield*. 'Fully exploited' indicates that the catch is approximately equal to the maximum sustainable yield; 'depletion' indicates that the catch exceeds the maximum sustainable yield. Many economically important fisheries, such as the Grand Banks cod fishery, have been closed to commercial fishing (Kurlansky, 1999). In this section, we offer an explanation, based on game theory, of how the problem has arisen, but before that we provide an economic model of fishing.

The fishery model has a biomass growth function—the biological growth of the fish stock—and a relationship giving catch as a function of fishing effort (a measure of all the inputs used in fishing, such as the number of boats and the hours at sea) and the stock. To simplify the model, we assume that the fishery is always run in a 'steady state' where the catch equals biomass growth; this means that the stock remains constant. This allows us to derive a relationship between the catch and the harvest effort that does not include the stock, but accounts for the effect of stock size on the catch per unit of fishing effort. In fishery economics, this is called the yield–effort curve.

In any fishery, the key relationship is how the fish stock changes through time; that is, the growth function. In our model, fishers share a fishery in which the stock of fish changes through reproduction, mortality, and growth according to a logistic growth curve given by

$$g(x) = \gamma(1 - x/K)x. \tag{7.1}$$

In biology, this is a standard way of representing the growth of a population. Here, $g(x)$ is the growth function, which gives the rate of stock growth per unit of time; x is the stock of fish, in tonnes; γ is a growth parameter; and K is the carrying capacity of the marine ecosystem. The parameters can be interpreted as follows: the growth parameter, γ, gives the rate of change of the stock when the stock is very low (close to zero). In that case, the rate of stock growth is approximately γx. Thus if $\gamma = 0.5$, the rate of stock growth is equal to half the stock per period. At higher stock levels, the term $(1 - x/K)$ acts to reduce the growth rate, until the stock reaches a carrying capacity K and the growth rate is zero. The carrying capacity is the maximum biomass of a given species that the ecosystem can support. Note that if $x = 0$, then $(1 - x/K) = 1$; and if $x = K$, then $(1 - x/K) = 0$.

The firm's catch (qi) is given by the following function:

$$q_i = \theta h_i x. \tag{7.2}$$

In economics, this is a production function in which there is a relationship between inputs, fishing effort h_i (measured, for example, as a number of standard trawler days at sea) by fishing firm i and the stock of fish. Later on, we allow for the possibility that there is more than one fishing firm. The other parameter, θ, represents how easy fish are to catch. Note that this equation can rearranged so that $q_i/h_i = \theta x$; that is, the catch per unit of effort is proportional to the stock size: the larger the value of θ, the easier fish are to catch. This relationship also encompasses the status of technology in the fishery, as new fishing technology makes the fishing effort more effective by increasing the value of θ. An important aspect of the production function is that the catch of fish for a given harvest effort depends upon the fish stock; if there are more fish, it is cheaper to catch a fish.

We now bring together fish biomass growth with harvesting. We do this by assuming that the fishery operates in a 'steady state equilibrium', where the quantity of fish caught equals the growth in biomass. Thus:

$$g(x) - q_i = 0.$$

Substituting in equations (7.1) and (7.2), the above steady state equation can be written as follows:

$$\gamma x(1 - x/K) - \theta h_i x = 0,$$

and by solving for x and substituting back into equation (7.2), we obtain the yield effort curve:

$$q(h_i) = \theta h_i K(1 - \theta h_i/\gamma) \tag{7.3}$$

(see Box 7.2 for the derivation). This is a modified version of equation (7.2) that accounts for the steady state of stock.

We have described the technical aspects of a simple fishery, so now we introduce prices and an expression of profit to define an economic problem. First, if we multiply the catch by a constant price p, we obtain the equation *total revenue* $= pq(h_i)$. If we multiply the fishing effort by the cost per unit of fishing effort, we obtain the total cost: *total cost* $= wh_i$, where w is the cost per unit of fishing effort measured as the cost of a trawler day. Profit is the difference between total revenue and total cost:

$$\pi_i = pq(h_i) - wh_i.$$

To maximize profit, the firm equates the marginal revenue per unit of harvest with the marginal cost of harvest at h^s in Figure 7.1. This represents a social optimum where the marginal revenue from fishing equals the marginal social cost. If a regulator were to choose how to manage a fishery to maximize, then a total harvest effort of h^s is likely to be optimal. It is the maximum level of profit that the fishery can generate, and if firms were able to co-operate, they would choose this level of harvesting and share the profit.

However, in an open-access fishery any firm can enter the fishery, attracted by the profits of those already fishing there. This is a common situation in many of the world's fisheries. The harvest effort increases by firms continuing to enter the fishery until the profits are driven down to zero, at which point there is no longer an incentive for additional firms to enter. This occurs where effort is h_∞, total revenue equals total cost, and profit is zero. Open access results in too much fishing effort and too few fish left in the sea.

7.2.3.1 A Nash equilibrium with two firms

We have now set up a simple economic model of a fishery and analysed two extremes: one profit-maximizing firm and a number (possibly a very large number) of firms that drive the profit down to zero. Now we consider an intermediate case where the resource is shared by two firms and there is no agreement between them to co-operate. Assume that there are two identical firms who share the fishery, thus their production functions are identical:

BOX 7.2 Derivation of the Nash Equilibrium for a Fishery

Read this box if you would like to understand how the Nash equilibrium is derived. Taking the yield effort curve shown in equations (7.1) and (7.2), if there are two identical firms in the fishery, the steady state total quantity caught is as follows:

$$x\gamma(1 - x/K) - \theta xh = 0.$$

Solving for x gives $x = f(h) = K(\gamma - \theta h)/\gamma$ and the yield effort curve—that is, the catch as a function of the harvest effort only (with the stock eliminated)—is:

$$q = \theta hK(\gamma - \theta h)/\gamma.$$

For two firms, $h = (h_1 + h_2)$, that is total effort in the fishery, using this definition, **(Unclear.)** we give the stock as a function of the total harvest $f(h)$. For more than two firms, the harvest of all other firms is given by h_{-i}; thus the total harvest is $h = h_i + h_{-i}$. If this is substituted into the firms' profit functions:

$$\pi i = p\theta h_i f(h) - wh_i,$$

and the firms are linked together by the shared stock through the term $x(h)$. The Nash equilibrium for firm i is defined where

$$\frac{d\pi_i}{dh_i} = p\theta(f(h) + hf'(h)) - w,$$

where the derivative $f'(h) = -\theta K/\gamma$.

This gives the response of firm i as

$$h_i = \frac{Kp\theta \ (\gamma - h_{-i} \ \theta) - w\gamma}{2Kp\theta^2}$$

This Nash response curve is given in Figure 7.2.

If there is a single firm,

$$h_i^c = \frac{\gamma(Kp\theta - w)}{2Kp\theta}$$

The two firms will continue to adjust their fishing effort along their response curves until the derivatives of both firms are zero:

$$h_i^N = \frac{\gamma(Kp\theta - w)}{(3Kp\theta)}$$

Define

$$\kappa = \frac{\gamma(Kp\theta - w)}{(Kp\theta)} \ .$$

The total fishing effort with both firms following a Nash strategy is

$$h^N = (2/3)\kappa.$$

With a single firm, the total effort is $h^c = (1/2)\kappa$. This gives the first result: the single-ownership firm always puts in less total harvest effort than the two competing firms, the stock from equation (a) is reduced, and the quantity caught may or may not be reduced. Finally, the total cost is $c = w(q/\theta x)$; thus reducing the stock increases the average cost of catching fish.

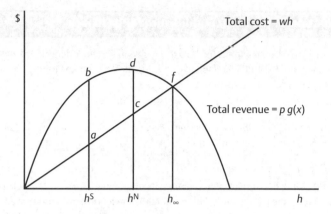

Figure 7.1 Fishery revenue and cost curves.

$$\pi_1(h_1 \mid h_2) = pq_1(h_1 \mid h_2) - wh_1; \qquad \pi_2(h_2 \mid h_1) = pq_2(h_2 \mid h_1) - wh_2.$$

The important point to note about these equations is that the profit of firm 1 is affected by the harvest of firm 2, and vice versa. For instance, the term $q_1(h_1 \mid h_2)$ indicates the catch of firm 1 *given* the fishing effort of firm 2. The form of this problem allows us to introduce the Nash equilibrium, a fundamental equilibrium concept in game theory. The profit of one firm acting independently depends upon what the other fishing firm does; therefore, the best a firm can achieve is to take the strategy of the other firm as given and maximize its profit on that basis. To reach a final equilibrium, firms may iterate towards a point at which neither firm wants to change.

If we choose some specific parameters for the fishery model: $K = 1000$, $\gamma = 1$, $\theta = 0.1$, $w = \$2,000$ per unit of effort per month, and $p = \$10,000$ per tonne of fish, we can produce the pay-off matrix shown in Table 7.2.

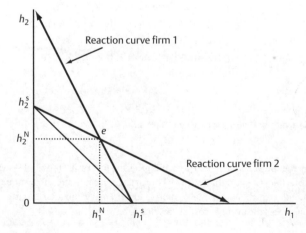

Figure 7.2 Fishery Nash equilibrium.

Table 7.2 The fisher's dilemma

		Firm 2 ($ million)	
		Nash (compete)	Co-operate
Firm 1 ($ million)	Nash (compete)	1.07, 1.07 NN_1, NN_2	1.35, 0.9 NC_1, NC_2
	Co-operate	0.9, 1.35 CN_1, CN_2	1.2, 1.2 CC_1, CC_2

By considering Table 7.2 with Figure 7.2, we see that the Nash equilibrium represents the best response to the other player's expected strategy. However, if both firms were able to co-operate, possibly through negotiated agreement, they would both be better off by $133,389. The Nash equilibrium is thus not optimal from the economy's point of view. Shifting the solution from the Nash equilibrium to a co-operative solution is said to be Pareto optimal, in that two firms are made better off and no firm or individual is made worse off. From Figure 7.2, the harvest rates h_1^s and h_2^s are the profit-maximizing efforts that the firm would choose if they had single and exclusive ownership of the resource. Reaction curves give the Nash response of one firm to the other firm's harvest effort; that is, they give the profit-maximizing harvest effort given the other firm's harvest effort. A Nash equilibrium occurs at e with an effort of $h_1^N + h_2^N$. At this equilibrium, there is no incentive for the firms to choose another strategy. The line from h_1^s to h_2^s shows a range of optimal 'co-operative' solutions. Along this line, the harvest effort is chosen so that firms maximize their *joint* profits. The total Nash equilibrium fishing effort, $h_1^N + h_2^N$, is greater than under single ownership, but the profit is less: therefore, this represents an inefficient outcome, as noted above. The solution is also illustrated in Figure 7.1, where $h^N = h_1^N + h_2^N$. Note also that the fish stock is greater under the profit-maximizing harvest at h^s. A fishery regulator should prefer the profit-maximizing solution, as it gives the greatest total welfare to producers and is therefore efficient. In a more general model, it would also maximize welfare to the economy as a whole—that is, producers and consumers—from the fishery.

There are two key results that emerge from this analysis. First, if the two firms co-operate, they stand to benefit by increasing their profit. The second point is that the problem of sub-optimal exploitation becomes worse as the number of firms increases, until the open-access equilibrium is reached, at which all firms earn zero profits. This gives a game-theoretic interpretation of Hardin's (1968) 'tragedy of the commons'. A prisoner's dilemma characterizes the outcome for two or more firms, but the problem becomes more severe when there are a large number of firms. With a small number of firms, a co-operative outcome may emerge as an equilibrium, especially when the game is repeated a large number of times. We discuss this further below.

7.3 Self-governance—Escaping the Tragedy of the Commons

In his paper 'The tragedy of the commons', Hardin (1968) foretells of dire consequences for common-property resources. However, the situation he is describing is more akin to open-access than limited-entry common property. Using common grazing as an example, Hardin predicts that:

Each man is locked into a system that compels him to increase his herd without limit—in a world that is limited. Ruin is the destination toward which all men rush, each pursuing his own best interest in a society that believes in the freedom of the commons. Freedom in a commons brings ruin to all.

(Hardin, 1968: 1244)

A different view is offered by Elinor Ostrom (1990), who won the 2009 Nobel Prize for Economics for her work on common-property resources:

Elinor Ostrom has challenged the conventional wisdom that common property is poorly managed and should be either regulated by central authorities or privatized. Based on numerous studies of user-managed fish stocks, pastures, woods, lakes, and groundwater basins, Ostrom concludes that the outcomes are, more often than not, better than predicted by standard theories. She observes that resource users frequently develop sophisticated mechanisms for decision-making and rule enforcement to handle conflicts of interest, and she characterizes the rules that promote successful outcomes.

(Nobel Prize Committee, 2009)

Ostrom (1990) observed that a significant number of common-property resources have avoided the tragedy of the commons as a result of users developing institutions that increase the efficiency of resource exploitation. She argues that the predictions of the prisoner's dilemma and, more generally, Nash equilibrium are not an inevitable outcome for common-property resources, because the potential exists for communication between players before they take their decisions. Government intervention is one way of forcing producers to co-operate, but this is not necessarily the only way.

In one alternative, firms may be able to co-operate by agreeing to abide by the decisions of an external regulator or referee, who may even be appointed by the firms and paid a fee. The referee acts by imposing penalties to ensure that the firms do not play their Nash strategies. This offers an escape route from the inefficient Nash equilibrium and thus from the prisoner's dilemma. Firms now have an incentive to co-operate so long as each firm's share of the fee is less than the difference between the co-operative solution and Nash equilibrium, which is $(1.2 - 1.08) = 0.12$ from Table 7.2. The penalty agreed by the firms should be large enough so that there is no incentive to cheat on the agreement; for instance, an amount greater than the difference between the profit rates—that is, \$133 thousand—should give an adequate incentive, especially if non-compliance is always detected.

Ostrom (1990) found that voluntary institutions work effectively in managing common-property resources where a relatively small number of firms share the resource. Common-property institutions tend to break down when the number of firms involved increases, or when there is a lack of family and community ties between the appropriators of the resource. Examples of where voluntary institutions have been successful include Turkish inshore fisheries (see Box 7.3), lobster fisheries in Maine, and irrigation schemes in the US Midwest (Ostrom, 1990).

7.4 Repeated Fishing Games

In Section 7.3, we concluded that the mismanagement of common-property resources is not inevitable. Some shared resources have been well managed without private ownership.

BOX 7.3 An Example of Self-organization in a Common-property Resource

Bodrum is located about 400 km west of Alanya on the Aegean Sea. The inshore fishery (Berkes, 1986) is relatively small, with about 100 local fishers operating two- to three-person boats. In the early 1970s, the fishery was in a depressed state. Conflict existed amongst the local fishers due to unrestrained access to the fishery, and local fishers devoted resources to competing for the best fishing spots, which tended to increase production costs.

In response to this situation, members of the local fishing co-operative began to experiment with a system for allotting fishing sites. After almost a decade of refinement, the resulting system is as follows.

Each year, a list of eligible fishers is drawn up. The fishing locations are named and listed. In September, the fishers draw lots and are assigned a location, but on each day of the fishing season, from September to May, they shift east to the next location. This gives the fishers equal opportunities to catch the migratory fish stock.

This system means that no resources are wasted by the fishers fighting over preferred locations; and the system is self-policing, with the fishers enforcing the system themselves by reporting fishers who are in the wrong location. The fishery is managed efficiently with the tacit support of the Turkish government, but no direct policy intervention.

One other explanation is that the players are brought together in long-term competition rather than a single 'one-shot' game such as that analysed in our simple fishing example. Over time, players may develop a system of sharing the resource by agreement, but agreement would only come about because the firms expect to benefit in the long term from showing restraint. This describes a repeated game where a sequence of games is played through time. Repeated games have a much larger number of potential strategies than one-shot games. There is the potential for observing how the other firms play over time, and for tacit agreements to co-operate or punish to emerge. If the prisoner's dilemma is played a large number of times, then co-operation can emerge as equilibrium. This equilibrium is reinforced by the threat that if one player stops co-operating, everyone will be punished by a return to a disadvantageous non-cooperative equilibrium. This is called a 'tit-for-tat' strategy, and it was found by Axelrod (1984) to be a frequently selected strategy in experiments where people play repeated prisoner's dilemma games.

In many real strategic interactions, such as water resource sharing or negotiations over fishing rights, games are repeated over and over again. It is an equilibrium to 'confess' in the one-shot prisoner's dilemma, because there is no possibility of repercussions at a later stage of the game. The key result in this literature is that when a game is repeated many times, co-operation may emerge as a competitive equilibrium. However, if the game is repeated just a few times, then the equilibrium is the same as for the one-shot game. If the game lasts only a few turns, then the players will reason as follows: in the last stage of the game, the other player has no incentive to do anything other than not co-operate, because in the last stage we have a one-shot game. On this basis, moving to the previous stage, there is no scope for retaliation, so the player chooses a Nash strategy and so on, back to the start of the game. Thus in this finite game we conclude that the outcome is to play the Nash strategy in all periods. If the game is repeated indefinitely, discounting ensures that the final period is of no importance, but the prospect of retaliation is important—in the sense that the optimal outcome is a policy where each player co-operates until the other deviates and then deviates for the remainder of the game. The reason for this is that the most the player can gain from deviating is a one-period improvement in his or her pay-off, which is followed by a reduction in pay-offs for the remainder of the game.

Consider what happens if the fisheries game in Table 7.2 is repeated a large number of times and the players adopt a tit-for-tat strategy. The pay-offs from the fishery game from Table 7.4, where CC_1 indicates that both firms co-operate and gives the pay-off to firm 1, CN_2 indicates that firm 1 co-operates while firm 2 plays a Nash strategy and gives the pay-off to firm 2. The present value of firm 1 co-operating for a long time is discussed in Box 7.4.

For the firms to gain by deviating, this equation would have to be positive. The gain from deviating lasts for only one period, when they receive $(NC_1 - CC_1)$, but they are then penalized for all periods after that $(NN_1 - CC_1)$. The present value of punishment forever is $(NN_1 - CC_1)/r$, where r is the discount rate (see Box 7.4). From this, it is obvious that

---

BOX 7.4 Revision on Discounting

How do we evaluate decisions that give costs and benefits over time? The problem is that $1 today is worth more than a $1 in a year's time, because we can invest that $1 in the bank or in the stock market and earn interest. So when evaluating a flow of net benefits (benefits minus costs), we cannot simply sum the net benefits in each year to give a total net benefit. This total would not take account of the lost investment opportunities. Instead, we calculate the present value of net benefits, which converts $1 in future years to its value today. For instance, if we compare $1 today with $1 in a year's time, the value of $1 in a year's time needs to be adjusted downwards to account for the fact that $1 today can be invested and earn annual interest equal to r. Let us suppose that $r = 0.1$ (10%). Then, after a year, $1 equals $(1 + r) \times 1 = 1.1$. The relative value of $1 after a year is, therefore, $(1/(1 + r)) = (1/1.1) = 0.9090$. In other words, the present value of $1 after a year is about 91 cents. After 2 years of compound interest, the dollar now has grown to $(1 + r)^2 \times 1 = 1.21$, the relative value of a dollar after 2 years is $(1/(1 + r)^2) = 0.8264$. A general value for the discount factor is $\delta^t = 1/(1 + r)^t$, where δ is the discount factor and t is the number of years into the future.

If a resource or an environmental asset is expected to give a constant flow of net benefits (y_t) for the foreseeable future, then we can actually simplify the discounting formula. The present value of a flow of income is given by

$$PV_T = \delta^1 y_1 + \delta^2 y_2 + \ldots + \delta^T y_T.$$

If the income is constant, then the present value can be given as

$$PV_T = \delta^1 y + \delta^2 y + \ldots + \delta^T y.$$

We can rewrite this geometric progression as

$$PV_T - \delta^1 PV_T = \delta^1 y - \delta^{T+1} y$$

or

$$PV_T = y(\delta^1 - \delta^{T+1})/(1 - \delta^1).$$

Note that if $T = \infty$, $\delta^{T+1} = 0$, and thus

$$PV_T = y(\delta^1)/(1 - \delta^1) = y/r.$$

Therefore, the present value for a constant income over an infinite period is simply the net benefit divided by the discount rate.

deviating from co-operation only pays if the benefits of deviating are very high or the discount rate is very high. For the example given in Table 7.2, the gain from deviation is $(1.35 - 1.20) = 0.15$, but the punishment is $(1.20 - 1.07)/r$. The discount rate would have to be 80 per cent ($r = 0.8$) for deviation to be worthwhile, which implies a very low weight on future pay-offs. A typical discount rate even for a highly impatient individual would probably be less than 20 per cent.

7.5 Co-operative Games

Co-operative games are concerned with the formation and stability of coalitions. For instance in a European Union negotiation over sharing out EU fishing quotas, if France and Spain form an alliance and agree to work together to get a bigger share of the quotas in negotiations with other countries and coalitions of countries, this is an example of a co-operative game. Forming an alliance is a strategy. History also tells us that such alliances are not always stable. The fact that co-operative game theory focuses on alliances as strategies tends to simplify the description of the details of the rest of the game; for instance, how much fish is caught by France and Spain. Instead the focus is on the total pay-offs of a coalition.

Co-operative games arise where, for instance, instead of competing, players decide to establish coalitions. In relation to a common property, a group of fishers or graziers may decide to form a group or coalition that determines how the resource is shared. More formally, co-operative games arise where players can form binding agreements in pre-play negotiations. Strictly, co-operative games are a special case of non-cooperative games, in that a non-cooperative game can be extended to include the decision to form a coalition in which a group of players play as if they are single players. This could occur between fishers within a producer's co-operative, where they negotiate collectively for fisheries quotas and licences, but they then need to decide how they share the gains between co-operative members. Co-operative game theory focuses on the pay-offs that different 'coalitions' can achieve, rather than on the details of how the game might be played. The following is a non-technical account of the basics of co-operative game theory with reference to the following example (for more detail, see Hanley and Folmer, 1998).

Suppose that three countries share a groundwater reservoir. They have a choice of acting individually or collaborating in various coalitions, including a 'grand coalition' that includes all countries. Each country receives the pay-off indicated in Table 7.3.

Table 7.3 The groundwater co-operation game

Coalitions of countries	Value of coalitions ($ million)
A	10
B	20
C	30
A, B	50
A, C	60
C, B	70
A, B, C	100

Table 7.3 gives the pay-offs to different combinations of countries. Let us define a pay-off function, $v(.)$, that gives the value of the game to various coalitions; for instance, $v(\{A\}) = 10$ gives the value to country A resulting from 'going it alone', $v(\{A, B\}) = 50$ gives the pay-off from a coalition between countries A and B, and so on. The next question is which coalitions of players are likely to form. For instance, $v(\{A, B\}) = 50$ indicates that a coalition between A and B has a pay-off of 50 units, while the grand coalition has a pay-off of 100, and thus $v(\{A, B, C\}) = 100$. Therefore, in this game the grand coalition gives a bigger pay-off than all sub-coalitions, but we have to check whether the coalition is stable. In other words, do either A, B, or C have an incentive to leave the grand coalition?

Now that we have set out the basic structure of co-operative games, it remains to discuss solution concepts that determine how players divide the benefits of co-operation. The approach to this is to assume that the grand coalition forms and then assess if a pay-off $\pi(S)$ (where S is a single player or a group of players) can be set that provides an incentive for the coalition to continue. The first condition is a 'budget constraint':

$$\pi(A) + \pi(B) + \pi(C) = v(\{A, B, C\}) = 100.$$

This ensures that the pay-off is shared amongst the players. Next, we need to specify individual and group (or coalition) rationality. This assesses whether players are able to achieve higher pay-offs outside the grand coalition, either individually or in other coalitions. Individual rationality says that $\pi(A) \geq v(\{A\})$; in other words, the pay-off received by country A as part of the coalition must be no less than the amount that country A could achieve alone. This extends to group rationality as $\pi(\{S\}) \geq v(\{S\})$: thus the pay-off to the subset of players S under the grand coalition must be greater than the pay-off that could be achieved by S as a separate coalition, $v(\{S\})$.

Individual and group rationality defines a set of constraints on pay-offs that would be acceptable to all players. The set of all such pay-offs that satisfy individual and group rationality is called the *core* and sets of pay-offs are called *imputations*. These concepts can be illustrated for our specific game using a diagram. Figure 7.3 shows the shares of the grand coalition as a triangle. In each corner, one player receives a pay-off of 100 and the others nothing. The lines across the triangle indicate individual rationality. For instance, $v[\{A\}] = 10$; thus in

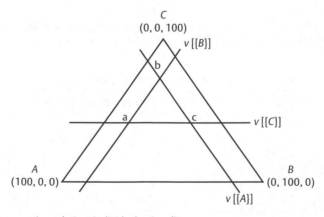

Figure 7.3 The co-operative solution: individual rationality.

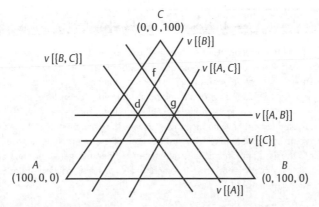

Figure 7.4 The co-operative solution: individual and group rationality.

terms of individual rationality, A must receive a pay-off of at least 10 due to individual rationality, which leaves 90 units to share between C and B. The smaller triangle abc is the set of pay-offs that satisfies the individual rationality constraints. Turning to Figure 7.4, we now introduce the group rationality constraints as well as the individual rationality constraints. This accounts for the pay-offs that the countries can obtain in sub-coalitions. The core dfg of the game represents a set of possible pay-offs that satisfy both the individual rationality and group rationality constraints. The actual solution would be determined by negotiation between the players and relative negotiating power (see also Box 7.5).

Co-operative game theory is a useful tool in environmental and natural resource economics, as it helps to explain why groups with similar preferences form alliances and agree to negotiate together. For instance, alliances have tended to emerge in global climate change negotiations in Cancun and Copenhagen between countries with similar interests (see Chapter 12). It also allows us to analyse how stable these alliances are and which alliances may form in the future.

7.6 Game Theory and Transboundary Pollution Control

7.6.1 Introduction

Transboundary pollution concerns emissions that cross international boundaries. We choose to analyse this problem here because it includes elements of both co-operative and non-cooperative game theory. Non-cooperative game theory analyses the outcome in the absence of negotiation, whilst co-operative game theory analyses how countries form coalitions and how stable these coalitions are. Transboundary pollution problems are of three broad types:

- First, there are unidirectional externalities, where an 'upstream country' affects a 'downstream' country. This form of externality is characterized by water pollution, where a country pollutes a river and hence imposes costs on the downstream country.

- Second, regional reciprocal externalities are typical of public goods such as European air quality, as measured by SO_x and NO_x levels. The actions of a country affect not only its own costs or benefits, but have impacts in other countries as well: emissions of

BOX 7.5 Self-enforcing International Environmental Agreements

International environmental agreements (IEA), such as the Montreal Protocol, for ozone-depleting substances and the Kyoto Protocol to limit emissions of greenhouse gases, have been characterized by protracted negotiations and partial agreements. The lack of a 'higher authority' makes international environmental agreements difficult to negotiate and police. Barrett (1994b, 2005) proposes that international environmental agreements should be self-enforcing, which means that the group of countries that sign the agreement have no incentives to leave the agreement and those that are non-signatories have no incentive to join. The condition for self-enforcement for a group of N identical countries is similar to the group rationality constraint from co-operative game theory. Countries divide into signatories (s) or non-signatories (n) to an IEA such that $N = n + s$. A coalition of signatories is stable if the following conditions are satisfied:

incentive to leave the agreement: $\pi_n(n + 1) \leq \pi_s(s)$;   (1)

incentive to join the agreement: $\pi_n(n) \geq \pi_s(s + 1)$;   (2)

where the pay-off to signatories is $\pi_s(s)$, and the pay-off to non-signatories is $\pi_n(n)$. A coalition is stable if there is no incentive for a country to accede to the IEA and no incentive for a country to leave. Condition (1) above says that there is no incentive to leave the coalition because the pay-off to a signatory is greater than the pay-off to a non-signatory when the number of non-signatories is increased by 1. Condition (2) says that there is no incentive to join, as the pay-off to a non-signatory is greater than a pay-off to a signatory when the number of signatories is increased by 1.

  The implications of this theoretical model are rather depressing. They imply that self-enforcing IEAs only include a large proportion of the countries when the benefits of co-operation are relatively small. Where the benefits of co-operation over non-cooperation are large, then the equilibrium tends to include only a relatively small proportion of the countries. The implication of this result is that it is going to be very difficult for countries to agree to IEAs, and we may see partial agreements where one group of countries joins and another group remains outside the agreement.

sulphur oxides from the United Kingdom acidify UK lakes and streams, but also impact on Swedish and Norwegian lakes and streams (see Box 7.6).

- Third, global externalities are subdivided into those that involve physical interactions between countries and those that do not. For instance, by thinning the ozone layer, chlorofluorocarbon emissions have the potential to cause detrimental health effects on most of the human population. Likewise, greenhouse gas emissions will, through global warming, affect everyone (see Chapter 9). Non-physical effects relate to a range of goods with non-use values. These bring in issues related to the conservation of global biodiversity (see Chapter 12).

All of these pollution problems involve a strategic interaction between countries and can be analysed by game theory. We explore this using an acid rain example.

7.6.2 The acid rain game

This section uses a simple hypothetical two-country 'acid rain game' to illustrate the application of game theory to transboundary pollution problems. This problem introduces concepts from both co-operative and non-cooperative game theory. We start off by specifying the problem. There are two countries, the United Kingdom (subscript 1) and Sweden (subscript 2),

BOX 7.6 The Montreal Protocol

Chlorofluorocarbons (CFCs) have been implicated in depleting the stratospheric ozone shield since the 1970s. The depletion of the ozone layer is a truly global pollution problem in that all countries are likely to be affected, to some degree, by the health problems that the resulting elevated levels of ultraviolet light will cause. In September 1988, twenty-four countries signed the Montreal Protocol (Barrett, 2005: ch. 8) to restrict their production and consumption of CFCs to 50 per cent of 1986 levels by 30 June 1998. In London during July 1990, fifty-six countries agreed to further tighten restrictions on the use of these chemicals. This agreement involved the phasing out of halons and CFCs by the end of the twentieth century. An interesting aspect of this agreement is that a fund of $240 million was established to assist poorer countries to comply with this agreement. This amounts to a side payment to ensure that a negotiated settlement is achieved. The restrictions were further tightened at the fourth meeting in 1992 in Copenhagen, with a ban on CFC products brought forward to 1996, from 1999, and a ban on trade in these substances.

The agreements over the reduction in substances that damage the stratospheric ozone layer represents a relatively successful international environmental agreement, perhaps because the environmental costs were potentially large and shared by all countries and the costs, due to the development of new products, were declining through time. The use of side payments also facilitated the inclusion of poorer countries in the London agreement. This outcome contrasts with the current state of disagreement over the right course of action in relation to climate change (see Chapter 9). The stability of the Montreal Protocol is strengthened by the threat of trade sanctions if countries are found to be non-compliant or refuse to sign the protocol. This has been an effective deterrent against free-riding.

both of which generate sulphur dioxide from coal-burning. Emissions from the UK affect Sweden and vice versa. This is a reciprocal externality. Each country has a benefit-of-emissions function due to profits derived from burning coal (e.g. for electricity generation) and an external cost function due to damages caused by acid rain. These functions can also be given as abatement cost functions (which represent the emission benefit function) and an abatement benefit function. To make this example more concrete, we use the specific functional forms and parameter values in Table 7.4, but, if you prefer, look at the diagrams that come later.

The Nash equilibrium is where each country only takes account of its own external costs. The equilibrium (national) level of abatement for the UK is where

$$MAC_1(a_1) = MBA_1(a_1 \mid a_2);$$

that is, the marginal abatement cost $MAC_1(a_1)$ is equated with the marginal benefit of abatement in country 1, the UK, given the amount of abatement in (and thus the level of emissions from) country 2, Sweden, $MBA_1(a_1 \mid a_2)$. If the two countries agree to co-operate, then each country takes account of the other's benefits of abatement. Thus, for the UK:

$$MAC_1(a_1) = MBA_1(a_1 \mid a_2) + MBA_2(a_1 \mid a_2).$$

Using the numerical example given in Table 7.5, the results of a Nash strategy and a co-operative strategy are given in that table and Figure 7.5.

Table 7.5 gives the pay-off and the abatement level for all the combinations of strategies. Starting with the strategy in which both countries co-operate, this gives the highest overall abatement of 482.8 and the highest aggregate welfare of 38.8. However, without a binding co-operative agreement, both countries have an incentive to follow an unco-operative strategy—especially the UK, which is less affected by acid rain than Sweden.

Table 7.4 The acid rain game

Private costs and benefits	External costs and benefits
Private benefit of emissions: $\quad B_i^e(e_i) = b_{0i}e_i - b_{1i}e_i^2$ $\quad e_i^* = b_{0i}/2b_{1i}$ where e_i^* is the private benefit-maximizing emission Abatement: $a_i = (e_i^* - e_i)$ Private abatement costs: $C_i^a(a_i) = (B_i^e(e_i^*) - B_i^e(e_i^* - a_i))$ that is, the difference between maximum private benefits and benefits with abatement Parameter values: $\quad b_{01} = 150; b_{02} = 150;$ $\quad b_{11} = 0.15; {}_ib_{12} = 0.15$	External costs: $\quad C_i^e(e) = c_i^e e^2$ Total emissions: $\quad e = e_1 + e_2$ $\quad e^* = e_1^* + e_2^*$ Aggregate abatement: $\quad a = e^* - (e_1 + e_2)$ Abatement benefit function: $\quad B_i^a(a) = C_i^e(e^*) - C_i^e(e^* - a)$ $\quad c_1^e = 0.02; \quad c_2^e = 0.05$

For the co-operative solution to hold, there would have to be a side payment from Sweden to the UK to make the agreement stable. This is a concept from co-operative game theory, where it is necessary to ensure that players receive at least as much through co-operation as they do from not co-operating. In this example, a side-payment transfer to the UK means that Sweden gains sufficiently from co-operation to compensate the UK and still be better off. However, there may be a problem of countries 'pre-committing' to side payments in a believable way, which can harm prospects for co-operative agreements. However, promises of side payments can be used to entice countries into becoming part

Table 7.5 Transboundary pollution—the acid rain game

Sweden / UK	Nash	Co-operate
Nash	Pay-off (£ millions) UK: 27.0 S: 6.5 UK+S: 33.5 Abatement (million tonnes SO_2): UK: 90.9 S: 227.3 UK + S: 318.2	Pay-off (£ millions) UK: 27.3 S: 6.3 UK + S: 33.7 Abatement (million tonnes SO_2): UK: 89.2 S: 241.4 UK+S: 320.6
Co-operate	Pay-off (£ millions) UK: 22.3 S: 15.9 UK + S: 38.2 Abatement (million tonnes SO_2): UK: 241.4 S: 189.7 UK + S: 431.1	Pay-off (£ millions) UK: 23.4 S: 15.4 UK + S: 38.8 Abatement (million tonnes SO_2): UK: 241.4 S: 241.4 UK + S: 482.8

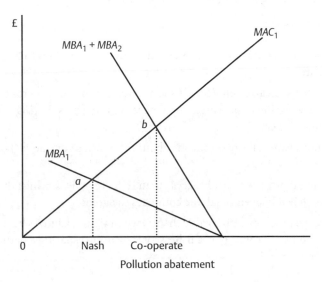

Figure 7.5 Transboundary pollution: the acid rain game

of international environmental agreements (IEAs) on transboundary pollution. Side payments were used during the negotiation process for the Montreal Protocol on the phasing out of CFCs. Side payments are also likely to be important in future global agreements on biodiversity conservation, and in greenhouse gas emission agreements.

Summary

In this chapter, we have introduced game theory as an approach to modelling the strategic interaction of a small number of economic agents. Situations in which small numbers of agents or coalitions of agents interact arise in environmental economics, where resources are shared. Environmental resources include global commons such as the atmosphere, regional air quality, and natural resources such as fisheries and grazing areas. The attributes of these problems are shared rights of ownership or poorly defined property rights, where agents compete to appropriate the benefits of a resource. Game theory enables us to analyse what the outcomes of these interactions might be.

An important game is the prisoner's dilemma, where the equilibrium is one where both players are worse off than they would be if they were to co-operate. Repeated games offer a new perspective on the problem, in that co-operation may actually emerge as an equilibrium, because—through time—players can punish defections by other players.

Co-operative game theory is about the formation and stability of coalitions between players. The approach can be viewed as complementary to competitive games, in that it considers only the best that players can achieve in different coalitions and abstracts from the mechanics of how a solution to a game is derived.

Game theory informs us how environmental conflicts and problems might be resolved, and it also goes some way towards explaining why problems have arisen in the first place—in particular, where individuals behave rationally, but counter to the common good.

Tutorial Questions

7.1 Why are the predictions of the prisoner's dilemma so important to natural resource management?

7.2 Distinguish between an open-access fishery and a common-property fishery. Would you expect overfishing to be worse when there are fifty firms sharing a fishery or two firms sharing a fishery?

7.3 Why is Elinor Ostrom more optimistic about the world's commons than Garrett Harding?

7.4 Why was the Montreal Protocol successful in reducing CFCs, whilst the Kyoto Protocol has failed to even get all the countries to agree?

7.5 With reference to co-operative game theory, why might coalitions be unstable in relation to producer groups (e.g. a fishers' organization) sharing a natural resource?

References and Additional Readings

Axelrod, R. (1984). *The Evolution of Cooperation* (New York: Basic Books).

Barrett, S. (1994a). 'The biodiversity supergame', *Environmental and Resource Economics* 4: 111–22.

—— (1994b). 'Self-enforcing international environmental agreements', *Oxford Economic Papers* 46: 878–94.

—— (2005). *Environment and Statecraft: The Strategy of Environmental Treaty-making* (Oxford: Oxford University Press).

Batabayal, A.A. (1995). 'Leading issues in domestic environmental regulation—a review essay', *Ecological Economics* 12(1): 23–39.

Berkes, F. (1986). 'Local-level management and the commons problem: a comparative study of Turkish coastal fisheries', *Marine Policy* 10: 215–29.

Dixit, A.K., Skeath, S., and Reiley, D.H. (2009). *Games of Strategy*, 3rd edn. (New York: W.W. Norton).

FAO (2008). *Review of the State of Fishery Resources: Marine Fisheries* (Rome: FAO).

Fudenberg, D., and Tirole, J. (1991). *Game Theory* (Cambridge, MA: The MIT Press).

Hanley, N., and Folmer, H. (1998). *Game Theory and the Environment* (Cheltenham: Edward Elgar).

Hardin, G. (1968). 'The tragedy of the commons', *Science* 162: 1243–8.

Kurlansky, M. (1999). *Cod* (London: Jonathan Cape).

Levhari, D., and Mirman, L.J. (1980). 'The great fish war: an example using a dynamic Cournot–Nash solution', *Bell Journal of Economics* 11: 322–44.

Maler, K.-G. (1989). 'The acid rain game', in H. Folmer and E. van Ireland (eds.), *Valuation Methods and Policy Making in Environmental Economics* (Amsterdam: Elsevier).

Mesterton-Gibbons, M. (2000). *An Introduction to Game-theoretic Modelling*, 2nd edn. (Providence, RI: American Mathematical Society).

Mueller, D.C. (1989). *Public Choice II* (Cambridge: Cambridge University Press).

Nobel Prize Committee (2009). Press Release, http://nobelprize.org/nobel_prizes/economics/laureates/2009/press.html.

Normile, D. (2010). 'U.N. Biodiversity Summit yields welcome and unexpected progress', *Science* 330: 743–4.

Ostrom, E. (1990). *Governing the Commons* (Cambridge: Cambridge University Press).

Russell, C.S. (1990). 'Game models for structuring monitoring and enforcement systems', *Natural Resource Modeling* 4(2): 143–73.

Von Neumann J., and Morgenstern, O. (1944). *Theory of Games and Economic Behaviour* (Princeton, NJ: Princeton University Press).

8 Trade and the Environment

Since 1970, trade liberalization has generated a rapid increase in trade volume and has driven economic growth and prosperity. At the same time, increased globalization due to trade is blamed for widespread environmental degradation, especially in developing countries. This chapter shows how economists have analysed these issues. This chapter:

- Reviews trade theory and shows why economists often promote freer trade.
- Extends a simple trade analysis to include possible impacts of trade on the environment.
- Considers the empirical evidence on the effects of trade policy on the environment.
- Discusses international trade policy and its role in environmental policy.

8.1 Introduction

International trade, the exchange of goods across national borders, can profoundly change the production, consumption, and welfare of a country. Inevitably, any change in the spatial distribution of production and consumption affects the environment locally, nationally, and globally.

Since Adam Smith in 1776 and David Ricardo in 1817, many economists (Krugman and Obstfeld, 2009) have believed that countries, as a whole, benefit by an increase in welfare from freer trade and suffer a reduction in welfare when trade is restricted by policies such as quotas and tariffs. Cline (2004: 180) estimates that the world would benefit by a 0.93 per cent increase in gross domestic product (GDP) through a move to freer trade. The modest size of this increase is probably due to the fact that by 2004, trade was already relatively free (Krugman and Obstfeld, 2009: ch. 9). This is not to say that freer trade will benefit everyone: some people engaged in producing tradable goods and services may suffer a reduction in income as a result of trade liberalization. Trade allows countries to specialize in producing goods for which they have the lowest opportunity cost. This means that they can achieve a higher level of consumption than they could achieve without trade. These principles have underpinned global trade negotiations under the General Agreement on Tariffs and Trade (GATT) and the World Trade Organization (WTO), which succeeded GATT in 1995 with the Marrakech Agreement. For the foreseeable future, we can expect to see a continued expansion in the volume and value of world trade that will tend to increase global production and consumption (see Figure 8.1). The relationship between trade and world GDP is not straightforward, but the fact that trade allows countries to specialize and increase the value of their output leads to economic growth, as measured by the rate of change in real GDP per capita (Frankel and Rose, 2005). In turn, as GDP grows then the demand for imported goods also increases.

Economic growth itself, whether induced by trade or not, can be expected to effect the environment by changing spatial patterns of polluting production and natural resource use, but it is hard to say whether it will be beneficial or detrimental, as we saw in Chapter 6. On the negative side, the first law of thermodynamics predicts that more output, by increasing the quantity of material used, will increase global pollution. The process of trade itself, which involves the transportation of goods to different countries, is also polluting. Trade liberalization may lead to production reallocating to countries with lax environmental regulations, the so-called *pollution havens hypothesis* (Eskeland and Harrison, 2003; Copeland and Taylor, 2004; Taylor, 2004). Environmental benefits from increased trade include that trade may lead to a reallocation of production to countries better able to deal with the environmental side-effects of production, whilst increased income may lead to consumers demanding higher environmental standards. Trade also results in a reallocation of production and consumption, moving the location of relatively polluting activities spatially from importers to exporters (Kander and Lindmark, 2006).

From Chapter 3, there is a clear recommendation that if a country aims to regulate pollution, it should target policy instruments such as regulation, emission taxes, or tradable emission permits directly on emissions. Restricting production inputs or outputs is a second-best policy, because these variables may not be directly related to the level of emissions or to environmental damage. Trade policy, in terms of tariffs and restrictions on the quantity and quality of goods sold in a country, deals with production inputs and outputs. Therefore,

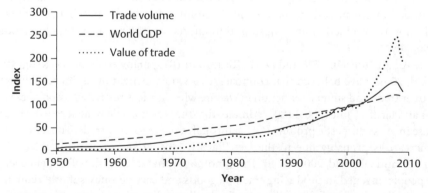

Figure 8.1 World gross domestic product (GDP), trade volume, and value.
Source: World Trade Organization (2010); 2000 = 100.

restricting trade in inputs and outputs is a sub-optimal approach to environmental policy. The fact that trade policy is sometimes justified on the grounds of environmental protection should be viewed with suspicion: a trade restriction on environmental grounds may be little more than a disguised measure to protect domestic producers. Examples of trade measures to protect the environment and consumers include the European Union ban on hormone treated beef on the basis of the Agreement on the Application of Sanitary and Phytosanitary Measures under the WTO arrangements in 1996 (Petersmann and Pollack, 2003), which was deemed unjustified in 2008 by the WTO appeals panel. The 1991 GATT ruling on the United States–Mexico tuna–dolphin dispute (Esty, 1994), where the United States banned imports of tuna from Mexico not produced in a way that avoided dolphin deaths, is a similar case. The 1998 WTO ruling against the USA for banning shrimp exports from countries not adopting technologies to protect sea turtles is a further example of countries being prevented from using environmentally motivated trade restrictions in a way that might benefit domestic producers (WTO, 2006).

In a perfect world, a country's domestic environment should be protected by national environmental policies, and the global environment protected by international environmental agreements enforced through national policies. Both domestic and global policies should target emissions, not consumer goods and production inputs. However, in some situations, restrictions to trade may be warranted as the only available sanction on a country causing an international environmental problem. For instance, the CITES (International Convention on Trade in Endangered Species) convention established in 1973 aims to protect species by reducing the demand for live animals and animal products. However, this Convention does not address the source of the problem, which is often the loss of habitat supporting the endangered species, due to the opportunity costs of habitat conservation.

The Basel Convention on the Transboundary Movements of Hazardous Waste (ratified in 1992) aims to protect developing countries from becoming a dumping ground for toxic waste. This agreement acknowledges a potential failure in some countries to protect the environment from the dumping of hazardous waste from other countries.

In the remainder of this chapter, we analyse these issues from a number of perspectives. In Section 8.2, using a simple general equilibrium model we show why gains from trade can occur. We then introduce domestic environmental policy into this model, to see how the outcome might be changed. Section 8.3 introduces predictions from a more sophisticated general equilibrium model and discusses the empirical evidence on links between trade and the environment. Section 8.4 discusses multilateral trade treaties and the environment.

8.2 Why do Countries Gain from Trade?

In this section, we introduce a simple general equilibrium (or whole-economy) model to provide an initial analysis of the effects of environmental policy and trade on the economy. A general equilibrium approach is warranted as trade liberalization affects the whole economy. The analysis starts with the idea of absolute advantage and then introduces comparative advantage as the 'driving force' of country specialization and trade.

Table 8.1 Trade and absolute advantage

Labour input needed per unit of output	UK	USA
Food	5 (5/2 cloth)	3 (3/6 cloth)
Cloth	2 (2/5 food)	6 (6/3 food)

Note: Opportunity costs are given in parentheses per unit of output.

In 1776, Adam Smith wrote:

What is prudence in the conduct of every private family, can scarce be folly in that of a great kingdom. If a foreign country can supply us with a commodity cheaper than we ourselves can make it, better buy it off them with some part of the produce of our own industry, employed in a way in which we have some advantage. The general industry of the country, being always in proportion to the capital which employs it, will not thereby be diminished . . . but only left to find out the way in which it can be employed with the greatest advantage.

(Adam Smith, 1776: book IV, ch. 2)

Here, Smith introduces the idea of *absolute advantage*; that is, a country specializing in the good that it can produce at the lowest cost. Consider the example in Table 8.1, in which two countries produce two goods, food and cloth, using a single factor of production, labour. Assume that transport costs are zero and that labour can be freely allocated between the two sectors.

If each country is endowed with 120 units of labour and under *autarky* (no trade) both countries, on the basis of what consumers demand, allocate 60 units of labour to each sector, this means that the United Kingdom will produce 12 units of food and 30 units of cloth (12, 30) and the USA 20 units of food and 10 units of cloth (20, 10).

If trade now opens up between the countries, which allows the UK to specialize by allocating all labour to cloth and the USA by allocating all labour to food production, this increases world production from (32 (food), 40 (cloth)) to (40 (food, USA), 60 (cloth, UK)). As long as the exchange rate of cloth for food between the two countries is less than the domestic opportunity cost of the good, there is a gain from trade. The opportunity cost is the amount of food that must be sacrificed to produce an extra unit of cloth and vice versa. Thus if trade between the UK and the USA opens at an exchange rate (terms of trade) of between 0.5 units (the opportunity cost of a unit of food in the USA) of cloth per unit of food and 2.5 units (the opportunity cost of food in the UK) of cloth per unit of food, trade will be mutually beneficial.

A more important concept than absolute advantage is that of *comparative advantage*, which was introduced by Ricardo in around 1817 (Sraffa, 1951–73: vol. I). This states that countries can gain from trade so long as the opportunity cost of producing goods is different between potential trading partners, even when there is no absolute cost advantage to one of the countries. Consider Table 8.2. The UK now has an absolute cost advantage in both sectors; however, total production can be increased if the UK transfers labour from food to cloth and the USA transfers labour from cloth to food. The outcome is illustrated in Figure 8.2.

Table 8.2 Trade and comparative advantage

Labour per unit of output	UK	USA
Food	5 (5/2 cloth)	6 (6/12 cloth)
Cloth	2 (2/5 food)	12 (12/6 food)

Note: Opportunity costs are given in parentheses.

Figure 8.2 shows the production possibility frontiers for the UK (PPF_{UK}) and the USA (PPF_{USA}). The consumption possibility frontiers for the UK (CPF_{UK}) and the USA (CPF_{USA}) show the possible rates of exchange between the two countries and the global production possibility frontier. In the absence of trade (autarky), the production possibility frontier also determines what a country can consume. Consider the diagram for the UK. The production possibility frontier gives the maximum combinations of cloth and food that can be produced. The slope of the production possibility frontier also tells us how much cloth the UK has to give up if it wishes to produce an extra unit of food. This is the opportunity cost of a unit of food in terms of cloth. How is this calculated? One unit of food requires 5 units of labour and cloth requires 2 units of labour per unit; therefore an extra unit of food means that the UK must forgo 2.5 (5/2) units of cloth.

Figure 8.2 also shows the consumption opportunities that a country has with free trade. The global production possibility frontier (PPF) adds together the UK PPF and the USA PPF.

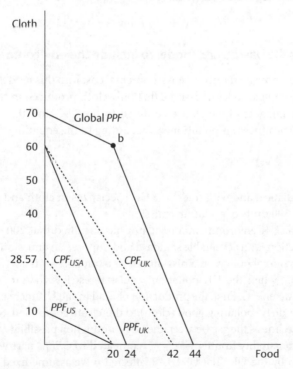

Figure 8.2 Comparative advantage.

Thus the maximum cloth production is 70 units, which includes 60 from the UK and 10 from the USA; whilst the maximum food production is 44, which includes 24 from the UK and 20 from the USA. However, which country should specialize in food and which in cloth? It is now that we compare the opportunity costs in the two countries. The opportunity cost of food in the USA is 0.5 units of cloth, while in the UK it is 2.5 units of cloth. Thus the USA specializes in food production and the UK in cloth. At point *b* in Figure 8.2 on the global *PPF*, the USA specializes completely in food and the UK completely in cloth.

Trade opens up between the countries and there is an exchange rate that gives the units of cloth per unit of food. A country will trade at any exchange rate that is less than the opportunity cost of production. For instance, the UK will accept an exchange rate for cloth of less than 2.5 units of cloth per unit of food and the USA will accept an exchange rate of greater than 0.5 units of cloth per unit of food.

Let us assume that trade opens between the two countries at an exchange rate of 0.7 units of food per unit of cloth, and that this implies 1.43 units of cloth per unit of food. This exchange rate is represented by the consumption possibility frontiers (CPF_{UK}, CPF_{USA}). The slope of these lines gives the exchange rate as cloth per unit of food. The gains from trade are measured as the vertical distance between the *PPF* and the *CPF*; that is, the extra cloth that can be consumed for any given level of food consumption.

This section has established that if a country has a comparative advantage in a good, then it can specialize in that good and gain by trading with another country. The gain is in terms of increased global output and thus consumption. Next, we consider how this outcome changes when one or more of the goods generate external costs, such as pollution, in its production process.

8.2.1 Extending the basic trade model to include the environment

What happens if we now introduce an environmental cost into this model? This could make the model quite complex, so let us assume that only cloth produced in the UK imposes an external cost, the impacts of which are confined to the UK, and that everything else is unchanged. Cloth produces air pollution e_{UK} according to the equation:

$$e_{UK} = 5Cloth_{UK}.$$

Thus without regulation and with trade, the UK specializes in cloth and produces 60 units of cloth, and thus 300 units of polluting emissions.

Imagine that the UK environmental regulator has specified that 200 units of emissions from cloth production is an acceptable standard and imposes an emission standard through a command-and-control policy, an emission tax, or a tradable emission permit scheme.

From Figure 8.3, when the UK pollution regulator restricts the production of cloth to 40 units, this has two effects. First, the production of food in the UK increases as resources are switched from the 'dirty' polluting good (cloth) to the 'clean' good, food. Second, gains from trade for the UK decline as the gap between the UK's production possibility frontier PPF_{UK} and the consumption possibility frontier $CPF_{UK(reg)}$ compared to CPF_{UK} narrows for each level of food consumption by the UK. The USA is unaffected if we assume fixed terms of trade for cloth; however, if the reduction in cloth by the UK means that there is an increase in the terms of trade for cloth (more food is required per unit of cloth), then the CPF_{USA} will pivot back towards the origin, and consumption of cloth at any given level of food production will fall.

It is not possible to conclude from the analysis presented in Figure 8.3 that the pollution regulation is welfare reducing. This is because the reduction in pollution may be of greater value to the population of the UK than the reduction in gains to trade. Our conclusions might also change if pollution is associated with the consumption of a traded good, rather than its production.

8.2.2 Trade and the environment

We have now established the basic concept of comparative advantage and analysed one possible effect of domestic environmental policy on trade. Copeland and Taylor (2003) explore the interactions between trade, growth, and the environment using a general equilibrium model (whole economy) for a small open (open to trade) economy. From this theoretical base, they develop a framework for empirical analysis of trade patterns. The full version of their model is quite complex; therefore our analysis presents a simplified version.

A *production possibility frontier*, *PPF*, gives the maximum output of goods that can be produced in a country given its resources (capital and labour) and technology. Figure 8.3 shows a more typical *PPF* than the linear *PPFs* given in Figure 8.1. As we already know, the slope of a *PPF* gives the opportunity cost of good *X* in terms of good *Y*; however, in Figure 8.3 the *PPF* has a concave shape that indicates that as resources are switched from one good to another,

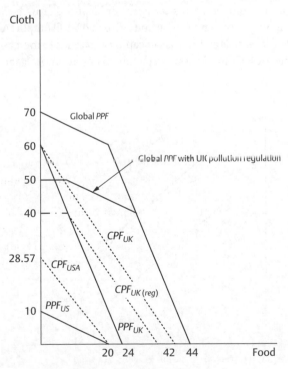

Figure 8.3 The effects of domestic environmental policy on trade.

the opportunity cost of producing more is increasing. This is because the resources switched from producing Y to producing X are progressively less well suited to the production of X.

Where does a country choose to produce on its *PPF*? Price signals will dictate the mix of X and Y, and with free trade these prices will be determined on world markets. Here, we assume that a country aims to maximize revenue or national income given by

$$G = p_x X + p_y Y.$$

National income is represented in Figure 8.4 as the line labelled p, and for any level of national income this line has the slope $-(p_x/p_y)$. Thus the highest attainable national income is where the line p is just tangent to the *PPF*. In other words, the price ratio that gives the exchange rate of Y for X just equals the opportunity cost of an extra unit of X in terms of output forgone of Y. The slope of the *PPF* is called the marginal rate of transformation. In Figure 8.4, the equilibrium is a point a. Other solutions, such as any point along the price line p', are sub-optimal as national income can be increased by moving out to the frontier, while output combinations along p'' are infeasible.

To introduce the environment into this model, we assume that one good X generates pollution Z, whilst producing the other good Y is clean. Therefore growth—for instance, as a result of *trade liberalization* that leads to an increase in the output of X—will increase pollution, if everything else in the economy is kept the same. Following on from Grossman and Krueger (1993), Copeland and Taylor (2003) distinguish between different effects of growth on the economy and environment. The *scale effect*, or balanced growth effect, involves equal proportional increases in labour and capital and a rise in overall output. A *composition effect*, or capital accumulation, entails an increase in capital and tends to increase output in capital-intensive dirty industries. Composition effects can also refer more generally to changes in

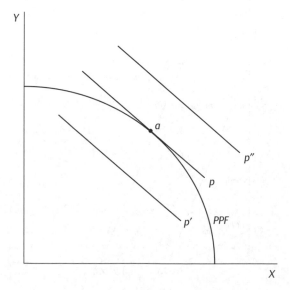

Figure 8.4 The production possibility frontier and national income.

the structure of a domestic economy because of trade, and the effects on pollution that this leads to: for example, if expanding exporting industries are relatively 'dirty', or if trade results in the import of dirty products and reduction in domestic production (Runge, 1995). The *technique effect* involves a policy change that leads to firms switching to less pollution-intensive production techniques. Such a policy change may be induced by increased consumer income that results in pressure upon politicians to reduce pollution. This is an example of how trade may induce an environmental Kuznets curve (EKC, see Chapter 6). We consider each of these effects in turn using diagrams.

The scale of the economy is measured as the total value of X and Y at fixed world prices. The *scale effect* is illustrated in Figure 8.5(i). An increase in capital and labour pushes the *PPF* outwards, this leads to an increase in output of both goods and an increase in pollution shown in the bottom panel of the diagram. The equilibrium shifts from a to b and the pollution increases (downwards in the bottom panel) from Z_a to Z_b. Note that the price of the dirty good X is adjusted to account for the costs of paying an emission tax.

The *composition effect* involves capital accumulation and a shift in share of output from the clean output Y to the capital-intensive polluting output X. From Figure 8.5(ii), the equilibrium shifts from a to b and pollution increases from Z_a to Z_b.

The *technique effect* can come from a policy shift that, by increasing an emission tax (say), induces firms to adopt a technology that reduces emissions per unit of output. This change in techniques is represented in the lower panel. Changing technique with a constant output reduces emissions from Z_a to $Z_{a'}$, but the resources used for abatement pivot the *PPF* towards the origin along the X-axis. This leads to a new equilibrium at b and a lower final level of pollution with the new technique of $Z_{b'}$.

These three effects measure how the economy changes in response to growth (scale and composition effects) and policy (technique effects). Technological changes may also result

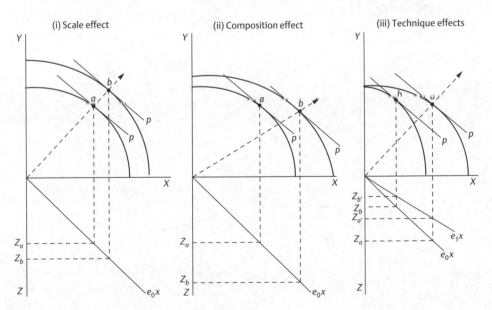

Figure 8.5 Scale, composition, and technique effects.

from other factors (such as exogenous technological change, or changes in consumer preferences). The model developed by Copeland and Taylor (2003) is also a basis for determining an
optimal level of pollution. In their model, pollution is viewed as an input into the production
of X. It could also be treated equivalently as a joint output, but let us treat it as an input. Like any
other input then, the amount demanded of the pollution input depends upon its price. The
price of emissions is an emission tax (or the price in a tradable emission permit market). The
economy will continue to demand pollution up to the point at which the marginal benefit of
pollution is equal to the emission tax. More specifically, the marginal benefit is the change in
the national income $G(p, K, L, z)$ with respect to pollution where pollution is treated as an input,
shown by G_z. The equilibrium demand for pollution is illustrated in Figure 8.6.

Thus we have established a demand curve, but for equilibrium we also need to consider
the marginal costs, or supply, of pollution. The marginal damage MD for a representative
(typical) consumer is given by their willingness to pay (WTP) to reduce emissions by one
unit. As income increases, it is expected that the willingness to pay for MD will increase.
Consumers face a trade-off, as pollution tends to increase their incomes and thus their utility, but by degrading the environment pollution is also utility reducing. Define the total willingness to pay as $N.MD$, where N is the population of the country. In conventional
microeconomics, supply curves for a firm are the marginal cost (above the average variable
cost), whereas here the supply cost is society's marginal damage (cost) from pollution. Thus
society's willingness to allow pollution depends upon the marginal cost of pollution.

As we saw in Chapter 6, the EKC analyses a relationship between income and pollution.
A common assumption is that as growth occurs and income increases pollution initially
rises, but as income increases beyond a level then society prefers a reduction in pollution,
causing emissions to fall. From Figure 8.6, an increase in income per capita would shift the

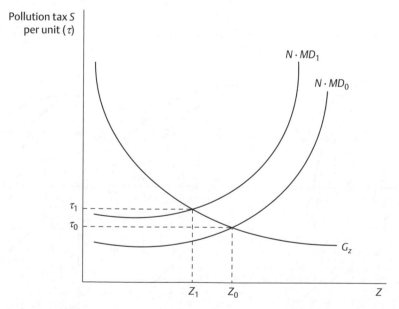

Figure 8.6 Optimal pollution.
Source: Copeland and Taylor (2003).

supply curve for pollution upwards as higher incomes increases the WTP and thus marginal damages. This is shown in Figure 8.6 as the new equilibrium at (τ_1, Z_1). This demonstrates the theoretical possibility of an EKC in an open economy. A complication is that growth can shift both G_z and $N.MD$ simultaneously, leading to outcomes that may also increase pollution. This analysis is found in Copeland and Taylor (2003: ch. 3).

8.3 Empirical Evidence on the Trade Effects of Environmental Regulation

There have been numerous studies of links between trade and the environment (for reviews, see Copeland and Taylor, 2003; Sheldon, 2006). Figure 8.7, from Frankel and Rose (2002), summarizes the links and possible causality, and poses a set of hypotheses relating to links between trade and the environment.

1. The link between trade openness and real income per capita is expected by comparative advantage to be strongly positive.
2. As GDP increase represents an increase in output, this is expected to have a positive effect on pollution (a detrimental effect on environmental quality) due to the scale of production.

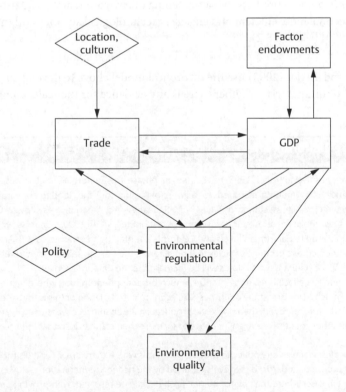

Figure 8.7 Possible causal links between trade and the environment.
Source: Based on Frankel and Rose (2002: 9).

3. If a country achieves a high income per capita, this raises the public's demand for environmental quality, and if the country's political institutions (the 'polity') are effective, leads to tighter environmental regulations. At the same time, pollution per unit of output may be modified by the composition effect and reduced by the technique effect. A negative effect of growth on the environmental is expected at low incomes, whereas the positive effect dominates at high incomes.

4. At a given level of GDP per capita, are more open economies better or worse for the environment? This may be viewed as the main trade effect and a test of the effects of globalization. One hypothesis is a so-called *regulatory chill*, where governments are reluctant to introduce new environmental regulation that will make domestic industry less competitive. This may become a *race-to-the-bottom* hypothesis, where countries progressively relax their environmental regulations in competition for inward investment. An alternative hypothesis is the *gains from trade* hypothesis (Frankel and Rose, 2005). Here, countries use open trade to reduce the detrimental effects on the environment of their domestic firms and also to obtain market goods (for an alternative hypothesis known as the California effect, see Box 8.1).

5. The *pollution haven hypothesis* predicts that trade openness leads to multinational companies switching production to developing countries with lax environmental regulations. This entails capital moving from one country to another.

6. The *Porter hypothesis* predicts that a tightening of environmental standards will induce firms to become more efficient and engage in technological advance and innovation (Porter, 1990) (see Box 8.2).

Copeland and Taylor (2003) use the theoretical model above to develop an econometric model of pollution that tests whether there is any evidence for the scale, composition, and

---

BOX 8.1 The California Effect

The political scientist David Vogel (1995) has coined the phrase 'the California effect' to describe the situation in which environmental standards for a group of trading countries tend to converge upon those of the country with the highest standards. The 1970 US Clean Air Act Amendments allowed California to enact stricter automobile emission standards than the rest of the USA. In 1990, Congress brought national emission standards up to Californian levels and California adopted tighter standards still. American automobile manufacturers produce vehicles to the California standard to sell to that market, and also in anticipation that the standards in all states will be increased to the Californian level.

The term 'California effect' is used to describe a much broader phenomenon where tighter regulatory standards are matched in competing countries. The economic explanation of this is that as one country's product standards are improved, then domestic producers have an initial competitive advantage in the market, so that other countries have an incentive to increase their standards so that their producers can compete.

Vogel advocates a *laissez-faire* policy to product standards where there are incentives for countries to increase their product standards to the levels required by the richer, greener nations. However, this effect is only relevant in cases where the environmental problem can be resolved by improving product standards.

BOX 8.2 The Porter Hypothesis

In an article in *Scientific American*, Porter (1990) challenges the notion that tight environmental policies inevitably lead to increased production costs, which reduce the competitiveness of a country's industry and therefore reduce its export competitiveness. Instead, he claims that tighter environmental standards trigger innovations that may increase a firm's competitiveness and outweigh short-run costs to firms of complying with the regulation. The so-called 'Porter hypothesis' is supported by evidence from case studies, which shows that some firms operating under strict environmental regulations have shown relatively high levels of performance. The empirical evidence in Tobey (1990) and Jaffe et al. (1995) indicates that there is very little evidence to indicate that tighter environmental regulations significantly reduce competitiveness, which may be largely explained by the small proportion of costs associated with complying with pollution standards.

The two reasons why Porter's hypothesis may be correct: first, environmental regulations make firms aware of opportunities for changing production activities in ways not previously identified; second, firms subject to stricter environmental standards than their foreign competitors may be at a competitive advantage when environmental standards are tightened in their competitors' markets.

Arguments against the Porter hypothesis include: first, why should rational firms need to be prompted by environmental regulation to find new techniques that improve their competitiveness; second, if environmental regulations are not tightened, the firm operating under the lax environmental standard has a permanent competitive advantage.

At present, there is no theoretical justification (Xepapadeas and de Zeeuw, 1999) for the Porter hypothesis and no conclusive empirical evidence. However, it received widespread attention because it provided an attractive model to policy-makers attempting to justify tighter environmental regulations to industrialists.

---

technique effects. The dependent variable to be explained is the concentration (parts per million) of sulphur dioxide pollution in a selection of cities from 1971 to 1995. Sulphur dioxide is chosen as an important pollutant that has detrimental effects on human health and causes environmental damage through acid rain. Sulphur dioxide is also correlated with a range of other air pollutants, such as nitrogen oxides and particulates.

The general equilibrium effects mentioned above are measured by a set of proxy variables; thus the scale effect is measured as the GDP per square kilometre, to measure the intensity of economic activity. Composition effects are measured by the capital-to-labour ratio; thus if (K/L) is relatively large, this would tend to favour pollution-intensive industries. The technique effect is measured indirectly as an income effect. The results are given in Table 8.3 in elasticity form; that is, as the percentage increase in sulphur dioxide emissions for a 1 per cent increase in the value of a variable. Elasticities are calculated at the mean values.

Table 8.3 Elasticities of SO_2 emissions

	Elasticity
Scale effect (measured by GDP per km²)	0.315
Composition effect (capital/labour)	0.993
Technique effect (per capita income)	−1.577
Trade intensity (exports plus imports)/GDP	−0.394

Source: Copeland and Taylor (2003: 25, table 7.4).

We can see that a 1 per cent increase in the scale of economic activity leads to a 0.315 per cent increase in sulphur dioxide concentrations. The technique effect indicates a strong policy response, as income increases on average lead to a reduction in pollution. Similarly, a country that has higher trade (exports plus imports) as a large proportion of GDP tends to have lower emissions. The analysis lends little support to the pollution haven hypothesis, which predicts that with trade liberalization, rich countries will shift dirty industries to poor countries with lax environmental policy. Instead, the composition effect indicates that dirty industries are shifting to the developed countries. This is because these industries are capital intensive, and thus a factor endowment effect is dominating a pollution haven effect. The overall conclusion of the study is that pollution as measured by sulphur dioxide has been reduced by more open trade. However, the authors also conclude that there is no simple relationship between trade, income per capita, and pollution.

The work by Copeland and Taylor (2003) depends critically on the pollutant selected, the time period(s), and the countries/jurisdictions included. Frankel and Rose (2005) identify a potential issue in that pollution and trade are determined simultaneously, and therefore it is not possible to determine directly how trade affects the environment. Using data from 1990, the authors estimate the following function:

$$Environmental\ damage = f(GDP\ per\ capita, (GDP\ per\ capita)^2,$$
$$Trade\ intensity, Polity, Land\ per\ capita).$$

Environmental damage stands for a range of pollutants and environmental effects, such as deforestation. *GDP per capita* is a measure of income, the purpose of the squared term being to pick up an EKC effect, whereby as income increases beyond a point environmental damage starts to decline. *Trade intensity* is estimated as the sum of imports plus exports divided by GDP, and *Polity* measures how democratic a country is. Finally, *Land per capita* is a measure of a country's capacity to assimilate pollution.

The results for three pollutants SO_2, NO_2, and particulate matter (PM) all lend strong support to an EKC, in that the square term on GDP is negative and statistically significant: thus countries start to reduce these pollutants once per capita income reaches a critical point. The key focus of this analysis is on trade openness: here, the trade intensity tends to reduce SO_2 and NO_2 and has no effect on PM. When the environmental damage variable is CO_2, trade intensity has a negligible effect on emissions, but the EKC never 'turns down'. According to the authors, this indicates that a global agreement will probably be needed to address CO_2 emissions, as there is no indication that as incomes increase, CO_2 emissions will be reduced by domestic environmental regulation.

The results discussed are not able to test for a pollution haven effect; that is, if net exports of dirty goods are deterred by tougher environmental regulations in developed countries. The pollution haven hypothesis predicts that pollution-intensive industries will relocate to developing countries as environmental regulation is made more stringent in the developed countries (Taylor, 2004). The presence of a pollution haven effect could be a precursor to pollution-intensive firms shifting overseas. There is evidence for the pollution haven effect (Levinson and Taylor, 2008) from data for Mexico, Canada, and the USA. The results show that industries with the largest increase in abatement cost also had the largest increase in net

BOX 8.3 Testing the Pollution Haven Hypothesis

For a multinational firm, a decision to disinvest in a home market and shift production to another country involves a number of considerations. To illustrate their theoretical model, Eskeland and Harrison (2003) consider the example of a steel producer. The government introduces tighter environmental regulations; this shifts the firm's average cost up and will reduce profits in the short run. In the long run (when capital investments can be made), the firm will consider investing in new steel furnace capable of meeting the emission standards or will switch investment to an overseas market. This decision will depend upon all the factors that determine the firm's profitability, including the costs of environmental compliance.

In their empirical analysis, Eskeland and Harrison (2003) take patterns of foreign investment in four developing countries: Mexico, Morocco, Ivory Coast, and Venezuela. They explain foreign investment as a function of variables such as abatement costs (in the investing country), market size, wage rates, and regulatory barriers. The results from a regression analysis yield no evidence that foreign investment in the selected developing countries relates to abatement costs in industrialized countries that are the source of foreign investment. Further, they find that foreign plants (as a result of foreign investment) are significantly more energy efficient and use cleaner types of energy than the domestic companies. The authors conclude that:

> The relationship between investment and regulation is not as simple as assumed in a naive model. It depends on a number of factors, the combined effects of which may be positive, zero or negative. We also find that foreign firms are less polluting than their peers in developing countries. This does not in any way mean that 'pollution havens' cannot exist, or that we should cease to worry about pollution in developing countries. However, our research does suggest that policy makers should pursue pollution control policy focusing on pollution itself, rather than on investment or particular investors.

(op. cit.: 22)

The pollution haven hypothesis remains a controversial concept in economics, in politics, and amongst environmentalists.

imports. This suggests that there is the potential for firms to take production of 'dirty goods' to other countries with lower abatement costs (for a study with a different conclusion, see Box 8.3).

However, Taylor (2004), in reviewing a range of other empirical studies (Ederington et al., 2004; Elbers and Withagen, 2004; Fredriksson and Mani, 2004), concludes that there is no strong evidence for the pollution haven hypothesis, and that the decisions by firms to locate in a country depend on a range of factors—such as labour costs—that are probably more important than the costs of pollution control.

8.4 International Trade Agreements and the Environment

8.4.1 International trade agreements

Multilateral trade negotiations under the General Agreement on Tariffs and Trade have their origins after the Second World War, when memories of the damaging protectionism of the 1930s led the UK and the USA to plan for more stable trade relations. The Bretton Woods Conference in 1944 proposed setting up three international organizations, the International Monetary Fund (IMF), the International Trade Organization (ITO), and the International Bank for Reconstruction and Development (IBRD). While negotiations were taking place on the form of the ITO, a group of countries recognized the need for immediate reductions in tariffs. The USA took the lead by drafting a general agreement on tariffs and trade, and later this was agreed to by twenty-three countries, as the GATT. Despite subsequent negotiations, the ITO never came into existence, leaving the GATT as the most important framework for trade relations. In 1995, 100 countries accounting for 80 per cent of world trade were signatories to the GATT. An additional twenty-nine countries abided by GATT rules.

In 1995, the GATT was replaced by the World Trade Organization, which inherited from the GATT the following objectives: first, to provide a forum for multilateral trade negotiations; second, to provide a framework for eliminating trade barriers; and third, to provide agreed rules to reduce unilateral trade-restricting action. These objectives are pursued by a set of thirty-eight Articles, which form the basis for resolving disputes. These Articles embody three basic principles:

- Non-discrimination, or the most-favoured nation (MFN) clause—which binds WTO signatories to treat all sources of imports for a good equally. Thus if one country reduces the tariff on timber from another country, it must extend this new tariff to all countries. This principle acts as a disincentive to bilateral trade agreements.

- Reciprocity—the principle that if one country agrees to reduce tariffs, then another country should agree to reduce tariffs, in order to leave their bilateral balance of trade unchanged.

- Transparency—a principle that, in most cases, involves the elimination of quantitative trade restrictions in favour of tariffs. It is argued that tariffs should be clear to exporters and domestic consumers.

When the GATT was established, there was no explicit reference to environmental issues, and it is only recently that the GATT and WTO have been asked to adjudicate on barriers to trade justified on environmental grounds. The GATT/WTO approach is best illustrated with some examples. Most product-related environmental policies do not conflict with WTO rules provided that they apply equally to domestic and imported products. This is the principle of the most favoured nation; thus if Germany requires domestic cars to carry catalytic converters and seat belts, it can impose these standards upon importers, but it cannot require imported cars to comply with more stringent standards. Countries can also adopt a range of policies to protect the domestic environment, including restrictions on emissions to air and water, but they cannot extend these standards to imported products unless they physically affect the final product. An imported product should not be treated differently from an identical domestic product on the grounds that the production process is different.

This basic principle has led countries wishing to restrict trade on the grounds of process and products to invoke Article XX, which allows for exceptions to general GATT principles where 'necessary to protect human, animal or plant life or health' (Article XX(b)) and where relating to the conservation of an exhaustible natural resource, if such measures are made in conjunction with restrictions on domestic production or consumption (Article XX(g)). The application of this article is informative in the case of the dolphin–tuna dispute between the USA and Mexico.

In eastern tropical areas of the Pacific Ocean, schools of yellowfin tuna are often found swimming beneath dolphins. When the tuna is harvested with purse seine nets, some dolphins become trapped and often die unless released quickly. The US Marine Mammal Protection Act set out fishing methods that the American fishing fleet must comply with and which extend to other countries fishing in the American zone of the Pacific Ocean. A country exporting tuna to the USA must prove that it meets the dolphin protection standards; otherwise, an embargo will be placed on all fish exports from that country.

In particular, the USA banned tuna exports from Mexico and also a number of intermediary countries handling Mexican tuna *en route* to the USA on the grounds that Mexican fishing methods were not dolphin friendly. Mexico requested a GATT panel in February 1991 and this reported in September 1991. The panel concluded that the USA could not embargo imports of tuna products from Mexico simply because Mexican regulations on methods of tuna fishing were less strict than American regulations. However, the USA could apply its regulations to the quality of the product. It also concluded that GATT rules did not permit one country to use trade policy as a means of coercing another to enforce its domestic laws in another country.

This ruling is important in that it reinforced the principle that products should be judged on their quality alone, not on the process used in their production. However, the panel deemed it acceptable for the USA to allow advertising to identify brands of tuna as being 'dolphin-friendly'. Mexico's complaint was upheld by the panel, but the panel's report was not adopted and the disagreement was eventually resolved bilaterally between the USA and Mexico. Trade disputes due to domestic environmental regulation have also arisen in the European Union: for an example, see Box 8.4.

In 1995, the World Trade Organization was established as the successor to the GATT, providing the framework under which multilateral trade negotiations take place. In the preamble to the Marrakech Agreement (1994) that set up the WTO, reference is made to sustainable development and environmental preservation. The WTO has become more involved in resolving conflicts where trade policy and environmental concerns interact. To this end, the WTO has established a Trade and Environment Committee to bring environmental and sustainable development issues into the mainstream of WTO work (WTO, 2004). It remains to be seen whether it is feasible for a trade organization to become involved in environmental policy. The WTO makes it clear that it has a limited role in environmental policy: 'WTO Members recognize, however, that the WTO is not an environmental protection agency and that it does not aspire to become one. Its competence in the field of trade and environment is limited to trade policies and to the trade-related aspects of environmental policies which have a significant effect on trade' (WTO, 2004: 6).

8.4.2 Multilateral environmental agreements and trade

The theoretical models presented in Section 8.2 predict that trade restrictions offer a second-best, or sub-optimal, solution to local, transboundary, and global environmental problems. The first-best or optimal solution is found by either taxing emissions or introducing a tradable permit system. Multilateral environmental agreements should be coupled with optimal national environmental policies to achieve the agreed standard. This principle holds for both transboundary and global pollution problems.

BOX 8.4 European Environmental Regulation and Trade

Article 30 of the 1957 Treaty of Rome aimed to foster the freedom of trade between the member states of the European Community by preventing 'quantitative restrictions on trade', but Article 36 of the same treaty states that trade may be restricted on the grounds of 'public morality, public policy or public security' or for the 'protection of health and life of humans, animals or plants'. Thus it allowed countries to restrict trade so long as it was justified on one of these counts. So when is a domestic environmental policy little more than a form of disguised protectionism?

In 1981, Denmark enacted legislation requiring all beer and soft drinks to be sold in a range of reusable containers accredited by the Danish environmental protection agency. Containers used by exporters to Denmark often did not meet the strict Danish recycling requirements and their sale was prohibited. The foreign companies complained that the extra costs involved in modifying their containers and arranging collection and transportation in Denmark would reduce their competitiveness. Manufacturers took their case to the European Commission, who ruled that the Danish law contravened Article 30. Not satisfied by Denmark's modification of the law in 1984, in December 1986 the European Commission took the case to the European Court of Justice. This step was taken because there was a fear that countries would justify protectionist laws on environmental grounds.

In September 1988, the Court ruled that Denmark's deposit and return system was legal under Article 36, because there was no alternative means of reducing the amount of waste. However, Denmark was required to remove the restrictions on the type of container: any container could be used so long as it was recycled.

This ruling was highly significant: for the first time the Court had sanctioned an environmental regulation that restricted trade. This led the German government to enact very strict recycling laws, which were also restrictive to trade. The implication was that, even within the Single European Market, countries could introduce legislation that restricted trade so long as it was justified on environmental grounds. For a fuller account, see Vogel (1995: ch. 3).

Unfortunately, there is little evidence that national economic policies—even in relatively green developed countries—are close to being optimal, and in many developing countries environmental policies may be weak or ineffectively enforced. The first-best optimum is therefore unattainable and regulators are compelled to choose from among second-best policies an option that, at least partially, achieves environmental objectives. This argument goes some way to explaining why multilateral environmental agreements include trade restrictions as the primary policy instrument. Examples include the Montreal Protocol and CITES, discussed below. Trade flows, because they involve movement across national boundaries, provide an opportunity for monitoring and restricting the flow of materials. This may curtail the environmental damage due to a particular product in the absence of effective national policies. We have also seen in Chapter 7 how difficult it is to set up voluntary international agreements for the control of global pollutants or the protection of global public goods, since countries have an incentive to free-ride on such agreements. Trade sanctions provide a means of encouraging participation in agreements and penalizing signatories that step out of line. The following policies provide examples.

The United Nations Convention on International Trade in Endangered Species of Wild Fauna (CITES) was ratified in 1973. It regulated trade in species that are threatened with extinction (Appendix 1 species) and those species that may become extinct unless trade is strictly regulated (Appendix 2 species). Trade is regulated by a system of export and import permits: the requirement for an import permit before an export permit is issued is an attempt to prevent exporters from sending live animals or animal products to countries that are not party to the convention. This policy aims to reduce the incentive to exploit rare or endangered species through trade, but can be seen as a second-best substitute for effective national policies that protect species and their habitats within countries.

The 1987 Montreal Protocol is an application of the 1985 Vienna Convention regarding substances that cause depletion of the ozone layer. The parties to the original protocol agreed to reduce chlorofluorocarbons (CFCs) by 50 per cent by 1999. Negotiations in London in 1990 led to agreement that production of CFCs should cease in 1996. Further meetings in Copenhagen (1992) and Montreal (1997) increased the list of substances subject to restrictions (for details, see http://ozone.unep.org/new_site/en/index.php). The Copenhagen (1992) meeting agreed not to export or import restricted substances and to ban imports of products containing CFCs by 1993. This policy includes both agreements over domestic production and consumption of these products, and is also backed up by trade measures that prevent countries that have not ratified the treaty from becoming potential markets for these products. This is an example of where a trade policy is used as an effective complement to multilateral environmental agreements and effective domestic policies. Trade policy is only used to prevent non-parties to the agreement eroding the effectiveness of the restrictions agreed, and signatories from defaulting on their commitments.

The Basel Convention on the Control of Transboundary Movements of Hazardous Waste and their Disposal allows restrictions to trade in hazardous waste. It forces countries to focus on national solutions to industrial waste problems and protects export countries from being used as dumping grounds. Thus the convention establishes that exports of waste should only be with the importing country's permission (as distinct from importing companies). If an exporting country believes that waste will not be disposed of in an environmentally sound manner, then it should not be exported. Trade with non-signatory countries is not allowed (UNEP, 2011).

Summary

Trade flows have a profound effect on national economies and must therefore have a significant effect on national environments. Simplistically, trade increases economic growth, production, and consumption, and due to the fact that more production requires more natural resources, an increase in trade is likely to lead to an increase in pollution. However, increased trade also leads to a specialization of production, which may occur in countries where inputs are used more efficiently or in 'pollution havens', countries with lax environmental standards. The empirical evidence suggests that the effects of stringent environmental standards on a country's competitiveness is rather slight, and that countries with lax environmental standards will not necessarily become pollution havens because firms place more importance upon factors other than environmental costs when deciding where to locate.

From the theoretical and empirical analysis, there is no clear justification for restricting trade on environmental grounds. Free trade for most countries is welfare-increasing and, so long as countries have effective domestic environmental policies, there is no reason why it should be more damaging to the environment than restricted trade. Trade policies are almost always sub-optimal instruments for protecting a country's environment and should be replaced by domestic environmental policies. The question arising from this is thus why are trade restrictions used as a major component of environmental policies? First, environmental justifications for trade restrictions are sometimes little more than covert protectionism. Second, in the case of international environmental agreements, they are a sub-optimal alternative where the failure of countries' domestic environmental policies may have consequences on the global environment. Examples include, the Montreal Protocol, CITES, and the Basel Convention on Hazardous Waste. In all these cases, using trade restrictions might be the best approach that is available.

Finally, in a world in which countries compete both for inward investment and for global market shares, it is not surprising that environmental policies are sometimes used as ways of helping to achieve these objectives. But this could be consistent both with an increasing level of environmental protection (competing for 'green' consumers or green inward investment) and a lowering of standards, as for the pollution havens hypothesis.

Tutorial Questions

8.1 You have been invited to take part in a debate with the proposal that 'Globalization is Bad for the Environment'. What would your three main points be if you were to argue for the proposal? Which three arguments would you have against the proposal?

8.2 Distinguish between the pollution haven hypothesis and the Porter hypothesis in relation to trade and the environment.

8.3 When is it justifiable to use trade tariffs and trade quotas as a substitute for domestic environmental policy?

8.4 Distinguish between the scale effect and the composition effect of trade liberalization.

8.5 What is the link between trade and the environmental Kuznets curve?

References and Additional Readings

Cline, W. (2004). *Trade Policy and Global Poverty* (Washington, DC: Institute for International Economics).

Copeland, B.R., and Taylor, M.S. (2003), 'Trade growth, and the environment', *Journal of Economic Literature* 62: 7–71.

— and — (2004). *Trade and the Environment: Theory and Evidence* (Princeton, NJ: Princeton University Press).

Ederington, J., Levinson, A., and Minier, J. (2004). 'Trade liberalization and pollution havens', *Advances in Economic Analysis and Policy* 4(2), Article 6.

Elbers, C., and Withagen, C. (2004). 'Environmental policy, population dynamics and agglomeration',

Contributions to Economic Analysis and Policy 3(2), Article 3.

Eskeland, G.S., and Harrison, A.E. (2003). 'Moving to greener pastures? Multinationals and the pollution haven hypothesis', *Journal of Development Economics* 70: 1–23.

Esty, D.C. (1994). *Greening the GATT: Trade, Environment, and the Future* (Washington, DC: Institute for International Economics).

Frankel, J.A., and Rose, A.K. (2002). 'Is trade good or bad for the environment? Sorting out the causality', NEBR Working Paper No. 9201.

— and — (2005). 'Is free trade good or bad for the environment? Sorting out the causality', *Review of Economics and Statistics* 87: 85–91.

Fredriksson, P., and Mani, M. (2004). 'Trade integration and political turbulence: environmental policy consequences', *Advances in Economic Analysis and Policy* 4(2), Article 3.

GATT Panel (1987). 'United States—taxes on petroleum and certain imported substances 1987. Report of the Panel, 17 June 1987', GATT Doc.L/6175,BISD 34S/136 (Geneva: GATT).

Grossman, G.M., and Krueger, A.B. (1993). 'Environmental impacts of a North American free trade agreement', in P.M. Garber (ed.), *The US–Mexico Free Trade Agreement* (Cambridge, MA: The MIT Press): 13–56.

Hudec, R.E. (1996). 'GATT legal restraints on the use of trade measures against foreign environmental practices', in J. Bhagwati and R.E. Hudec (eds.), *Fair Trade and Harmonization: Prerequisites for Free Trade?* (Cambridge, MA: The MIT Press): 95–174.

Jaffe, A.B., Peterson, S.R., Portney, P.R., and Stavins, R.N. (1995). 'Environmental regulation and the competitiveness of US manufacturing: What does the evidence tell us?' *Journal of Economic Literature* 33: 132–63.

Jaunky, V.C. (2011). 'The CO_2 emissions–income nexus: evidence from rich countries', *Energy Policy* 39: 1228–40.

Kander, A., and Lindmark, M. (2006). 'Foreign trade and declining pollution in Sweden', *Energy Policy* 34: 1590–9.

Krugman, P.R., and Obstfeld, M. (2009). *International Economics: Theory and Policy*, 8th edn. (Boston, MA: Pearson Addison-Wesley).

Levinson, A., and Taylor, M.S. (2008). 'Unmasking the pollution haven effect', *International Economic Review* 49: 223–54.

McGuire, M.C. (1982). 'Regulation, factor rewards and international trade', *Journal of Political Economy* 17: 335–54.

Petersmann, E., and Pollack, M.A. (2003). *Transatlantic Economic Disputes: The EU, the US, and the WTO* (Oxford: Oxford University Press).

Porter, P.R. (1990). 'America's green strategy', *Scientific American* 264: 168.

Runge, C.F. (1995). 'Trade pollution and environmental protection', in D.W. Bromley (ed.), *The Handbook of Environmental Economics* (Oxford: Blackwell).

Sheldon, I. (2006). 'Trade and environmental policy: a race to the bottom?' *Journal of Agricultural Economics* 57(3): 365–92.

Smith, A. (1776). *The Wealth of Nations*, book IV: 2 (New York: Modern Library edition).

Sraffa, P. (1951–73). *The Works and Correspondence of David Ricardo*, 11 vols (Cambridge: Cambridge University Press).

Taylor, M.S. (2004). 'Unbundling the pollution haven hypothesis', *Advances in Economic Analysis and Policy* 4, Article 8.

Tobey, J.A. (1990) 'The effects of domestic environmental policies on patterns of world trade: an empirical test', *Kyklos* 43: 191–209.

UNEP (United Nations Environment Programme) (2011). Basel Convention, http://www.basel.int/convention/about.html (accessed 24 June 2011).

Vogel, D. (1995). *Trading Up: Consumer and Environmental Regulation in the Global Economy* (Cambridge, MA: Harvard University Press).

WTO (World Trade Organization) (1997). 'Taxes and charges for environmental purposes—border tax adjustments', Committee on Trade and the Environment, WT/CTE/W/47 (Geneva: WTO).

—— (2004). *Trade and the Environment* (Geneva: WTO).

—— (2006). 'India etc. versus US: "Shrimp-turtle"', *Environment: Disputes* 8, http://www.wto.org/english/tratop_e/envir_e/edis08_e.htm (accessed 1 May 2011).

—— (2010). 'Australia—Measures affecting the importation of apples from New Zealand', *Dispute Settlement: Dispute DS367*, http://www.wto.org/english/tratop_e/dispu_e/cases_e/ds367_e.htm (accessed 1 May 2011).

Xepapadeas, A., and de Zeeuw, A. (1999). 'Environmental policy and competitiveness: the Porter hypothesis and the composition of capital', *Journal of Environmental Economics and Management* 37: 165–82.

Part II

Applying the Tools

9 The Economics of Climate Change

We first explore the idea of climate change as a global environmental risk. We then discuss the challenge of finding an international agreement on how to control climate change risk. The next two sections examine the costs and benefits of international co-operation to control carbon emissions. Finally, we discuss the economic trade-off that exists in climate stringency and flexibility to hit this given emissions target.

9.1 Introduction

Imagine an invisible quilt covering the earth. Its warmth allows us to grow food, build shelters, and clothe ourselves. But a potential problem exists. Natural scientists warn us that the earth is getting warmer, and human actions have impacted the climate to its detriment: developing land, raising livestock, and burning fossil fuels are disrupting the planet's atmosphere—and the consequences could be devastating. The scientists base their argument on observed trends. First, the earth has warmed by 0.5°C, or 1°F, over the past 100 years. At the same time, atmospheric concentrations of greenhouse gases have increased by about 30 per cent over the past 200 years (see Table 9.1). These greenhouse gases consist principally of CO_2, methane, and N_2O; the latter two are expressed as 'carbon equivalents' when we measure a country's contribution to global warming.

Science has made a connection between these trends—or more precisely, scientists cannot reject the hypothesis that human-driven climate change exists today. This view is reflected by the scientists working for the Intergovernmental Panel on Climate Change (IPCC)—the international panel that has been assessing climate change for past two decades. The IPCC has concluded that the balance of evidence points towards human influence on the global climate. Many natural scientists and policy-makers continue to advocate for a worldwide reduction in greenhouse gas emissions. The implications of climate change policy are significant: restrictions on carbon emissions will affect everyone on the planet.

Today, climate change dominates environmental policy discussions. People need to understand and address the risks posed by climate change and the choices we have to reduce them. Economics offers a unique perspective to help frame the discussion about the costs and benefits of climate change policy. Investments to protect human and environmental

Table 9.1 Total carbon dioxide emissions of Annex 1 parties in 1990, for the purposes of Article 25 of the Kyoto Protocol

Party	Emissions (Gg)	Percentage
Australia	288,965	2.1
Austria	59,200	0.4
Belgium	113,405	0.8
Bulgaria	82,990	0.6
Canada	457,441	3.3
Czech Republic	169,514	1.2
Denmark	52,100	0.4
Estonia	37,797	0.3
Finland	53,900	0.4
France	366,536	2.7
Germany	1,012,443	7.4
Greece	82,100	0.6
Hungary	71,673	0.5
Iceland	2,172	0
Ireland	30,719	0.2
Italy	428,941	3.1
Japan	1,173,360	8.5
Latvia	22,976	0.2
Liechtenstein	208	0
Luxembourg	11,343	0.1
Monaco	71	0
Netherlands	167,600	1.2
New Zealand	25,530	0.2
Norway	35,533	0.3
Poland	414,930	3
Portugal	42,148	0.3
Romania	171,103	1.2
Russian Federation	2,388,720	17.4
Slovakia	58,278	0.4
Spain	260,654	1.9
Sweden	61,256	0.4
Switzerland	43,600	0.3
UK	584,078	4.3
USA	4,957,022	36.1
Total	13,728,306	100.0

Note: Data based on the information from the thirty-four Annex 1 parties that submitted their first national communications on or before 11 December 1997, as compiled by the secretariat in several documents (A/AC.237/81; FCCC/CP/1996/12/Add.2 and FCCC/SB/1997/6). Some of the communications included data on CO_2 emissions by sources and removals by sinks from land-use change and forestry, but since different ways of reporting were used these data are not included.

Source: Report of the Conference of the parties on its third session, held at Kyoto from 1 to 11 December 1997 FCCC/CP/1997/7/Add.1.

health from climate change can be thought of as 'planet insurance'. Planet insurance captures the idea that societies need to spend money today to help reduce future risks and damages. This chapter examines how we can use economics to understand how invest in planet insurance cost-effectively.

9.2 A Global Environmental Risk

Life on earth is possible because certain gases trap sunlight in our atmosphere and keep us warm—as in a greenhouse. Carbon dioxide (CO_2), mainly released from burning fossil fuels, is one such greenhouse gas. But in excess, those gases may work against us, holding in too much heat, blocking outward radiation, and altering our climate. Scientists warn that such changes could affect agricultural yields, timber harvests, and water resource productivity. Results might include a rise in sea level, saltwater contamination of drinking water, and more storms and floods. Human health could be threatened by more heat waves and spreading tropical diseases. Defining the risk of such outcomes is crucial for good climate policy. Reducing the risk of climate change suggests that we must wean ourselves off of the fossil fuels we have used to build our stock of wealth (also see Krugman, 2010).

Good policy should also distinguish between stock and flow pollution. Stock pollution is concentration—the accumulated carbon in the atmosphere, like water in a bathtub. Flow pollution is emissions—the annual rate of emission, like water flowing into the tub. Because risk comes from the total stock of carbon, our focus should be on projected concentration levels. Greenhouse gases remain in the atmosphere decades before they dissipate, so different rates of emission could generate the same concentrations by a given year; policy-makers have options regarding how they hit a given concentration target.

One policy option to reduce emissions, as identified by economists, is to start slowly and then increase the rate of emission reductions after several decades. That would allow for a natural rate of capital depreciation and the replacement of high-carbon energy sources—such as coal—with low-carbon sources such as wind and solar. The 'broad, then deep' path is recommended by many researchers and policy-makers: broad participation by both developed and developing countries, and a gradual emission reduction path to achieve a long-term concentration target (Shogren, 1999). Olmstead and Stavins (2012) again stress these points in their discussion of effective post-Kyoto international climate policy. They argue that three elements are essential: a structure that incorporates both developed and developing nations to participate, a focus on a gradual time path for emissions targets, and the use of flexible incentive systems to reduce costs and promote cost-sharing.

Good policy should also account for alternative risk-reduction strategies—mitigation, adaptation, and insurance. Mitigation involves investments to reduce the probability of damages due to carbon emissions; mitigation is a public good determined by the sum of all nations' efforts to reduce carbon. Mitigation is a public risk-reduction strategy in which the benefits of reduced risk accrue to all nations Adaptation involves investments to reduce the severity of realized damages. Adaptation is a private good in which the benefits of reduced severity accrue to one nation—and usually to certain sectors of this nation (World Bank, 2010). Insurance involves investments that transfer wealth from good to bad states of nature given a bad event has been realized.

Climate policy acknowledges that the climate is a global public good: everybody uses the same one. It is the sum of all the carbon emitted around the globe that matters. This is crucial because the biggest emitters of greenhouse gases will change over the next few decades. Today, the industrialized world accounts for the largest portion of emissions; soon, transitional economies in China and India will be the world's largest emitters. That is why international co-operation is essential.

9.3 The Challenge of International Coordination

The world community began responding in 1979 with the First World Climate Conference, held in Geneva and sponsored by the World Meteorological Organization. In 1988, the IPCC held its first meeting to begin to address the state of scientific knowledge on climate change. The IPCC consists of some 2,500 scientists, natural and social, who are charged with evaluating potential impacts and finding cost-effective solutions. At the Rio Earth Summit in 1992, 154 countries singed the United Nations Framework Convention on Climate Change—the signatories agreed to stabilize greenhouse gas emissions voluntarily at 1990 levels by the year 2000.

By the mid-1990s, most observers knew that the Rio emission reduction target was unlikely to be realized. In 1997, in Kyoto, Japan, 150 countries signed the Kyoto Protocol, which binds the major industrialized nations (i.e. the 38 Annex 1 countries) to emissions reductions below 1990 levels by 2008–12. Basic provisions were made for international trading of emissions allowances and for sinks, but no agreement was reached about the responsibilities of developing countries or financial incentives to them, and no concrete measures for enforcement of the agreements were determined (on the Kyoto Protocol, see Box 9.1). The Kyoto Protocol became international law in 2005 after Russia's ratification pushed emission reductions over the 55 per cent mark.

In 2007, the IPCC released its Fourth Assessment Report (FAR), stating that human-driven climate change is 'unequivocal' (see Pachauri and Reisinger, 2007). The Copenhagen Accord emerged in 2009. One of the Accord's key achievements was to unite the United States and China—the two largest emitters of greenhouse gases—in a commitment 'to reduce global emissions so as to hold the increase in global temperature below 2°C'. But the Accord is not a legally binding agreement, and there was no global target for emission reductions by 2050.

Today, achieving meaningful international co-operation remains an 'insurmountable opportunity'. Even though nations have a common interest in climate change, many are reluctant to reduce carbon voluntarily. They realize that they cannot be prevented from 'free-riding': benefitting from reductions in emissions whether they contribute or not. Free-riding is complicated further in developing countries, where clean water and a stable food supply seem more urgent than climate change policy. The developing world also has less financial and technical capacities to act, and different perceptions about what constitutes equitable distributions of effort.

Economists use game theory as a tool to examine the climate coordination problem, as we saw in Chapter 7. The typical approach to model strategic interaction in climate policy is to think of it as a public good (or prisoner's dilemma) game. Since a credible 'climate police

BOX 9.1 The Kyoto Protocol on Climate Change

The Kyoto Protocol represents a major international environmental agreement—one of the most significant attempts to coordinate voluntary and binding global action on climate change policy. About 150 countries met in Kyoto, Japan in December 1997 at the Third Conference of the Parties (COP-3) to the United Nations Framework Convention on Climate Change (UNFCC) (see United Nations, 1992). Their task was to create a legally binding international agreement for climate protection—the Kyoto Protocol. The Kyoto Protocol (United Nations, 1997) was the culmination of years of negotiations to strengthen the first international climate change treaty signed by over 160 countries at the 1992 Earth Summit in Rio de Janeiro. The original treaty, the UNFCC, called on industrial nations to voluntarily reduce their greenhouse gas emissions to 1990 levels by 2000.

What does the Kyoto Protocol say?

Targets and timetables (Article 3). The protocol set a legally binding target for thirty-nine of the world's most developed countries to reduce greenhouse gas emissions in aggregate by 5.2 per cent from a 1990 baseline for the period 2008–12. The targets are differentiated by nation, ranging from an 8 per cent reduction (the EU) to a 10 per cent increase (Iceland) from 1990 levels. The USA agreed to a target of 7 per cent reduction; Japan a 6 per cent reduction (see Table 9.2). The goal was for each party to show demonstrable progress towards meeting its target by 2005.

Nations can act jointly to hit their target (Article 4). The Protocol lets a group of nations form a multi-country 'bubble', in which the group has an overall target to reach. Each nation inside the bubble has its own commitment to the rest of the group. The bubble met the EU's demand that it should be able to comply as a group. The bubble does require the EU to adjust its commitment if its membership enlarges.

Greenhouse gases (Article 3: Annex 1). The Protocol covers six greenhouse gases—carbon dioxide, methane, nitrous oxide, hydrofluorocarbons (HFCs), perfluorocarbons (PFCs), and sulphur hexafluoride (SF6)—as a 'basket'. The latter three use a 1995 baseline instead of 1990. The inclusion of the six gases allows for some flexibility in reaching the target. Reductions in one gas can be used to substitute for reductions in other gases.

Emission trading (Article 16). The Protocol allows for emission trading among the nations to fulfil their commitments. An emission-trading programme provides greater flexibility for a nation to achieve its target.

The joint implementation/clean development mechanism (Articles 6 and 12). Joint implementation (JI) is when one nation gets credit for implementing a project to reduce carbon emissions in another country. A new device, the clean development mechanism (CDM), was developed for joint projects with developing nations through the payment of a special administrative fee by developed nations.

Carbon sinks. The protocol allows for carbon sinks—land and forestry practices that remove carbon emissions from the atmosphere. Sinks could play an important role for some nations because they represent a low-cost option. Sinks are ambiguously defined in the Protocol, and will be a challenge to measure.

No harmonization of actions. The Protocol allows each nation to figure out its own best strategy to meet its commitment. Not everyone sees this as a good thing: some critics have argued that the world would have been better served by a common action rather than a common target.

What didn't the Kyoto Protocol achieve?

Developing country participation. No agreement was reached in Kyoto on what commitments they should assume to reduce their greenhouse gas emissions. But everyone agrees that climate protection requires the participation of the developing countries, because by the middle of the next century, they are predicted to generate the largest share of carbon emissions. Developing nations have no incentive to reduce their economic growth. In 2011, China was the largest emitter just ahead of the USA, but its per capita emissions are about a seventh of those in the USA. A Chinese delegate captured the sentiment underlying the opposition: '[W]hat they [developed nations] are doing is luxury emissions, what we are doing is survival emissions.' Compensation might be required to induce necessary participation of these emerging economies.

BOX 9.1 (Continued)

Table 9.2 Kyoto Protocol Annex 2. Quantified emission limitation or reduction commitment (percentage of base year or period)

Australia	108
Austria	92
Belgium	92
Bulgaria[a]	92
Canada	94
Croatia[a]	95
Czech Republic[a]	92
Denmark	92
Estonia[a]	92
European Community	92
Finland	92
France	92
Germany	92
Greece	92
Hungary[a]	94
Iceland	110
Ireland	92
Italy	92
Japan	94
Latvia[a]	92
Liechtenstein	92
Lithuania[a]	92
Luxembourg	92
Monaco	92
Netherlands	92
New Zealand	100
Norway	101
Poland[a]	94
Portugal	92
Romania[a]	92
Russian Federation[a]	100
Slovakia[a]	92
Slovenia[a]	92
Spain	92
Sweden	92
Switzerland	92
Ukraine[a]	100
United Kingdom	92
United States	93

[a] Countries in transition to a market economy.

force' does not exist to enforce an international environmental agreement, this implies that an agreement must be voluntary and self-enforcing. But recall that in a public good game each player has an incentive to deviate from the co-operative solution—each country wants to 'free-ride' on the abatement actions of others (or each prisoner gives up the other prisoner). These free-riders capture all the benefits of climate protection and pay none of the costs. In this case, the Nash equilibrium—the outcome in which no one has a unilateral incentive to deviate—is for all countries to free-ride.

In reality, what we have witnessed are partial international environmental agreements—a *coordination game* with multiple equilibria (ranging from good to bad) rather than a public good game with a single worst-case outcome (see DeCanio and Fremstad, 2011). If coordination games better capture climate policy, the open question is whether it is better to have a partial co-operation, in which some nations do a lot and others do nothing (co-operation-limited), or to have full co-operation, in which all nations do a little but not the optimal amount (co-operation-lite). Which scenario leads to the most total abatement? In our example in Figure 9.1, it is co-operation-lite that has the greatest total abatement, but the opposite could also hold. This issue deserves more attention.

Game theory suggests that sub-optimal coordination can be alleviated if conforming nations can retaliate against violators with trade sanctions. But the force of this deterrence is blunted in several respects. First, a nation's incentive to deviate from the agreement depends on how it views a short-term gain from cheating compared to the long-term losses from punishment. Nations that must deal today with other problems, such as the supply of clean water, might discount the threat of sanctions. Second, conforming nations must see a gain in applying punishment; otherwise, their threats are not to be believed. And since many forms of sanctions exist, nations need to select a mutually agreeable approach—not a trivial negotiation. Alternatively, one could argue that the process of negotiation itself can help reinforce mutual expectations for co-operation. This perspective recognizes that unilateral confidence-building moves by some countries could inspire like-minded actions by others, and communication itself can reinforce positive expectations.

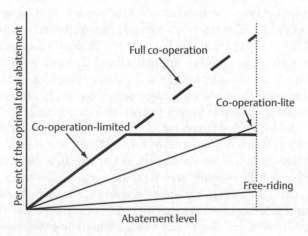

Figure 9.1 Voluntary contributions to abatement.

Good international climate policy should also address the implementation of cost-effective risk-reduction strategies, such as carbon taxes or carbon emission trading. Carbon taxes fix the cost of carbon, and allow the quantity of emissions to be determined by the private sector. Emission trading fixes the quantity of emissions and allows people to trade emission permits at a price set by the market. Such flexible mechanisms may increase the likelihood of international co-operation.

First, consider the carbon tax. A carbon tax adds a fee to the price of fossil fuels according to their relative carbon content. The tax could be collected in various ways: as a severance tax on domestic fossil fuel output plus an equal tax on imports; as a tax on primary energy inputs levied on refineries, gas transportation systems, and coal shippers; or further down-stream to homeowners and car or truck owners. The further upstream the tax is levied, the less carbon 'leaks' out through uncovered activities such as oilfield processing. A fossil fuel tax also would not be that difficult to administer, given the existing tax collection apparatus in the USA and the European Union. Several countries now have a carbon tax: Denmark, Sweden, Norway, and the United Kingdom. The UK carbon tax was imposed on electricity generation in the 2011 budget, and is set initially at a level of £16 per tonne of CO_2, rising to £30 per tonne in 2020. This tax is called the 'carbon floor price', since it operates in tandem with the EU carbon trading system. Policy-makers use this carbon tax to change the relative prices between renewable and non-renewable energy resources; electricity generation via wind and solar now become cheaper relative to non-fossil fuel sources.

A carbon tax provides incentive to emitters to reduce emissions when the marginal abatement cost was less than or equal to the tax, as we saw in Chapter 2. A tax can stimulate several responses. Firms might reduce their tax exposure by reducing CO_2 emissions. Fossil fuel users would have an incentive to improve energy efficiency, use less carbon-intensive fuels, and consume less of the goods and services produced in carbon-intensive ways. Taxes would trigger the diffusion and development of new technologies that emit less carbon. The tax is cost-effective because it sets up the institutional structure so that the marginal abatement costs are the same across all sources—there are no gains from trade remaining to be had. One downside is that a carbon tax does not guarantee a specific emissions reduction goal.

A carbon tax could be extended to other greenhouse gases. The appropriate tax on natural gas entering the pipeline system could account for leakage, and the greater relative potency of methane. Levies also could be placed on methane releases from coal mines and landfills, and on hydrochlorofluorocarbons, on the basis of their expected venting to the atmosphere through sources such as automobile air-conditioners. Extending taxes to agricultural sources of methane is conceivable, but given the decentralized and difficult-to-measure nature of these sources, such an extension might be problematic in practice.

Second, we consider a tradable permit system; also called cap-and-trade. The Kyoto Protocol establishes quantitative targets for reductions in the emissions of carbon dioxide by signatory countries. Many countries have promoted the use of tradable permit markets to achieve these targets. Why? If economics has one key insight, it is that value is created by trade. High-cost firms can buy permits to emit carbon from low-cost firms—both gain from the exchange. Tradable permits are attractive since they create mutual gains between trading partners, guarantee a fixed level of emission reductions, and produce less political flak than green taxes. As Box 9.2 explains, an extensive carbon trading system was introduced by the EU in 2005.

BOX 9.2 The EU Emissions Trading Scheme

The EU Emissions Trading Scheme was launched in January 2005, covers about 45 per cent of UK emissions, and is mandatory for power generators, metal and minerals industries, and pulp and paper plants (see Ellerman and Buchner, 2007). The system covers 12,000 CO_2 producers across the whole EU. They use the National Allocation Plans (NAP) to determine baseline allocation, with grandfathering under Phase 1 (2005–7) for 95 per cent of permits, and 5 per cent allocated by auction. These NAP are supposed to be consistent with individual-country Kyoto targets. We are currently in Phase 2, from 2008 to 2012, which will then be followed by Phase 3 (2013–20). The EU system is the largest permit trading scheme ever, and one that includes the option to trade across borders, and it is linked to 'flexible mechanisms' under Kyoto. German sources (ZEW) predicted that EU-wide costs of hitting Kyoto targets would be higher by €79 billion without permit trading:

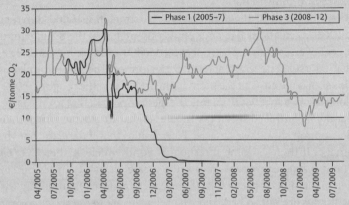

Source: Ellerman and Buchner (2007).

A big difference in Phase 2 is a reduction of between 5 per cent and 10 per cent in the emissions permits granted. City analysts believed that this would lead to a big increase in the market price of carbon. Deutsche Bank expected forward prices to rise from the 2007 level to €35. These predictions were made before the recent global recession, however, which has seen prices fall (the current price is €13 per tonne). The system also allows for banking and borrowing of permits between Phases 2 and 3. More auctions are planned in Phase 3, and Phase 3 will see the scheme extended to commercial airlines flying in European airspace.

Some economists, however, have questioned whether cap-and-trade is the best approach given the uncertainty attached to the costs of reducing CO_2. They have promoted the use of a carbon tax. A nation sets a tax (or price) on emissions of CO_2, or on actions that produce the fossil fuels that generate the CO_2 emissions. Producers respond to the tax by seeking out the lowest means of production, internalizing the costs of CO_2 emissions. Several European nations have introduced carbon taxes during the 1990s and 2000s, including Denmark, Finland, France, the Netherlands, Norway, Sweden, Switzerland, and the UK. In the summer of 2012, the Australian government will introduce a new carbon tax aimed at reducing carbon emissions, which implies that firms and people will probably have to reduce their use of fossil fuels.

If no uncertainty existed over future control costs, tradable quantity controls and carbon taxes would produce similar outcomes. But there is considerable uncertainty over how big carbon control costs will be in the future due to three factors: (i) we have little experience with such large cuts in emissions; (ii) we do not know what future technological options will be; and (iii) we do not know what the 'do nothing' level of emission will be, relative to which achievements are measured and targets set.

Pizer (2002) constructed a scenario in which uncertainty exists over control costs, and that these costs turn out to be greater than thought. Under a permit system, emissions stay constant, but costs of control rise. Under a tax system, emissions are cut by less, even though the price per tonne stays constant. Permit systems result in more uncertainty about costs than emission reductions, whilst this situation is reversed with taxes. Under certainty, emissions by 2010 for either a $80 per tonne carbon tax or a permit market with 8.5 gigatonnes or total allowances are about equal.

Pizer tested the strength of these alternatives by simulating 1,000 different predictions based around IPCC calculations. He finds emissions are below the 8.5 gigatonnes of carbon level in 75 per cent of cases with the tax, but exceed it in the remaining cases. The permit market ensures that emissions never go above 8.5 gigatonnes. The same simulation of possible future scenarios shows the costs of the permit scheme to be in the range of 0.0–2.2 per cent of global gross domestic product (GDP), a much larger range than that for the tax, at 0.2–0.6 per cent. The variation of control costs is much greater under the permit system than with a tax.

Which policy option should we choose? Pizer argues that it depends on what we believe about the damage. If there is some threshold beyond which further CO_2 emissions will impose high (and maybe irreversible) costs, the greater certainty over emission levels that comes with permit markets is preferable. If, instead, damage rises smoothly with increasing emissions, the threats are not so bad, and we prefer the greater certainty over control costs that comes from taxes. This preference for taxes over permits is reinforced when one remembers that it is not current emissions that most worry us about climate change, but the overall stock of greenhouse gases in the atmosphere, which changes slowly.

Nordhaus (2008) makes the case for an internationally harmonized carbon tax over a permit system. His argument is that a carbon tax is likely to be a more efficient incentive device because of its conceptual simplicity. A harmonized carbon tax is a method to help coordinate policies across countries. The tax will hold the advantage over permits if the goals are to maintain the flexibility needed to promote economic growth, to minimize inefficiencies due to highly non-linear damages, to avoid the volatility that can arise in permit prices, and to encourage the idea of a 'double dividend'—to raise revenues through the carbon tax while reducing taxes on other goods or inputs. The potential downside of a harmonized carbon tax is that implicit carbon prices will differ across countries due to different opportunity costs. This suggests that richer nations will have to make large transfer payments to poorer countries to offset any differences in carbon prices. Landis and Bernauer (2012) estimate that for a global carbon price of $35 per tonne of CO_2, the transfer payments could range from $15 billion to $48 billion per year. As a comparative benchmark, the Development Assistance Committee of the OECD provided $134 billion in official development assistance in 2011.

But carbon taxes are politically unpopular, and unlikely to be widely used. What to do? Economists have argued for a hybrid system—one that combines taxes and permits. In this system, the government first allocates a number of limited life permits freely, and then makes additional supplies available at a price—a 'trigger price'. This trigger price works like a tax on emissions or a safety valve, and can be increased over time if we want to tighten up progressively on climate policy.

9.4 The Benefits and Costs of International Co-operation

The conventional economics approach to assessing climate change policy is to calculate the benefits and costs of action or inaction. As noted by Pindyck (2011), most economic analyses of climate change policy compare costs and benefits in five steps: (a) defining a 'business as usual' (BAU) carbon emissions benchmark against which we can compare any policy options; (b) the potential temperature changes that might arise from staying on the BAU benchmark path, either at a global average or at a regional level; (c) the estimated losses to the world economy (GDP) due to the higher temperatures from the BAU path—some estimates include human adaptation, some do not; (d) the estimated costs associated with reducing BAU emissions to some reduced target level of emissions; and (e) presumptions about how society values these changes today and off into the future.

The benefits from climate policy are determined by what losses we avoid with lower concentrations of carbon: severe weather patterns, hobbled ecosystems, less biodiversity, less potable water, loss of coastal areas, rises in mean temperature, more infectious diseases such as malaria and cholera. Climate change could benefit some parts of agriculture and forestry with longer growing seasons and more fertilization. These benefits from a climate agreement are most likely to accrue to the future generations in developing nations because their economies depend relatively more on climate (e.g. agriculture, forestry, and fishing). As stressed by Schelling (1997), climate policy boils down to a wealth transfer from today's industrial nations to future generations in emerging economies.

These gains (or losses) can be categorized into four broad sets that are increasingly difficult to quantify: the avoided losses to market goods and services, non-market goods, ancillary effects, and catastrophes. People judge the benefits of climate protection as the incremental reduction in human and environmental risks compared to the 'business as usual' baseline. Under BAU, modellers have estimated that carbon concentrations might be expected to double pre industrial levels within the next half century, with mean temperatures predicted to rise by about 1°C by 2050, and 2.5°C by 2100. With Kyoto, concentrations are still likely to double, with temperatures increasing by about 0.1°C by 2050 and 0.5°C by 2100.

By most estimates produced in the 1990s and early 2000s, climate change could reduce gross world product by around 1 or 2 per cent. The impact on GDP in the USA has been estimated to be between plus or minus 1 per cent. Most industries in the developed nations are separate from climate: less than 3 per cent of US livelihoods, for instance, are earned in agriculture and other climate-sensitive activities. If one included the potential non-market damage, the market and non-market benefits to the USA might be at most about 2 per cent of GDP.

Tol (2012) recently reviewed the estimated range of total economic impacts due to global warming (estimated between 1994 and 2006). He finds that most estimates suggest that a doubling of atmospheric concentrations would lead to moderate economic decline, a decrease of 1 or 2 per cent of GDP. The overall pattern that emerges from these economic estimates is that of moderate economic gains with a modest increase in temperature, but then significant economic losses with more substantial temperature increases, over 3°C.

These estimates include the 2006 Stern Review on the Economics of Climate Change, which changed the political debate on the range of damages to the global economy. Without action to reduce global emissions, the Stern Review estimated that world GDP could fall by 5 per cent every year for the long run; potentially, under the worst-case scenario, GDP loss might be as high as 20 per cent per year. The Stern Review raised the political costs of doing nothing. The main conclusion was that the benefits (i.e. avoided damages) of extreme and immediate climate protection outweigh the costs. The estimated damages could be reduced if the global community took early and strong action to reduce emissions, actions that would cost about 1 per cent of world GDP. Krugman calls this action the 'climate policy big bang' approach.

Critics of the Stern Review challenge both the estimated costs and benefits of climate action. They argue that the estimated future damages are too high, given the report's use of unjustifiable low social discount rates. Economists use a discount rate to compare economic impacts that arise at different times. A social discount rate captures how today's generation values the benefits and costs that accrue to future generations—an ethical statement about how we value present and near-present costs relative to the distant future. The Stern Review argued that a low social discount rate (e.g. not much more than zero) was ethical and therefore appropriate. Critics such as Nordhaus argued that such a low rate was inconsistent with the implied discounting rates that are consistent with today's marketplace.

Critics also argued that the costs of climate protection are too low—more reasonable estimates would raise the costs of mitigation. The costs of mitigation are lower if one makes favourable assumptions about rapid technological change and institutional responsive to implement energy efficiency policy. If people and institutions are assumed to readily adopt new low-carbon technologies without a price shock, the costs of mitigation are much lower. Many new low-carbon technologies exist already; the open question is how quickly these options will penetrate into the economy. Economists believe that a price shock in energy is a necessary requirement to speed up adoption of new technologies.

In addition, there are two topics that arise in the non-market arena that are likely to trigger debates over costs and benefits of climate change: human health and ecosystem/ endangered species services. Potential threats to human health include thirty diseases and infections new to medicine, such as *E. coli*, hantavirus, and HIV, plus old scourges such as cholera, plague, yellow and dengue fever, tuberculosis, and malaria. How do we quantify such threats? It is another challenge to estimate the social value of ecosystem services and endangered species. Despite the extraordinary analytical difficulties associated with measuring the social value of preserving each species, determining at least a range for these values is essential if we are to make judgements about the benefits of preservation.

One way to increase the size of the benefits of the Kyoto Protocol is to add in the potential ancillary benefits that might come from discouraging fossil fuel consumption. The Kyoto Protocol would reduce emissions of such air pollutants as carbon monoxide, sulphur and nitrogen oxides, and toxic trace pollutants in exhaust gases, thereby reducing their damage to health, visibility, materials, and crops. Studies in Europe and the USA have estimated that

---

BOX 9.3 Stated Preference Evidence from the USA

In a recent stated preference study of 1,651 US households, Lee and Cameron (2008) estimated the willingness to support/pay for 'large' mitigation policies that maintain current climate. They investigate whether this WTP depends on: (i) how seriously people take the 'do nothing' scenario; (ii) how much mitigation costs; and (iii) who pays these costs (how they are distributed), both domestically and internationally. They implement the question of who pays (domestic) by looking at how costs are divided across energy taxes, income taxes, falling investment returns, and higher consumer prices; they implement who pays (international) by considering global cost shares between (i) India and China, (ii) 'other developing countries', (iii) the USA and Japan, and (iv) other industrialized countries.

   Their results confirm *ex ante* expectations that the WTP depends on perceived severity of impacts of climate change; on how much of the costs are borne by increased energy taxes; on how much the USA and Japan pay as their share of global costs; and on which sectors experience the biggest effects (e.g. agriculture, health, ecosystems). For example, the average WTP per household per month in higher energy taxes to reduce the risk of 'moderate harm' or 'substantial harm' is as follows: (a) $6 or $456 if the USA/Japan pay 100 per cent; and (b) $271 or $728 if the USA/Japan pay 31 per cent and India/China pay 17 per cent. Overall, across the entire sample, the mean and median WTP if the USA/Japan pay all costs are $151 and $62 per month, respectively.

---

the non-climate benefits might be as large—or larger—than the direct benefits from avoiding climate change. Box 9.3 shows some results from a study of the willingness to pay (WTP) of US citizens to mitigate carbon emissions, and shows that these depend on which other countries join in the effort, and on which sectors are likely to experience the biggest impacts.

Finally, although modellers typically presume that climate change will be gradual—a slow and steady rise in temperature or precipitation—some have raised the spectre of catastrophe. They suggest that the risk of a sudden rupture is real; for example, a structural change in ocean currents or the melting of the Western Antarctic ice sheet. The problem is that researchers do not have any reasonable estimates of the odds that these events will come to pass, but making informed policy judgements requires knowing those odds.

There has been a range of estimated costs of climate protection. Some studies suggest that the world could reduce emissions at negligible cost; others call climate change policies an 'economic disarmament'. In the early 2000s, a report from the US White House stated that the costs to the USA of meeting its Kyoto target were 'likely to be modest' if reductions were efficiently pursued with domestic and international emissions trading, joint implementation, and the Clean Development Mechanism (a system in which developed nations can buy the carbon reductions in developing nations). By 'modest', the report means an annual GDP drop of less than 0.5 per cent (roughly $10 billion); no expected negative effect on the trade deficit; increased gasoline or petrol prices of about 5 cents a gallon in the USA; lower electricity rates; and no major impacts on the employment rate.

But other estimates suggest that the US GDP could take an annual hit of nearly 3 per cent, or about $250 billion a year, with intra-nation emission trading. Also, the trade deficit would increase by billions of dollars; gasoline prices would increase by 50 cents a gallon; electricity prices would nearly double; and two million US jobs would disappear. The net global costs have been estimated at over $700 billion, with the USA bearing about two-thirds of those costs.

The effects of international climate policy on world trade patterns are not well understood. Many leaders envision a 'pollution haven' hypothesis, as outlined in Chapter 8: a domestic industry relocates to a developing-country 'haven' that has weaker regulations on emissions. This scenario seems unlikely on economic grounds. Except for the biggest polluting industries, the costs of complying with environmental regulations are a small fraction of total costs, and are outweighed by international differences in labour costs, capital costs, material costs, and exchange rate changes. The differences between developed nations' environmental regulations and those of most major trading partners are not that big. Besides, developed-nation firms build state-of-the art facilities abroad regardless of the host nation's environmental regulations.

Leaders also fear that carbon policy will affect the demand for domestic energy-intensive goods and cause the trade balance to deteriorate. But studies have not supported this idea. A related notion is the 'leakage effect'—cuts in domestic emissions are offset by shifts in production and increases in emissions abroad. The early research range of estimates on carbon leakage: unilateral emissions-reduction policies in OECD countries predict leakage rates of anywhere between 3.5 and 70 per cent. A recent study by Aichele and Felbermayr (2012) has arrived at a more definitive and pessimistic story. They examine the *carbon footprint* for countries that committed to the Kyoto Protocol. A carbon footprint is defined as a measure that accounts for all carbon emissions generated by a nation's citizens, regardless of where the good was produced. Calculating the carbon footprint between 1995 and 2007, they estimate that the Kyoto Protocol generated significant carbon leakage. Countries committed to Kyoto have reduced domestic emissions, but given the relocation of production, they have not reduced their carbon footprint. This result supports the 'broad, then deep' idea for international climate agreements. Again, this suggests broad participation by developed and emerging economies, with a gradual emission reduction path over a long period—what Nordhaus calls the 'climate-policy ramp'.

Finally, cost estimates are likely to be on the low side for several reasons. Models presume the most efficient possible climate control programme. The models assume that the control programme is announced early and maintained indefinitely, even though governments will be hard pressed to maintain consistent control over the decades. Many models focus on long-term equilibrium and do not address the short-run adjustments, such as the oil shocks of the 1970s, which could raise cost estimates by a factor of between one and four. This factor would cause Kyoto to reduce GDP by 1–10 per cent from baseline. Compare that to the 2 per cent of GDP that the USA now spends on all environmental programmes combined.

9.5 Economic Issues Underlying Benefit and Cost Estimates

How one accounts for the benefits and costs of international co-operation depends on what one believes about the nature of three elements that underlie climate protection: the chance of a catastrophe, the degree of flexibility in finding low-cost solutions for mitigation and adaptation, and the origins of technological advance. We now take a brief look at each of these issues.

If you believe that catastrophe is imminent, or at least more likely than previously believed, emission reductions need to start now. If you do not, it is harder to justify the likely costs of rapid climate protection without global trading. Reliable information is needed to help people understand the nature of climate change. Science does not know with certainty which regions will get warmer or cooler, which will get wetter or drier, which will get stormier or calmer. Climate policy discussions also consider whether a model has accounted for the likelihood that a change in the ecosystem will be discontinuous—a catastrophe. Most modellers acknowledge that their models do not address the potential of structural change such as discontinuous shocks, like a sudden shift in the Gulf Stream or an unravelling of natural systems from biodiversity losses.

The risk of climate change catastrophe has triggered a debate about how to evaluate the benefits and costs of climate change under uncertainty over climate variability. This is the so-called 'fat tails' argument. A fat tail reflects the idea that the probability of an extreme-impact event is not as rare as believed under the 'business as usual' climate scenarios. A 'fat tail' is the term used to capture the idea that societies cannot rule out the possibility of an extreme event due to climate change. So-called 'deep structural uncertainty' exists about the nature of climate system and its variability. This structural uncertainty means that the chance of extreme-event damages are not zero—there is a positive chance of an absolute catastrophe due to climate change. In this case, standard cost–benefit analysis is unhelpful, because the benefits of avoiding infinite damages will always outweigh the costs of climate protection (see Weitzman, 2011).

In addition, extreme events and structural uncertainty about climate change induce a behavioural response from regular people—we all tend to overestimate low-probability events. Experience tells people little about low-probability risks such as climate change. They rely on outside sources of information to help them make judgements about the likelihood that a bad event will come to pass. If that information stresses severity without giving some notion of the odds, people systematically bias their risk perceptions upwards. Numerous studies have revealed that people overestimate the chance that they will suffer from a low-probability/high-severity event; for example, a nuclear power accident.

Second, the costs to meet a policy depend on how quickly society wants to change its energy systems and capital structure. A stringent, inflexible carbon policy will induce greater economic burden than a loose, flexible policy, since more flexibility allows firms greater agility to search out the lowest-cost alternatives. Estimates suggest that any agreement without the flexibility provided by trading will at least double the costs.

Flexibility means the ability to reduce carbon at the lowest cost, and three issues are relevant. We first need to work through how the trading system would be designed before alternative policies can be evaluated. The business of defining the rules for flexibility incentive systems is wide open, and experimental economists could play an important role in reducing the uncertainty. This holds for joint implementation and the clean development mechanism as well.

We need to address the role of 'carbon sinks', which remain the wild card in the search for flexible, low-cost solutions. A sink is a process that destroys or absorbs greenhouse gases, such as the absorption of atmospheric carbon dioxide by trees, soils, and other types of vegetation. In the USA, forests are an important terrestrial sink, since they cover about 750 million acres. A few studies have found that carbon sequestration through sinks could cost as little as $25 per tonne in the USA, although this figure is likely to vary substantially across types of forest, across land types, and according to how forests are managed (Read et al., 2009). The United Nations REDD programme (Reducing Emissions from Deforestation and Forest Degradation) is another ongoing effort to create financial value for carbon storage, especially in forests in developing countries. Started in 2008, the REDD programme is designed to provide technical assistance to implement strategies to reduce deforestation (also see Chapter 7). But serious uncertainties remain about how to measure and account for estimates of net carbon sequestered in forests, whilst enhancing forest carbon sequestration might have mixed effects on other public goods associated with forestry, such as biodiversity (Caparrós et al., 2010).

We also need to consider that the existing tax system might accentuate the costs of climate protection. Labour and capital taxes distort behaviour because they reduce employment and investment levels to below what they would have been otherwise. If we add on a carbon tax that discourages consumption and production, we further reduce employment and investment, which then exacerbates the labour and capital tax distortions, perhaps by as much as 400 per cent. One could reduce these extra costs by channelling the revenue from the carbon tax, if any existed, to reduce the labour and capital taxes.

Finally, the costs of climate protection depend on what one chooses to believe about the origins of technological diffusion. Some people argue that those origins are rooted in non-price responses: people will do the right thing for the right reason. Economists disagree with such optimistic scenarios—the majority of people do not adopt technologies that cost more just to protect the environment. People have other more immediate needs. Economists see the origins of technological advance as driven by changes in relative prices. Even if new technologies are available, people do not switch unless prices induce them to switch. People behave as if their time horizons were short, perhaps reflecting their uncertainty about future energy prices and the reliability of the technology. High initial investment costs also slow down the adoption of new technologies—for example, replacing all household light bulbs at once with energy-efficient lights—whilst transaction costs also set barriers on the take-up of low carbon technologies by households.

If people adopted new technologies—such as compact fluorescent light bulbs, improved thermal insulation, heating and cooling systems, and energy-efficient appliances—without a price shock, carbon emissions could be eliminated at lower cost (see Gillingham et al., 2009). The open question is whether people can be 'nudged' into adopting climate-friendly technologies without a sustained price increase in energy. While some people adopt new technologies on their own, economists estimate that higher energy prices are typically associated with significantly more adoption of energy-efficient equipment. For example, Chakravorty et al. (1997) argue that if historical rates of cost reduction in the production of solar energy are maintained (30–50% per decade), more than 90 per cent of the world's remaining coal will never be used. In their simulations, the world economy makes the transition to solar from coal and oil even without a carbon tax. Global temperatures will increase by 1.5–2.0°C by around 2050, and will then decline to pre-industrial levels.

9.6 A Flexibility–Stringency Trade-off

In the end, the economics of climate change rests on the trade-off between the stringency of a country's emissions reduction path and how much flexibility this country has to reach its

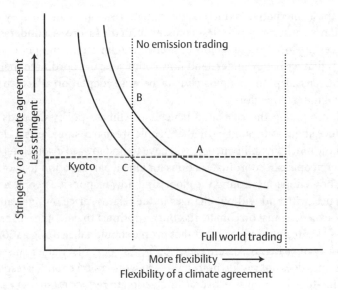

Figure 9.2 The flexibility–stringency trade-off.

target. A stringent, inflexible carbon policy creates a greater economic burden than a loose, flexible policy. If the goal is to keep costs down to an acceptable level, the push for a more stringent target requires flexibility in how a nation can achieve the target. If market or institutional imperfections restrict flexibility, policy-makers can loosen the stringency of the target to keep the costs down. Figure 9.2 illustrates this stringency–flexibility trade-off; the iso-cost curves represent different combinations of flexibility and stringency that generate the same given cost to the economy.

Now consider the policy options from a post-Kyoto agreement, using points A and B in the figure. Both points are on an iso-cost curve representing a relatively low cost to the economy. Point A could represent China going into post-Kyoto negotiations. Point B represents the same total cost to the economy, except that now emissions trading is prohibited. This point is consistent with the negative reaction of many developed and developing countries towards emissions trading. To maintain the same cost as at point A, point B must involve a weaker target. If you lose flexibility, you have to give up some stringency to keep costs fixed. What emerged instead from the original Kyoto process was something like point C, with both less policy flexibility than some nations initially sought and a somewhat more ambitious emissions control target. Point C is on an iso-cost curve, with higher cost to the economy than points A and B.

Summary

Climate change is a historical fact, and its connection to human actions is better understood now. Today, economists do not debate over the need for climate policy; rather, we make cases for different levels of stringency in abatement of carbon emissions and when these policies should begin to go from loose to strict targets. Economics offers insight into how people value these alternative reductions in climate risk—how much they are willing to sacrifice in today's consumption for less climate risk in the future. An understanding of this trade-off is necessary to help design more cost-effective climate change policy. Cost-effective policy requires that we better understand how countries can coordinate their actions, and how private citizens adapt to changing climate, because adaptation affects the effectiveness of international mitigation efforts.

In the end, estimating the costs and benefits of climate policy depends on what you choose to believe about four points: whether people are increasing the real risk of a climate catastrophe; how much flexibility people will have to find low-cost solutions (e.g. cap-and-trade); whether people can coordinate actions for global participation to avoid a shell game of moving carbon emissions around the globe; and how responsive people are to adopting new technologies, with and without changes in the relative price of high- and low-carbon energy. If you are a pessimist on climate risk but an optimist that people will react rationally, the economics of climate change suggest that people should take strong action right now—the climate policy big bang. If you are catastrophic risk optimist but a realist about human actions, economics does not say 'do nothing'—it suggests a slower policy response, in which we follow a climate policy ramp-up over a long period to reduce fossil fuel use.

Tutorial Questions

9.1   Describe the major economic benefits of reducing climate change risk.

9.2   Describe the key drivers that will either increase or decrease the costs of climate policy around the globe.

9.3   Suppose that you are asked to put a price on carbon emissions. Explain why you prefer a global carbon tax or a global cap-and-trade system.

9.4   How does the idea of a 'fat tail' extreme event affect the economics of climate change?

9.5   Explain the challenges that countries face when considering how to coordinate over an international environmental agreement such as the Kyoto Protocol.

References and Additional Readings

Aichele, R., and Felbermayr, G. (2012). 'Kyoto and the carbon footprint of nations', *Journal of Environmental Economics and Management* 63: 336–54.

Blinder, A. (1997). 'Needed: planet insurance', *New York Times*, 22 October.

Caparrós, A., Cerdá, E., Ovando, P., and Campos, P. (2010). 'Carbon sequestration with reforestation and biodiversity', *Environmental and Resource Economics* 45: 49–72.

Chakravorty, U., Roumasset, J., and Tse, K. (1997). 'Endogenous substitution among energy resources and global warming', *Journal of Political Economy* 105: 1201–34.

DeCanio, S., and Fremstad, A. (2011). 'Game theory and climate diplomacy', *Ecological Economics*, http://www.sciencedirect.com/science/article/pii/S0921800911001698.

Ellerman, D., and Buchner, B. (2007). 'The European Union Emissions Trading Scheme: origins, allocation, and early results', *Review of Environmental Economics and Policy* 1: 66–87.

Gillingham, K., Newell, R., and Palmer, K. (2009). 'Energy efficiency economics and policy', NBER Working Paper No. 15031.

Heal, G. (2009). 'Climate economics: a meta-review and some suggestions', *Review of Environmental Economics and Policy* 3: 4–21.

Krugman, P. (2010). 'Building a green economy', *New York Times Magazine*, 7 April, http://www.nytimes.com/2010/04/11/magazine/11Economy-t.html?pagewanted=all (accessed 11 November 2011).

Landis, F., and Bernauer, T. (2012). 'Transfer payments in global climate change', *Nature Climate Change* 2: 628–33, http://www.nature.com/nclimate/journal/vaop/ncurrent/full/nclimate1548.html (accessed 1 June 2012).

Lee, J.J., and Cameron, T.A. (2008). 'Popular support for climate change mitigation: evidence from a general population mail survey', *Environmental and Resource Economics* 41(2): 223–48.

Nordhaus, W. (2008). *A Question of Balance: Weighing the Options on Global Warming Policies* (New Haven, CT: Yale University Press).

Olmstead, S., and Stavins, R. (2012). 'Three key elements of a post-2012 international climate policy architecture', *Review of Environmental Economics and Policy* 6: 65–85.

Pachauri, R.K., and Reisinger, A. (eds.) (2007). *Climate Change 2007: Synthesis Report. Contribution of Working Groups I, II and III to the Fourth Assessment Report of the Intergovernmental Panel on Climate Change* (Geneva: IPCC).

Pindyck, R. (2011). 'Uncertain outcomes and climate change policy', *Journal of Environmental Economics and Management* 63: 289–303.

Pizer, W. (2002). 'Combining price and quantity controls to mitigate global climate change', *Journal of Public Economics* 85: 409–34.

Plambeck, E., and Hope, C. (1996). 'An updated valuation of the impacts of global warming', *Energy Policy* 24: 783–93.

Read, D.J., Freer-Smith, P.H., Morison, J.I.L., Hanley, N., West, C.C., and Snowdon, P. (eds.) (2009). *Combating Climate Change: A Role for UK Forests. The Synthesis Report*, (Edinburgh: Stationery Office).

Schelling, T. (1997). 'The costs of combating global warming', *Foreign Affairs*, November/December: 8–14.

Shogren, J. (1999). The *Benefits and Costs of the Kyoto Protocol* (Washington, DC: American Enterprise Institute).

—— and Toman, M. (2000). 'Climate change policy', in P. Portney and R. Stavins (eds.), *Public Policies for Environmental Protection*, 2nd edn. (Washington, DC: Resources for the Future): 125–68.

Stern, N. (2006). *Review on the Economics of Climate Change*, HM Treasury, UK, October, http://webarchive.nationalarchives.gov.uk/+/http://www.hm-treasury.gov.uk/sternreview_index.htm (accessed 30 May 2012).

Tol, R. (2012). 'On the uncertainty about the total economic impact of climate change', *Environmental and Resource Economics* (online).

United Nations (1992). *United Nations Framework Convention on Climate Change* (New York: United Nations).

—— (1997). *Kyoto Protocol to the Convention on Climate Change* (New York: United Nations).

Weitzman, M. (2011). 'Fat-tailed uncertainty in the economics of catastrophic climate change', *Review of Environmental Economic Policy* 5: 275–92.

Wigley, T., Richels, T., and Edmonds, J. (1996). 'Economic and environmental choices in the stabilization of atmospheric CO_2 concentrations', *Nature* 379: 240–3.

World Bank (2010). *Economics of Adapting to Climate Change* (Washington, DC: The World Bank).

10   Forests

This chapter gives an economic analysis of the market and non-market value of forestry. This includes natural forests, modified natural forests, and timber plantations. The reason why we treat forests in a separate chapter is that they are critically important in providing a range of ecosystem services, especially as a host to biodiversity and a store of carbon.

- We review the costs and benefits of conserving natural forests.
- We analyse why natural forests are being cleared.
- We consider how the optimal area of forest might be determined.
- We discuss local and international policy responses to the problem of deforestation.

10.1 Introduction

The destruction of large areas of natural forest, especially tropical rainforest, has become a major environmental issue. Many environmentalists believe that natural forests are being converted to other land uses too rapidly, and that this process is causing profound damage to the world's environment and ecosystems. In addition to forest loss, there is also widespread forest degradation as a result of fragmentation and the disturbance of vegetation.

A different view of deforestation is that it is a necessary and inevitable part of the development process: land under natural forest is converted to more economically productive uses including agriculture, commercial forestry, and urban expansion. The countries with high rates of deforestation are repeating a pattern of development followed in medieval Europe, seventeenth- to nineteenth-century North America and nineteenth- and twentieth-century Australia, where forests were cleared on a massive scale for agriculture, mining, and urban uses.

From an economist's viewpoint, natural forests may be excessively depleted due to a failure of market price signals to reflect the wide range of local, national, and global benefits that natural forests provide. In contrast, the benefits of deforestation *are* expressed through timber markets and agricultural commodity markets, and without government intervention, rates of deforestation may continue to be above the social optimal level in many countries. Government policies can also increase deforestation rates; for example, by subsiding investment and tying land ownership to land clearing. The benefits of conserving forestry are as follows.

10.1.1 **Local benefits**

For instance, tropical forests are home to many millions of people, including numerous indigenous groups. The forests provide a range of outputs, including timber and other wood products as well as non-timber forest products (NTFP) such as edible fruit, oils, latex, fibre, and medicines, which can be consumed or sold. Estimates of the number of people who utilize NTFP are between 0.955 and 1.455 billion (Scherr et al., 2004). They utilize the forest in many ways. The largest proportion, 50–75 per cent, are those who manage remnant forest for subsistence and income as part of a farm. Others, approximately 25 per cent, depend on the forest for supplementary and 'safety-net' income, especially when their main source of income, possibly agriculture, is adversely affected by drought, for instance. People that depend largely on the forest as a source of income for hunting and gathering are between 4 and 6 per cent of the total. Standing forests through renewable NTFP are capable of yielding higher net returns per hectare than timber (Peters et al., 1989; Shackleton et al., 2011). Local people often make their living practising shifting cultivation and collecting a wide variety of forest products to sell in local markets. The income of poor landless farmers depends in many tropical regions on the availability of forest resources for shifting cultivation, bushmeat, and supplies of fuelwood. This type of benefit is not restricted to tropical rainforests: many natural and partially modified forests across the world provide similar market and non-market benefits. In Box 10.1, we discuss the nature and extent of ecosystem services derived by farmers in the Bragantina region of Brazil.

10.1.2 **National benefits**

At a regional level, forests perform complex ecosystem functions, including the regulation of flows of surface and groundwater, and the protection and enrichment of soils through reduced erosion and nutrient recycling. Forests act as a sponge, releasing water at a steady rate and evening out variable precipitation rates (for a discussion and a more complex story that indicates that forests are good at moderating minor floods, but have little effect on major flood events, see FAO, 2005). Once a rainforest is cleared, rainfall runs off the land more rapidly, potentially causing increased flooding and soil erosion. Tropical forests also maintain a balance of species by providing pest control services, and they regulate surface temperatures and local and regional climates through evapotranspiration.

10.1.3 **Global benefits**

Greenhouse gas emissions. Forests make a significant contribution to climate regulation through their role in the global carbon cycle. Forests store carbon in vegetation and the soil and take carbon out of the atmosphere. Deforestation and forest degradation release stored carbon into the atmosphere as carbon dioxide emissions. Forest growth sequesters carbon

BOX 10.1 Forest Ecosystem Services to Shifting Cultivation in Brazil

Secondary regrown tropical rainforest is important in many areas of Brazil, where the original forest has been cleared many years ago, but farmers engaging in slash-and-burn agriculture allow forest fallow; that is, a period when cultivation ceases and the forest is allowed to regenerate. Forest fallow provides many of the same market and non-market ecosystem services as the original forest: it sequesters carbon, reduces soil erosion, increases soil fertility, and reduces the damage due to flood events. Klemick (2011) interprets forest fallow for between 3 and 8 years as providing private benefits to the farmers with forest fallow on their land and positive externalities, in the form of reduced flood frequency and intensity, to neighbouring farmers that share the same water catchment.

Bragantina is a shifting cultivation region of the Brazilian Amazon. The author combined farm survey data with satellite land cover data to estimate a production function to explain the value of farm output. In a simplified version, the production function is as follows:

Farm output $\$ = f$(on-farm fallow (ha), all-other farms fallow,
        cultivated land, labour, fertilizer).

The study estimated a Cobb–Douglas production function that regresses the logarithm of output on the logarithm of all the variables. This means that the coefficients of the regression can be interpreted as elasticities. The results find that a 1 per cent increase in the area of fallow on farm increases the value of output by 0.135 per cent (Klemick, 2011: 101, table 3, model (3)). The positive external benefit derived by the farm from a 1 per cent increase in the upstream fallow area is 0.355 per cent.

Determining the optimal allocation of land to fallow requires an investment analysis that accounts for the opportunity cost of land in fallow (in terms of lost output) and the opportunity cost of labour (required to clear the fallowed land at the end of the fallow period). Farmers allocate land efficiently between cultivation and fallow if the marginal benefits of cultivated land minus the marginal costs in terms of land clearing, forgone soil quality, forest products, and positive externalities to other farms equal zero.

Evidence from Bragantina using the results from the estimated production function is that, if anything, farms over allocate land to fallow and take account of the positive externality that they have on other farmers. This slightly surprising result may be due to the fact that Bragantina farmers have well-established private tenure of their land and are therefore willing to invest in soil conservation through forest fallow and, possibly inadvertently benefit their downstream neighbours through the hydrological services provided by forest fallow.

from the atmosphere. Globally, the forest sector emits approximately 5.8 Gt of carbon dioxide a year from deforestation. The Eliasch Review (Eliasch, 2008) estimates that halving deforestation rates by 2030 would reduce global greenhouse gas emissions by 1.5–2.7 Gt of CO_2 per year. The same review estimates that halving emissions from the forestry sector from 2005 to 2030 could be worth between US$17–33 billion per year if forests were included in global carbon trading. The net present value of benefits is estimated at US$3.7 trillion between 2010 and 2200. This figure does not include the many other local, regional, and global benefits of forest ecosystems.

Biodiversity store. Tropical rainforests are a rich source of biodiversity: they cover 7 per cent of the earth's surface but contain 50 per cent of all species (Brown and Pearce, 1994). The gene base present in tropical rainforest is a commercially exploitable natural resource, which contains biologically active compounds with medicinal properties (see Chapter 12).

10.2 Forest Distribution and Losses

Forests can be classified according to tree type and physiognomy (overall physical structure or development stage) and phenology (concerning phenomena, such as leaf fall, and their relation to climate). The most aggregated classification, based on climate and tree type, is into: temporal and boreal needleleaf; temporal broadleaf and mixed; tropical moist and tropical dry; and parkland (Groombridge and Jenkins, 2002: 81). Trends in deforestation and reforestation vary regionally and according to forest type.

This section summarizes the main trends in the world's forests. The state of the world's forests is assessed every five years by the Global Forest Assessment (see, e.g., FAO, 2010). In 2010, the world's total forest area was estimated at slightly over 4 billion hectares, with just five countries—the Russian Federation, Brazil, Canada, the United States, and China—accounting for more than half of the total area (53%).

The loss of primary (undisturbed) forest and naturally regenerated forest remains alarmingly high. FAO (2010) estimates this as at around 13 million hectares of forest lost each year from 2000 to 2010. The land is either converted to agriculture or lost due to natural causes such as bushfires. This is actually a reduction in the even higher rate of loss that occurred in the 1990s, of 16 million hectares in each year. The loss of 13 million hectares of forest entails a major loss in biodiversity, as it is often the undisturbed forest that is lost. Offsetting some of these losses is an expansion in natural forests and an increase in plantation forests. This gives a net annual forest loss of 5.2 million hectares.

The distribution of forest area and forest loss is given in Table 10.1. This shows that although the rate of net forest loss is slowing, especially in South America and Asia, the rate of loss is still greatest for the tropical nations that host the forests with the highest level of biodiversity.

One issue with considering data such as that presented in Table 10.1 is that sums across different forest types simplify the patterns of forest loss and gain. Plantation forest may be a close substitute for primary and natural regenerating forest in terms of timber and some ecosystem services, such as moderating soil erosion and the local hydrological system, but a poor substitute as a host for biodiversity. Thus the continued loss of primary forest in Brazil, at an average rate of 2.3 million ha per annum between 2005 and 2010 (FAO, 2010: table 8), and its corresponding loss in biodiversity is not compensated for by a similar increase in, for instance, the area of planted forest in China (2.0 million ha expansion per annum, 2005–10) (FAO, 2010: table 9).

10.3 Why is Rainforest Lost? Economic Theories of Deforestation

Rudel and Roper (1997) assess two competing economic explanations of deforestation, the *frontier model* and *the immiserization model*. The frontier model assumes that capital investment is the main determinant of deforestation, with the timber industry playing a key role. The immiserization model assumes that increasing population and impoverishment is driving the conversion of forestry to agriculture. We now consider each of the models in more detail.

Table 10.1 Regional forest area and change

Area	Forest area (1,000 ha)			Country area (1,000 ha)	Annual change rate					
	1990	2000	2005	2010		1990–2000		2000–2005		2005–2010	
						1,000 ha/yr	%	1,000 ha/yr	%	1,000 ha/yr	%
Eastern and Southern Africa	304,312	285,906	276,679	267,517	1,022,650	−1,841	−0.62	−1,845	−0.65	−1,832	−0.67
Northern Africa	85,123	79,224	79,019	78,814	955,540	−590	−0.72	−41	−0.05	−41	−0.05
Western and Central Africa	359,803	343,434	335,770	328,088	1,053,297	−1,637	−0.46	−1,533	−0.45	−1,536	−0.46
Africa	749,238	708,564	691,468	674,419	3,031,487	−4,067	−0.56	−3,419	−0.49	−3,410	−0.50
East Asia	209,198	226,815	241,841	254,626	1,176,421	1,762	0.81	3,005	1.29	2,557	1.04
South and South-East Asia	325,423	301,143	299,327	294,373	897,996	−2,428	−0.77	−363	−0.12	−991	−0.33
Western and Central Asia	41,489	42,207	42,880	43,513	1,108,056	72	0.17	135	0.32	127	0.29
Asia	576,110	570,164	584,048	592,512	3,182,473	−595	−0.10	2,777	0.48	1,693	0.29
Europe	989,471	998,239	1,001,150	1,005,001	2,306,276	877	0.09	582	0.06	770	0.08
Caribbean	5,902	6,434	6,728	6,933	23,474	53	0.87	59	0.90	41	0.60
Central America	25,717	21,980	20,745	19,499	52,161	−374	−1.56	−247	−1.15	−249	−1.23
North America	676,764	677,083	677,823	678,961	2,199,178	32	n.s.	148	0.02	228	0.03
North and Central America	708,383	705,497	705,296	705,393	2,274,813	−289	−0.04	−40	−0.01	19	n.s.
Oceania	198,744	198,381	196,745	191,384	856,143	−36	−0.02	−327	−0.17	−1,072	−0.55
South America	946,454	904,322	882,258	864,351	1,783,040	−4,213	−0.45	−4,413	−0.49	−3,581	−0.41
World	4,168,399	4,085,168	4,060,964	4,033,060	13,434,232	−8,323	−0.20	−4,841	−0.12	−5,581	−0.14

Source: FAO (2010, Global Tables, tables 1 and 3).

The frontier model identifies networks of entrepreneurs, companies, and small farmers as the chief agents of deforestation. Together, this group has sufficient power to raise private capital and obtain assistance from the state to open up regions for timber extraction, settlement, and deforestation. For an initial period, while roads are being established and land-ownership is contested, farmers have a strong incentive to clear land rapidly to state a claim or to extract resources before they are appropriated by others. This is an example of an open-access resource (for a more detailed analysis, see Chapter 7). Investment-driven deforestation will open up whole regions to settlement and agriculture; however, once this process has taken place, there may be a pattern of more gradual deforestation as farmers incrementally expand their cultivated area.

In this form of deforestation, population growth increases the size of the surplus labour force that is willing to enter remote regions and clear land. Gross national product (GNP) is a measure of the funds available to invest in large capital projects such as road-building and timber companies. Timber companies contribute to deforestation directly by harvesting,

---

BOX 10.2 Deforestation in Rondonia: An Example of the Frontier Model

The Amazon encompasses the world's largest moist forest region, at 5.5 million km². Of this, roughly 3.8 million km² lie within Brazil. The Brazilian forests are home to as many as one-fifth of the world's plant and animal species. Brazil has the world's largest remaining tropical forest, and by far the largest area of annual deforestation.

In Brazil, most of the extensive deforestation can be traced directly to government-financed programmes and subsidies. Cattle-ranching has been the foremost cause of forest conversion, with small farm settlements (mainly government promoted) the second largest cause of deforestation. Small farms have accounted for about 11 per cent of the Amazon's total deforestation up to 1983. Other large projects developed partly to alleviate Brazil's foreign debt crisis have deforested more areas. These include several huge hydroelectric investments such as the Tucurui Hydroelectric Project, which cost US$4 billion, and flooded 2,160 km² of forested land.

The government of Brazil has engaged in massive efforts to colonize its tropical forests with small farms; for example, along the Transamazon Highway. The Northwest Development Programme (Polonoroeste) encompasses the entire state of Rondonia and part of the Mato Grosso. The government undertook to demarcate plots and establish land titles, and by mid-1985 the responsible agency had awarded 30,000 titles, mostly for 100 ha farms. Settlers only paid a nominal fee for their land (US$1) and could recover their relocation costs by selling timber. Once they had obtained title to the land, they become eligible for subsidized agricultural credits. It has been estimated that subsidized settlers cleared almost 25 per cent more forests than those not benefiting from government programmes (Repetto, 1988).

Polonoroeste was intended to promote sustainable farming systems, based on tree crops, and to include environmental protection. Instead, unguided colonization took place. Settlers poured into the state of Rondonia increasing its population at an average rate of 14 per cent a year from 1980. The wave of settlers in Rondonia cleared and burnt the forest, and accelerated the rate of deforestation from an area equating to 3 per cent of Rondonia in 1980, to an area that accounting for 24 per cent by 1985 (Repetto, 1988). The deforestation was in part a direct result of existing government policies. First, clearing the land was required as evidence of 'land improvement'. The settlers were then able to claim title to an amount of land in direct proportion to the area of forest cleared. Poor settlers who did not benefit from tax incentives offered at the time gained more by clearing the land, selling it to large cattle-ranchers, and moving on.

and indirectly by building roads, which are then used by farmers and ranchers to gain access to remote areas (see also Box 10.2).

The immiserization model assumes that individual farm household decisions are the source of deforestation. In a country with low levels of GNP, foreign debt and tight fiscal policies lead to a low level of growth in non-farm employment and income. The lack of off-farm opportunities and increasing household size mean that the opportunity cost of labour is low and this provides the household with an incentive to expand the cultivated area to more marginal land areas. The immiserization model has strong Malthusian over-tones (see Chapter 6), in that Malthus predicted that population growth will continue until the family drives its per capita food consumption down to subsistence levels, leading to a 'dismal' equilibrium where the family just meets it subsistence needs. Walker (1993) con-cludes that deforestation due to poverty amongst farmers tends to be more local and incre-mental than the frontier model, in which whole regions are opened up to deforestation (see also Box 10.3).

In the immiserization model, economic growth, as measured by GNP, will reduce the rate of deforestation in two ways: growth increases off-farm opportunities so that labour moves out of agriculture, and this reduces the incentives for deforestation. A country's debt burden affects deforestation in two ways. First, the government's requirement for foreign exchange to pay debts encourages expansion of export sectors, which include cash crop production and timber. Second, the devaluation of local currency that often accompanies a debt crisis tends to increase the profits of timber companies and leads to increased investment and expansion of logging activities. Finally, an increase in the rural population leads to the movement of agriculture to more fragile marginal land.

Testing the models. On the basis of a cross-country study, Rudel and Roper (1997) con-clude that the evidence gives more support to the immiserization model than the frontier model. The main justification for this conclusion is that economic activity, as measured by

---

BOX 10.3 Deforestation in the Ivory Coast and the Discount Rate: An Example of Immiserization

The Ivory Coast has lost tropical rainforest at the rate of 300,000 ha per year during the 1980s and of an original area of 16 million ha, only 3.4 million ha remains. Deforestation is due to an increased demand for land for shifting cultivation. This demand is driven by population growth, rising poverty, and ill-defined property rights over forest land. Deforestation has led to soil erosion, a reduction in agricultural productivity, and the siltation of waterways. Attempts by government to define protected areas have been frustrated by the continued loss of forest to slash-and-burn agriculture.

In their paper, Ehui and Hertel (1989) estimate the costs of deforestation through average agricultural yields. As deforestation proceeds, average yields across cultivated land decline due to soil erosion and a reduction in soil fertility. The socially optimal equilibrium is where both the forest area and the average agricultural yield are constant. The outcome is highly sensitive to the discount rate. For instance, if the discount rate is 3 per cent ($r = 0.03$), the optimal forest area is 5.4 million ha, which implies some reforestation. If, however, the discount rate is 11 per cent ($r = 0.11$), then the optimal forest area is 2 million ha. In a country that is prone to economic instability, high interest and discount rates tend to be the norm. On the basis of this analysis, without government protection the rainforest area in the Ivory Coast will continue to decline.

the GNP per capita, is not found to be a significant determinant of deforestation: this counts against the frontier model as an explanation. However, the choice between the two models is not clear-cut and explanations of deforestation vary from country to country. In low-income countries with small remnant forest areas—for instance, the Ivory Coast—population growth appears to increase the rate of deforestation. In countries such as Brazil, with large blocks of forest, the frontier model is more appropriate. It is also possible to discern a progression, where initial deforestation is due to capital investment in roads, which is then followed by agricultural expansion that may be driven by population growth. Different pressures for deforestation may wax and wane, depending upon the cycles in a country's economy. If the economy is growing strongly, then this leads to frontier expansion and reduced dependence on subsistence agriculture. If the economy moves into recession, then frontier development declines, but deforestation for subsistence agriculture increases as a large proportion of the labour force turns to agriculture for a livelihood as the availability of urban jobs declines.

To generalize this relationship, Rudel and Roper predict the relationship, shown in Figure 10.1, between the proportion of the forest area logged and GNP:

- *Stage 1*. At low levels of GNP, deforestation is due to impoverished peasant farmers clearing more land to meet their subsistence food needs. Funding is not available to finance an expansion in the frontier and open up whole regions for deforestation. As the GNP increases and off-farm labour opportunities improve, then the rate of deforestation declines as labour moves out of agriculture.

- *Stage 2*. As economic development proceeds, investment capital becomes available from government and the private sector, and the frontier is opened up by investment in roads and other infrastructure.

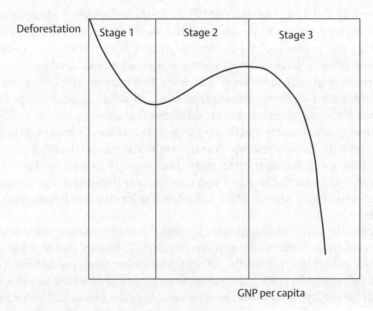

Figure 10.1 The deforestation environmental Kuznets curve.

- *Stage 3*. The level of wealth increases such that consumers have a demand for forest protection, and the labour force is less dependent on agriculture due to the development of jobs in manufacturing and service sectors.

Rates of deforestation may thus follow an environmental Kuznets curve (EKC). The possibility of a positive relationship between environmental protection at high income levels is a recurring theme that has already arisen in Chapter 6 and Chapter 8 in relation to trade. Other studies have confirmed the results of Rudel and Roper. There is evidence from cross-country studies by Ehrhardt-Martinez et al. (2002) and Shandra (2007) to support the presence of an EKC: the former find an inverse relationship between the rate of deforestation and income per capita in a country, whilst the latter finds that, on average, higher rates of population growth increase the rate of deforestation.

10.4 Tropical Deforestation and Poverty

The UN established the Millennium Development Goals in 2000 to address key measures of development, with a deadline of 2015 for the world community to achieve these goals. The goals relate poverty and hunger alleviation, education, gender equality, child health, HIV/AIDS prevention and treatment, environmental sustainability, and global partnership (largely concerned with opening markets to exports from developing countries). In the context of this chapter, a key question is: what role does forestry have in fostering development and, specifically, the reduction of poverty? In a review paper, Sunderlin et al. (2005) conclude that this is a complex question, as in some cases conserved forests reduce poverty and in others deforestation, by increasing the availability of agricultural land, reduces poverty and hunger.

Who depends on tropical rainforests? Some forest dwellers are traditional/indigenous peoples and their poverty is often 'primordial' (Sunderlin et al., 2005) and is not due to economic change. By 'primordial', the authors mean that the forest dwellers were relatively impoverished prior to large-scale deforestation and economic development. Incoming migrant farmers migrate to forest areas to increase their incomes and in this case the forest provides potential for increasing income. Forests are in some regions a refuge for landless people, as the forests are often treated as open-access resources.

For all these groups, the ability of forestry to provide income depends upon how the people interact with the forestry resource. The use of forestry can be classified as hunting and gathering, shifting cultivation, and sedentary cultivation. These uses can be seen as a progression from livelihoods that require a high forest density (hunting and gathering) through a moderate level of forest cover (shifting cultivation), to low levels of forest cover (sedentary agriculture).

Forests have the potential to contribute to market and non-market based determinants of poverty reduction. Timber sales worldwide (2003–7) had an annual value of US$100 billion (FAO, 2010: 120). In 2005, the value of non-timber forest products was estimated at US$18.5 billion (FAO, 2010: 120). Values from timber production do not always benefit the poor, as they typically do not have ownership of the resource. Timber production is capital and skills intensive, and this can exclude impoverished forest dwellers from employment in the industry. The more significant beneficial effects of forestry to farmers are through the positive externality due to increased ecosystem services and access to non-timber forest products.

It may be that the extraction of timber generates the highest short-term monetary (market) income and it is relatively straightforward to assign ownership to timber through timber concessions. This is in marked contrast to retained forest that provides non-monetary (non market) ecosystem services to groups benefitting through hunting and gathering and shifting agriculture. These groups may be relatively poor and thus even a non-market valuation would tend to return a low willingness to pay (WTP)—even though the forest resources account for a significant part of their income. One policy solution proposed by Sunderlin et al. (2005) is to strengthen community ownership over the forest. This may mean that these non-timber values are taken into account in the decision to clear an area of forest. Community ownership may also benefit the relatively poor, although evidence on this is mixed (for a review, see Shackleton et al., 2011) (see also Box 10.4).

10.5 Forestry Management

In this section, we consider two problems: first, how should forests be managed when the standing forest is a commercial enterprise that is managed for its timber values alone; and, second, how should the standing forest be managed when it also has an external (non-timber) value?

Forest managed for timber value. The problem of how long trees should be left to grow (i.e. how long the *forest rotation* should be) to maximize the present value of profits for multiple rotations was solved in 1847 by a German forester called Martin Faustmann. As a stand of single-aged trees grows through time, so does its timber value $V(T)$. This is shown in the top half of Figure 10.2. The value of trees is set against their opportunity cost; that is, the return on money tied up in trees that could earn a rate of return r if invested elsewhere. The bottom half of Figure 10.2 shows the rate of return on trees as the percentage growth in value. This is given as the *marginal growth in value* (*MV*) divided by the value of the trees.

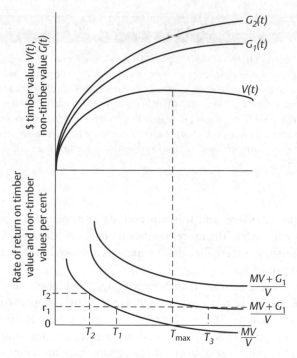

Figure 10.2 The optimal timber rotation.

This value is compared with r and when the two are equal, as at a in Figure 10.2, it is optimal to fell the forest and sell the timber. At this point, the present value of the forest is maximized. Note that this is a shorter time than T_{max}, the time when $V(T)$ reaches a maximum. The original Faustmann formula includes an adjustment for the *site value*; that is, the opportunity cost of the land, in terms of delaying the start of all future rotations. If the interest rate rises, then the optimal rotation length falls; for instance, at r_2, the length of the rotation reduces to T_2.

Forest managed for timber and non-timber value. If the forest has a non-timber value—for instance, in terms of its recreation value, or its value as a biodiversity refuge—then this changes the socially optimal forest rotation. Instead of maximizing the present value of timber, the forest is managed to maximize the present value of timber and non-timber values. Unlike the timber value, which is only realized at the time when the forest is clear-felled, the non-timber value is given as a flow of benefits in each year. The line $G_1(t)$ in the upper half of Figure 10.2 shows the value of these non-timber benefits. Note that the non-timber benefits $G_1(t)$ continue to increase with the rotation length, reflecting the fact that wildlife habitat values tend to increase with the length of the rotation. This contrasts with the timber value $V(T)$, where the forest is assumed to reach an age at which it starts to have a declining timber value due to tree death and senescence. The optimal rotation, at which the rate of return on the total value equals the discount rate $((MV + G_1)/V) = r$, at discount rate r_1, is now longer than the yield-maximizing rotation T_{max} at T_3. It may be optimal to never harvest the timber because of the size of the non-timber benefits; this is illustrated for a level of non-timber benefits G_2 in Figure 10.2.

10.6 How Much Natural Forest Should be Preserved?

10.6.1 The optimal area of natural forest for a region

In most regions, the loss of native forest is either entirely or partially irreversible. Natural forests have much in common with non-renewable resources like oil where extraction permanently depletes the stock. Once a forest has been cleared and the land converted to agriculture or abandoned, soil changes and the long time period required for the forest to return to its original state means that the natural forest is effectively lost for good. This is a simplification, since in some regions partial regeneration is possible and some of the biodiversity and ecosystem services of the original forest might be recovered in a period of 10–30 years.

The annual benefits from a forest comprise three components. The aggregate market benefits (net of costs) of the annual area of forest felled q_t given as a function $h(q_t, x_t)$, where x_t is the remaining forest area at time t. The market net benefits derive from the net benefits of logging and increased agricultural productivity, as more land becomes available for agriculture. For any given level of deforestation, the marginal benefits to the farmer of clearing decreases with the cumulative area logged. This is explained by forest clearance moving to land of progressively lower agricultural value. The benefits of preserving forest derive from two sources. Local benefits include the market and non-market benefits derived from forest products and flood protection $b^L(x_t)$. Global benefits include the benefits of biodiversity, which include the possibility of discovering new pharmaceutical products, and the existence values to citizens of other countries derived from knowing that the forest is protected, this benefit being given by the function $b^G(x_t)$. Both benefit functions are an increasing function of the forest area, with a declining marginal benefit. Thus as the cumulative area cleared increases, the marginal benefit of preserving the last hectare increases. Together, the net benefits of preservation are as follows:

$$b(x_t) = b^L(x_t) + b^G(x_t).$$

A socially optimal forest area is one in which the marginal benefits of clearing equals the present value of the marginal benefits of preservation. The marginal benefits of clearing in terms of timber and agriculture are assumed to be generated over a relatively short period: immediately for timber and over a relatively short period, say five periods, for agricultural land. The benefits of preservation are assumed to be forever. Therefore, the present value of preservation benefits is given by the formula $b(x_t)/r$, where r is the discount rate (see Box 7.3 about discounting), as in the Krutilla–Fisher model of wilderness conservation. The social optimum is where the present value of the marginal benefit of harvesting, mh, equals the present value of the marginal benefits of preservation, mb:

$$mh = mb/r = (mb^L + mb^G)/r. \tag{10.1}$$

The social optimum is illustrated in Figure 10.3. The initial forest area is x_0. The optimum solution that accounts for the local and global benefits of preservation is at c, with a conserved forest area of x^* where the condition in equation (10.1) holds. If, however, there is no mechanism to account for (to pay forest owners for), the global values of rainforest

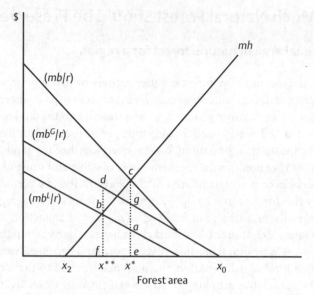

Figure 10.3 The equilibrium natural forest area.

preservation, the equilibrium is b at a lower level x^{**}. If the forest is open access and there are no effective policies for its protection in place, the equilibrium is driven down to x_2 where $mh = 0$. Note, from equation (10.1), that the discount rate is a key parameter: if this is high, then the present value of preservation is reduced. An example of this is given in Box 10.3, for the Ivory Coast. The discount rate on which firms base their decisions will be biased upwards if there are imperfections in the capital market or the government, in planning natural resource use, adopts a discount rate that does not reflect society's true rate of time preference. There is also no incentive for the country to account for the benefits that other countries derive from the forest. This problem has much in common with the problems of providing public goods discussed in Chapter 2. Putting all of these factors together goes a long way to explaining why forest losses across the globe have been excessive and represent a market failure.

10.7 Policies for Rainforest Conservation

10.7.1 International policy

Forestry has been an international policy priority since the 1992 United Nations Conference on Environment and Development (UNCED). UNCED led to a *Non-legally Binding Authoritative Statement of Principles for a Global Consensus on the Management, Conservation and Sustainable Development of all Types of Forests*, also known as the 'Forest Principles', and Chapter 11 of Agenda 21, 'Combating Deforestation'. This was followed by the Intergovernmental Panel on Forests (IPF), from 1995 to 1997, and the Intergovernmental Forum on Forests (IFF), from 1997 to 2000, both under the UN Commission on Sustainable

Development. These have led to the IPF/IFF Proposals for Action. The IPF/IFF proposals are not legally binding, but they do provide organizations in participant countries with a rationale for improving national forestry policy.

The UN Forestry Forum (UNFF) was established by ECOSOC Resolution/2000/35 to build on IPF and IFF processes. The resulting *Non-legally Binding Instrument on All Types of Forests* was adopted in 2007 by the UN General Assembly (Resolution 62/98). The purpose of this resolution is as follows:

a. To strengthen political commitment and action at all levels to implement effectively sustainable management of all types of forests and to achieve the shared global objectives on forests.

b. To enhance the contribution of forests to the achievement of the internationally agreed development goals, including the Millennium Development Goals; in particular, with respect to poverty eradication and environmental sustainability.

c. To provide a framework for national action and international co-operation.

10.7.2 The Global Environment Facility (GEF), REDD, and REDD+

The Global Environmental Facility (GEF) was established in 1991 to provide funds to address global environmental issues. Since 1991, the GEF has allocated US$9.5 billion of core funding and leveraged approximately US$42 billion in co-financing (GEF, 2012a). Most of the Focal Areas for GEF 5 are directly and indirectly related to natural forest protection (GEF, 2012b) (see also Box 10.5).

The UN–REDD Programme is the United Nations Collaborative Initiative on Reducing Emissions from Deforestation and Forest Degradation (REDD) in developing countries. The programme was established in 2008 to provide funds to developing countries to prepare projects that reduced greenhouse gas (GHG) emissions from deforestation. REDD also involves the Food and Agriculture Organization of the United Nations (FAO), the United

---

BOX 10.5 The Example of the GEF Project for Tropical Rainforest Conservation in Brazil

The GEF project, the *Amazon Region Protected Areas Program*, has three specific objectives:

1. To identify and create new strict protected areas.
2. The effective establishment of these new areas.
3. To develop long-term sustainable management tools and mechanisms for effective protection within all Amazonian strict protected areas.

The project emerges from a Government of Brazil commitment to extend strict protection in the Amazon to cover at least 10 per cent (37 million ha) of the biome (370 million ha). Although it is expected that all costs associated with the project will be of global benefit and incremental, GEF grant funds will act as seed capital to catalyse additional funds. The total cost of the project from GEF and other sources was US$82 million (GEF, 2012b).

> **BOX 10.6 The Noel Kempff Mercado National Park, Bolivia: A Case Study of a Carbon Offset Project**
>
> The Noel Kempff Mercado Climate Action Project (NKMCAP) is a deforestation avoidance project established in 1997, in the Santa Cruz Department of north-eastern Bolivia. It is a pilot project under the Kyoto Protocol Clean Development Mechanism and also an example of how REDD and REDD+ may operate. The project, by buying out logging concessions, expanded the area of the Noel Kempff National Park by 70 per cent (Pereira, 2010), with the primary aim of reducing carbon emissions by storing carbon that would have been released by timber harvesting and other forms of deforestation (NKMCAP, 2008).
>
> NKMCAP is a partnership between the Bolivian government, the Nature Conservancy (an international NGO), a Bolivian NGO (Fundación Amigos de la Naturaleza), and four multinational energy corporations (American Electric Power, British Petroleum Amoco, and PacifiCorp). The energy companies contributed to the US$11 million cost of the project. In return, they received carbon offsets. A community of 237 indigenous families were supported to apply for land title and also received other economic benefits, including work in the park and work in the ecotourism industry. This project is an example of where a payment for ecosystem services is combined with carbon abatement.

Nations Development Programme (UNDP), and the United Nations Environment Programme (UNEP) (UN–REDD, 2008). Box 10.6 gives an example of how the REDD mechanism might work, with an example of where payments for environmental services are partially derived from carbon offsets.

Agreement was reached at the COP16 (Conference of Parties to the Convention on Biodiversity) in Cancun, Mexico, in 2010 to reinforce REDD through the REDD+ agreement. This scheme extended the REDD agreement to include multiple benefits of reduced deforestation, ecosystem services, and biodiversity protection, in addition to GHG emission reduction:

> REDD+ goes beyond deforestation and forest degradation, and includes the role of conservation, sustainable management of forests and enhancement of forest carbon stocks.
>
> (UN–REDD, 2010)

The funding for REDD+ is around US$30 billion and this represents a substantial investment in conserving forestry in developing countries.

10.7.3 How effective are international policies?

Are international treaties effective? On the basis of the current rate of deforestation, which is still running at above 13 million ha a year, the short answer to this question is 'no'. The longer answer is that, while deforestation rates remain very high, there are some reasons to be optimistic. The FAO (FAO, 2010: ch. 8) notes that international policies feed through into an increase in the number and scope of national forestry programmes and policies. Independent evidence comes from Schofer and Hironaka (2005), who find, from a statistical analysis of deforestation, that participation in international institutions such as the UNFF has led to a significant estimated reduction in the rate of deforestation.

In the same paper, the authors hypothesize that 'institutions affect outcomes when they are: 1) highly structured; 2) when they penetrate actors at multiple levels of the social system; and 3) when they are persistent over time' (ibid.: 25). The last of these conditions applies as the UNCD brought deforestation to centre stage almost 20 years ago. As with the biodiversity conventions discussed in Chapter 12, there is a danger that:

> states routinely sign treaties to support global environmental norms, conformity to external norms may be ceremonial, offering environmental protection in form but not in substance.
>
> (ibid.: 26)

There is evidence of an increase in the enactment of national forest policies since 2000, with around 70 per cent of countries enacting new forest programmes between 2005 and 2009 (FAO, 2010: 154). It is argued by FAO that this relatively large number of new items of legislation have been driven by commitments to the UNFP.

There remains a fundamental problem that tropical rainforest is largely controlled by developing tropical nations, whilst many of the benefits of preservation—including carbon sequestration and biodiversity conservation—are global. The developed nations have the technological capacity to take advantage of gene material, with commercial potential for new crops and medicines that may be discovered in preserved rainforests.

International policy to protect rainforests has a strategic dimension, as does any problem that involves the provision of a public good (Barrett, 2005). There is a strong incentive for countries to free-ride: that is, benefit from reduced deforestation without paying their share of the costs. Figure 10.3 illustrates a problem of strategic interaction. With no intervention from the international community, then the optimum is at *b*, since this is where only national benefits are recognized. However, this is an undesirable outcome and represents the situation if there is no binding agreement to pay tropical nations to protect more of their forest. If countries can agree to a side payment to the tropical nations, this payment must be at least the area *abc*, which represents the tropical nations' net costs in terms of the reduction in the benefits of clearing. The additional benefits to the international community would be *dgef*. The tropical country may negotiate hard to make the side-payment as large a share of the additional benefits as possible. A complication in this process is that some countries may try to avoid paying their share of the side-payment, in the hope that others will pay and allow them to benefit for free (for a more detailed analysis of this issue, see Sandler, 1993).

The policy response to rainforest loss has been at the international, national, and local level. National policies are the most important, as they determine the incentives that farmers and timber companies face when taking decisions to clear an area of forest. International policies have had a limited impact so far; this is largely because they express broad objectives, without the resources needed by the tropical nations to agree to reduce the rate of deforestation. However, international payments for forest conservation under REDD+ may go some way to addressing this failure in future, by increasing financial transfers to tropical countries conditional on reduced rates of deforestation and better forestry management.

10.7.4 National and local policies

International initiatives to conserve tropical forests depend critically upon national and local policies within tropical nations. The objective of national policies should be one of reducing the adverse effects of market failure and government failure (McKean, 1965).

Government failure, where government intervention actually makes matters worse rather than better, includes subsidies for forest clearing, the link between land title and clearing, and price support for agricultural outputs such as palm oil. Areas in which government policy may eliminate market failure include placing taxes on deforestation, establishing effective property rights over forest land, creating conservation areas, and banning or regulating clearance in sensitive areas.

Deforestation remains a major global environmental problem because of government and market failure. The most significant market failure is the failure to account for national and global non-market values. A further problem in many poor countries is that government policy may be only partially implemented. International funds might be provided for rainforest conservation but, due to corruption and weak administrative arrangements, may not be spent effectively.

Summary

The international community agrees that tropical rainforests are valuable—they regulate the local environment, shelter biodiversity, and store carbon. Market failure, market distortions, missing markets, and ineffective and unstable government in many tropical countries have led to rates of deforestation that are greater than socially optimal rates of deforestation.

Those who own or who have access to the forests will cease deforestation only when it is profitable to do so (Mendelsohn, 1994). This can come about through national governments offering incentives to stop deforestation. In turn, this may only happen if there are funds from the international community to account for the global public goods provided by tropical rainforests.

Tutorial Questions

10.1 What are the main drivers of forest loss in Brazil and the Ivory Coast?

10.2 When should a natural forest never be cleared?

10.3 Why should the developed countries consider compensating the poor nations to stop deforestation?

10.4 Why are non-timber forest products often not taken into account when governments decide to allocate logging concessions?

10.5 Is there any evidence for an environmental Kuznets curve for forestry?

References and Additional Readings

Barrett, S. (2005). *Environment and Statecraft: The Strategy of Environmental Treaty-making* (Oxford: Oxford University Press).

Brown, K., and Pearce, D. (eds.) (1994). *The Causes of Tropical Deforestation* (London: UCL Press).

Ehrhardt-Martinez, K., Crenshaw, E.M., and Jenkins, J.C. (2002). 'Deforestation and the environmental Kuznets curve: a cross-national investigation of intervening mechanisms', *Social Science Quarterly* 83: 226–43.

Ehui, S.K., and Hertel, T.W. (1989). 'Deforestation and agricultural productivity in the Côte d'Ivoire', *American Journal of Agricultural Economics* 71: 703–11.

Eliasch, J. (2008). *Climate Change: Financing Global Forests* (The Eliasch Review) (London. HMSO).

FAO (Food and Agriculture Organization) (2005). *Global Forest Resources Assessment, Main Report* (Rome: UN Food and Agriculture Organization).

—— (2010). *Global Forest Resources Assessment, Main Report* (Rome: UN Food and Agriculture Organization).

GEF (Global Environmental Facility) (2012a) 'What is GEF?', http://www.thegef.org/gef/whatisgef (accessed 15 November 2012).

—— (2012b). *The Greenline* (July 2012), http://www.thegef.org/gef/greenline/july-2012/progress-towards-impact-review-outcomes-phase-i-amazon-region-protected-areas-pr (accessed 15 November 2012).

Groombridge, B., and Jenkins, M.D. (2002). *World Atlas of Biodiversity: Earth's Living Resources in the 21st Century* (Berkeley, CA: University of California Press).

Klemick, H. (2011). 'Shifting cultivation, forest fallow, and externalities in ecosystem services: evidence from the Eastern Amazon', *Journal of Environmental Economics and Management* 61: 95–106.

McKean, R.N. (1965). 'The unseen hand in government', *American Economic Review* 55: 496–506.

Mendelsohn, R. (1994). 'Property rights and tropical deforestation', *Oxford Economic Papers* 46: 750–6.

NKMCAP (Noel Kempff Mercado Climate Action Project) (2008). Project summary, http://www.nature.org/ourinitiatives/urgentissues/global-warming-climate-change/places-we-protect/noel_kempff_case_study_final-1.pdf (accessed 6 June 2011).

Pereira, S.N.C. (2010). 'Payment for environmental services in the Amazon forest: how can conservation and development be reconciled?' *Journal of Environment and Development* 19: 171–90.

Peters, C.M., Gentry, A.H., and Mendelsohn, R.O. (1989). 'Valuation of an Amazonian rainforest', *Nature* 339: 655–6.

Repetto, R. (1988). *The Forest for the Trees? Government Policies and the Misuse of Forest Resources* (Washington, DC: World Resources Institute).

Rudel, T., and Roper, J. (1997). 'The paths to rain forest destruction: cross-national patterns of tropical deforestation', *World Development* 25: 53–65.

Sandler, T. (1993). 'Tropical deforestation: markets and market failures', *Land Economics* 69(3): 225–33.

Scherr, S.J., White, A., and Kaimowitz, D. (2004). *A New Agenda for Forest Conservation and Poverty Alleviation: Making Markets Work for Low-income Producers* (Washington, DC: Forest Trends).

Schofer, E., and Hironaka, A. (2005). 'The effects of world society on environmental protection outcomes', *Social Forces* 84: 1–25.

Shackleton, S., Shackleton, C., and Shanley, P. (eds.) (2011). *Non-timber Forest Products in the Global Context* (Heidelberg: Springer-Verlag).

Shandra, J. (2007). 'The world polity and deforestation: a cross-national analysis', *International Journal of Comparative Sociology* 48(1): 5–28.

Sims, K.R.E. (2010). 'Conservation and development: evidence from Thai protected areas', *Journal of Environmental Economics and Management* 60: 94–114.

Sunderlin, W.D., Angelsen, A., Belcher, B., Burgers, P., Nasi, R., Santoso, L., and Wunder, S. (2005). 'Livelihoods, forests, and conservation in developing countries: an overview', *World Development* 33: 1383–402.

UN-REDD (2008). UN collaborative programme on reducing emissions from deforestation and forest degradation in developing countries (UN-REDD), http://www.un-redd.org/Portals/15/documents/publications/UN-REDD_FrameworkDocument.pdf (accessed 15 November 2012).

UN-REDD (2010). About REDD+, http://www.un-redd.org/aboutredd/tabid/582/default.aspx (accessed 15 November 2012).

Walker, R. (1993). 'Deforestation and economic development', *Canadian Journal of Regional Science* 16: 481–97.

11 The Economics of Water Pollution

In this chapter, we will explore the economics of water pollution. Most of the chapter is taken up with analysis of the costs and benefits of reducing water pollution.

11.1 Introduction

What is 'water pollution'? For a natural scientist, water pollution is the discharge of a substance into a water-body (a river, stream, lake, or estuary, or an underground aquifer), which changes the functioning of the system. For example, the input of organic wastes to a river speeds up biological processes, and in the process uses up oxygen. The input of ammonia may be directly toxic to fish. Phosphate inputs to a lake lead to nutrient enrichment of the aquatic ecosystem, and can result in a build-up of toxic algae and lead to a change in plant and animal communities.

For an economist, however, we need to know more—precisely, we need to know whether water pollution adversely affects at least one person's well-being (e.g. people affected by sewage levels at their local beach) or adversely affects production (e.g. commercial fishers suffer reduced catches as a result of an oil spill). This is because pollution only becomes an external cost, and a source of market failure, if people suffer from its impacts. We classify water pollution problems into two types, each with different policy implications:

- point-source pollution; and
- non-point pollution.

Point-source pollution is defined as emissions that enter water-bodies from an easy-to-identify single source, such as a pipe from a factory or the outfall from a sewage works. These kinds of emissions can be monitored at low cost, and linked to the actions of individual firms or households. *Non-point* pollution, in contrast, enters water-bodies in a diffuse manner, such as surface run-off from farmers' fields or from forests, or as pollution seeping into groundwater aquifers. Non-point pollution emissions are hard to measure, since they cannot be traced to a single pipe or point of entry to the water-body. It is hard to assign responsibility for the emission of non-point pollutants to individual firms or households.

Water pollution may originate from many different sources, for example:

- from industry, in the form of point-source discharges of heavy metals, organic wastes, and other pollutants;
- from sewage treatment works or direct sewage outfalls;
- as acid drainage waters from old mines;
- as leachate from landfill sites;
- as pathogens washing off from fields in which cattle are kept;
- as run-off of oils and solvents from city streets;
- as run-off of fertilizers and pesticides, and soil erosion from farmland and forests; and
- as accidental (unplanned) spillages—for instance, from oil tankers.

In what sense is pollution harmful? Pollutants may have their main effect on aquatic organisms by reducing the dissolved oxygen (DO) content of water. The amount of oxygen dissolved in water is important for the support of fish. Alternatively, pollutants may be directly toxic: for example, if pesticides or chlorine are spilt in a river. Pollutants can also change the acidity of a river or lake, making it impossible for certain organisms to survive over time. Pollution can change water temperatures, or increase bacterial levels to the detriment of human health. Finally, pollutants can change the nutrient balance of a water-body, making it over-rich, a process known as eutrophication.

The impact of emissions on water quality may vary in space and time. Consider the discharge of sewage into the sea. The impact is measured in bacterial counts, and will depend on tide movements, temperature, and sunshine, and the overall direction of water circulation. This means that a given quantity of sewage discharged at two different points on the same coastline may have differing effects on water quality at a local beach. Another example is how organic discharges affect local water-quality levels (measured in DO) in an estuary. Again, the impact of one ton of effluent discharged at one point on the estuary will vary according to where it is measured (e.g. upstream or downstream). Pollutants whose impact varies spatially are called *non-uniformly mixed*. Some water pollutants do not have this property: for instance, if the concern is with nitrate levels in a lake, it is not important where in the catchment nitrate originates—cutting any source will have roughly the same impact on eutrophication. Whether pollutants are uniformly or non-uniformly mixed is important for the design of policy, since this determines whether our control policies need to discriminate between polluters according to their location.

11.1.1 Trends over time

In many early-industrializing countries such as the United Kingdom and Germany, most water-quality indicators have shown improving trends over the past 40 years. This follows periods of decline associated with earlier industrialization and urbanization. For instance, the earliest legislation passed in England (the 1876 Rivers Act) followed on from the closure of Parliament during the 'Great Stink' on the River Thames in London in 1858. Gross discharges from industrial and municipal sources (sewage works) have now largely been brought under control, as a result of legislation such as the Control of Pollution Act (1974) in the UK, the Water Framework Directive of the European Union, and the Water Quality Act (1965) in the United States. In the UK, for example, the length of rivers classified as 'grossly polluted' fell from 2,000 km in England and Wales in 1958 to 800 km in 1980. Since then, progress has slowed. Many localized difficulties remain, whilst diffuse-source pollution has risen in significance worldwide (Foley et al., 2005) (see also Box 11.1).

Non-point pollution was the reason why many rivers failed to achieve a 'Good Ecological Status' in England and Wales in 2006, and it is the main cause of water-quality problems in the USA (Ribaudo, 2009). Table 11.1 shows the different reasons why water-bodies in Scotland were classified as 'at risk' of not achieving Good Ecological Status, from a 2005 audit. The main non-point pressures vary across type of water-body. Pollution of ground-water aquifers by pesticides, nitrates, chlorinated solvents, and chlorine-rich water from old mines, and the presence of newer, exotic pollutants such as TBT (tri-butyl tin) and poly-chlorinated biphenyls (PCBs), has raised relatively recent concerns. In contrast, in many developing countries, water pollution from 'traditional' point sources such as industry and sewage works is still a significant problem.

11.2 The Costs of Water Pollution Control

Market failures require corrective action (see Chapter 2). Water pollution is a classic example of a market failure. What could governments do to reduce water pollution, whether it be

BOX 11.1 Changes in River Quality over Time in Scotland

Prior to 1800 and rapid urbanization, Scotland's rivers were clean and healthy. However, by 1850, rivers such as the Clyde and the Almond were rendered foul by a combination of sewage and industrial waste and this trend continued into the twentieth century. Significant efforts in restoring Scotland's rivers did not start until 1965, but since then, progress has been considerable. The improvement has been due to a combination of causes; principally Scotland's shrinking heavy industrial base and the enforcement of new legislation.

A comprehensive assessment of trends in water quality since the mid-1970s is provided by SEPA (2010). Based on a system of 'harmonized monitoring stations', they look at trends in a large number of water-quality parameters. They also consider spatial and seasonal variations in water quality. The main conclusions reached are that '… improvements in many aspects of water quality have been delivered through environmental regulation, cleaner technologies, improved sewage treatment and changes in agricultural practice. This is most notable for parameters such as biochemical oxygen demand, ammoniacal nitrogen, lead and sulphate, which have all generally declined in river waters. Other parameters showed a more complex pattern of regional and seasonal trends' (SEPA, 2010: 7). Total phosphorus levels (due to a mixture of non-point pollution from farming and point-source pollution from sewage treatment work, for example), show improving trends in many parts of the country, but rising levels in northern rivers. The report suggests agricultural intensification as one reason for this trend.

See http://www.sepa.org.uk/science_and_research/data_and_reports/water/scottish_river_water_quality.aspx/.

Table 11.1 Sources at risk of not achieving Good Ecological Status for different water-body types, Scotland, 2005

Pressure	Rivers	Lakes	Estuaries	Coastal waters	Groundwater
Point discharges	14.2	12.3	45	24.7	16.0
Diffuse pollution	24.3	18.4	45	13.2	19.8
Abstraction	24.6	36.9	2.5	Not applicable	10.4
Physical changes	33.3	38.8	40	9.6	Not applicable
Overall percentage of water-bodies at risk	**45.5**	**54**	**57.5**	**28.7**	**23.6**

Source: SEPA (2005).

from point or non-point sources? Government intervention to reduce pollution can take three basic forms:

- *Regulation.* This works by setting technology or performance standards. For water pollution, a performance standard could be a quantitative limit on how much pollution firms were allowed to discharge to a river per day, enforced by law. Technology standards might include the specification of minimum technological standards for sewage works (e.g. the installation of nutrient stripping technology).

- *Voluntary means.* Households could be asked to use low-phosphate laundry products in a catchment suffering from excess nutrient levels in its streams and rivers; firms could be asked to achieve improvements in their emissions as their contribution to a catchment management plan.

- *Economic incentives.* This could include a tax on emissions of organic wastes to an estuary; or a tradable permit scheme for such wastes.

The costs of achieving a water-quality standard (such as a minimum concentration of dissolved oxygen, or a maximum concentration of ammonia) depends on which government intervention is used. In Chapter 2, we saw that aggregate reduction in pollution *at least cost* depends on the marginal costs of abatement (*MACs*) being equalized across sources; only economic incentives can achieve such an outcome (in the absence of an all-powerful, fully informed regulator who can impose the least-cost pollution on polluters by regulation). For a target reduction in some measure of water pollution in a lake, achieving the least-cost outcome means that:

- Marginal abatement costs are equalized between different categories of sources: for example, between farmers, paper mills, and sewage works, if all are sources of nutrient pollution.

- Marginal abatement costs are equalized across all firms or households within a particular source category—that is, for example, across all farmers.

The costs of reaching an aggregate pollution target will exceed the theoretical minimum if differences exist between and within source categories. If a system of performance standards means that *MACs* vary significantly across factories all discharging some pollutant, costs savings will emerge if firms could trade the right to emit—as occurs in a tradable permit scheme—so to take advantage of these differences. Suppose for example, BK Paper has marginal abatement costs of €2,000 per tonne at its current level of emissions and Ace Paper has marginal abatement costs of €5,000 per tonne. If BK cuts its emissions by an extra 100 tonnes and sells permits to Ace, Ace can increase emissions by 100 tonnes, and the total costs to the economy of achieving the target fall. A pollution tax can have a similar effect, as we have seen: both BK and Ace can increase or cut emissions until MAC is equal to the tax rate for each firm (see Figure 11.1).

One problem with using economic incentives for water pollution is when non-uniform mixing exists:

- When pollutants are non-uniformly mixed, a single tax rate is inefficient. This happens because the tax is levied on emissions rather than on their environmental impact (Muller and Mendelsohn, 2009). Firms that cause more damage per unit of emissions should be taxed at a higher rate than firms that cause lower per-unit-of-emission damage. At the limit, correcting this problem involves a unique tax rate for each firm. More pragmatically, suggestions have been made for 'banded tax rates'—where taxes vary according to the stretch of an estuary in which a firm is located, for instance—to try to control for non-uniform mixing to at least some degree.

- When pollutants are non-uniformly mixed, allowing permits to trade at a one-for-one rate may result in local violations of water-quality standards. Imagine two firms are thinking of trading. In Figure 11.2, firm A is a potential buyer from firm B. But because A is located upstream of B, each unit of emissions from A does more harm than each unit from B. If A buys 100 permits from B, total emissions remain constant—but

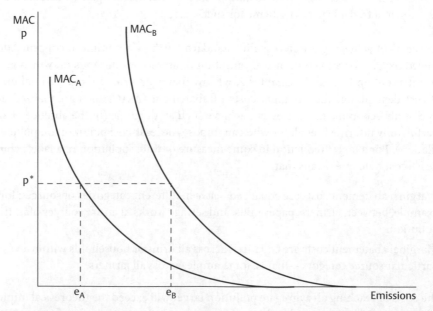

Figure 11.1 The effect of a pollution tax (t) on emissions from two firms, A and B. Note that each firm reduces emissions up to the point at which its marginal abatement costs (*MAC*) are equal to the pollution tax rate.

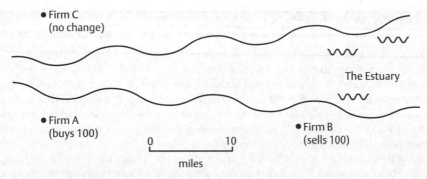

Figure 11.2 Permit trading in an estuary.

environmental damage rises, especially in the zone immediately downstream of A. This situation arises for many cases of water pollution control, and several solutions have been proposed. One is zonal trading, which might involve banning trades between A and B, and only allowing A to trade with C. But the more trade is restricted in this way, the lower the cost-saving potential of the scheme. Another idea is to use trading rules, which would govern the rate at which A and B can trade. Suppose that A's emissions are twice as harmful per unit as B's in terms of average water quality. An exchange rate of 0.5/1 could be imposed on trading between the two. Under this scheme, exchange rates would have to be calculated for all firms on the river, but this is possible using water-quality models. It remains a challenge to establish viable and reasonable trading ratios for the design of water-quality trading markets (Farrow et al., 2005).

Box 11.2 gives two empirical illustrations of the potential cost savings from introducing tradable permit systems for water pollution control.

11.3 Non-point Source Water Pollution: A Difficult Problem to Solve

We have pointed out that non-point pollution is an important source of water-quality problems in many countries. As point-source pollution is reduced, non-point emissions from farmland and other types of land cover become more important for governments trying to drive up water-quality standards. Worldwide, agriculture is now the main source of excessive nitrate and phosphate levels in fresh water and coastal waters (Foley et al., 2005). Like any form of pollution, non-point source (NPS from now on) pollution is amenable to management using regulation, voluntary measures, or economic incentives. One challenge for NPS pollution control is the costs of measuring and monitoring emissions (such as soil eroding from a hillside, or nutrients flowing into an estuary). An even more difficult task is to attribute these to the actions of an individual land manager. We use nitrate pollution to illustrate how the various policy options might work to control NPS pollution. Too high a nitrate concentration in water-bodies can result in eutrophication, and consequent fish deaths and loss of amenity. Farming is a major source of nitrates; artificial fertilizers and livestock waste are therefore potentially polluting inputs. If a stable relationship could be

BOX 11.2 Do Tradable Permits Save Money in Controlling Water Pollution?

Little empirical evidence exists on the ability of tradable permit systems to deliver actual cost savings with respect to water pollution control, since they have not be used that much (in stark contrast to their use in controlling air pollution). The Fox River, Wisconsin trading system was the subject of initial studies that suggested large cost savings from permit trading (O'Neil et al., 1983). In practice, however, the trading scheme was hamstrung by regulations that only one trade ever occurred. Most 'evidence' for cost savings from tradable pollution permits (TPPs) for water pollution control comes from simulation studies. In this box, we give brief details on two such studies in two European countries.

Scotland: the Forth Estuary. The Forth Estuary, in central Scotland, is a tidal water-body that is subject to many demands, including providing water for industrial cooling, for recreation, as a habitat for birds and as a sink for waste disposal. Most wastes come from industry, notably from a large petrochemical complex and from a yeast factory. A seasonal 'sag' in dissolved oxygen in the upper estuary due to excessive pollution has been noted in many summers: this has a bad effect on salmon migrating upstream. Control is exercised by the Scottish Environment Protection Agency, which uses performance standards to regulate discharges of pollution from firms and sewage works. Hanley et al. (1998) report results from a simulation exercise to study the potential cost savings from introducing a TPP system to improve DO levels. They found that such a system could generate large cost savings over regulation, although these were reduced once uncertainty over water-quality impacts was allowed for. For example, a TPP system could achieve a 20 per cent improvement in DO in the most polluted part of the estuary at one-ninth of the cost of uniform regulation. This large saving occurs because marginal abatement costs vary greatly over firms at the current level of control. Under uncertainty, the TPP system generates higher costs, but still achieves the target (in probabilistic terms) at a much lower cost than standards. These results were obtained by combining an economic model of polluters, based on abatement costs, with a water-quality model that allows for firms located in different parts of the estuary to have different impacts on DO per unit of emission.

Coastal water quality in Sweden: the pulp and paper industry. Paper and pulp mills have traditionally been seen as major sources of water pollution in many countries. In Sweden, more than 50 per cent of total discharges of oxygen-depleting pollutants, and almost all discharges of chlorine-containing material come from this industry. Most plants are located on Sweden's east coast, so a lot of these discharges end up in the sea. Discharges are regulated by non-tradable permits, set at the firm-specific level, as in the Scottish case. Runar Brannlund and colleagues studied the likely impact on abatement costs of allowing firms to trade these permits. Their results are based on a study of 41 pulp mills over the period from 1986 to 1990 (Brannlund et al., 1998). They find that moving from no trading to trading increases industry-level profits by around SEK1.2 billion in 1989, a 6 per cent rise, since firms with higher abatement costs can buy permits from firms with lower abatement costs, who can profit from such sales. Some thirty-two firms become permit sellers, and eighteen firms become buyers. The authors note that the permit system they model could result in increased environmental damages, since although *total* emissions are the same in the trading and no-trading cases, the impacts of these emissions may vary, since firms have different environmental impacts per unit of emission due to their physical locations (i.e. this is a problem of a non-uniform mixing pollutant).

found between inputs of nitrate fertilizer and nitrate levels in a polluted lake, control could be exercised on this use of input. This means that we need information about the 'pollution production function' (*g*), which relates inputs of fertilizer, N_i, from source i to water-quality levels at a range of monitoring points, Q_j:

$$Q_j = g(N_i, Z). \tag{11.1}$$

Here, Z represents all the other observable factors that determine nitrate concentrations in a lake at a given point in time, such as rainfall, and the type of crops being grown. Imagine that the state of knowledge is such that for a particular lake, we can estimate equation (11.1) using water-quality modelling.

The policy alternatives are the same as with point-source pollutants: a tax could be placed on N, or a tradable permits system set up for purchases/applications of N. Alternatively, farmers could be regulated in terms of how much N they are allowed to apply. In Figure 11.3(a), we show the impacts of a tax on nitrate fertilizer. The initial price is P_n, at which price farmers maximize profits by applying N_1 units, since at this point the marginal cost of N (its price) is equal to its marginal benefits, measured by the demand curve N^D. Introducing a tax of t raises the price to $(P_n + t)$, and nitrate applications fall to

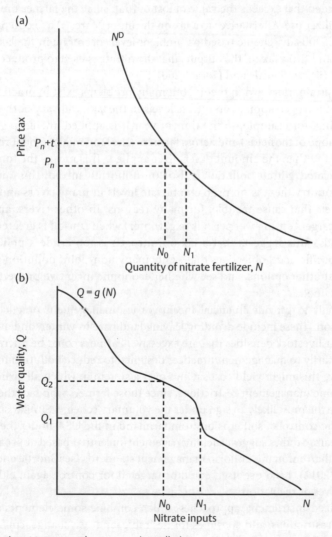

Figure 11.3 Using input taxes to reduce non-point pollution.

N_0. This reduction in fertilizer use is shown in Figure 11.3(b) as resulting in a reduction in nitrate inputs to the river from N_1 to N_0, improving water quality from Q_1 to Q_2.

The demand curve N^D can be interpreted as the farmer's marginal abatement cost curve for nitrogen use, since each unit less the farmer uses costs him in terms of forgone output (as yields fall). The fall in output will vary across farms, due, for instance, to variable land productivity, varying managerial skills, and variable climate. This means that the MAC curve for nitrate use varies across farms, just as with point-source pollution. Given such differences in MAC curves, an economic incentive approach such as a tax should give a desired reduction in emissions at a lower aggregate cost than regulation. In this instance, regulation would involve constraining all farms to apply no more than N_0 nitrogen to their land. But if the N^D curve varies across farms, then this uniform regulation will be more costly (less efficient) than a tax. We can also see that under the nitrates tax, the farmer incurs a financial burden that exceeds the value of lost output, since the farmer must also pay the tax on his fertilizer use. Alternatives to a tax on the input N are: (i) a tax on predicted emissions; (ii) a tax/subsidy scheme based on ambient levels of nitrate in the lake, known as a Segerson tax; and (iii) a tax on the outputs that the nitrate is used to produce. For a discussion of (i) and (ii), see Shortle and Horan (2001).

This seems straightforward in theory, but many problems exist in practice. The impact of each unit of nitrogen applied on nitrate levels in the lake will vary both within a given farm (according, for example, to the time of year it is applied, the crop growing in the fields, or the slope of the fields) and across farmers. The land management regime adopted may matter more than the amount of fertilizer applied. This means the function $Q = g(.)$ will be complicated. Nitrate pollution is also non-uniformly mixed. This implies for many areas of the country there is no problem: nitrate levels in many rivers and groundwater fall below levels that cause trouble, for many reasons. In other rivers, ambient nitrate levels exceed targets during wet periods (e.g. winter) when run-off is greater, but not during dry periods. This suggests that a tax on nitrogen is too crude a policy measure to achieve the specific, local objectives that typify many non-point pollution problems. We need to look at other options, and see whether economic incentive properties can somehow be maintained.

One option is to provide financial incentives for management practices that reduce nitrate pollution. These include avoiding leaving land bare in winter, and avoiding nitrate applications or livestock densities that are excessive. Farmers could be offered subsidies to sign up voluntarily to management practices designed to reduce pollution in specific areas of the country. This might yield cost savings over a system in which all farmers must conform to the same management restrictions, since those farmers who face the lowest abatement costs are the most likely to sign under the voluntary scheme. Similar subsidy systems are used for the control of soil erosion from farmland in the USA under the Conservation Reserve Program. Studies suggest such management-incentive-based approaches are more cost-effective than enforcing uniform management standards (see Shortle and Horan, 2001; Shortle et al., 2012). Land use itself could be targeted for control, again either using economic incentives or regulation.

Finally, 'mixed-instrument' approaches, which combine some elements of input taxes, management restrictions, and subsidies for desirable land-use change, could out-perform either a system based on either economic incentives only or regulation only. Aftab et al.

(2007) provide one illustration. They model policy options to reduce nitrate pollution in a catchment in eastern Scotland. A model of different farm types in the catchment was constructed, and linked to a water-quality model that related land use to nitrate levels in the river. The authors considered the following range of policy options:

- A tax on estimated nitrate run-off (estimated emissions)
- A tax on nitrate inputs
- Input quotas per hectare
- Limits on livestock density
- Set-aside requirements (a requirement to leave a certain fraction of farmland uncultivated)

They considered mixes of incentives to capture how regulators use more than one policy lever to achieve their objectives. The model was run to estimate the costs of hitting a target maximum concentration of nitrates (specified as how many weeks per year the target was allowed to be exceeded). Since nitrate pollution also depends on the weather, two scenarios were considered: an average and a wet year. Policy options were ranked by costs, and the results are shown in Table 11.2.

The pure economic instrument of an estimated emissions tax is always lowest cost. However, it is difficult and controversial to implement such a tax in practice, since farmers may object to the levels of emissions that were being attributed to them. A pure tax on inputs is relatively low cost, but a mix of instruments, such as combining stocking density restrictions with an input tax, can be better. In a wet year, the ranking changes slightly. Measures effective in reducing nitrate run-off in wet conditions (e.g. setting land aside from cultivation) are now relatively more attractive. These results suggest that regulators have good grounds to combine an economic instrument with more regulatory approaches for NPS pollution.

Another policy option for NPS pollution is *point–non-point* trading. In some water-bodies, nutrient pollution originates from both point sources such as sewage treatment works or factories, and from farmland. Allowing permit trading between point sources saves costs. Finding an efficient balance of emission reduction activities between point and

Table 11.2 Ranking of options to achieve a water-quality target according to cost

	Rank during an average year	Rank during wet years
Estimated emissions tax	1	1
Input tax	3	4
Input quota	4	5
SD restriction + input tax	2	8
Set aside + input tax	6	3
SD restriction, set aside + input tax	5	2
Set aside + SD restriction	7	7
Set aside	8	6

Note: SD = stocking density.
Source: Adapted from Aftab et al. (2007).

non-point sources requires that we either set a pollution tax that applies to both sectors, or we allow them to trade emission reduction rights. A local authority might find it cheaper to pay a group of farmers to reduce expected emissions from their land by, for example, switching to low input cropping, rather than investing in nutrient removal facilities at its treatment plants.

The scope for trading emission reduction rights across point and non-point sources depends on the extent of differences in marginal abatement costs between them. In principle, point–non-point trading of emission reductions could deliver pollution reduction targets at lower costs than in the absence of such a system. Box 11.3 gives an example of such systems. Several schemes that allow point–non-point trades are in operation in the USA, Canada, and New Zealand. Their success has been rather limited, due to several factors. These include regulatory uncertainty about how much emission reduction will be forthcoming from a particular set of actions by farmers; and that emissions from farmland depend on the weather and vary by season. It is a challenge to know the correct exchange rates between point and non-point sources. For a full discussion of the pros and cons of designing and implementing point–non-point trading schemes, see Shortle and Horan (2001) and OECD (2010). For a recent simulation of the winners and losers under a point–non-point trading scheme, see Lankowski et al. (2008).

BOX 11.3 Water-quality Trading in Practice

A review of water-quality trading schemes related to agricultural pollutants around the world is given in OECD (2010). Some twenty-six programmes worldwide where trading *could* occur were identified, although trading had not actually occurred in all of these. Most schemes were found in the USA, but similar policies also exist in Australia, Canada, and New Zealand, whilst trading programmes are being considered in Finland and Sweden.

A point–non-point trading programme for phosphorus management for the South Nation River in Ontario, Canada, is described. This allows fifteen municipalities and two industrial point sources of phosphorus (P) to offset their requirements for pollution reduction by funding projects to reduce emissions from agricultural sources. A trading rule requires an estimated 4 kg of P from agriculture to be cut to offset 1 kg of P from point sources. The programme is thought to result in cost savings, since reductions from agriculture, even with this trading rule, are cheaper than reductions from point sources via enhanced treatment. All point sources covered by the scheme have chosen to use these agricultural offsets, although there is no direct bargaining between farmers and point sources: trades are affected through an agency that contracts with farmers to engage in emissions reduction programmes, and then sells the offsets to point sources. Direct trading between *point* sources for pollution credits does, however, occur in the Hunter River Salinity Trading Scheme in Australia, via an online trading platform.

Other examples of non-point trading schemes in the USA include the California Grassland Areas Program (where trades are in reductions in selenium discharges from farmland), and the Greater Miami Watershed point–non-point trading scheme, established in Ohio in 2005. The California scheme is interesting since rather than being based on estimated emissions, it is based on actual selenium levels, monitoring of which is made possible due to the nature of the irrigation system within which the scheme works. The Ohio scheme features trading of nutrient reduction credits for nitrates and phosphorus between farmers and regulated point sources in the catchment.

11.4 Measuring Water-quality Benefits

Water-quality benefits can arise from the amelioration of many sources of impairment, including:

- non-point pollution from farmland and forests;
- changes to river morphology;
- hydroelectricity production;
- storm water overflows;
- point-source pollution from industry and sewage treatment works; and
- habitat loss and conversion.

Benefits arise from improvements to river appearance/aesthetics and flows; improvements in bankside vegetation; improvements to in-stream ecology; increases in biodiversity (water birds, otters, amphibians); and reductions in bad odours and health risks (e.g. from cyanobacteria: Hunter et al., 2012). These physical changes in water-bodies generate a range of economic benefits, involving both increased use values—for example, to fishers or kayakers (Johnstone and Markandya, 2006; Hynes et al., 2009), or to those living near a polluted water-body—and increased non-use values; for example, because of an improvement in the survival probabilities of rare species. Many benefits will not be directly reflected in market prices, so that non-market valuation methods must be used to estimate them.

Many methods have been used to measure the economic value of water-quality improvements, dating back to early work by Smith and Desvouges (1986). A recent overview of methods that can be applied within the context of the European Union's Water Framework Directive can be found in Birol et al. (2006). Consider three methods—contingent valuation, choice experiments, and revealed-preference approaches.

Starting with work in the 1980s, the contingent valuation method has been a popular tool to value changes in water quality (e.g. Mitchell and Carson, 1989). Loomis et al. (2000), for instance, use a contingent valuation survey to measure the benefits of restoring ecosystem service flows on the Platte River; Holmes et al. (2004) studied the benefits of ecosystem service restoration for the Little Tennessee River. Both studies were used as part of a cost–benefit analysis (CBA) of river restoration, showing in both cases that benefits outweighed costs (see also Box 11.4). In the UK, contingent valuation has been used to estimate the benefits of improvements to flow conditions in rivers subject to summer low flows (e.g. Hanley et al., 2003).

The second method is choice experiments. This method has proven itself attractive to water-quality researchers, since it enables separate values for different attributes of water quality (e.g. in-stream ecology, aesthetics, bankside vegetation). Such attribute values are seen as being useful from a management or policy context. Policy-makers like the detailed picture of the relative benefits of water-quality management options to be put together. Examples include Hanley et al. (2006), who looked at the value of improvements to two rivers in eastern Scotland, and Smyth et al. (2009), who study the benefits of

---

BOX 11.4 National Water-quality Benefits Assessment in the USA

Viscusi et al. (2008) report the results of a national stated preference survey aimed at measuring the economic value of changes in US water quality over the period from 1994 to 2000. How to quantify changes in water quality is one problem facing economists wishing to place monetary estimates on these changes. Viscusi et al. use the US Environmental Protection Agency's classification of water quality, based on what uses can be made of a particular water-body; for example, whether it is clean enough to swim in, and whether fish caught there can be safely eaten, or whether it is only suitable for boating. In their stated preference survey, they use two classes of water: 'Good' and 'Not Good'. Good quality was described as 'a lake or river suitable for all uses'. 'Not Good' meant 'a lake or river is an unsafe place to swim due to pollution, has fish that are unsafe to eat, or supports only a small number of fish, plants and other aquatic life'. Between 1994 and 2000, national water quality in the USA, defined on this basis, declined: there was a 6.2 per cent decline in the area of lakes and miles of river classified as 'Good'.

Some 4,527 members of the US public were questioned, using an Internet panel. Respondents were asked to make choices between moving to one of two possible new regions. Each pair of regions differed in terms of the annual cost of living and the percentage of lake acres and river miles that were of 'Good' quality. By observing people's preferences in repeated choice situations, the researchers could infer their willingness to pay (WTP) for a 1 per cent increase in the percentage of waters near their (hypothetical) residence that were of Good quality. On the basis of this, they estimated a mean figure of $196 per household per year on the economic cost of the water-quality decline from 1994 to 2000; this is equivalent to around $22 billion across all US households. In a benefit–cost analysis, this figure could be compared with the costs of restoring this length of degraded lakes and rivers to 'Good' status.

---

management actions for Lake Champlain. Attributes used in the Smyth et al. study include water clarity, beach closures, the spread of an invasive plant, and fish consumption advisories. An example of a choice experiment task, for the Hanley et al. (2006) study, is included as Table 11.3. Figure 11.4 shows in more detail how the varying levels of water-quality attributes can be portrayed to respondents. Table 11.4 shows typical results in terms of marginal values for improvements in river attributes, again from the Hanley et al. (2006) study. Box 11.5 reports on a study using both choice experiments and contingent valuation to study benefits of water-quality improvements in Iowa.

Table 11.3 An example of a choice card

Policy	Do nothing	A	B
Option impact			
Number of agricultural jobs lost or gained in the local area	No loss, no creation	Loss of five jobs	Creation of two jobs
Visual impact: number of months of low flow conditions in the river	5 months	2 months	3 months
Ecological condition of river	Worsening	Slight improvement	Big improvement
Increase in water rates per year	£0	£2	£40
Please tick the option you prefer	☐	☐	☐

Source: Hanley et al. (2006).

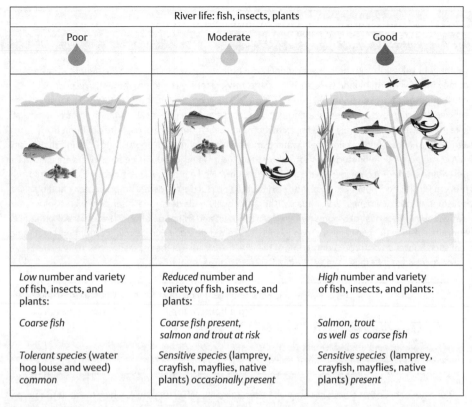

Figure 11.4 Explaining varying levels of an attribute.
Source: Stithou (2011).

A third type of valuation procedure that has been applied to water-quality improvements involves revealed-preference methods. These methods are used to measure changes in recreational use values. An example is the work reported by Johnstone and Markandya (2006), who relate anglers' choice of total fishing trips in a year, and where those trips were made,

Table 11.4 Example outputs from a choice experiment for two rivers in Scotland. The units are pounds sterling per household per year. Bid vehicle: local water taxes. Figures in parentheses are 95% confidence intervals

	Motray River	Brothock River	Pooled data
Local farm jobs	3.52	3.63	3.65
	(2.38; 4.66)	(2.41; 4.98)	(2.81; 4.48)
River flow conditions, per month improvement	3.87	2.70	3.00
	(2.52; 5.07)	(0.90; 4.21)	(1.74; 4.25)
Ecology, slight improvement	8.97	10.53	9.45
	(5.41; 12.38)	(4.57; 17.19)	(6.25; 12.93)
Ecology, big improvement	24.03	28.26	25.91
	(18.53; 31.08)	(19.65; 40.57)	(21.10; 31.74)

Source: Hanley et al. (2006).

BOX 11.5 Comparing Contingent Valuation and Choice Experiment Values for Water-quality Improvements

Contingent valuation and choice experiments have both been used to measure the benefits of water-quality improvements. But do we obtain the same answers for a given improvement, irrespective of which method of measurement we use? Christie and Azevedo (2009) investigate this issue, looking at the specific case of improvements to water quality in Clear Lake, Iowa. Clear Lake is the third-largest natural lake in Iowa, and is intensively used for recreation. However, non-point phosphate pollution from agriculture has resulted in a decline in water clarity, an increase in algal blooms, and a fall in fish diversity.

A contingent valuation study was administered to 900 Iowa residents. Three scenarios were used, each describing a different change in water quality. Plan A involved a programme of measures that would prevent further declines in water quality. Plan B would produce a 'moderate' improvement, and plan C a 'substantial' improvement in water quality. The water quality was described in terms of water colour and clarity, the number of algal blooms per year, water odour, and fish populations. These were also the attributes used in the choice experiment, which was administered to 600 people. Respondents were told that such improvements could only come at the expense of a rise in their taxes.

The following table shows the WTP estimates from the two methods:

	Contingent valuation ($ per household)	Choice experiment ($ per household)
Plan A—further declines	−1,327	−2,341
Plan B—a moderate improvement	1,093	385
Plan C—a substantial improvement	1,642	2,692

As can be seen, both methods show a welfare loss (negative WTP) for plan A, which the authors interpret as how much worse off people would be if water quality declined below the current level. Both methods give a welfare gain (positive WTP) for improvements in water quality, which are bigger for the larger improvement. However, the two measures give significantly different mean WTP values for any given change. Christie and Azevedo then test whether the preferences underlying these responses differ between the choice experiment and contingent valuation. They do this by combining the three contingent valuation scenarios into one data set. They find that there are no statistically significant differences between the marginal values that people place on the four attributes used in the design (water colour and clarity, number of algal blooms per year, water odour, and fish populations), which they see as encouraging in terms of the 'convergent validity' between these two stated preference methods.

to water-quality parameters such as the number of taxa within the river, organic pollution levels, habitat quality, and the number of fish species. Separate models were estimated for lowland, upland, and chalk streams in England, based on a survey of anglers. They found that both the number of angling trips and the distribution of these trips across sites were significantly related to most of the water-quality measures used, although parameter signs are sometimes unexpected. They then used the combined participation and site choice model to measure welfare benefits (changes in consumer surplus per trip) for a 10 per cent improvement in water-quality measures. Table 11.5 shows some of their results. However, one problem with applying travel-cost models to valuing water-quality improvements is that researchers find a high degree of multi-collinearity between measures of water quality,

Table 11.5 Economic benefits to anglers in England from water-quality improvements, as given by change in consumers' surplus per trip in pounds sterling for a 10 per cent improvement in statistically significant river attributes

	Upland rivers	Lowland rivers	Chalk rivers
Number of fish species		2.49	
BOD	−0.43		
Ammonia		−0.13	
DO	2.09		0.29
Flow	1.97	3.70	0.15

Note: The mean consumers' surplus across all three rivers under current conditions was £25 per trip.
Blank cells imply that the water-quality parameter was not significant in the choice model at 95%.
Source: Adapted from Johnstone and Markandya (2006).

making it difficult to identify individual effects. This was an issue in the Johnstone and Markandya study.

Hedonic pricing (HP) is a revealed-preference approach that relates variations in water quality to variations in house prices, as a way of measuring aspects of the benefits of improvements in quality. Leggett and Bockstael (2000) look at the effects of varying faecal coliform levels in coastal waters on property prices in Anne Arundel County, Maryland. The irregularity of this coastline means that water-quality levels vary substantially within the housing market. The analysis was based on house sales data of waterfront properties from 1993 to 1997. The authors argue that faecal coliform counts are a good measure of water quality to use in HP studies, since it is something that people are likely to care and know about, especially if they engage in water-based recreation such as swimming and boating, due to the health risks. High levels of faecal matter also make the water smell and look bad, and pose health risks to users. Leggett and Bockstael explore different functional forms for the hedonic price equation, including linear, double-logarithmic, semi-logarithmic, and inverse semi-logarithmic. With the exception of the linear form, the measure of faecal coliform concentration is significant and negative as an explanatory variable. Welfare changes from reducing faecal coliform pollution are then estimated. Taking one polluted stretch of coastline, where the levels range from 135 to 240 coliforms per 100 ml of water, the authors find that property values would rise by $230,000 if levels were cut to 100 coliforms per 100 ml, a 2 per cent gain in value (based on the inverse semi-log hedonic price equation).

11.5 Problems for Cost–benefit Analysis of Water-quality Improvements

Two broad classes of problem exist when using cost–benefit analysis for water-quality issues:

1. Identifying the water-quality change to be valued.
2. Valuing the water-quality change, once identified.

11.5.1 Identifying the water-quality change to be valued

Economists start by assuming that the change in water quality or quantity is well established. But this is a strong presumption. Welfare economics operates on the assumption that the 'initial' and 'subsequent' amounts of a public good are known, so that willingness to pay can be measured. But two issues exist in applications to water-quality management, for instance, in terms of assessment of a new policy to reduce water pollution. First, a CBA must identify what changes would have taken place over time without this measure in place—the 'business as usual' scenario. This can be tricky, since many factors determine future water quality. For example, the closure of factories due to an economic downturn could lead to water-quality improvements independently of a clean-up programme, as could the requirements of other pieces of legislation. Whilst households might not care why their river has become cleaner, the application of CBA to a programme of measures requires the analyst to separate cause and effect.

Second, the impacts of a programme of measures on water quality will be uncertain. The reduction of dairy herds should improve water quality in a catchment, but these predictions are made with error bounds implicitly or explicitly attached. Should respondents in a WTP study be made aware of this uncertainty over the water-quality outcomes of, say, a tax on fertilizer use, or the installation of buffer strips alongside watercourses? Finally, researchers may be unsure how long an aquatic ecosystem will take to recover from some pollution episode and subsequent remediation (e.g. liming of acidic lakes: Banzhaf et al., 2006). This will affect the time profile of benefits that form part of the CBA, and that constitute aspects of the benefits scenario within which respondents are asked to state their preferences. How should this uncertainty be conveyed to those who might benefit?

11.5.2 Problems in pricing the environmental change, once identified

Three problems will be reviewed here. First, the way in which water quality is measured by scientists does not describe how it is perceived by ordinary people, either in terms of what it is important to measure, or whether actual quality (in terms of health risks, say) corresponds to perceived quality. Yet it is perceived quality that determines behaviour and helps determine WTP (Adamowicz et al., 2003). This mismatch between how water quality is measured by scientists and regulators and how it is perceived by ordinary people creates problems for the application of CBA to water policy and water management.

Second, aggregate benefits in a CBA depend both on per-person or per-trip measures of water-quality improvements, and the number of people or number of trips that are impacted by this change. Economists tend to focus on the per-person or per-trip measurement problem, rather than the 'how many people benefit?' problem. One solution to this problem in the water-quality context is the estimation of distance-decay functions, which try to find a spatial relationship between who is willing to pay for an improvement and how far away from the river and so forth they live (Bateman et al., 2006): Figure 11.5 shows examples of two such functions for water-quality improvements to the River Mimram, England and for the Manchester Ship Canal in England.

(i) River Mimram

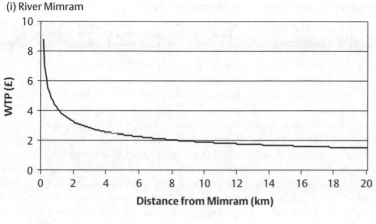

(ii) Manchester Ship Canal

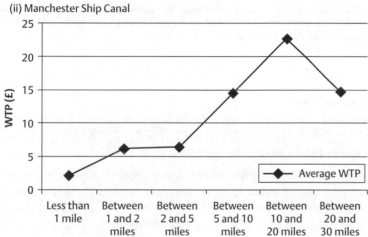

Figure 11.5 Examples of distance-decay functions for English water-bodies.
Sources: Hanley et al. (2003); Hanley and Colombo (2008).

Summary

The economics of water pollution offers an interesting contrast between policy and economic theory. Despite the arguments of economists, governments have been reluctant to adopt economic instruments rather than regulation to reduce water pollution. Examples of water pollution taxes exist, but on the whole, economic instruments have gained less 'traction' in water pollution control than in air pollution control. This might be because of the difficulties of applying taxes or tradable permits to non-point sources of water pollution, and because of the way in which even point-source emissions map on to ambient quality levels is complex and locale-specific. In contrast, the economic ideas of cost–benefit analysis and benefits assessment have gained relatively more prominence in both project and policy appraisal for water pollution; for example, in the context of the EU Water Framework Directive (see Box 11.6).

BOX 11.6   Who Faces the Costs and Who Gets the Benefits of Water-quality Improvements?

Water-quality improvements impose costs on sectors responsible for water pollution. Depending on the market structure, a proportion of these costs will fall on consumers, Those paying the costs of clean-up are likely to differ from those benefitting from better water quality. A nice illustration of this concerns a study by Fezzi et al. (2008), on the costs and benefits of improving water quality in rivers in Yorkshire. A major source of nitrate pollution in this area is agriculture: measures to reduce nitrate pollution impose costs on farmers in terms of lost profits. Benefits accrue to those who value water-quality improvements, including recreational users of the catchment. Using a combination of Geographic Information Systems and a range of environmental valuation methods, Fezzi et al. find that most benefits accrue to urban households in the area. For an improvement in water quality required under the Water Framework Directive, they find that benefits are in the order of £12.5 million, whilst the costs to farmers are in the order of £5.5 million. So whilst (urban) households gain from the water-quality improvement, the costs are felt by farmers as lost income due to their forgoing more profitable cropping activities. This study is a good example of the use of integrated modelling to measure benefits and costs of water pollution reductions, and on whom these benefits and costs fall.

Tutorial Questions

11.1 What are the main types and sources of water pollution? Why might the source of the problem matter for policy design?

11.2 What problems would a regulator face in using a system of pollution taxes to improve water quality in a river, where the main problem is point-source discharges from factories and sewage treatment works? What would be the main potential benefits of using such a tax approach, relative to regulation?

11.3 How could economic instruments be used to reduce pollution from non-point sources in an estuary? In what way does the nature of the pollution source impose additional policy design problems for the government?

11.4 How could you use (i) choice experiments and (ii) hedonic pricing to estimate the benefits of an improvement in river-water quality in an urban area?

11.5 What are the problems of undertaking a cost–benefit analysis of a planned improvement in coastal water quality through improvements in sewage treatment?

References and Additional Readings

Adamowicz, W., Swait, J., Boxall, P., Louviere, J., and Williams, M. (2003). 'Perceptions versus objective measures of environmental quality in combined revealed and stated preference models of environmental valuation', in N. Hanley, D. Shaw, and R. Wright (eds.), *The New Economics of Outdoor Recreation* (Cheltenham: Edward Elgar).

Aftab, A., Hanley, N., and Kampas, A. (2007). 'Co-ordinated environmental regulation: controlling non-point nitrate pollution while maintaining river flows', *Environmental and Resource Economics* 38(4): 573–93.

Banzhaf, H.S., Burtraw, D., Evans, D., and Krupnick, A. (2006). 'Valuation of natural resource improvements in the Adirondacks', *Land Economics* 82(3): 445–64.

Bateman, I., Day, B., Georgiou, S., and Lake, I. (2006). 'The aggregation of environmental benefit values: welfare measures, distance decay and total WTP', *Ecological Economics* 60: 450–60.

Birol, E., Karousakis, K., and Koundouri, P. (2006). 'Using economic valuation techniques to inform water resources management: a survey and critical appraisal', *Science of the Total Environment* 365: 105–22.

Brannlund, R., Chung, Y., Fare, R., and Grosskopf, S. (1998). 'Emissions trading and profitability: the Swedish pulp and paper industry', *Environmental and Resource Economics* 12: 345–56.

Christie, M., and Azevedo, C. (2009). 'Testing the consistency between standards contingent valuation, repeated contingent valuation and choice experiments', *Journal of Agricultural Economics* 60(1): 154–70.

Farrow, R.S., Schultz, M., Celikkol, P., and Van Houtven, G. (2005). 'Pollution trading in water quality limited areas: use of benefits assessment and cost effective trading ratios', *Land Economics* 81(2): 191–205.

Fezzi, C., Rigby, D., Bateman, I.J., Hadley, D., and Posen, P. (2008). 'Estimating the range of economic impacts on farms of nutrient leaching reduction policies', *Agricultural Economics* 39: 197–205.

Foley, J.A., DeFries, R., Asner, G.P., Barford, C., Bonan, G., Carpenter, S.R., Chapin, F.S., Coe, M.T., Daily, G.C., Gibbs, H.K., Helkowski, J.H., Holloway, T., Howard, E.A., Kucharik, C.J., Monfreda, C., Patz, J.A., Prentice, I.C., Ramankutty, N., and Snyder, P.K. (2005). 'Global consequences of land use', *Science* 309: 570–4.

Hanley, N., and Colombo, S. (2008) 'Benefits of potential water quality improvements on the Manchester Ship Canal', Unpublished report, Economics Division, University of Stirling.

——, Colombo, S., Tinch, D., Black, A., and Aftab, A. (2006). 'Estimating the benefits of water quality improvements under the Water Framework Directive: are benefits transferable?' *European Review of Agricultural Economics* 33: 391–413.

——, Faichney, R., Munro, A., and Shortle, J. (1998). 'Economic and environmental modelling of pollution control in an estuary', *Journal of Environmental Management* 52: 211–25.

——, Schlapfer, F., and Spurgeon, J. (2003). 'Aggregating the benefits of environmental improvements: distance–decay functions for use and non-use values', *Journal of Environmental Management* 68: 297–304.

Holmes, T.P., Bergstrom, J.C., Huszar, E., Kask, S.B., and Orr, F. III (2004). 'Contingent valuation, net marginal benefits, and the scale of riparian ecosystem restoration', *Ecological Economics* 49: 19–30.

Hunter, P., Hanley, N., Czajkowski, M., Mearns, K., Tyler, A.N., Carvalho, L., and Codd, G.A. (2012). 'The effect of risk perception on public preferences and willingness-to-pay for reductions in the health risks posed by toxic cyanobacterial blooms', *Science of the Total Environment* 426: 32–44.

Hynes, S., Hanley, N., and O'Donoghue, C. (2009). 'Alternative treatments of the cost of time in recreational demand models: an application to whitewater kayaking in Ireland', *Journal of Environmental Management* 90(2): 1014–21.

Johnstone, C., and Markandya, A. (2006). 'Valuing river characteristics using combined site choice and participation travel cost models', *Journal of Environmental Management* 80: 237–47.

Lankowski, J., Lichtenberg, E., and Ollikainen, M. (2008). 'Point/nonpoint trading with spatial heterogeneity', *American Journal of Agricultural Economics* 90(4): 1044–58.

Leggett, C.G., and Bockstael, N. (2000). 'Evidence on the effects of water quality on residential land prices', *Journal of Environmental Economics and Management* 39: 121–44.

Loomis, J., Kent, P., Strange, L., Fausch, K., and Covich, A. (2000). 'Measuring the total economic value of restoring ecosystem services in an impaired river basin: results from a contingent valuation survey', *Ecological Economics* 33: 103–17.

Mitchell, R., and Carson, R. (1989). *Using Surveys to Value Public Goods: The Contingent Valuation Method* (Washington, DC: Resources for the Future).

Muller, N.Z., and Mendelsohn, R.O. (2009). 'Efficient pollution control: getting the prices right', *American Economic Review* 99(5): 1714–39.

OECD (2010) *Water Quality Trading in Agriculture* (Paris: OECD).

O'Neil, W., David, M., Moore, C., and Joeres, E. (1983). 'Transferable discharge permits and economic efficiency: the Fox River', *Journal of Environmental Economics and Management* 10: 346–55.

Ribaudo, M. (2009). 'Non-point pollution regulation approaches in the U.S.' In J. Albiac and A. Dinar (eds.), *The Management of Water Quality and Irrigation Techniques* (London: Earthscan): 83–102.

SEPA (Scottish Environment Protection Agency) (2005). *Scotland River Basin District: Characterisation and Impacts Analyses Required by Article 5 of the Water Framework Directive—Summary Report* (Stirling: SEPA).

——(2010). *Trends in Scottish River Water Quality* (Stirling: SEPA).

Shortle, J.S., and Horan, R. (2001). 'The economics of nonpoint pollution control', *Journal of Economic Surveys* 15(3): 255–89.

Shortle, J.S., Ribaudo, M., Horan, R., and Blandford, D. (2012). 'Reforming agricultural nonpoint pollution policy in an increasingly budget-constrained environment', *Environmental Science and Technology* 46(3): 1316–25.

Smith, V.K., and Desvouges, W. (1986). *Measuring Water Quality Benefits* (Boston, MA: Kluwer Nijhoff).

Smyth, R.L., Watzin, M.C., and Manning, R.E. (2009). 'Investigating public preferences for managing Lake Champlain using a choice experiment', *Journal of Environmental Management* 90: 615–23.

Stithou, M. (2011). 'The economic value of improvements in the ecology of Irish rivers due to the Water Framework Directive', Unpublished PhD dissertation, Economics Division, University of Stirling.

Viscusi, K., Huber, J., and Bell, J. (2008). 'The economic value of water quality', *Environmental and Resource Economics* 41(2): 169–87.

12 Biodiversity

The decision about what species and habitats to protect and how they should be protected is a major issue for society, as terrestrial and marine habitats hosting high levels of biodiversity are being irreversibly lost or degraded on a massive scale. In economic terms, biodiversity is becoming scarcer as some species are lost and others become more vulnerable to extinction. The ecosystems that we depend upon to provide life-support functions are losing the species that maintain these functions. We approach this topic by addressing a series of questions.

- What is biodiversity?
- What is the objective of biodiversity conservation?
- How is biodiversity valued, especially in terms of its contribution to ecosystem services?
- And how can we design policies to ensure consumers, farmers, foresters and fishermen have an incentive to protect biodiversity cost-effectively?

12.1 Introduction

Throughout the ages, the processes of evolution have driven innumerable species to extinction and, by mutations, have created new species better suited to the evolving environment. For most species, this process has proceeded gradually. Evidence from fossil records suggests that millions of years may separate one distinct species from another, and new species are often only slightly genetically different from their predecessors. Periodically, there have been mass extinctions (Raup, 1988; Stork, 2010) when a large number of species have disappeared. It is estimated that there have been five mass extinctions in the last 600 million years when 65–95 per cent of species known in earlier fossils have disappeared (Raup, 1988). The last of these was due, it is thought, to meteorite strikes that briefly plunged the whole earth into an extended winter. Many biologists (May et al., 1995; Stork, 2010) believe that we are currently witnessing a mass extinction, but this time the sudden loss of biodiversity is due to human actions.

Biodiversity can be defined as: the variability among living organisms from all sources, including *inter alia*, terrestrial, marine, and other aquatic ecosystems, and the ecological complexes of which these are a part. This includes diversity within species, between species, and of ecosystems (Convention on Biological Diversity, 1992, Article 2). Thus biodiversity represents the variety of life, whether in terms of different species of birds and mammals, and the variability across ecosystems.

The exact rate of species extinction is difficult to assess because we do not know how many species there are, and thus it is difficult to estimate how many have been lost (see Box 12.1). Estimates range from 5 to 30 per cent of species loss per decade (for a review, see Stork, 2010). The IUCN (2010) predicts that the rate of extinction that we are currently witnessing is 100 to 1,000 times the average rate measured in the fossil record. The key determinant of the rate of species loss is the destruction of high-biodiversity habitats, which include rainforest, Mediterranean vegetation communities, and coral reefs (Myers et al., 2000).

In ecology, a key concept in discussions relating to biodiversity, conservation, and extinction is the species–area curve. A species–area curve is a relationship between the area of a habitat and the number of species found within that area. Larger areas tend to contain more species than smaller areas, but as the area considered increases the marginal (extra) increase in species declines (MacArthur and Wilson, 1967). The curve typically follows a non-linear relationship such as that depicted in Figure 12.1. For concreteness, let us suppose that this curve represents the number of species of higher plants in a given area of rangeland habitat. The curve predicts that, as habitat area is lost, initially very few species are lost. For instance, if the area lost is from a_0 hectares down to a_1, then we can see from

BOX 12.1 How Many Species Are There and How Many Have Been Lost?

There are two surprisingly difficult questions in relation to measuring the state of biodiversity and the loss of biodiversity due to extinction: First, how many species are there on earth? Second, how many species have gone extinct due to habitat loss?

So far, 1.7 million species have been described by science (Stork, 1996). These include about 250,000 plants, 44,000 vertebrates, and 751,000 insects. We know with some confidence that the 4,000 mammals described are an accurate estimate of the total, but the numbers of described insects, spiders, fungi, and other primitive species are a gross underestimate of the total number of species. Other groups such as viruses, bacteria, and algae have been relatively unexplored (Colwell, 1996) and their species number probably exceeds that of all other species combined.

Current estimates are between 5 and 15 million species—this evidence is reviewed in Stork (2010). Of this large number of species, about 85-95 per cent have not been described by science. There are four approaches to estimating extinctions: species–area based estimates, estimates from empirical data of known extinctions, estimates from the use of Red Data lists (IUCN, 2010), and co-extinctions. The species–area curve shown in Figure 12.1 is used as a statistical modelling approach to estimating extinctions due to habitat loss. Thus as a rainforest or coral reef habitat is progressively lost, the rate of species loss is expected to accelerate. Co-extinction occurs when if a species becomes extinct, then all the species that depend upon it also become extinct. Climate change is also predicted to be an important driver of species loss (Opdam and Wascher, 2004).

The more comprehensive species–area curve estimates of extinction estimate a rate of extinction per decade of between 5 per cent and 30 per cent of all species on earth (Stork, 2010: table 1). More recent estimates tend to predict a lower rate, because it has been found that some species have been able to 'hang on' in regrowth forest. For instance, for the critical Amazonian rainforest region, by 2050 there is expected to be a 12-24 per cent reduction in forest habitat and this is expected to lead to 5-9 per cent of species becoming extinct (Feeley and Silman, 2009).

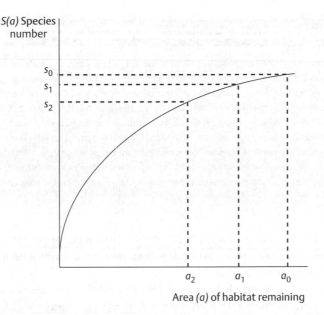

Figure 12.1 The species–area curve.

the vertical axes that the corresponding species loss is the difference between s_0 and s_1. A further habitat loss of the same area results in a greater species loss that is, the difference between s_0 and s_1 is smaller than the difference between s_1 and s_2 for an identical reduction in area. The implications of this fundamental ecological concept for conservation planning are that if a conservation agency wants to protect the maximum number of species, they may need to allocate more resources towards relatively rare habitats and less towards common ones.

Biodiversity loss involves more than the loss of a few high-profile species such as elephants and black rhinoceros; it concerns any regional loss of species or any reduction in the geographical range of species that reduces their genetic diversity.

Why is this accelerated biodiversity loss a cause for concern? The loss of a species is a cost to society for three reasons. First, the species lost may have a direct value as a source of knowledge that can be used to locate genetic material for food crops, or as a source of active chemical compounds for new medicines. Second, a species may play a critical role in maintaining an ecosystem and providing humanity with a range of 'life-support' ecosystem services, such as nutrient cycling and water catchment regulation. Finally, a species may have aesthetic and non-use benefits; for instance, people like to see 'charismatic' species such as birds and butterflies in the wild, and place a value on knowing that a valued ecosystem is functioning and protected. The Economics of Ecosystems and Biodiversity (TEEB) project recently highlighted the potential economic consequences of current rates of loss in biodiversity (TEEB, 2010).

Why are species lost? The main threat to biodiversity is a loss of habitat by conversion of land to other uses, especially agriculture, and the degradation of habitat, especially through fragmentation. Particularly at threat are rainforests, old-growth temperate forests, rangelands, heathlands, and coral reefs, which together provide habitats for over

---

BOX 12.2 Noah's Library

Metrick and Weitzman (1998) employ the following metaphor to explain the problem of choosing which species to preserve. Consider a species as if it were a library full of books. Each book is a gene. Common books (genes) are housed in many libraries (species); others in only one. Resources can be used to protect libraries and reduce the probability of destruction by fire, but at a cost. The problem, then, is to determine how the fire-fighting resources should be distributed amongst the different libraries.

A library has two attributes, the building (the phenotype of the species) and the information contained within it (the genes). We value the species for its aesthetic appeal or its use value. We may value the books (genes) for the diversity that they bring to species in terms of colour and form, or we may place a utilitarian value upon them for the ideas that they may contain for future medicines and food crops.

---

50 per cent of known species (Stork, 2010). An additional factor is climate change, which may drive species to premature extinction because they are not able to evolve rapidly enough to adapt to a new climate.

By deciding to protect some habitats and depleting others, man decides which species are destined to become extinct and which survive. Collectively, human society acts in the role of Noah, deciding which species should be allowed on the 'Ark of survival' and which should be allowed to perish (see Box 12.2).

Human actions have increased the rate of extinction; therefore economics should be involved in finding solutions. Shogren et al. (1999) highlight the importance of economics to decisions that society makes concerning biodiversity: economic activity determines the risk that a species faces of extinction; whilst protecting a species has an opportunity cost in terms of reduced resources for other valued public and private goods. In other words, resource scarcity means that we often face choices over what biodiversity to prioritize for conservation. Finally, economics can offer guidance into the most cost-effective way of conserving biodiversity; for example, in the design of agri-environment schemes, or international schemes for biodiversity conservation in developing countries (Ferraro and Pattanayak, 2006; Claassen et al., 2008).

12.2 What to Conserve?

Active conservation of biodiversity has a cost in terms of lost economic opportunities and the allocation of resources to conservation. Given the large number of threatened species, we cannot save everything; thus society must make difficult choices about how limited resources are allocated to biodiversity conservation rather than other public goods. This chapter explores society values for biodiversity and ecosystem services, and how society may make these choices.

12.2.1 Economic insights into conservation objectives

The issue of which species to preserve might, in economic terms, be judged on the basis of whether the benefits of preservation exceed the costs. This calculation is complex, because both the benefits and the costs are difficult to estimate. Weitzman (1992) developed a theory of which species should be preserved, based on a measure of distinctiveness (see also Metrick and Weitzman, 1998). Distinctiveness can be interpreted as the 'genetic' difference between a species and its closest relative. However, distinctiveness says nothing about how much people actually like a species or how effective a species is in providing ecosystem services; it may say something, in the case of higher plants, about its potential medicinal value or about its importance in filling a particular niche within an ecosystem.

Policy-makers often have to make choices between species or ecological communities when allocating resources for conservation. In an ideal world, they might be able to use the following formula:

$$w_i(a_i) = p_i(a_i)\{v_i^d + v_i^e + u_i\} - c_i(a_i), \tag{12.1}$$

where the term $w_i(a_i)$ is the expected net benefit over a long time horizon of conserving a species or a particular ecosystem i.

Natural species populations are often highly variable and it is impossible to ensure that a species will survive. The term $p_i(a_i)$ gives the probability of a species surviving. The probability of survival depends upon the decisions of landowners and policy-makers to conserve the habitat. In this simple model, it is an increasing function of the remaining area of habitat a_i.

The value of conserving a species or an ecological community has three components. The direct value of distinctiveness v_i^d is due to the expectation that a species will provide 'information'–that is chemical information about potential drugs or genetic material with commercial value; for instance, in agriculture. This is an expected value, because we cannot be certain that a species or a group of species will provide commercially valuable material. We consider the nature of this component of value later in this chapter. Species distinctiveness determines this value as it measures how close a species is to related species with similar properties. If two species have very similar genotypes, then they may be close substitutes in terms of their chemical constituents.

The other component of value, the ecosystem service value v_i^e, gives the contribution of the species to ecosystem services by increasing ecosystem resilience and underpinning the functioning of ecosystems. As we discuss later, this value depends upon how many substitute species there are within an ecosystem capable of taking over the niche occupied by a species: a species with many close substitutes is in general less valuable than a species with few or none.

Finally, the aesthetic and non-use value u_i (we outlined this concept in Chapter 3) depends upon society's preferences for a species or an ecological community. The species contributes to the aesthetic value of the conserved area. The total value of a species is therefore $v_i^t = \{v_i^d + v_i^e + u_i\}$.

Costs $c_i(a_i)$ are in terms of the direct costs of conservation and the opportunity costs of forgone development opportunities as a function of the area of habitat preserved. This reflects the fact that as the area of habitat increases, then this increases the opportunity cost of lost development opportunities. Opportunity costs could, for example, consist of forgone profits from conversion of rainforest to cattle grazing. Figure 12.2 shows the trade-off between costs and the probability of survival. In this diagram, the current habitat is given by a_0. Habitat can be increased by restoration and increased conservation management. There may be an asymmetry of costs, in that if land is lost to save conservation costs, say from a_0 to a_1, going back from a_1 to a_0 by restoration will entail a far greater cost than conservation, that is $c'_0 > c_0$ in Figure 12.2.

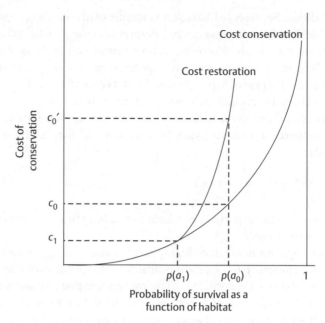

Figure 12.2 The trade-off between cost and probability of survival.

As more habitat is preserved, or even re-created, then the probability of survival approaches, but it never reaches one because there is always some possibility that a species will become extinct whatever conservation actions are undertaken. The cost curve becomes steeper as society allocates progressively more valuable land, from agriculture, forestry, or development, to restore the habitat. In fact, due to the irreversibility of destruction for many habitats, it may be impossible to restore some of the original habitat at any cost. It is also a general rule that re-creating habitat is many times more expensive than conserving existing habitat. Prach and Hobbs (2008) make this point in relation to land restoration following mining.

12.2.2 Allocating resources between species and ecosystems

A problem often faced by government agencies with responsibility for conservation is how to share a budget allocation between one species or another, or between spending on different habitats. Equation (12.1) gives the objective function related to a single species or habitat, but in reality there are often many species and threatened ecosystems, and a choice has to be made of allocating resources between them. Let us set up a simple version of this problem, in which the regulator has to pay farmers the opportunity cost for conservation and limited funds are allocated between just two species. We will name the species after two Australian endangered species, the chuditch (also known as the western quoll), *Dasyurus geoffroii* (a small marsupial predator endangered by introduced predators such as the fox and cat and loss of habitat, and now confined to the lower south-west of Australia), and the bilby, *Macrotis lagotis* (an endangered omnivorous marsupial threatened by loss of habitat and predation, and now confined to remote arid regions of northern Western Australia).

The Department of Environment and Conservation (DEC) in Western Australia has a budget to allocate between these species. The problem they face is as follows. They would like to maximize the expected net benefit from the conservation of both species:

$$J(a_{bilb}, a_{chud}) = w(a_{bilb}) + w(a_{chud})$$
$$= p_{bilb}(a_{bilb})v_{bilb}^t + p_{chud}(a_{chud})v_{chud}^t - c_{bilb}(a_{bilb}) - c_{chud}(a_{chud}), \qquad (12.2)$$

where the area allocated to bilby habitat is a_{bilb} and the area allocated to chuditch habitat is a_{chud}. The total value of each species is v_{bilb}^t and v_{chud}^t. The budget constraint, assuming all funds are allocated, is given by

$$M = c_{bilb}(a_{bilb}) + c_{chud}(a_{chud}), \qquad (12.3)$$

where M is the total budget available in dollars and $c_{bilb}(a_{bilb})$ is the opportunity cost of providing a given area of bilby habitat and $c_{chud}(a_{chud})$ the same for chuditch.

If the DEC wishes to maximize the objective function in equation (12.2) subject to the budget in equation (12.3), what rule might they use? One approach would be to consider the gains from providing one more hectare of bilby habitat compared to one more hectare of chuditch habitat. To this end, the marginal net benefit of bilby habitat is as follows:

$$MNB_{bilb} = (\Delta p_{bilb} v_{bilb}^t - \Delta c_{bilb})/\Delta a_{bilb}, \qquad (12.4)$$

and the marginal net benefit of chuditch habitat is

$$MNP_{chud} = (\Delta p_{chud} v_{chud}^t - \Delta c_{chud})/\Delta a_{chud}. \qquad (12.5)$$

The term Δ is used to indicate the change in a term with respect to the corresponding area. If we consider very small changes, then this is interpreted as a derivative.

As proposed by Metrick and Weitzman (1998), these terms can be compared to provide a criterion to guide investment in habitat. Thus if, for instance, $MNB_{bilb} > MNP_{chud}$, this would imply that there should be more resources from the budget allocated to bilby conservation and less to chuditch.

The example presented here is highly simplistic, but since the use of systematic conservation planning has become more common (Margules and Pressey, 2000), so has the inclusion of the opportunity cost of conservation in terms of land or marine resources such as fish catch (see Box 12.3). Examples of this approach include Fernades et al. (2005) for the Great Barrier Reef and Polasky et al. (2001) for cost-effective terrestrial ecosystem conservation in Oregon. It is more challenging to put a value on the biodiversity and the probability of survival. We consider the value of biodiversity in the next section.

12.3 Values of Biodiversity

The total value of all biodiversity is the sum of all human welfare for current and all future generations. Without any biodiversity, humanity would cease to exist. In this sense, the

BOX 12.3 How Hot Are Biodiversity Hotspots?

In a paper in *Nature,* two ecologists—Possingham and Wilson (2006)—question biodiversity conservation priorities and recognize the importance of cost in conservation decision-making:

> The variety of life on Earth is in rapid decline and global spending on nature conservation is inadequate to arrest that decline. Consequently, resources for conservation must be allocated to secure the 'biggest bang for our buck'. In recognition of that need, scientists have identified biodiversity hotspots, where extraordinary concentrations of biodiversity exist.

Biodiversity hotspots (Myers et al., 2000) combine high biodiversity with a high risk of biodiversity loss. Wilson and Possingham propose that the allocation of funds to biodiversity hotspots around the world should depend on how much they cost to conserve. Without information on such costs—including the opportunity cost of land set aside for protection—money spent could be less cost-effective in terms of conserving a given number of species.

economic value of global biodiversity is infinite. However, this self-evident truth does not help us with more relevant questions about the value of marginal changes in biodiversity, which species should be protected and which neglected. Commercial activities that may push species to extinction, such as agricultural expansion and intensification, deforestation, and urbanization, have costs and benefits that, at least in part, are measured by market prices. Valuing a loss of biodiversity is more difficult, because markets for its preservation are either missing or incomplete. The key economic questions concern the marginal value of biodiversity itself and the benefits of preserving a particular part of a habitat. As noted earlier, the benefits of preservation derive from three sources: first, direct values due to medicine and agriculture; second, ecosystem services such as recycling nitrogen, filtering sediment, and decomposing waste; and third, aesthetic use and non-use values. We consider each of these sources of value in more detail.

12.3.1 Direct values

Currently, we use approximately 40,000 species of plants, animals, fungi, and microbes (Elridge, 1998; Heal, 2000). Organisms have a vast range of uses, some of which are often taken for granted. For instance, the bacteria actinobacteria is used to produce a common form of antibiotics. From fungi, we obtain the common mushroom, whilst *Genea hispidula* provides the structure in legumes for nitrogen fixation. Useful insects include silkworms, bees (which provide pollination services to agriculture), and ladybirds that predate upon aphids. Useful animals include sheep for food and fibre, and buffalo, which provide meat, milk, draft power, transportation, leather, and fertilizer. The higher plants provide crop plants, timber, insecticides, and fodder, and are also an important source of traditional and modern medicines. These compounds have provided the basis of many common drugs, including aspirin, which comes from willow bark, and taxol, a cancer treatment, derived from the Pacific yew.

Over time, we have become adept at finding and developing species that are useful to us, and this continues as we search for new crops, and new genetic material for existing crops and new medicines. Biotechnology has made it possible to take traits such as disease resistance from close relatives to crop plants, and incorporate these traits into commercial varieties. For these genes to be discovered, they must already exist in wild or cultivated species. By destroying a habitat, we may inadvertently destroy a close relative to a crop species that contains valuable genetic material. An example is *Zea diploperennis* (Iltis et al., 1979), a rare relative of commercial maize (*Zea mays*), which was unknown and on the verge of extinction in its last remaining habitat in the Sierra de Monantlán in Mexico. This plant shows resistance to many of the diseases that affect the commercial crop, and is currently starting to provide genetic material for new commercial maize varieties.

As diversity amongst wild relatives of crop plants is lost, we are in danger of becoming dependent on an increasingly small number of 'supercrops'. But in the future these are at risk from disease and from pest species that can evolve resistance to pesticides. Without genetic diversity from older crop varieties and wild relatives, the plant breeder is restricted to the gene pool available in known varieties. Loss of crop genetic diversity over the last 50 years has been so rapid that there has been a call to establish a 'Red List' of endangered crop species (Hammer and Khoshbakht, 2005), based on the IUCN (2010) Red List for endangered species.

12.3.2 Bioprospecting for drugs

The genetic codes of organisms contain the instructions to synthesize biologically active chemicals. Some of these chemicals can be exploited as the blueprint for drugs that are then produced synthetically. Often, the naturally occurring substance gives the medicinal chemist a 'lead' to the likely form of promising molecules, but these need to be modified before they can be used as medicines. Preservation of biodiversity maintains the number of species that are available to be used in this way (for a related example in which biodiversity is exploited commercially, see Box 12.4). However, there is also substitutability between

---

BOX 12.4 Bioprospecting in Costa Rica

By collecting and cataloguing the endemic plant species of Costa Rica's rainforests, the Instiuto Nacional de Biodiversidad (INBio) in Costa Rica (see Aylward et al., 1993) hopes to be able to market genetic information as a means of financing conservation. In addition to government support, INBio has commercial contracts with Merck & Co. and the British Technology Group for the exclusive rights over tested samples.

This type of contract is unlikely to provide significant funds for conservation until the host countries derive more benefits from the discovery of such material (Swanson, 1994). Despite its financial backing and worldwide publicity since 1991, INBio has generated a surplus of US$2.5 million from bioprospecting. This does not suggest that the total value of the institute's work in helping conserve the biodiversity of Costa Rica is equal to this amount. However, it does show some of the difficulties of converting unique genetic material into substantial profits through commercial contracts.

A case study for the Tapanti National Park puts the value of bioprospecting in perspective. Bernard et al. (2009) undertook a cost–benefit analysis of the forest to estimate values through stakeholder surveys on ecosystem services for the 58,000 ha national park. The provision of ecosystem services related to hydrological regulation and drinking water were estimated at US$2.5 million per year. Bioprospecting was undertaken in the park by INBio, but was yet to return any funds through the discovery of a new compound. This illustrates that the value of bioprospecting is likely to be low relative to other ecosystem services.

organisms in an ecosystem. First, organisms may occur across a wide ecological range. Second, different plants may produce chemicals that have similar medicinal properties. This implies that the value of the active ingredients cannot be entirely related to the preservation of a local population of a particular plant.

The value of a new drug is measured by its contribution to improving the treatment of disease. For instance, a new cancer drug, such as taxol derived from the yew tree, may increase remission rates, reduce the costs of treatment, and improve the quality of life. Its value is measured by how much better the new drug is than its closest substitute in treating disease.

Consider the following simple analysis of the value of species (Simpson et al., 1996). The value of a new product is given by the return R from the new drug and the costs of analysing a specimen c. The probability of success in finding a new drug is given by p. Therefore, the expected value of analysing a single plant specimen, $v(1)$, is the expected revenue less the costs. That is:

$$v(1) = pR - c.$$

For instance, if $R = \$10$ million, $c = \$0.5$ million, and $p = 0.1$, so that there is a 10 per cent chance of finding a substance that will form the basis of a new drug, the expected value of the specimen is $(0.1)10 - 0.5 = \$0.5$ million. If there is more than one candidate organism to produce a similar drug, then we identify a search procedure, in which searching stops when a discovery is made. Therefore, with two organisms, the expected value is given by

$$v(2) = pR - c + (1 - p)(pR - c),$$

where the second term gives the expected value of the second organism and the term $(1 - p)$ is the probability of no compound being found in the first organism. For instance, if $p = 0.1$, then the probability of the second organism needing to be analysed is 0.9, or 90 per cent. The value of having this extra species to analyse is simply the expected value of the second species, $(1-p)(pR-c)$.

The formula can be generalized to give the expected value of any number (n) of species, as follows:

$$v(n) = pR - c + (1 - p)(pR - c) + (1 - p)^2(pR - c) + \ldots + (1 - p)^{n-1}(pR - c).$$

The value of the 'marginal' species is

$$(1 - p)^n(pR - c),$$

that is, the expected value of having one more species to test for the medicinal product. The expected value of the marginal species is inversely related to the probability of success and the number of species. For instance, if there are 1,000 species and a 10 per cent ($p = 0.1$) probability of finding a medicinal product, $(1 - p)^n = 1.747 \times 10^{-46}$ (a very small number). In percentage terms, the success rate is the number of plants, on average, in a hundred that have a biologically active substance that could form the basis of a new drug. If the probability of finding a product is only one-tenth of 1 per cent ($p = 0.001$), then $(1 - p)^n = 0.3677$; at the same time, the $(pR - c)$ term declines, but not as quickly as $(1 - p)^n$ increases. If the number of species is reduced from 1,000 to 100, and assuming a one-tenth of 1 per cent success rate, then $(1 - p)^n = 0.905$. In ecosystems, there are often large numbers of species, and as the number of candidate species increases, then the value of the marginal species falls close to zero. This implies that the 'bioprospecting' values for the marginal species in a rainforest, say, may be quite low.

Consider the following example. The higher plants have, historically, produced the largest number of new drugs. So how do we value the conservation of one plant species in terms of its potential medicinal value? Simpson et al. (1996) suggest the following approach and parameters. There are about 250,000 (n) species of plants known to science (Wilson, 1988). On average between 1981 and 1993, 23.8 new drugs per annum were approved by the US Food and Drug Administration. This is an approximate measure of world discovery rates, as drugs first sold in other countries need to gain approval before being sold in the United States. Of these new drugs, approximately one-third are derived from higher plants (Chichilnisky, 1993); thus about eight new drugs (k) are discovered from higher plants each year. The cost of discovering a new product is around US$300 million. The expected revenue (R) is US$450 million, which assumes that the drug companies make a 50 per cent return on research costs. The cost of evaluating a single sample (c) is US$3,600. Use of the formula for the value, v, of an individual species, gives an estimate of the value of preserving an individual plant species on the basis of its medicinal value of US$7,109. Is this value significant in preserving an additional hectare of rainforest? The answer depends critically on how common plant specimens are. If a plant is widespread, a hectare of rainforest may contribute little to its long-term survival. If, instead, a relatively small area of rainforest is the host to many rare species, it could be highly valuable. On the basis of providing specimens for drug prospecting alone, as rainforest is cleared and the remaining species are found in a smaller and smaller area, this value becomes more significant to the conservation value of a hectare of rainforest. For a discussion of this point relating to Costa Rica, where the value of bioprospecting accounts for a small proportion of the ecosystem value of one forest area, see also Box 12.4.

12.3.3 Ecosystem service values

In simple terms, the ecosystems that surround us 'sustain and fulfil human life' (Daily, 1997: 3). As made clear in the Millennium Ecosystem Assessment (2005), ecosystems provide us with numerous direct and indirect services, including waste assimilation, water purification, and nutrient cycling (MEA, 2005). Complex ecosystems provide these services, but we are often unable to assess the value of a particular species within an ecosystem.

Ecosystem cycles relate to energy input, circulation of the elements essential to life—carbon, nitrogen, hydrogen, and so on (biogeochemical cycles)—and water circulation. All living organisms require energy to maintain their vital functions and grow. Energy in terrestrial and most marine ecosystems must be constantly renewed from the sun. Plants capture the sun's energy through photosynthesis to produce tissue. Plants are called autotrophs: they live on inorganic elements, such as carbon dioxide and water. All animals, insects and micro-organisms are directly or indirectly fed by plants, and are called consumers or heterotrophs. For example, a rabbit eats grass and produces waste, which feeds the

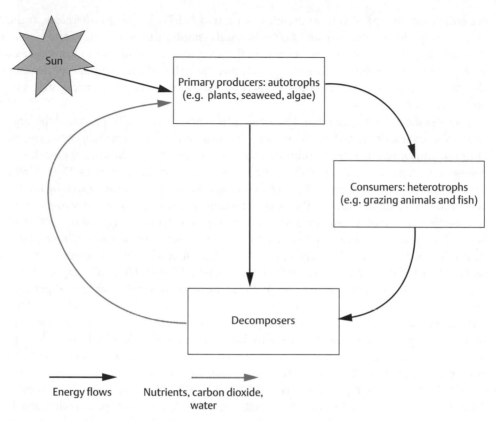

Figure 12.3 Ecosystem cycles.

decomposers. A fox that eats the rabbit benefits indirectly from plants. Organic matter circulates in a food chain, is transformed, and decomposed into basic elements (CO_2, water, nitrogen, etc.) that are available for plants to use. The energy captured in the food cycle is dissipated at each stage as heat.

The number of species in an ecosystem occupying these roles varies. Diverse ecosystems may have a large number of species in a particular role, and may be able to survive the loss of a number of species and continue to function. Damage to one part of the ecosystem may be compensated for by adjustment in another part. One way of thinking about an ecosystem is as flows of energy through a web of interacting species. If one of these energy pathways in the web becomes blocked—for instance, by a species becoming extinct—then it may not affect the whole system so long as other pathways remain open. Hopkin (quoted in Putman and Wratten, 1984: 350) uses the analogy of the blood circulation system. If a capillary is blocked or damaged, the body adapts by developing more capillaries or using existing capillaries. If main veins or arteries become blocked, then the body is damaged and finds it impossible to adapt. Thus diversity leads to resilience, and resilience is important if the system is to continue functioning when subjected to a shock such as loss of land to agriculture or an extreme climatic event. In contrast, impoverished ecosystems tend to be more fragile and less resilient to the loss of key species.

Consider some examples of ecosystem services and how they might be affected by species loss. Trees in a rainforest act like a sponge, and moderate the local water cycle by retaining water in the soil and transpiring (evaporating) rainfall. In this way, they reduce the frequency and intensity of floods. The loss of forest tree species would significantly reduce this ecosystem service, whereas the local loss of a species of monkey may not directly affect this service. Coral reefs provide protection to coastal areas and protect delicate coastal wetlands and mangrove swamps from storms. The loss of a significant part of the coral reef by pollution, sedimentation, or a sea-level rise due to climate change would result in a significant loss of ecosystem services, whereas the local loss of a species of fish would not directly.

The general point here is that the fewer close substitutes a species has in terms of its ecosystem functions and productivity, the more damaging is its loss. For instance, mangrove trees are critical to the functioning of coastal swamps, as they stabilize sediments and filter the water. The loss of a species of mangrove, the primary producer in that ecosystem, would have a devastating effect on the local marine environment, since there are no close substitutes for this species in its role as a primary producer capable of surviving in salt water and stabilizing the sediment in coastal swamps (see Box 12.5).

Functioning ecosystems provide society with a range of benefits to people, including natural resources, flood mitigation, pollination for agriculture, carbon sequestration, and reduction in soil erosion. These benefits have been termed 'ecosystem services' (Bateman et al., 2011). These services include goods such as fish or fuel wood, and services such as recreational opportunities, storm reduction, water purification, and cultural benefits, all of which have economic value (UK National Ecosystems Assessment, 2010). The link between the provision of ecosystem services and biodiversity is that, typically, biodiverse ecosystems are more resilient to environmental shocks and are often better able to provide ecosystem services in a range of climatic conditions. Biodiversity can also play a key role in the functioning of ecosystems, and thus in the quantity of services that they deliver.

BOX 12.5 Mangrove Fisheries Linkages in the Campeche of Mexico

The high productivity of the Gulf of Mexico fishery is partially attributed to the extensive areas of coastal lagoons and estuaries, which are dominated by the mangroves. Mangroves provide ideal breeding grounds for commercially exploited shrimps and finfish. In this region of Mexico, mangrove is under threat from mariculture (the development of shellfish farms) and urban encroachment. In their study of the Campeche fishery, Barbier and Strand (1998) estimate that, on average, the fishery loses 0.19 per cent of its annual revenue for each km^2 of mangrove deforestation. This estimate is based upon a simulation model that assumes that the loss of mangrove swamp reduces the carrying capacity of the coastal shrimp fishery, which benefits from the nursery function provided by the mangroves.

An interesting conclusion of the study is that the costs of mangrove deforestation—and, indeed, of the fishery as a whole—would be greatly increased if the fishery was converted from open access to a regulated fishery. This problem is an example of two missing markets: there is no market for the ecosystem services provided by the mangrove forests and there is no market for the shrimp stocks. The lack of a market for shrimp stocks, due to open access, leads to a reduced value of protecting the mangrove swamp.

12.3.3.1 Case study: marine ecosystems in Alaska

Economies and ecosystems are complex, interrelated systems. This complexity means that, often, the parts of an ecosystem/economy complex are analysed separately by economists and ecologists rather than analysing the whole system. An exception is a recent study of the Alaskan economy and its underpinning ecosystem (Finnoff and Tschirhart, 2008). The outline of their model gives an insight into how the ecosystem links to the economy, the determinants of value, and the role of biodiversity.

The Alaskan economy depends heavily on renewable and non-renewable natural resources to support its economy. A large number of Alaskan firms engage in commercial fishing and tourism activities that depend directly on the marine and terrestrial ecosystems. The total value of output of the Alaskan economy is US$32 billion, comprising a fishery output of US$659 million (2 per cent of total output), an aggregate recreational output of US$1,661 million (5 per cent of total output), and a composite good output of US$30 billion (93 per cent of total output).

The model developed by Finnoff and Tschirhart (2008) considers two equilibria, one for the economy, using a computable general equilibrium (CGE) model that accounts for the allocation of labour and capital among the three sectors in the economy subject to resource constraints, and a general equilibrium ecosystem model (GEEM). The models are represented in Figure 12.4.

The economic model includes production functions that link inputs, labour, capital, and natural resources to the level of sectoral outputs. The fishery sector is also regulated by a total allowable catch restriction and a limit on the time for which the fishery is open. The recreation sector also uses labour and capital, but its output is in terms of the number of recreational trips sold. In turn, the number of trips sold depends upon the population of charismatic predators (killer whales, seals, and sea otters). The computable general equilibrium model determines an equilibrium allocation of resources between the three sectors by commodity and factor price adjustments.

The general equilibrium ecosystem model determines the equilibrium species populations accounting for predation and harvesting. The ecosystem equilibrium is determined by maximizing behaviour for individual species in the acquisition of energy. For instance, individual stellar sea lions have the following net energy equation for preying on pollock:

$$R_{pred} = (e_{pred} - e)x_{pred} - r_{pred}(x_{pred}) - \beta_{pred}.$$

In this equation, R_{pred} is the net energy flow in kcal per unit of time; e_{pred} is the energy per biomass unit (kcal/kg); e is the energy expended in locating, attacking, and consuming pollock; x_{pred} is the biomass consumed, in kg per unit of time; $r_{pred}(x_{pred})$ is the respiration energy as a function of the level of predation; and β_{pred} is the resting metabolic rate (Tschirhart, 2004). If a predator's problem is assumed to be net energy maximization, then it will continue to increase its biomass consumed until the net energy per kg $(e_{pred} - e)$ equals the marginal increase in respiration. This gives an interpretation of the behaviour of predators as equating marginal benefit with marginal cost; however, instead of being measured in money per unit time, the benefits and costs are measured in terms of energy per unit of time. Other components of the model include energy expenditure from the predator avoiding larger predators;

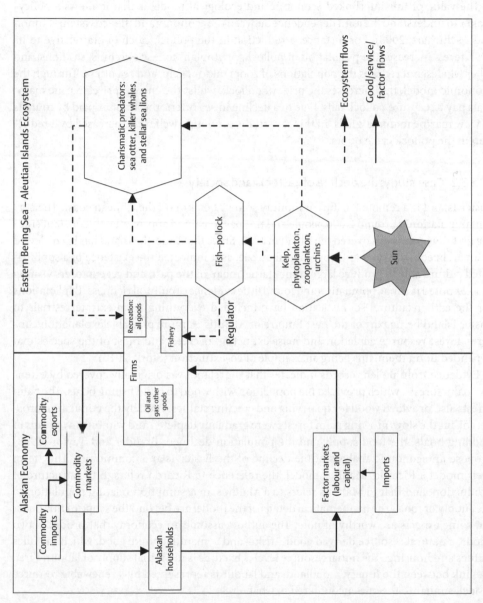

Figure 12.4 Marine ecosystem services in Alaska.

in this case, stellar sea lions being captured by killer whales. There is an equilibrium that states that the total biomass demanded by the predator must equal the total amount available from the prey. Finally, this is linked to a population growth model that determines the population of sea lions and pollock, the economically important fish stock, in each period.

The value of this interlinked economic and ecological model is that it allows a policy-maker to understand the joint dependence between the economy and the ecosystem (Finnoff and Tschirhart, 2008). For instance, a reduction in the pollock catch quota relative to its 1997 levels increases the population of pollock, phytoplankton, sea urchins, sea lions, and killer whales, but reduces the populations of zooplankton, kelp, and sea otters. Through the economic model, this increases the price of pollock, whilst the energy 'price' marine mammals pay to capture pollock falls. Due to a decline in sea otters, the amount paid by tourists to view marine mammals falls. In this case study, economic welfare is increased by a reduction in the pollock catch quota.

12.3.3.2 Case study: the decline of Easter Island society

Easter Island is a remote Pacific community some 2,000 km off the Chilean coast. The current population is around 2,000 people and this has remained approximately constant since the first Europeans discovered the island in 1722. Since that time, the island has been viewed as an archaeological and anthropological puzzle, as it indicated the existence of a sophisticated culture able to produce large stone statue 'moai' in the past, and yet explorers visiting in 1722 noted its small population and found little evidence of cultural richness. Explanations for the earlier cultural sophistication have included everything from extraterrestrials to Easter Island being part of the Lost Empire of Atlantis. A more plausible explanation concerns forest resource depletion and mass extinction of trees, and most of the species that depended upon them, this being an example of co-extinction (Stork, 2010).

Evidence from pollen records indicates that the island was originally covered by extensive palm forests, which provided the population with wood to build fishing boats. The palm forests also provided wood for quarrying and erecting statues. Initially the population prospered, but the slow-growing palm forests were gradually depleted and without any means of building boats, the food supply and the population declined. Brander and Taylor (1998) propose an economic analysis of the decline of the Easter Island community. They term their model a Ricardo–Malthus model: the reference to Ricardo refers to the structure of production, and that to Malthus refers to a Malthusian assumption relating population to the supply of food. The mathematical details of the model are beyond the scope of this book, but some aspects are worthy of note. The authors assume an economy that produces two goods, a natural resource derived good—fish—and a 'manufactured' good, which includes statues and housing. The initial resource level is fixed, as is the initial supply of labour. First, the link between the fishery, woodland, and labour is represented by a renewable resource model, similar to the one encountered in Chapter 8:

$$dx/dt = g(x) - h;$$

that is, the change in the stock x of the natural resource (dx/dt) equals the growth of stock $g(x)$ less the harvest rate h. In turn, the harvest is given by the Schaefer (1957) model:

$$h = \alpha x L_h,$$

where α is a parameter, and L_h is the labour used in harvesting. The palm forest and the fishery are open access, thus the labour input into the fishery will increase to the point at which the price of an extra fish equals cost per unit of labour.

The Malthusian component of the model is the link between the population growth and the food supply:

$$dL/dt = L(b - m + \phi[h/L]).$$

This equation states that the change in population (dL/dt) (and total labour supply) L is due to the birth rate b and death rate m plus a fertility adjustment term that gives the harvest (food) per capita [h/L] multiplied by a parameter ϕ. It is this last Malthusian term that incorporates the link between the food supply and population growth. A steady state in this model is where there is no change in the population or in the natural resource stock; however, there is no guarantee that it will be a 'desirable' steady state, as there is no regulatory policy in the model to ensure that the forest stock is conserved. In their paper, Brander and Taylor (1998), using parameters calibrated for Easter Island, predict a population peak in the early thirteenth century, accompanied by a collapse in the natural resource base followed by a gradual population decline, as people overexploited the natural resource basis of their economy.

It is tempting to draw wider conclusions from the Easter Island example about the dire consequences for society of overexploiting natural resources today and removing the biodiversity that supports a society. To an extent, this may be appropriate: however, there were a number of features of Easter Island that make it unusual. First, there was the relatively long time period, between 40 and 60 years, required for the Easter Island palm trees to start producing fruit. Second, the island depended heavily on a limited natural resource base. For a fascinating update on this Easter Island story, and how it relates to current debates over climate change policy, see Taylor (2009).

12.3.4 Aesthetic use and non-use values

We derive utility from observing species in the wild, or even knowing that a particular species is being protected. People value individual species, such as bald eagles, tigers, elephants, and whales, and whole ecosystems, such as rainforests, prairies, and heather moorland. For a summary of values that have been estimated for individual species, see Richardson and Loomis (2009). These values tend to favour the more 'charismatic' species and ecosystems. Thus large mammals, birds, and brightly coloured flowering plants tend to be valued more highly than insects, fungi, amphibians, and grass species, even though these species may be essential to the functioning of an ecosystem (Jacobsen et al., 2008). This is not to say, however, that people do not reveal positive willingness to pay (WTP) for less well-known and uncharismatic species—as shown, for example, in Christie et al. (2006).

What is likely is that we obtain estimates of the amenity value of individual species and/ or individual habitats, rather than of biodiversity itself (Hanley et al., 1995). These values may be either use or non-use values (see Chapter 3). Approaches taken to estimating these

---

BOX 12.6 The Value of Biodiversity in Poland

Biodiversity in Poland is largely located in the forests, which cover roughly 30 per cent of the land area. The Białowieża Forest is considered the last natural lowland forest in temperate Europe and is especially regarded for its species richness, and its ecological structures and functions.

For this reason, Czajkowski et al. (2009) selected this forest as the case study region to explore how Polish respondents valued different attributes of biodiversity conservation. Some ecologists suggest that the highest priority from a policy perspective should be the protection of all forms of biological variability within the Białowieża Forest, including landscape, habitats and their components, and species, as well as biological and ecological processes. Such a policy would allow for long-term observation of flora dynamics, succession and regression, fluctuation, degeneration and regeneration, as well as seasonal changes. Most transformed and actively managed temperate forests in Poland and elsewhere in Europe do not allow for observations of all these processes, which makes the Białowieża Forest unique. Almost 40 per cent of currently known species present in Poland (over 11,000) can be found in the Białowieża Forest. The forest's habitats are characterized by the presence of a large volume of dead wood, so that many endangered species that are dependent on this resource are still present. One of the flagship endangered species that exists here is the European bison (Żubr). The Białowieża Forest has played an important role in the recovery of this species.

There are two broad approaches to valuing biodiversity: either as a whole, using a contingent valuation method, in which individuals are asked to provide a WTP for a discrete change in the forest area of management; or through a choice modelling approach that presents alternative management options as sets of attributes. The authors applied the second approach and presented four attributes to respondents: natural ecological processes (conservation that allowed the forest to express dynamic processes of ecological succession facilitating scientific study); rare species of flora and fauna (conservation targeted at rare species); ecosystem components, which was concerned with the provision of biotopes and niches within the forest); and, finally, the cost of protecting the forests, in the form of additional tax payments. All options were compared with a status quo, which was characterized as what would happen if the forest management was not changed to enhance conservation. The results suggested €20 per household per year in Poland for a maximum improvement in all attributes, but also that respondents seemed to be willing to pay to protect complex ecological aspects of biodiversity in the forest.

---

values including travel costs, contingent valuation, and choice modelling. Box 12.6 gives an example of where values on different attributes of biodiversity are assessed using choice modelling: another example is to be found in Christie et al. (2006).

12.4 Biodiversity and Conservation Policy

Declining levels of biodiversity have led to policy responses at three levels: international, national, and local. International agreements on biodiversity often provide a guiding framework for national and local policies. In the future, international policies may become more important in providing funds for conservation in developing countries where biodiversity is concentrated.

Conserving biodiversity policy concerns securing optimal investment in a global public good. In common with any public good, there is an incentive for individuals and nations to free-ride and hope that the good is provided by others. Since the Convention on Biological Diversity (CBD) brought biodiversity loss into sharp focus, success in stemming the rate of biodiversity loss has been limited. The Millennium Ecosystem Assessment (2005) concluded that 60 per cent of ecosystem services worldwide have become degraded, most in the past 50 years. Past targets introduced as part of the CBD's efforts to reduce the rate of biodiversity loss by 2010 have not been met. In fact, the rate of biodiversity loss has continued to accelerate. In a commentary on the 2010 COP 10 talks in Nagoya, Moony and Mace (2009) state that

> Even the most conservative estimates suggest that an area of tropical rainforest greater than the size of California has been destroyed since 1992, mostly for food and fuel. Species extinction rates are at least 100 times those in pre-human times and are expected to increase.

(op. cit.: 1474)

What is going wrong? The problems appear to be, first, a poor targeting of resources for conservation; second, a lack of funds, given the scale of the problem; and, third, a problem of designing policies that give private farmers and fishermen incentives to protect biodiversity (Ferraro and Pattanayak, 2006). It is often overlooked that whilst international treaties and the national policies inspired by them may have scientifically justifiable objectives, if the farmers or fishers whose actions directly affect biodiversity has no economic incentive to modify his or her practices, then biodiversity will continue to be lost.

The challenge in designing conservation policy for private land was put succinctly by Shogren et al. (1999: 1260) in their economic critique of the US Endangered Species Act 1973:

> Just as policy makers cannot ignore the laws of nature, neither can they ignore the laws of human nature when protecting endangered species. Economic behavior matters in protecting and recovering endangered species. Effective federal and local policy requires that we adjust our perspectives and better integrate knowledge about human actions and reactions to species risk into the mix of influences on endangered species policy.

Significant progress has been made in understanding the nature of conservation science; however, finding cost-effective policies in developed and developing countries has proved elusive, despite significant expenditure.

12.4.1 International policy

In Rio de Janeiro on 5 June 1992, the Convention on Biological Diversity came into being at the United Nations Conference on Environment and Development (UNCED). The convention was signed by 154 countries, and recognized the need to preserve biodiversity not only in terms of reducing the rate of species extinction, but also in terms of preserving ecosystems and genetic variability. The broad objectives of the convention are the conservation of biological diversity, the sustainable use of its components, and the fair and equitable sharing of benefits from the use of genetic resources.

The objectives of the convention are far-reaching, but what tangible benefits have there been? There is a danger that a convention with such sweeping objectives, backed up by limited funding, will be ineffective. There is a need to translate international policy into national and local policies that provide additional incentives for biodiversity protection.

The CBD includes the General Environmental Facility (GEF), which provides funding from developed countries for projects in developing countries to protect biodiversity. The economic rationale for transferring funds to developing countries to preserve biodiversity is that biodiversity is a global public good, that should be paid for by all countries—not only those countries that 'host' the biodiversity. The principle behind this fund is that it pays for the incremental costs of projects that provide additional global benefits. Between June 1992 and November 1998, the GEF has provided a total of US$1.74 billion for biodiversity projects (COP, 1998). The replenishment of the fund was expected to be in the region of US$2.75 billion. However, this sum is small relative to the size of the problem and the potential value of biodiversity. Research indicates that the global funds available will not be sufficient to compensate the developing countries for the likely costs, including the opportunity cost, that they face in conserving biodiversity.

The 10th Conference of the Parties meeting, held in Nagoya, Japan in 2010, confronted the failure of the international community to reduce the rate of biodiversity loss and meet the targets set in 2002 to reduce the rate of biodiversity loss by 2010. This failure has been assessed by a range of indicators of biodiversity (Butchart et al., 2010). Indicators are classified as state indicators, which measure the state of biodiversity—for instance, the area of natural forest, pressure indicators, which include agricultural nitrogen use, and response indicators that measure how countries are responding to biodiversity loss. Almost all indicators are heading in the wrong direction for biodiversity; in other words, measures of the state of biodiversity are declining and pressure is increasing. Some of the response indicators, including aid tied to biodiversity projects, are increasing, and the area protected is increasing.

In response to this dire state of affairs, the revised CBD includes a new Strategic Plan for Biodiversity for the Period 2011–20—'Living in harmony with nature'—and a new protocol related to access and benefit sharing. In his commentary (Harrop, 2011: 119) proposes that the CBD

> … is an example of a 'hard' international law that possesses a 'soft' nature. [However …] The obligations in the text are for the most part textually diluted or heavily qualified leaving extensive discretion to Member States in the manner of their implementation.

Thus while 190 countries have signed up to a binding convention, the way in which it is worded means that it is effectively not binding on countries. However, some significant progress has been made on sharing the commercial benefits of biodiversity with the countries that host the biodiversity (see Box 12.7).

International Convention on Trade in Endangered Species (CITES). The International Convention on Trade in Endangered Species is perhaps the most important international agreement relating to the protection of biodiversity. The convention was signed in March 1972 and came into force 3 years later. It aims to protect endangered species by restricting trade in those species, effectively reducing or withdrawing demand for a species through trade. The mechanism is that endangered species are listed in Appendix I and potentially threatened species are listed in Appendix II. These lists are revised at biennial meetings. An Appendix I species requires a permit from the exporting country to ensure that trade will not be detrimental to the survival of the species, and a permit from the importing country to guarantee that the species will not be used for commercial purposes. This is effectively a

> **BOX 12.7 Valuable Viper Venom**
>
> It was known that people bitten by a Brazilian pit viper (*Bothorps jararaca*) suffered an often sharp drop in blood pressure, and blood thinning that often led to victims bleeding to death. The venom was extracted by a Brazilian biochemist, Mauricio Rocha de Silva, in the 1960s. Initial work by a British pharmacist, John Vane, and then an extended period of commercial and academic development led in 1975 to a synthetic compound being identified that mimics the effect of the snake venom. The resulting hypertension drug Captopril, sold by Bristol-Myers Squibb and launched on the US market in 1981, now has a sales revenue that runs into billions of dollars. However, the Brazilian research institute that originally isolated the venom did not receive a share of this revenue; nor did the region that hosts the snakes. The COP 10 agreement on access and benefit sharing aims to rectify similar cases in the future, by putting in place a protocol for the sharing of benefits. This is important for biodiversity conservation, as it provides countries with an incentive to protect biodiversity as a source of information for future drugs. For a more detailed account, see Patlak (2004).

ban on commercial trade. An Appendix II listing is less restrictive: it only requires a permit from the exporting country. The CITES Secretariat is also an important source of information on the state of endangered species, as it receives annual reports from member states on the level of trade in listed species (Secretariat of the Convention on Biological Diversity, 2010). The listing is an official declaration that a species is endangered and this may be beneficial in reducing demand or, in the case of an Appendix II listing, may actually increase speculative demand. For a discussion on the role of trade policy in environmental protection, see Chapter 8.

Restrictions on trade provide, at best, a sub-optimal approach to wildlife conservation. By reducing demand, they provide no incentive for landowners or governments to devote resources to protecting habitats for the species. For instance, banning trade in ivory gives no incentive to rural populations to protect elephant habitat. However, in some instances, an Appendix II listing may be more effective in terms of conservation than an Appendix I listing, as there is some incentive in regulated trade to actually protect the habitat (Bulte and van Kooten, 1999).

Some of these unanticipated perverse incentive effects have started to be addressed by delegates from developing countries. The 1981 New Delhi meeting 'downlisted' some species from Appendix I to Appendix II for the purposes of managed exploitation. For instance, the Zimbabwean population of Nile crocodile was downlisted, so that its commercial utilization could be expanded to provide funds for habitat protection. In 1983, this approach was extended to include trade quotas; for instance, the African leopard was allocated a quota. This approach was further extended in 1985, when downlisting was allowed on a range of species so long as a quota on trade was accepted. In 2010, Tanzania and Zambia requested that trade in ivory from their elephants be allowed (Wasser et al., 2010). For a discussion of the effectiveness of the ban on the ivory trade, see Box 12.8.

12.4.2 National policies are more challenging

National biodiversity conservation policies are concerned with investing in an asset that provides a range of private and public goods. One approach to securing this good is through

BOX 12.8 Saving Elephants

In December 1989, CITES placed the African elephant on the Appendix I list of endangered species. This decision made trade in ivory with the main consuming nations—the USA, Japan, and the European Union—illegal. This decision was prompted by a 50 per cent decline in the elephant population between 1979 and 1989, reducing numbers to 609,000. The decline was due to illegal hunting for ivory and a loss of elephant habitat to agriculture.

Has the ban succeeded in increasing the probability of long-term elephant survival? The population estimates give a mixed picture. The Zimbabwe population has increased, and this led in 1997 to a downlisting by the parties of CITES to Appendix II. This allows trade with Japan subject to quotas. The situation in the other countries, apart from Kenya, is one of further population decline.

How can this be the case when the trade in ivory is banned? The answer is that as with any criminal activity, the level of poaching effort depends upon the potential cost and benefits. So long as an illegal world market remains in ivory and some countries are relatively lax in enforcing anti-smuggling and anti-poaching legislation, then an incentive remains for elephant hunting (Wasser et al., 2010).

Consider the following simple model. The expected profit from poaching is given by

$$\text{profit} = (1 - \text{prob})\,pq - \text{costs} - \text{prob fine};$$

that is, the profit from a poaching trip is equal to the revenue from ivory sales, where p is the price of ivory and q is the quantity of ivory. The costs are the costs of labour and transport on a poaching trip; 'prob' is the probability of getting caught and 'fine' is the fine charged for poaching when the poachers are caught (Burton, 1999).

To reduce the incentive for poaching to zero, the profit must be zero. How can this be achieved? First, by reducing the effective ivory price by making smuggling more expensive; second, by increasing the resources devoted to catching poachers, which increases the probability of being caught, 'prob'; and third, by increasing the size of the fines charged when a poacher is caught.

If a country is not committed to either catching poachers or imposing large fines or custodial sentences upon them when caught, then it is likely that poaching will remain profitable. One role of international agencies might be to provide resources to catch poachers. However, a more constructive approach is to provide local people with benefits for protecting elephants and elephant habitats. If this system works, then perhaps local people will sort out the poachers themselves!

land purchase and direct management through nature reserves and national parks, but this is a relatively high-cost means of achieving conservation targets and thus in most countries a significant area of habitat is on private land. Therefore, governments have taken to contracting with farmers to provide biodiversity conservation on private land.

Investing in biodiversity is complicated by two aspects of what is called asymmetric information: first, adverse selection—that is, it is not possible for the regulator to observe the farmers' costs of undertaking conservation actions so that the landowner can earn so-called 'information rents' by the regulator paying the farmer more than it costs; and second, moral hazard, where farmers may not actually undertake agreed-on conservation actions because the regulator is unable to observe directly what farmers do. For instance, if biodiversity conservation requires reduced use of fertilizers to protect water quality, a farmer can state that this has occurred and receive a compensation payment, but the regulator cannot validate this claim.

The approaches that regulators can take to solve this policy design puzzle are becoming increasingly sophisticated (Ferraro, 2008). Contracts for conservation actions tend to be based on inputs or management actions. Thus, if a farmer reduces grazing and fences an area of native vegetation, he or she receives a payment for changing management actions in the hope that an ecological improvement (here, an increase in the area of native vegetation conserved) will result. Alternatively, contracts can be based on ecological outcomes. It turns out that because ecological outcomes such as habitat condition are difficult to define, and also highly random through time due to climatic and environmental conditions, few contracts are outcome based. This is an aspect of policy that should be developed in the future, as it gives incentives for landowners to develop ways to make conservation more efficient (Ferraro, 2008; White and Sadler, 2012).

Contracts can be fixed-price; that is, actions receive a fixed amount. For instance, in the United Kingdom, the Country Stewardship Scheme (Natural England, 2011) provides fixed payments to farmers for conservation actions. The scheme is offered in two levels, an Entry Level and a Higher Level. The advantage of this scheme is that it is relatively straightforward to administer, but it will tend to attract farmers with low compliance costs rather than necessarily the highest marginal gain in biodiversity protection. An alternative is to use a price-discriminating reverse auction (an auction in which the bidders offer to sell something to a buyer). An example is the Bushtender auction in Victoria, Australia where farmers submitted tenders for biodiversity conservation projects on bushland that were assessed on the basis of an expected increase in a biodiversity metric (an approximate measure of biodiversity) per dollar of tendered amount (Stoneham et al., 2003). The advantage of this approach is that by getting farmers to compete for conservation projects, they can reduce the cost of conservation and make a limited conservation budget go further. However, the transaction costs will be higher for auctions than for fixed-price schemes.

US Endangered Species Act. In 1973, the Endangered Species Act (ESA) acknowledged that the 'ecological, educational, historical, recreational and scientific value' of species diversity was inadequately accounted for in the process of 'economic growth and development'. The stated purpose of the Endangered Species Act is 'to provide a means whereby the ecosystems upon which endangered and threatened species depend may be conserved'. The Act is administered by the Fish and Wildlife Service and the National Marine Fisheries Service. Administration involves: first, listing a species as endangered or threatened— endangered being at greatest risk; second, designating habitats critical to a species' survival; third, banning activities that threaten the species; fourth, developing and implementing a recovery plan; and fifth, removing a species from the list when its population has recovered sufficiently for it not to be in danger of extinction.

The stated intention of the Act is to save *all* species. Nothing in the original wording of the statute requires that benefits or costs of species extinction should be taken into account. Although the Act treats all species as equal, budgetary restrictions force the regulatory authorities to identify priorities and thereby run the risk of some species becoming extinct. Of the 1,104 species in the USA listed as threatened and endangered, by July 1997 just over 40 per cent had approved recovery plans. The existence of a recovery plan does not guarantee that funds will be available to implement its recommendations. Evidence from Carroll et al. (1996) and Tear et al. (1993) suggests that survival prospects for just less that 60 per cent of listed species are actually deteriorating. Further, some approved recovery plans entail significant risks of extinction.

Schwartz (2008) reviews the more recent evidence on the success of the ESA and is moderately optimistic. On the basis of the US Fisheries and Wildlife Service (USFWS) reporting, fourteen species have been recovered and been delisted, while seven have gone extinct (USFWS, 2008a). A total of twenty species have changed listing status, indicating recovery (from endangered to threatened) compared to seven shifting towards decline (from threatened to endangered) (USFWS, 2008b). To an economist (Shogren, 2004: ch. 1), the success of the ESA relates to efficiency: Is the maximum species protection being achieved from the substantial budget available, US$1.64 billion (as of 2010) (USFWS, 2012)?

The status of US wildlife is further complicated by a lack of information on a list of 3,600 'indefinite' species that may be threatened or endangered. The listing process itself is partly the product of the preferences of the specialists in the Office of Endangered Species, and this may account for the high proportion of mammals, birds, and flowering plants listed and the low proportion of spiders and amphibians. This situation was partially rectified by the 1982 Congress amendment, which required scientific 'objectivity'. This led to the development of an eighteen-point scale that included measures of the 'degree of threat', 'recovery potential', 'taxonomy', and 'conflict with development'. Recovery expenditure (Metrick and Weitzman, 1998) is correlated with the level of conflict between a habitat and development and whether or not the species is megafauna, such as bears, wolves, and eagles. This tendency is confirmed by Ferraro et al. (2007), but their results indicate that over time the scientific basis of species listing tends to outweigh the charismatic and political motivations for endangered species listing. These authors find, as their main result, that listing alone reduces the chance of a species recovering, but listing accompanied by funding increases the probability of survival. The negative effects of listing alone on species recovery may reflect a perverse incentive effect. Once listing has occurred or is expected to occur, a landowner may have an incentive to eradicate an endangered species from his or her land to avoid restrictions on land use or development.

Economic considerations are accounted for implicitly in species listing, since the role for economics only emerges at the stage at which a critical habitat is designated. Under a 1978 amendment, the Secretary of the Interior may exclude a critical habitat on cost–benefit grounds so long as that exclusion does not lead to extinction.

The power of the Act rests with its ability to restrict the activities of private parties and public agencies. Private parties cannot harass, harm, or wound a listed species, where 'harm' includes damaging the ecosystem. This is backed by fines of between US$1,000 and US$50,000, and jail sentences of between 10 and 1,170 days (GAO, 1995). For a fuller account of the US Endangered Species Act and its performance, see Brown and Shogren (1998) and Schwartz (2008).

Local policies. International and national conservation policies can be well intentioned, but if they have little support from local communities they are unlikely to be effective. This is critical, as the burden of the costs of conservation measures tends to fall upon the rural populations who previously benefited by exploiting the protected resources. In Africa and other developing countries, these are often amongst the poorest people. By establishing conservation areas through national parks and the like, we are excluding people from the resources that had previously sustained them by providing food or income. There is thus a strong incentive for these people to turn to poaching, or to allow their cattle to encroach on protected areas.

Is this outcome inevitable? Drawing on examples from Africa, McNeely (1993) proposes that the solution to the problem of providing biodiversity is to design conservation schemes which:

- provide incentives for local communities to protect resources;
- avoid perverse incentives that actually encourage people to exploit the resources more than they would otherwise;
- and establish disincentives that penalize damaging actions.

Let us consider some examples for conservation schemes in Africa.

Kasungu National Park in Malawi provides an example of positive incentives for conservation, where local people have been given the right to collect tree caterpillars and establish beehives in return for curbing damaging actions such as excessive firewood removal. The income from these activities, US$198/ha for tree caterpillars and US$230/ha for beekeeping, provides cash for agricultural inputs, which have allowed some farmers to produce more cash crops (Mkanda, 1992).

Ecotourism can also provide a strong incentive for conservation. Heal (2000) analyses ecotourism as a way of bundling a public good with a private good. In this scheme, the tourism revenues are taxed to provide funds to support the public good. Thus in Kenya, tourism revenues are used to support the Kenyan Wildlife Service.

Unfortunately, examples of *perverse incentives* are also common. Often, these represent government failure, where natural resource or agricultural policies give an incentive to degrade the environment. For instance, in Botswana, prices for export beef supported by the European Union combined with subsidized inputs including fencing, veterinary services, and borehole development have led to widespread overgrazing, which benefits a small number of ranchers (Perrings and Stern, 2000).

Incentives need to be reinforced by *disincentives* that discourage damaging actions. However sympathetic a conservation scheme is to the economic well-being of the local community, there is almost always an incentive for people to misappropriate open-access or common-property resources, to catch more fish than is their right, to poach, or to allow their cattle to overgraze. Hannah (1992) found that the stronger the enforcement procedures in place, then the more effective were conservation projects in relation to their objectives. Enforcement may be in terms of conventional monitoring backed up by legal action. Misappropriation of resources may also be reduced by community opprobrium. If a community has a sense of shared ownership over a resource, then the community itself is more likely to protect it.

Summary

The earth is currently undergoing a phase of mass species extinction. Unlike previous mass extinctions, this current episode is due to habitat loss and disruption. By appropriating rich and diverse habitats for agricultural production and other disruptive forms of land use, humankind determines which species survive, which thrive, and which are pushed to extinction. In taking these decisions, we are determining which species survive to provide future generations with new drugs, crops, genetic material, aesthetic values, and ecosystem services. These decisions are often taken without any sense of their gravity; instead, we often blunder on in profound ignorance of which species are being destroyed in terms of their genetic make-up, their form, their behaviour, and their role in the ecosystem in which they are embedded.

The economics of biodiversity should attempt to value biodiversity in all its complexity, including the possibility that a species contains information that is irreversibly lost by extinction. Unfortunately, we are a long way from being able to do this. We can assess the value of biodiversity in terms of its potential medicinal value. We can value some ecosystem services, especially where those are associated with market values. However, we have a problem in valuing a species or a group of species in terms of their role within a complex ecosystem. The other challenge for economists is to design policies that present landowners and land users with an incentive to protect valued species and habitats cost-effectively.

Tutorial Questions

12.1 In your own words, define biodiversity.

12.2 Why should society conserve biodiversity?

12.3 How do we decide which species to save and which to leave unprotected?

12.4 'Sometimes biodiversity conservation policies can make things worse.' Discuss this statement in relation to a specific policy.

12.5 Define what might represent a cost-effective conservation policy.

References and Additional Readings

Aylward, B.A., Echeverría, J., Fendt, L., and Barbier, E.B. (1993). *The Economic Value of Species Information and its Role in Biodiversity Conservation: Case Studies of Costa Rica's National Biodiversity Institute of Pharmaceutical Prospecting.* Report to the Swedish International Development Authority (London: Environmental Economics Centre).

Barbier, E.B., and Strand, I. (1998). 'Valuing mangrove-fishery linkages—a case study of Campeche, Mexico', *Environmental and Resource Economics* 12(2): 151–66.

Bateman, I.J. Mace, G.M., Fezzi, C., Atkinson, G., and Turner, K. (2011). 'Economic analysis for ecosystem service assessments', *Environmental and Resource Economics* 48: 177–218.

Bernard, F., de Groot, R.S., and Campos, J.J. (2009). 'Valuation of tropical forest services and mechanisms to finance their conservation and sustainable use: a case study of Tapantí National

Park, Costa Rica', *Forest Policy and Economics* 11: 174–83.

Brander, J.A., and Taylor, M.S. (1998). 'The simple economics of Easter Island: a Ricardo–Malthus model of renewable resource use', *American Economic Review* 88: 119–38.

Brown, G.M., and Shogren, J.F. (1998). 'Economics of the Endangered Species Act', *Journal of Economic Perspectives* 12: 3–20.

Burton, M. (1999). 'An assessment of alternative methods of estimating the effect of the ivory trade ban on poaching effort', *Ecological Economics* 30: 93–106.

Butchart, S.H.M. et al. (2010). 'Global biodiversity: indicators of recent declines', *Science* 328: 1164–8.

Bulte, E., and van Kooten, C. (1999). 'Marginal valuation of charismatic species', *Environmental and Resource Economics* 14: 119–30.

Carroll, R., Augspurger, C., Dobson, A., Franklin, J., Orians, G., Reid, W., Tracy, R., Willcove, D., and Wilson, J. (1996). 'Strengthening the use of science in achieving the goals of the Endangered Species Act: an assessment by the Ecological Society of America', *Ecological Applications* 6: 1–11.

Chichilnisky, G. (1993). 'Property rights and biodiversity and the pharmuceutical industry', Working Paper, Columbia University Graduate Business School, New York.

Christie, M., Hanley, N., Warren, J., Murphy, K., Wright, R., and Hyde, T. (2006). 'Valuing the diversity of biodiversity', *Ecological Economics* 58(2): 304–17.

Claassen, R., Cattaneo, A., and Johansson, R. (2008). 'Cost-effective design of agri-environmental payment programs: U.S. experience in theory and practice', *Ecological Economics* 65: 737–52.

Colwell, R.R. (1996). 'Microbial biodiversity and biotechnology', in M.J. Reaka-Kudla, D.E. Wilson, and E.O. Wilson (eds.), *Biodiversity II* (Washington, DC: James Henry Press).

Convention on Biological Diversity (1992). http://www.cbd.int/ (accessed 31 July 2011).

COP (1998). COP4 Report, http://unfccc.int/cop4/ (accessed 15 November 2012).

Czajkowski, M., Buszko-Briggs, M., and Hanley, N. (2009). 'Valuing changes in forest biodiversity', *Ecological Economics* 68: 2910–17.

Daily, G. (ed.) (1997). *Nature's Services: Societal Dependence on Natural Ecosystems* (Washington, DC: Island Press).

Elridge, N. (1998). *Life in the Balance: Humanity and the Biodiversity Crisis* (Princeton, NJ: Princeton University Press).

Feeley, K.J., and Silman, M.R. (2009). 'Extinction risks of Amazonian plant species', *Proceedings of the National Academy of Sciences of the United States of America* 106(30): 12382–7.

Fernandes, L., Day, J., Lewis, A., Slegers, S., Kerrigan, B., Breen, D., Cameron, D.F., Jago, B., Hall, J., Lowe, D., Innes, J., Tanzer, J., Chadwick, V., Thompson, L., Gorman, K., and Possingham, H. (2005). 'Establishing representative no-take areas in the Great Barrier Reef: large scale implementation of theory on marine protected areas', *Conservation Biology* 19(6): 1733–44.

Ferraro, P.J. (2008). 'Asymmetric information and contract design for payments for environmental services', *Ecological Economics* 654: 810–21.

—— McIntosh, C., and Ospina, M. (2007). 'The effectiveness of the US Endangered Species Act: an econometric analysis using matching methods', *Journal of Environmental Economics and Management* 54: 245–61.

—— and Pattanayak, S.K. (2006). 'Money for nothing? A call for empirical evaluation of biodiversity conservation investments', *PLoS Biology* 4: 482–8.

Finnoff, D., and Tschirhart, J. (2008). 'Linking dynamic economic and ecological general equilibrium models', *Resource and Energy Economics* 30: 91–114.

Gallai, N., Salles, J-M., Settele, J., and Vaissière, B.E. (2009). 'Economic valuation of the vulnerability of world agriculture confronted with pollinator decline', *Ecological Economics* 68(3): 810–21.

GAO (General Accounting Office) (1995). *Endangered Species Act: Information on Species Protection on Non-federal Lands*, GAO/RCED-95-16 (Washington, DC: USGAO).

Hammer, K., and Khoshbakht, K. (2005). 'Towards a "Red List" for crop plant species', *Genetic Resources and Crop Evolution* 52: 249–65.

Hanley, N., Spash, C., and Walker, L. (1995). 'Problems in valuing the benefits of biodiversity protection', *Environmental and Resource Economics* 5(3): 249–72.

Hannah, L. (1992). *African People, African Parks* (Washington, DC: Conservation International).

Harrop, S.R. (2011). ' "Living in harmony with nature"? Outcomes of the 2010 Nagoya Conference of the Convention on Biological Diversity', *Journal of Environmental Law* 23(1): 117–28.

Heal, G.M. (2000). *Nature and the Marketplace: Capturing the Value of Ecosystem Services* (Washington, DC: Island Press).

Iltis, H.H., Doebley, J.F., Guzman, R., and Pazy, B. (1979). *Zea diploperennis* (Gramineae)—new teosinte from Mexico, *Science* 203: 186–8.

IUCN (International Union for Conservation of Nature) (2010). IUCN Red List of threatened species, Version 2010, IUCN, Gland, Switzerland, http://www.iucnredlist.org (accessed 10 June 2010).

Jacobsen, J.B., Boiesen, J.H., Thorsen, B.J., and Strange, N. (2008). 'What's in a name? The use of quantitative measures versus "iconised" species when valuing biodiversity', *Environmental and Resource Economics* 39(3): 247–63.

MacArthur, R.H., and Wilson, E.O. (1967). *The Theory of Island Biogeography* (Princeton, NJ: Princeton University Press).

McNeely, J.A. (1993). 'Economic incentives for

conserving biodiversity—lessons for Africa',
Ambio 22(2–3): 144–50.

Margules, C.R., and Pressey, R.L. (2000). 'Systematic
conservation planning', *Nature* 405: 243–53.

May, R.M., Lawton, J.H., and Stork, N.E. (1995).
'Assessing extinction rates', in J. H. Lawton and R.
M. May (eds.), *Extinction Rates* (Oxford: Oxford
University Press).

MEA (Millennium Ecosystem Assessment) (2005).
*Ecosystems and Human Well-being: General
Synthesis* (Washington, DC: Island Press).

Metrick, A., and Weitzman, M.L. (1998). 'Conflicts
and choices in biodiversity preservation', *Journal
of Economic Perspectives* 12: 21–34.

Mkanda, C.X. (1992). 'The potential of Kasungu
National Park in Malawi to increase income and
food security in neighbouring communities',
Paper presented at IV World Congress on
National Parks and Protected Areas, Caracas,
Venezuela.

Moony, H., and Mace, G. (2009). 'Biodiversity policy
challenges: editorial', *Science* 325: 1474.

Myers, N., Mittermeier, R.A., Mittermeier, C.G., da
Fonesca, G.A.B., and Kent, J. (2000). 'Biodiversity
hotspots for conservation priorities', *Nature* 403:
853–58.

Natural England (2011). Environmental stewardship,
http://www.naturalengland.org.uk/ourwork/
farming/funding/es/default.aspx (accessed 3 June
2011).

Opdam, P., and Wascher, D. (2004). 'Climate
change meets habitat fragmentation: linking
landscape and biogeographical scale levels
in research and conservation', *Biological
Conservation* 117: 285–97.

Patlak, M. (2004). 'From viper's venom to drug
design: treating hypertension', *The FASEB Journal*
8: 421–34.

Perrings, C., and Stern, D.I. (2000). 'Modelling
loss of resilience in agroecosystems: rangelands
in Botswana', *Environmental and Resource
Economics* 16: 185–210.

Polasky, S., Camm, J.D., and Garber-Yonts, B.
(2001). 'An application to terrestrial vertebrate
conservation in Oregon', *Land Economics* 77: 68–78.

Possingham, H.P., and Wilson, K.A. (2006).
'Biodiversity: turning up the heat on hotspots',
Nature 436: 919–20.

Prach, K., and Hobbs, R.J. (2008). 'Spontaneous
succession versus technical reclamation in the
restoration of disturbed sites', *Restoration Ecology*
16: 363–6.

Putman, R.J., and Wratten, S.D. (1984). *Principles of
Ecology* (London: Croom Helm).

Raup, D. (1988). 'Diversity crises in the geological
past', in E.O. Wilson (ed.), *Biodiversity*
(Washington, DC: National Academy Press).

Richardson, L., and Loomis, J. (2009). 'The total
economic value of threatened, endangered and
rare species: an updated meta-analysis', *Ecological
Economics* 68(5): 1535–48.

Schaefer, M.B. (1957). 'Some consideration of
population dynamics and economics in relation to
the management of marine fisheries', *Journal of the
Fisheries Research Board of Canada* 14: 669–81.

Schwartz, M.W. (2008). 'The performance of the
Endangered Species Act', *Annual Review of
Ecology, Evolution, and Systematics* 39:
279–99.

Secretariat of the Convention on Biological Diversity
(2010). *Global Biodiversity Outlook 3* (Montreal).

Shogren, J.F. (ed.) (2004). *Species at Risk: Using
Economic Incentives to Shelter Endangered Species
on Private Property* (Austin, TX: University of
Texas Press).

—— Tschirhart, J., Anderson, T., Whritenour Ando,
A., Beissinger, S.R., Brookshire, D., Brown,
G.M. Jr, Coursey, D., Innes. R., Meyer, S.M., and
Polasky, S. (1999). 'Why economics matters for
endangered species protection', *Conservation
Biology* 13(6): 1257–61.

Simpson, R.D., Sedjo, R.A., and Reid, J.W. (1996).
'Valuing biodiversity for use in pharmaceutical
research', *Journal of Political Economy* 104:
163–85.

Spash, C., and Hanley, N. (1995). 'Preferences,
information and biodiversity preservation',
Ecological Economics 12: 91–208.

—— and Simpson, I. (1994). 'Utilitarian and
rights-based alternatives for protecting sites of
special scientific interest', *Journal of Agricultural
Economics* 45(1): 15–26.

Stoneham, G., Chaudhri, V., Ha, A., and
Strappazzon, L. (2003). 'Auctions for
conservation contracts: an empirical
examination of Victoria's BushTender trial',
*Australian Journal of Agricultural and Resource
Economics* 47: 477–500.

Stork, N.E. (1996). 'Measuring global biodiversity
and its decline', in M.J. Reaka-Kudla, D.E.
Wilson, and E.O. Wilson (eds.), *Biodiversity II*
(Washington, DC: James Henry Press).

—— (2010). 'Re-assessing current extinction rates',
Conservation Biology 19: 357–71.

Swanson, T.M. (1994). *The International Regulation of Extinction* (Basingstoke: Macmillan).

Taylor, S.M. (2009). 'Environmental crises: past, present and future', *Canadian Journal of Economics* 42: 1240–75.

Tear, T., Scott, J., Hayward, P., and Griffith, B. (1993). 'Status and prospects for success of the Endangered Species Act: a look at recovery plans', *Science* 262: 976–7.

TEEB (The Economics of Ecosystems and Biodiversity) (2010). *The Economics of Ecosystems and Biodiversity: Mainstreaming the Economics of Nature—A Synthesis of the Approach, Conclusions and Recommendations of TEEB*, http://www.teebtest.org/ecological-and-economic-foundations-report/ (accessed 15 November 2012).

Tschirhart, J., Anderson, T., Whritenour Ando, A., Beissinger, S.R., Brookshire, D., Brown, G.M. Jr, Coursey, D., Innes. R., Meyer, S.M., and Polasky, S. (1999). 'Why economics matters for endangered species protection', *Conservation Biology* 13(6): 1257–61.

Tschirhart, J. (2004). 'Integrated ecological–economic models', *Annual Review of Resource Economics* 1: 381–407.

UK National Ecosystems Assessment (2010). http://uknea.unep-wcmc.org/ (accessed 3 August 2011).

UNEP (United Nations Environment Program) (1993). *Guidelines for Country Studies on Biological Diversity* (Nairobi: UNEP).

—— (1998). Conference of the Parties to the Convention on Biological Diversity, Fourth Meeting, Bratislava.

Wasser, S. et al. (2010). 'Elephants, ivory and trade', *Science* 327: 1331–2.

USFWS (US Fishery and Wildlife Service) (2008a). *Conservation Plans and Agreements Database* (Washington, DC: USFWS).

—— (2008b). *Summary Reports to Congress on the Recovery Program for Threatened and Endangered Species* (Washington, DC: USFWS).

—— (2012). 'Budget at a glance', http://www.fws.gov/budget/2012/PDF%20Files%20FY2012%20Greenbook/04.%20Budget%20at%20a%20Glance%202012.pdf (accessed 12 May 2012).

Weitzman, M.L. (1992). 'On diversity', *Quarterly Journal of Economics* 108: 157–83.

White, B., and Sadler R.J. (2012). 'Optimal conservation investment for a biodiversity rich agricultural landscape', *Australian Journal of Agricultural Economics* 56: 1–21.

Wilson, E.O. (1988). 'The current state of biological diversity', in E.O. Wilson and F.M. Peter (eds.), *Biodiversity* (Washington, DC: National Academy Press).

13 Non-renewable Natural Resources and Energy

Economists have long been concerned with the efficient use of scarce natural resources. Adam Smith examined the nature of capital for land, mines, and fisheries; Ricardo explored how land quality matters for economic rent; Malthus worried about population, poverty, and the limits of agricultural resources; and Jevons feared the social consequences of the depletion of coal quantity and quality. These classical economists treated natural resources as a factor of production provided freely by nature, which made it distinct from costly capital and labour. The general mindset framed the problem as one in which a resource owner made choices to maximize the net present value of the natural resource.

At the start of the twentieth century, economics started to treat natural resources as something more distinct than just as a free factor of production. Theorists such as Gray and Hotelling argued that an additional intertemporal cost for extracting or harvesting natural resources existed. They argued that a resource owner should account for an additional cost above and beyond the cost of extraction and processing—the opportunity cost of depletion or harvesting sooner rather than later. After the Second World War, fishery economists explained how weakly defined property rights can lead people to overexploit resources that inhabit the commons. In the late 1970s and early 1980s, economics began to examine the social inefficiencies associated with stock pollutants such as carbon emissions and climate change, the loss of services from reductions in the stock of global biodiversity, and the risks to life support and aesthetic services provided by natural resources left unpriced by the market.

Today, natural resource economics continues to turn these early and new insights into mature theories that can help explain how people and societies choose to manage and use their limited resources, both non-renewable resources such as minerals and fossil fuels, and renewable resources such as fisheries (Chapter 7) and forests (Chapter 10). The field considers how societies makes choices to (mis)manage their stocks of biological diversity cost-effectively, to reduce risks from climate change efficiently, and to value natural resource services that are not bought and sold in the marketplace.

This chapter examines how people develop and conserve their scarce non-renewable resources and renewable energy resources; and how these resources are transformed into energy. Many questions arise when thinking about natural resources and our usage: Are we running out of resources? Do resources get depleted too fast as countries try to maximize their profits too quickly? What are the predictions for the future of world energy demand and supply? In this chapter, we will examine these questions by:

- Discussing what is meant by 'resources'.
- Explaining an economic model of how resource extraction should be managed.
- Evaluating alternative measures of resource scarcity.
- Examining the special role of energy in the economy.
- Discussing what a nation's energy policy has to address.

13.1 Natural Resource Types

What do we mean by 'natural resources'? A distinction is often made between 'material' and 'energy' resources. This distinction relates to the conventional end-uses of these resources, in that material (or mineral)[1] resources are used as part of the physical constituency of commodities (iron ore, converted into steel, in car bodies, or copper in pipes); whilst energy resources are converted into heat and other forms of energy. The chemical energy in natural gas is converted into heat energy when gas is burnt in domestic central-heating boilers. Some resources are used both as materials and as energy sources: oil is the prime example here, being used for propulsion in internal combustion engines, and to make plastics. Conversion of material resources into usable forms also requires inputs of energy resources (for smelting and mining). There are some eighty-eight minerals occurring on earth. Of these, only twelve make up 99 per cent of the earth's crust: the most common elements in these minerals are silicon (27%), aluminium (8%), and iron (6%).

One obvious distinction between resource types is by their potential for natural growth. A fishery is different from a deposit of iron ore; fish have a natural rate of growth, iron ore does not. Most economists distinguish between 'renewable' and 'non-renewable' resources, with the renewable classification reserved for those resources exhibiting a positive natural rate of growth. This is a cleaner distinction than the classification into 'exhaustible' and 'non-exhaustible' resources, since even a renewable resource can be exhausted (by continuing to harvest in excess of the natural rate of growth, for example), and a non-renewable resource may not be exhausted if it becomes uneconomic to extract.

13.2 The Extraction of a Non-renewable Resource

In this section, we focus on how economists think about using non-renewable resources such as oil and coal. We focus on the classic Hotelling model of resource extraction as our benchmark case. We next consider whether the owner of the resource has a monopoly on the resource, and finally we examine how economic behaviour changes once we add extraction costs.

---

[1] A mineral is defined as a solid crystalline chemical element or compound in fixed composition. Rocks are aggregates of one or more minerals. A mineral deposit is an accumulation of a specific mineral.

13.2.1 **The baseline case–an introduction to Hotelling's rule**

Consider an oil market made up of a large number of firms, each one owning its own oil well. All firms want to maximize the *present value* of their profits, where profit is the price of oil times the quantity extracted. We assume, for the time being, that oil can be produced at zero cost. The problem that the firms face is how much oil to supply in each time period. The use of a present value of profit implies that delaying oil extraction has an opportunity cost in terms of the return (r) that money tied up in oil reserves could earn from alternative investments (such as money in interest earning deposits in a bank or invested in stocks and shares). So why do these firms not empty their oil wells in the first year and live off their investments?

A similar question led Hotelling (1931) to develop a model of how non-renewable natural resources are extracted through time. The key result is now known as *Hotelling's rule*. The general version of the rule is complex: see Hanley et al. (2007: ch. 7) for a fuller introduction, but the basic idea can be explained in a simple two-period example. We define an equilibrium in which the producer is indifferent between selling the last unit of oil in the current period or in the next period. For this to be the case, the present value of a barrel of oil would have to be the same in both periods. If the price in period 1 is given as p_1 and the price in period 2 is given by p_2, then the equilibrium condition is given by

$$p_1 = p_2(1/(1 + r)), \tag{13.1}$$

where $(1/(1 + r))$ is the discount factor. What does this condition imply? Suppose the discount rate is 10 per cent ($r = 0.1$); this implies (by rearranging this formula) that

$$(1 + r)p_1 = p_2,$$

where the price in period 2 must be 10 per cent greater than the price in period 1 for the firm to be in equilibrium. Another way of representing this formula is by rearranging to give:

$$\frac{p_2 - p_1}{p_1} = r, \tag{13.2}$$

which states that the proportional price rise for oil equals the discount rate. Hotelling's rule predicts that the oil price will rise through time. The next question is what actually drives the price increase? The answer is market demand combined with all firms reducing their output through time. In aggregate, firms extract at a rate in each period that ensures that the equilibrium shown in equation (13.2) holds.

We now have a basic condition to determine the price and the quantity of oil produced in each period. This is not enough, however, to determine the life cycle of oil reserves, since we also need to know the initial stock of oil and the price at which demand falls to zero. The price at which demand falls to zero is known as the 'backstop price' and it can be interpreted as the price of a substitute for the non-renewable resource. For instance, in the case of oil it might be the price at which demand switches to a renewable alternative such as fuel made from ethanol.

Once we know the backstop price and the initial stock, on the basis of Hotelling's rule, we can calculate the price and quantity through time. This can be represented in a four-quadrant diagram (Figure 13.1). The north-west quadrant of Figure 13.1 gives the demand curve, and the north-east quadrant the extraction path. Note that through time the quantity extracted falls and reaches zero at the end time T when the resource is exhausted. The area under the extraction curve is the total initial stock, which is the sum of all extraction through time. As the rate of extraction falls then the price, in the south-west quadrant, rises at a rate that satisfies Hotelling's rule, until at time T it reaches the backstop price p^b, when demand falls to zero. The south-east quadrant contains a 45-degree line that simply transfers time from one axis to the other.

Is this resource extraction plan socially optimal? The discount rate reflects the current generation's preferences for resource use through time. If this is accepted, so long as the discount rate is the social time preference rate, then the resource extraction path is at least efficient. But if firms face imperfect capital markets and interest rates, or returns on other assets are distorted, this may lead firms to extract the non-renewable resource either too rapidly or too slowly. In many countries, the interest rate tends to be higher than the social discount rate due to the inclusion of a premium to cover risk. This implies that firms may be inclined to extract a non-renewable resource too rapidly. This is predicted by Hotelling's rule: high discount rates lead to more rapid rises in the price and a more rapid decline in the rate of extraction and a shorter time to economic exhaustion of the resource.

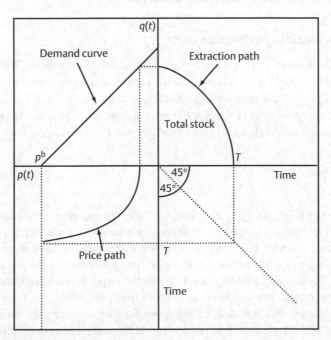

Figure 13.1 The Hotelling model of resource extraction.

13.2.2 Resource extraction and the monopolist

In contrast to the competitive market example in the previous section, the structure of many non-renewable resource industries is highly concentrated in one or two countries. For instance, as an oil cartel, the Organization of Petroleum Exporting Countries (OPEC) represents a significant proportion of world oil production, and the same holds for South Africa and diamonds. An interesting question is: How would a monopoly decide to extract a non-renewable resource? The answer is that the profit-maximizing zero-cost monopoly follows a slightly different version of Hotelling's rule. Instead of equating the present value of price through time, it equates the present value of the marginal revenue. Remember that marginal revenue is the change in total revenue when we increase output by one unit:

$$\frac{MR_2 - MR_1}{MR_1} = r. \tag{13.3}$$

The implication of this rule is that if the marginal revenue increases at the discount rate, then this implies that the monopoly price starts higher than the competitive price, but rises more gradually through time. Remember that a higher price implies a lower level of demand. In practice, the monopoly acts as a price discriminator where the market is separated through time. The implication of this rule is that a monopoly extracts relatively slowly compared with firms in greater competition with each other. In fact, we may view the activities of members of OPEC as being 'conservationist' in the sense that by acting as a cartel they reduce the supply of oil and extend the life of the resource.

13.2.3 Model including extraction costs

Hotelling's rule has been given for a zero-cost firm, which is unrealistic. The model can be easily modified to include costs. Note that in the zero-cost case, the price can be interpreted as the marginal profit—the addition to profits for each extra unit extracted. If we introduce costs, then the marginal profit becomes the price minus the marginal cost, given as $M\pi = p - MC$. Hotelling's rule with costs is then given as follows:

$$\frac{M\pi_2 - M\pi_1}{M\pi_1} = r.$$

Instead of the price increasing by the discount rate, the marginal profit increases by the discount rate. This means that the rate of increase in prices now depends partly on how costs change over time. Costs for non-renewable resource firms are typically given as an increasing function of the rate of extraction (q) and a declining function of the remaining reserves (x), $c = c(x, q)$. This form of cost function explains the physical reality of many mineral and petroleum reserves, that extraction tends to move to progressively more costly deposits as reserves are depleted. For instance, mines move further underground and this tends to increase costs. Oil extraction tends to reduce the pressure in oil reservoirs and this increases the cost of production (see Box 13.1). The marginal profit ($M\pi = p - MC$) also gives a measure of resource scarcity, in that it is the value of the marginal unit of the resource stock. We

BOX 13.1 Testing Hotelling's Rule

Hotelling's rule is remarkable as an example of a dynamic model that is able to trace out the life cycle of a non-renewable resource industry from the current time to the time when the last drop of oil worth extracting is extracted. As a model, it has two possible applications. It can be used prescriptively to inform non-renewable firms how they should schedule resource extraction through time, or it can be used to predict how firms actually behave. In the first of these roles, the model might be useful as a guide to extraction rates, so long as the firm can predict how the oil price changes through time. However, even a monopoly firm faces a demand curve that changes through time due to changing tastes, technology, and general economic conditions. Many authors have tested how good Hotelling's rule is at predicting the behaviour of firms (for a review, see Hanley et al., 2007: ch. 8). The overall conclusion is that the standard form of Hotelling's is not good at explaining how firms actually behave. Why should this be?

In a review paper, Livernois (2009) concludes that scarcity by itself is not sufficient to drive prices upwards through time: 'It appears that other factors, notably technological change, revisions to expectations regarding the resource base, and market structure, have had a more significant influence on the evolution of price.' A recent analysis of trends in non-renewable resource prices (Lee et al., 2006) for eleven major commodities concludes that for most series there is no clear upward trend; in fact, the trend from 1870 to 1990 includes periods of rising, falling, and constant real prices, with a number of structural breaks. The results confirm the findings of Krautkraemer's review (1998). It seems that if we want to understand the workings of non-renewable resource markets, we need to understand demand and supply responses through time and the critical role of price expectations (Pesaran, 1990).

can see that scarcity increases as the price increases, but falls as the marginal cost increases. Measures of scarcity are discussed in the next section.

13.3 Measuring Resource Scarcity

One of the most common questions in debates over the use of natural resources is 'are we running out?' For any non-renewable resource, a positive rate of extraction means that the physical stock of the resource is reduced in size. However: (i) there are major problems in defining what this physical stock represents; (ii) the economic measure of the size of reserves is not the same as the physical size of the reserves; (iii) the value of the economic reserve will change over time; and (iv) there are alternative measures for the *scarcity* of this economic reserve, which may well give different answers to the above question.

Consider Figure 13.2. The figure shows a more realistic representation of a non-renewable resource through time in terms of marginal costs and prices. This diagram can be considered as a modified version of the south-west quadrant of Figure 13.1. At any one time, there is a range of marginal costs of extraction for a resource such as oil. The International Energy Agency (2008) analysed the global oil supply curve on the basis of production costs per barrel: the lowest-cost reserves are found in the Middle Eastern and North African oilfields, at $6 to $28 per barrel; the most expensive are oil from oil shales, at between $58 and $113 per barrel.

In Figure 13.2, the upper and lower limits of the distribution of marginal costs change through time. The lower marginal cost rises due to extraction, but the rate of rise may be reduced by new technology that makes extraction cheaper. The higher marginal cost falls

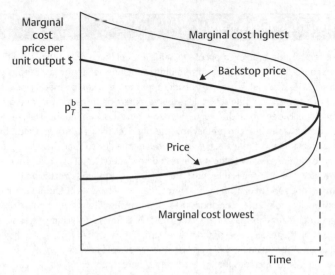

Figure 13.2 Resource extraction, technological innovation, and exploration through time.

Note: The 'marginal cost lowest' is the expected lowest marginal cost of extracting from the known proven resource stocks; the 'marginal cost highest' is the expected marginal cost from extracting from possible resource stocks; the price is the expected market price and the backstop price gives the price of alternate technology.

due to new technology that makes, for instance, extraction of oil from remote areas less expensive. Note that most expensive reserves (highest marginal cost) are not extracted until the end of the resources' life.

The backstop price generally falls through time due to new technology. Non-renewable resource firms may anticipate this trend and extract more rapidly.

The term 'economic reserves' is often used to describe that portion of a deposit (or collection of deposits) that it is profitable to extract, given current prices and costs. Costs depend partly on the state of technology, and on cumulative extraction: these costs change over time. Prices will also change in response to the decisions of extractors over extraction rates (which might depend, for example, on the agreement reached by a cartel of producers, such as OPEC), demand for the material, and government intervention on prices. In Figure 13.2, the economic reserves are those reserves with a marginal cost less than the price and above the lowest marginal cost.

The diagram shows that reserves in the economic reserve change through time. For example, the minimum concentration of copper in a copper deposit required for profitable extraction fell from 3 per cent in the 1800s to 0.5 per cent in the mid-1960s with technological progress, which at constant real prices would result in the size of the economic reserve increasing over time.

Uncertainty also exists over the actual amount of a resource in a given geographical area. For example, it is not known with certainty how much oil lies under the North Sea. Some oil deposits have been found and are in production; others have been found and are not in production. Other deposits are thought to exist given the nature of the surrounding geology. But the total size of deposits may be greater than this. But even with respect to defining the physical size of a deposit, or of all deposits for a particular material, difficulties arise. For example, should all amounts of copper be counted, irrespective of their concentration, or of the form in which they are present?

Several writers argue for a crucial concept called the 'mineralogical threshold' (e.g. Harris and Skinner, 1982). Below this threshold, minerals occur as silicates, in that they are chemically bonded to silica. The total amount of a mineral that exists on earth is known as its 'crustal abundance', also referred to as the resource base. However, only a small fraction (roughly 3% on average) of the crustal abundance of most minerals exists in non-silicate form, as oxides, sulphides, or carbonates. For some minerals, few deposits exist that are in non-silicate form. Skinner (1976) calls these minerals 'geochemically scarce'.

To take the example of lead, its average concentration in the earth's crust is 0.001 per cent, but extraction currently takes place in ore deposits where lead is found in concentrations of between 2 and 20 per cent. Once these ore deposits have been extracted, then vastly more energy would be required to extract lead from its silicate form, where it is trapped by atomic substitution. The extraction of the deposits would also produce large quantities of geochemically abundant minerals as a by-product. Geochemically scarce minerals include copper, lead, mercury, and gold (Anderson, 1985). For geochemically abundant minerals, such as iron, the energy required to extract the mineral increases smoothly as the purity of the ore declines, as Figure 13.3 shows; for geologically scarce minerals, energy use jumps at the mineralogical threshold. A prediction from the mineralogical threshold model is that geochemically abundant minerals will be substituted for geochemically scarce minerals as the threshold is approached.

Table 13.1 gives recent estimates of world total reserves, the countries with the largest deposits, the number of years of consumption remaining (at current consumption levels) (Gordon et al., 2006; Cohen, 2007), and also the percentage of consumption met from

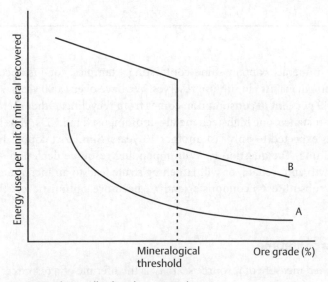

A. Geochemically abundant minerals
B. Geochemically scarce minerals

Figure 13.3 The mineralogical threshold.

Table 13.1 Abundance, regional concentration, and recycling for metallic minerals

	Uses	Stock	Units	Country with largest reserves (%)	Years reserves remaining at current consumption	Percentage supply from recycling
Aluminium	Cans, white goods	32,350	mt	Guinea (27)	1,027	49
Antimony	Drugs	3.86	mt	China (62)	30	0
Chromium	Chrome plating	779	mt	Kazakhstan (60)	143	25
Copper	Wire, coins, plumbing	937	mt	Zambia (38)	61	31
Gold	Dentistry, jewellery	89,700	t	South Africa (40)	45	43
Indium	LCDs	6,000	t	Canada (33)	13	0
Lead	Pipes, batteries	144	mt	China (25)	42	72
Nickel	Batteries, turbine blades	143	mt	Australia (19)	90	35
Phosphorous	Fertilizer	49,750	mt	Morocco and Western Sahara (42)	345	0
Platinum/ rhodium	Jewellery, catalytic converters	79,840	t	South Africa (88)	360	0
Silver	Jewellery, catalytic converters	569,000	t	Poland (25)	29	16
Tantalum	Cell phones, camera lenses	153,000	t	Brazil (48)	116	20
Tin	Tins, solder	11.2	mt	China (31)	40	26
Uranium	Power generation	3.3	mt	Australia (23)	59	0
Zinc	Galvanizing	460	mt	USA (20) and China (20)	46	26

Source: Cohen (2007).

recycling. The minerals contain some contrasting examples; for instance, the world is unlikely to ever exhaust its aluminium reserves. We have over 1,000 years' reserves of aluminium, and 49 per cent of consumption comes from recycling. Other metals are more of a concern. For instance, one high-tech metal—indium, used in LCDs—has limited known reserves and is expected to only last another 13 years. Similarly, copper has 61 years of reserves remaining. The question is: Will impending resource depletion seriously affect economic growth and welfare, or will Hotelling's rule lead to an increase in prices and a drive to find substitutes? Economists tend to be more optimistic on this issue than geologists.

13.3.1 Resource lifetime

A frequently cited measure of resource scarcity is the lifetime of a resource. This is usually expressed as the economic reserve of a resource divided by its current annual consumption rate, with perhaps an allowance for a predicted growth in this rate over time. Fisher (1981) quotes (but does not endorse) a measure of 45 years for copper in 1974: a prediction that by the year 2019, the world will run out of copper. The most immediate problem here is that if we instead divided the total resource base by annual consumption, we would arrive at a much larger figure, one that allows for higher-cost deposits being brought on line as prices rise—but which measure is correct?

The answer is neither. As a resource gets scarcer, its price will, other things being equal, tend to rise. This will reduce consumption (by substitution, for example), and increase production. These changes will change the lifetime measure. What is more, as prices rise producers will be encouraged to engage in more exploration, which will increase the resource base if finds are made. Lifetime measures for many resources have been found to be approximately constant over time, and have been argued by Fisher to say more about firms' attitudes to holding inventories of minerals than about scarcity.

13.3.2 **Unit cost measures**

The earliest arguments in natural resources economics about scarcity centred around the costs of extraction. As a mine is depleted, the miners have to travel further and further underground to recover ores or coal, causing labour costs per unit of output to rise. As a country mines its copper, it has to move on to less and less pure grades of ore. Cumulative production increases average costs, which are an indicator of scarcity.

In the 1960s, Barnett and Morse (1963) studied trends in average costs over the time period 1870–1957 for a variety of primary products. With one exception (forestry), they found that an index of real unit (capital plus labour) costs had declined over the period, indicating decreasing scarcity: real capital-plus-labour inputs had declined by 78 per cent for the minerals sector and by 55 per cent for the total extractive sector. Barnett and Morse's work was repeated by Johnson et al. (1980), who found that, if anything, the rate of decline in unit costs had increased over the period from 1958 to 1970.

Are these results proof that these materials were becoming less scarce over this time period? Unfortunately, this unit cost measure has problems. First, technological progress has undoubtedly reduced unit costs over this time period (for empirical evidence from the oil sector, see Norgaard, 1975). This will also have the effect of increasing the size of economic reserves. Second, the unit cost hypothesis relies on the assumption that firms will always deplete the lowest-cost deposit first; yet to know which deposit is the lowest-cost one implies a perfect knowledge of the characteristics of all deposits, some of which are yet to be discovered. Norgaard (1990) has termed this the 'Mayflower problem':

> [I]f the pilgrims knew where the best places for an agricultural colony were, they would not have gone to Plymouth Rock. Many generations passed before American agriculture shifted from the relatively poor soils of the east coast to the more productive mid-west.

Third, while unit capital and labour costs may have been falling, this might be due to substitution of some other input for capital and labour. The obvious missing input here is energy. Hall et al. (1986) recomputed Barnett and Morse's figures for the coal and petroleum sectors, including energy use with capital and labour use: they found that whilst the Barnett and Morse data showed a 35 per cent decline in unit costs for the petroleum sector, the inclusion of energy use changed this to a 10 per cent *increase*. Fourth, unit costs are a poor predictor of future scarcity, since they are based entirely on past experience, and are not 'forward-looking': technological advances could increase future economic reserves even if, historically, unit costs have risen.

13.3.3 **Real prices**

Prices are well established in conventional microeconomics as indicators of scarcity. For natural resources, a rising real price has been argued by many to be a potentially good measure of increasing scarcity (e.g. Fisher, 1981). This will be so when prices signal all future and current opportunity costs of using up a unit of a non-renewable resource today. In basic versions of the Hotelling model, the price of a resource rises at the rate of interest along an optimal depletion time path, until it is equal to the price of the 'backstop resource'—its closest substitute.

Several empirical studies have looked at real price data. The earliest comprehensive study was by Barnett and Morse (1963), who found that for most primary products, real prices had remained approximately constant from 1870 to 1957. Slade (1982) suggested that the time path of prices might follow a U-shape, as an initial decline in prices due to technological progress was eventually overcome by the tendency for increasing cumulative production to increase costs, and by the desire of resource extractors to see user rents rising at the real rate of interest. Slade found that a U-shape fitted the price series of twelve materials better than a linear form, indicating that for aluminium, for example, real prices started to rise in the 1960s. Finally, Moazzami and Anderson (1994) repeated Slade's analysis, using a somewhat different statistical technique. They found strong evidence of increasing scarcity for some materials (such as coal and copper), but only weak evidence of increasing scarcity for others (such as aluminium and iron).

But many criticisms can be levelled at the use of real prices as scarcity measures. First, the influence of producer cartels on prices of primary products can be significant, and yet not reflect scarcity changes. For example, the large oil price increases produced by OPEC in 1974 and 1979 were more to do with a voluntary reduction in supply to increase oil revenues than an increase in scarcity. Other commodities (such as tin) have been similarly affected. Second, governments intervene in resource markets, imposing price controls that distort price signals. An example here is the action taken by the United Kingdom government in the 1970s and 1980s to keep gas prices high, to reduce a loss in sales by the nationalized electricity companies (gas is a substitute for electricity in domestic heating and cooking). Tietenberg (1992) documents distortions caused by the imposition of maximum prices (price ceilings) by the US government for natural gas.

Third, natural resource prices do not measure social opportunity costs, partly because producers are not forced to pay for the environmental damage caused by the extraction and processing of these resources. For example, oil prices could be argued to be too low since not all of the external costs associated with oil-drilling and refining are imposed on producers; whilst a similar statement could be made for aluminium extraction (via bauxite-mining) and processing. Natural resource prices do not measure one element of social opportunity costs; namely, the environmental benefits forgone in their production.

13.3.4 **Economic rent**

Economic rent (or user rent or resource rent) is defined as the difference between price and marginal cost. One result from the Hotelling model is that an efficient depletion path involves resource rents rising at the rate of interest. The intuition behind this is clear: if resource rents represent the rate of return on 'holding' a non-renewable resource deposit, then this should be equal at the margin to the return on holding any other kind of asset, such as a savings bond. Rising rents are an indicator of scarcity.

But several problems exist with this measure. First, empirical data are scarce. Economic rents are the difference between price and marginal extraction costs, but are not the same as accounting profits. Neither firms nor governments are in the habit of recording these data. Empirical economists have relied on proxy measures, such as exploration costs. The argument here is that rational firms will spend no more on exploration than the expected net benefits (i.e. the expected future rents) to be gained. Devarjan and Fisher (1980) measured average exploration costs for oil in the United States over the period from 1946 to 1971, and found them to be rising, an indicator of increasing scarcity despite the fact that no such trend exists in oil prices over that period. Yet as expected prices are a component of expected rents, the criticisms of the real price measure given in the previous section also apply to the rent measure.

Second, the use of rent as a scarcity measure assumes that firms are following optimal depletion plans (Faber and Proops, 1993). Yet there is little evidence that this is so in reality (see Box 13.2). What is more, to be able to follow the optimal depletion plan, firms need to be fully informed about future prices and extraction costs: a rather more extreme version of the Mayflower problem (although it is certainly possible to define a best-depletion programme under conditions of uncertainty). Interest rate movements will also affect optimal depletion programmes, such that changes in rent will pick up these macroeconomic effects too. Rent is perhaps the best scarcity indicator from a theoretical point of view. After all, it shows that gap between what society is willing to pay for one more unit of the resource and the cost of extracting that unit. But it suffers from empirical drawbacks. It is possible for the rent on a resource to *decrease* even though its physical abundance is falling.

BOX 13.2 Why Is Resource Scarcity so Difficult to Measure?

The value of a unit of resource stock in the ground is the marginal profit that it earns:

$$M\pi = p - MC.$$

We can approximately measure resource scarcity by either costs or prices, but neither is ideal, as the discussion in Section 13.3 suggests. Empirical studies tend to arrive at conflicting conclusions: Why might this be?

Farzin (1992) explores the impact that new technology has on costs. The cost curve for a renewable resource firm depends on the rate of extraction, q, the remaining reserves, x, and the state of cost-reducing technology, z. The cost function is $c(q, x, z)$, where costs are increasing in q, decreasing with the size of the stock, and decreasing in z. The reason why costs are decreasing with the size of the stock is that as extraction proceeds, the firm shifts to reserves that are more costly to exploit. What happens to costs through time? New technology reduces costs, and increases the value of the resource stock. This might be characterized as a 'race' between depletion and technological change to keep costs down.

What is the evidence? Lasserre and Ouellette (1991) show that, even with technical change, the decline in the grade of asbestos ore extracted still increased marginal costs.

13.3.5 **Hotelling and the oil market**

If we consider a graph of the oil price (Figure 13.4) from the 1970s to 2010, we see that prices are not monotonically increasing, and that there is no straightforward evidence (Krautkraemer, 1998; Livernois, 2009) to support Hotelling's rule. The question then arises: What drives price movements in non-renewable resource markets? This section considers the case of oil and follows the recent analysis of Smith (2009).

Oil is the leading commodity in world trade, accounting for 13 per cent of commodity trade by value (United Nations, 2008) and the oil price has a profound effect on the economies of most countries. The market structure is imperfectly competitive with OPEC, which includes nine countries—Saudi Arabia, Nigeria, the United Arab Emirates, Nigeria, Venezuela, Iran, Kuwait, Iraq, and Libya—operating as a cartel. These countries account for a significant proportion of supply, 55 per cent in 2007, and a larger proportion of reserves, 87 per cent in reserves (*Petroleum Intelligence Weekly*, 2008; Smith, 2009). It is also notable that a large proportion of the world production and supply is from state-owned companies; for instance, Saudi Aramco in Saudi Arabia (see Box 13.3).

It is notable from Figure 13.4 that since 1972 the oil market has shown extreme price volatility (variability) that cannot be explained by a market price driven by resource scarcity.

Smith (2009) explains this volatility in terms of demand and supply shifts. The demand elasticity for oil is relatively low. For instance, the US demand elasticity has been estimated to range from –0.05 for the short run to –0.30 in the long run (OECD, 2004; US Energy Information Administration, 2007). These elasticity values mean the demand for oil is unresponsive to price changes. The US supply elasticities are estimated to range between 0.04 (short run) and 0.35 (long run) (OECD, 2004; US Energy Information Administration, 2007). The peak in oil prices in 2008 was due to a 33 per cent increase in demand from 2003 to 2008, set against a fall in supply from non-OPEC countries and a small rise in OPEC supplies (as measured, OECD, 2004, by Smith 2009).

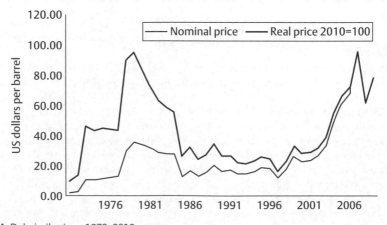

Figure 13.4 Dubai oil prices, 1972–2010.

Source: Platts, as reported in http://www.eia.gov/cfapps/ipdbproject/IEDIndex3.cfm?tid=44&pid=44&aid=1/.

> **BOX 13.3 Energy Facts**
>
> According to the US Energy Information Administration 2010 database:
>
> - Global oil production has increased to 86.8 million barrels per day (bbl/day), with Saudi Arabia leading production at 10.5 million bbl/day; Russia at 10 million bbl/day, and the USA at 9.7 million bbl/day. The USA consumes over 19 million day bbl/day of petroleum, China 9 million bbl/day, Japan 4.4 million bbl/day, and India 3.1 bbl/day.
> - The USA is the leading consumer of natural gas, and Russia follows, and together they account for 43 per cent of world demand.
> - World coal production is just under 8 billion short tons. China is the largest consumer of coal, using 1.31 billion short tons, followed by the USA, which consumes 1.04 billion short tons, India, Russia, and Germany.
> - Canada, the USA, Brazil, China, and Russia are the five largest producers of hydroelectric power. Their combined hydroelectric power generation accounts for 51 per cent of the world total.
> - The USA leads the world in nuclear electric power generation, France is second, and Japan ranks third.
> - The USA leads the world in biomass, geothermal, solar, and wind electric-power generation. Japan is second, followed by Germany, Brazil, and Finland. These five countries account for 65 per cent of the world's biomass, geothermal, solar, and wind electric-power generation.

In 2008, Hubbert's (1956) hypothesis of 'peak oil' came to the fore as an argument to explain the price peak. The geology-based model is aptly described by Smith:

> Hubbert's idea was that, in the case of oil production, prices and other incentives are superfluous; it is all a matter of time. His resulting model of production behaves like a ballistic missile, first rising and then falling of its own accord.

(2009: 161)

The problem with this model is that it does not address the economic effects that high prices have on supply and demand. Smith points out that estimates of remaining reserves are currently at an all-time high. In addition, if we consider other sources of oil, such as shale oil, we may have up to another 160 years of oil supply.

The International Energy Agency (2008) presents a field-by-field analysis of expected oil production up to 2030. It expects that demand for oil will increase from 82.3 million barrels per day (bbl/day) in 2007 to 103.8 million bbl/day in 2030. The share of the OPEC countries in the global output increases from 44 per cent in 2007 to 51 per cent in 2030. The new supply will come from natural gas liquids and new methods of oil recovery.

The same report analyses the long-term oil supply: approximately 2.4 trillion (10^{12}) barrels of conventional oil were available before any production commenced. To date, we have extracted 1 trillion barrels, and another 2–3 trillion barrels remain as currently accessible reserves. That leaves another 5–6 trillion barrels as currently uneconomic reserves in the form of 'oil shales natural gas to liquid' and 'coal to liquid'. The point is that as conventional oil supplies are depleted and if prices rise, these backstop technologies will become economic.

In the next section, the analysis is broadened to show how the set of non-renewable energy resources contribute to the global energy market. At one time, oil was the key energy resource, it is still the most important, but the energy market is evolving to reduce the dependence on oil and to include a wide range of non-renewable and renewable resources.

13.4 Global Energy Demand and Supply

People focus on natural resource scarcity in part because these resources are the source of the energy and material needed to drive modern economies. From an economics perspective, energy plays three key roles in our lives:

- *Energy is a consumer good.* The energy derived from renewable and non-renewable resources such as petroleum, natural gas, coal, hydro, nuclear, biomass, geothermal, solar, and wind helps us grow and cook our food, warm and light our homes, and power our cars.

- *Energy is a factor of production.* Energy, combined with capital, labour, and land, is an essential input in the production of nearly all goods and services around the globe.

- *Energy is a strategic resource.* Energy also has enormous strategic value for a nation, and the threat of its loss has led to war. People and governments follow energy prices with intense interest, because it is so vital to our daily lives.

Today, the world produces and consumes nearly 500 quadrillion (10^{15}) Btu (British thermal units) of power. Global energy use is expected to increase by another 50 per cent over the next two decades. As a comparative benchmark, energy use four decades ago in 1970 was about 200 quadrillion Btu. China, Russia, and the USA are the biggest producers and consumers of world energy. Five nations—Canada, China, Russia, Saudi Arabia, and the USA—currently produce about half of the world's energy. The USA produces over 70 quadrillion Btu of energy; Russia and China produce over 40 and 33 quadrillion Btu. And five nations—China, Japan, Germany, Russia, and the USA—consume nearly half of the world's energy. The USA consumes nearly 95 quadrillion Btu, three and four times that demanded by China and Russia, at 34 and 26 quadrillion Btu, respectively. The next big consumers are Brazil, Canada, France, India, and the UK.

As the world economy grows, so does the demand for energy. Emerging economies demand more energy. Consider now how energy supply and demand has changed by region over the past three decades, from 1980 to 2008. The largest regional increase in energy production occurred in the Asia and Oceania region—production increased by nearly 100 quadrillion Btu in three decades (Table 13.2). The energy consumption in this region tripled with an increase of 114 quadrillion Btu, again the largest change during this period (Table 13.3). This increase in energy use matches the rapid growth in this region's economies over the past three decades.

In North America, overall energy production and consumption have not grown as fast, but have still increased by about 19 and 30 quadrillion Btu. The Middle East has increased its production and consumption by 26 and 20 quadrillion Btu, respectively. Africa has increased its production and consumption by 20 and 10 quadrillion Btu, respectively. In Central and South America, we see production and consumption increased by 17 and 14 quadrillion Btu. Europe has increased supply and demand by about 6 and 14 quadrillion

Table 13.2 World primary energy production (quadrillion Btu)

Region	1980	1995	2008
North America	83.3	90.3	101.7
Central and South America	12.1	22.5	29.6
Europe	40.2	49.0	46.5
Eurasia	56.5	51.9	71.7
Middle East	42.3	48.3	68.2
Africa	17.4	24.1	37.5
Asia and Oceania	35.9	72.9	134.3
World total	287.5	357.6	489.5

Source: US Energy Information Agency, http://www.eia.gov/cfapps/
ipdbproject/iedindex3.cfm?tid=44&pid=44&aid=1&cid=ww,r1,r2,r3,r4,r5,
r6,r7,&syid=2004&eyid=2008&unit=QBTU.

Btu. In Eurasia, energy production has declined and then increased by about 15 quadrillion Btu; energy consumption, however, has declined slightly, the only region to witness a decline in energy demand.

Energy is not a homogeneous input. Different primary energy sources will be used based on the relative energy prices. Cheaper energy sources will dominate the mix, and continue to do so until there is a change in relative prices—either through increased scarcity or a change in technology. People made changes in their energy mix and use when the OPEC cartel restricted oil supply, causing energy prices to spike in the 1970s. Technological progress and innovation also induce people to switch towards less expensive energy sources over time, as old capital is retired and new technologies prove themselves to be effective and reliable.

What is the current mix of primary energy supply around the world? Table 13.4 shows that the non-renewable resources of petroleum, coal, and natural gas are the big three energy sources today. Petroleum remains the most important source of energy (168 quadrillion Btu in 2006): Saudi Arabia, the USA, and Russia are the three largest suppliers. Coal is second,

Table 13.3 World primary energy consumption (quadrillion Btu)

Region	1980	1995	2008
North America	91.6	109.3	121.9
Central and South America	11.5	17.6	25.8
Europe	71.8	76.7	85.8
Eurasia	46.7	42.2	45.8
Middle East	5.8	13.8	25.5
Africa	6.8	10.7	16.1
Asia and Oceania	49.0	95.1	163.5[a]
World total	283.2	365.4	493.0

[a] Data for 2007

Source: US Energy Information Agency, http://www.eia.gov/cfapps/ipdbproject/
iedindex3.cfm?tid=44&pid=44&aid=1&cid=ww,r1,r2,r3,r4,r5,r6,r7,&syid=2004&
eyid=2008&unit=QBTU.

Table 13.4 World production of primary energy by energy type (quadrillion Btu), 1980–2006

Energy type/country group	1980	1990	2000	2006
Petroleum	133	136	156	168
Dry natural gas	55	76	91	107
Coal	71	91	90	129
Net hydroelectric power	18	22	26	30
Net nuclear electric power	8	20	26	28
Net geothermal, solar, wind, and wood and waste electric power	0.5	2	3	5
US production of biomass, geothermal and solar energy not used for electricity generation	2	2	2	3
Total energy	288	350	396	469

Source: Energy Information Administration, *International Energy Annual 2006*, http://www.eia.gov/emeu/international/energyproduction.html.

with 129 quadrillion of production: China and the USA are the leading producers. Natural gas ranks third, supplying about 107 quadrillion Btu, and has increased its share over the past decade: Russia is the leading producer. The remaining energy sources—hydro, nuclear, biomass, geothermal, solar, and wind—make up the balance. Together, they accounted for a combined total of 66 quadrillion Btu. While currently a small share, these other sources of energy have begun to increase over the past decade.

An understanding of how prices drive the mix of energy has implications for the future of global energy use. As we showed earlier in the chapter, the most relevant economic model is Hotelling's rule for the pricing of non-renewable energy resources. So how well has Hotelling's rule explained price movements? Economists have had mixed success in empirically validating the rule. The needed data are difficult to come by, and have forced most studies to use proxies for user rents and expectations of future interest rates. Since user rents are usually confidential and we do not observe expectations in practice, whether the Hotelling rule is a reasonable guide for the future remains an open question.

Table 13.5 World estimated recoverable coal, 2008

Region	Recoverable reserves	Share of recoverable reserves (%)
USA and Canada	243.9	28.3
Russian Federation	157.0	18.2
China	114.5	13.3
Europe (incl. Turkey)	110.4	12.8
Australia	76.4	8.9
India	60.6	7.0
Kazakhstan	33.6	3.9
South Africa	30.2	3.5
All other	34.3	4.0
World total	860.9	100

Source: World Energy Council estimates of proved recoverable reserves (hard coal and lignite) at end-2008 (billion metric tons).

What does the future of energy demand look like? The US Energy Information Agency's *International Energy Outlook 2012* (IEO2012) predicts that world energy demand will increase by about 44 per cent over the next two decades. The outlook forecasts that world-wide energy use could increase to over 770 quadrillion Btu in 2035, from 505 quadrillion Btu in 2008. While the developed nations have long been the dominant users of energy, emerging economies such as China and Russia are predicted to drive much of the future growth in demand. Energy use in Asia and Central and South America is projected to more than double.

What does the mix of energy sources look like into the future? Oil currently supplies the largest share of world energy consumption, about 86 million barrels per day in 2010. The IEO2012 predicts that worldwide oil demand will hit about 113 million barrels per day by 2035. Growth in oil use in the developed nations should come from the transportation sector, since the few alternative sources are expensive. Oil demand in the developing countries could come from both transportation and heating demand. Table 13.6 gives reserves of fossil fuels.

Natural gas will remain the fastest-growing component of world energy demand. The IEO2012 predicts that natural gas use could increase to 153 trillion cubic feet (tcf) in 2035, from 113 tcf in 2010. In 2012, many experts see the emergence of shale gas as a 'game changer' in US natural gas energy markets. Shale gas can now be recovered cost-effectively from low-permeability geological areas, given new advances in hydraulic fracturing. According to one estimate supplied by the US Energy Information Agency, shale gas reserves could be about 750 trillion cubic feet in the USA alone.

Coal is predicted to grow at about 0.9 per cent between 2008 and 2035, increasing from 139 to 175 quadrillion Btus. The main reason why coal will continue to grow is to meet the expanding energy demands in Asian nations. China and India are predicted to account for most of the increased world demand for coal. The future of *nuclear power* is less clear. The IEO2012 shows an increase in nuclear power from 2,600 to 4,900 billion kilowatt hours from 2008 to 2035. Nuclear power remains one of the key substitute energy sources given climate change policy, but fears of nuclear meltdown remain in many people's minds, especially after the Fukushima Daiichi nuclear accident in 2011.

Renewable resource development will be slow if the expected price of fossil fuels remains relatively low in the near future. Renewables cannot compete with low fossil fuel prices, but this is changing as relative costs are declining. The IEO2012 projects a doubling of energy through hydroelectric projects—world consumption is predicted to increase to 102 quadrillion Btu in 2035, from 55 in 2010. The report also suggests that the installed wind-powered generating capacity could more than double; increasing to over 520 gigawatts in 2035, from 180 in 2010. Similarly, the solar generating capacity is estimated to increase to 117 gigawatts in 2035, from 25 in 2010.

13.5 Global Issues in Energy Policy

We care about the future energy trends because energy plays such a crucial role in the modern world. Governments remain tempted to intervene in energy markets. Policymakers have long wanted to control energy for national security reasons. Many reasonable arguments exist to justify government intervention on national security grounds; that is,

Table 13.6 World crude oil and natural gas reserves (March 2009)

Region/country	Crude oil (billion barrels) *Oil and Gas Journal*	Crude oil (billion barrels) *World Oil*	Natural gas (trillion cubic feet) *Oil and Gas Journal*	Natural gas (trillion cubic feet) *World Oil*
North America	209	57	308	314
Central and South America	122	104	267	245
Europe	14	14	169	169
Eurasia	98	126	1,993	2,104
Middle East	746	727	2,592	2,570
Africa	117	115	494	504
Asia and Oceania	34	40	430	528
World total	1,342	1,184	6,254	6,436

Source: US Energy Information Agency, http://www.eia.gov/emeu/international/reserves.html.

to reduce the odds of another 'energy crisis', to promote the public good of research and development into new technologies. Now policy-makers have added environmental concerns as a justification for intervening in energy markets. As we have read throughout this book, private markets can fail to provide the socially desired level of a good or service, and energy markets are no exception.

Global climate change, regional acid rain, and local air pollution problems are all linked to fossil fuel use. Petroleum and coal, no matter how efficiently burned, all produce the carbon dioxide feared to be warming the planet to unacceptable levels; they also produce the sulphur oxides and nitrogen oxides that lead to the acidification of soils and surface water; they also produce smog and particulate matter that affect human health. People have also worried about the health and safety issues from the actual mining of energy sources—for example, black lung disease—and the impacts of strip mining.

The question is should governments intervene in energy markets for environmental protection, and if so, how? Justifiable intervention for environmental protection depends on whether one can reasonably argue that the gains of new rules and regulations outweigh the risks of slowing down the productivity that drives the development of an economy. If the gains dominate the costs, there are three general ways in which the government can intervene in energy markets: by changing economic incentives through taxation of fossil fuels and the subsidization of renewable fuels; by expanding technological options through the promotion and subsidization of research and development (R&D); and by providing information about options that promote energy efficiency.

Changing economic incentives. Relative prices drive the mix of energy demand. Energy prices encourage people to make the least costly adjustments based on their own personal information. Governments that wish to alter this mix can change the relative prices through economic incentives such as taxes and subsidies. Energy policy could provide economic incentives in a variety of ways. A typical economic incentive policy is to increase the private cost of fossil fuels, forcing users to address the social costs of emissions. This policy raises the price of emissions, by taxing emissions on the basis of their potential to cause environmental harm, removing existing subsidies that increase fossil fuel use (e.g. parking subsidies), or adding new subsidies that promote renewable fuels and lower-emissions fuels or

BOX 13.4 Renewable Energy in the UK: Promotion and Impacts

The UK Renewable Energy Advisory Group has defined renewable energy as 'those energy flows that occur naturally and repeatedly in the environment and can be harnessed for human benefit' (REAG, 1992). Europe has a great and largely untapped potential for the generation of power and heat from renewable sources of energy. Renewables currently supply 5.3 per cent of the European Union's energy consumption, but only 1 per cent in the UK. In a 1996 green paper, the European Commision suggested a target to increase renewables' share of gross energy consumption to 12 per cent by 2010 (ENDS, 1996). Achievement of this target would reduce the EU's annual carbon dioxide emissions by around 250 million tonnes (ENDS, 1997). Although renewable energy technologies are being continually developed, many are still significantly underutilized due to financial, technical, environmental, and social factors.

Private-sector development of renewable energy is promoted in the UK by guaranteeing a certain portion of electricity demand from electricity supply companies for renewable sources, and offering a higher payment to renewable operators per kilowatt supplied, compared to the price of fossil fuel electricity. This difference is funded by a fossil fuel levy on consumer's electricity bills. The two schemes that implement this policy (in England and Wales, the Non-Fossil Fuel Obligation, and in Scotland the Scottish Renewables Orders) have been successful in increasing private-sector investment in renewables. In Scotland, this has mainly taken the form of wind farms, biogas plants, and small-scale hydropower schemes.

But while the environmental benefits of renewable energy are well known (mainly avoided emissions from fossil fuel power stations), the environmental costs of renewables receive less attention (European Commission, 1995). In Scotland, these include landscape impacts from wind farms, local dis-amenities from waste-to-power schemes, and ecosystem impacts from hydro plants. Hanley and Nevin (1999) report some results from a study of these environmental costs for a range of alternative renewable energy investments in the crofting community of Assynt, in the north-west Highlands. This is an interesting case, since the investments would be made on behalf of the local community. However, there is a concern that tourists could be put off by such changes. An energy audit and environmental impact analysis were carried out, which resulted in three main viable options being identified: a small wind farm, a small-head hydro, and a biomass planting scheme. Contingent valuation was used to study impacts on local residents: this revealed community views that differed across the three options. A tourist survey was also undertaken to estimate the differing impacts of each option on tourist spending. The results were then presented as a ranking of options.

The following table shows the energy options and potential tourism effects:

Renewable energy option	Possible effect on total season's income from tourism (£) if trips were shortened by 1 day	Possible effect on total season's income from tourism (£) if trips were shortened by 0.5 days	Implied ranking
Wind farm at Raffin	−2,590	−1,295	1
Small-scale hydro on Loch Poll	−17,208	−8,604	2
Biomass schemes at Culkein/ Stoer	−26,829	−13,415	3

The next table shows the energy options and the willingness to pay (WTP) of residents.

The relationship between support for renewable energy options and number of years in residence on the estate was interesting. With respect to both the wind and hydro options, there was less support amongst those who had lived on the estate for 10 years or less. In contrast, a low level of support for biomass development was evident among residents who had lived in the area for many years. The taking of land from traditional crofting areas that this option would require may have been a factor in this result.

BOX 13.4 (Continued)

Renewable energy option	Percentage in favour of scheme	Proportion of those opposed who would accept compensation[a]	Implied community WTP (per annum)[b] (£)	Implied ranking
Wind farm at Raffin	78	3/10	13,585	2
Biomass schemes at Culkein/Stoer	42	7/26	6,642	3
Small-scale hydro on Loch Poll	87	0/6	14,282	1

[a] The sum of those willing to accept personal income compensation and local jobs compensation.
[b] Based on population of 260 adults living on the estate.

technologies (see Box 13.4). Another policy to change relative prices is to limit emissions or energy use, and let people trade permits to pollute.

Changing the relative price of fossil fuels would give people an incentive to reduce their energy consumption—they would drive less, and they would turn down the thermostat. People would also have incentives to buy more energy-efficient equipment; for example, more insulation or a car with better fuel consumption. Sellers would also adjust if the demand for energy-inefficient goods declined. Everyone has incentives to develop more energy-efficient technologies, and find low-emission energy sources.

However, economists argue that these energy savings will not be as high as predicted by engineering models. People who buy energy-saving products experience a 'rebound effect'; people who drive cars with better fuel consumption drive more miles, since they get a better mileage per gallon. This rebound effect works based on both a substitution and an income effect. Increased fuel efficiency reduces the costs of fuel consumption, which—due to the substitution effect—increases consumption of fuel. In addition, since fuel is cheaper, the consumer has more real income, which allows him or her to consume other goods and services that also use energy.

Expanding technological options. Governments can intervene in the energy market by promoting the R&D of new technologies that address the environmental problems associated with fossil fuel use. The private sector generally underinvests in this type of R&D, because it cannot capture all the benefits. These public programmes include government-funded programmes and subsidies for private R&D. Options include R&D into fossil fuel technologies with greater conversion efficiencies and non-fossil fuels such as biomass, wind, solar, geothermal, and nuclear energy.

Information programmes. Governments can also try to alter the energy market by providing information to people about different energy-efficient options. Policies that promote the market penetration of new technologies include information and outreach programmes, green programmes (e.g. offering electricity supplies from renewable sources at higher tariffs), market identification, and targeting. Governments can form partnerships with industry and others to promote less environmentally damaging fuels. For example, governments can try to overcome the information problems associated with landowners and renters. Neither has any incentive to invest in energy efficiency, because the landowner does not pay the utility bill, while the renter might not get reimbursed for investments in energy efficiency.

The ability to cause much change through information is an open question. Unexploited opportunities to use cost-reducing technologies might exist, but other factors impede the realization of these opportunities. People typically respond to changes in energy prices and clearer information on the potential to remove the hidden costs of technology switching not addressed in engineering cost estimates. The choice of energy technology offers no free lunch. Even if new technologies are available, many people are unwilling to experiment with new devices at current prices. Factors other than energy efficiency also matter to consumers, such as quality, and the time and effort required to learn about a new technology and how it works. People behave as if their time horizons are short, perhaps reflecting their uncertainty about future energy prices and the reliability of the technology. Some people use less fossil fuel because it is, in their opinion, the right thing to do; others will need more convincing, based on climate change risks or a change in energy prices.

Summary

Adam Smith said in *The Wealth of Nations* that '[e]very man endeavours to supply by his own industry his own occasional wants as they occur. When he is hungry, he goes to the forest to hunt; when his coat is worn out, he clothes himself with the skin of the first large animal he kills: and when his hut begins to go to ruin, he repairs it, as well as he can, with the trees and the turf that are nearest it.' What was true then is true now. People use natural resources for their own benefit, sometimes at their own expense, sometimes at the expense of others. The goal of natural resource economics is to address these human needs and natural resources limits—to define the constraints, to confront them, and to design rules to increase the efficient use of land, forests, and fisheries. Natural resource economics has shown why physical and biological constraints matter to economic reasoning about the efficient nature of capital stocks; how natural resource economic reasoning can alter management strategies when one accounts for the additional opportunity costs of depletion or not harvesting a resource; and what challenges remain, including defining durable property rights systems, designing effective regulatory tools through incentives, and valuing changes in the non-market services provided by natural resources such as climate change and biodiversity.

The energy that we derive from natural resources help drive the global economy. In this chapter, we have taken an economic perspective to explore how resource extractors *should* manage their resource deposits—given certain simplifying assumptions. We have also reviewed different measures of resource scarcity. We have presented the case as to why 'resource lifetimes' is a flawed measure of scarcity. We have examined the role of energy in the world economy, and potential changes in global supply and demand. Finally, we have looked at alternative tools with which governments can implement an energy policy that tries to reduce the environmental costs of energy. An economic perspective provides a useful mindset to help understand the factors that either limit or promote the switch towards a more sustainable energy future.

Tutorial Questions

13.1 Economists believe that energy plays three key roles in our lives. Explain.

13.2 Explain the economic model of how society should extract its natural resources.

13.3 Why do the predictions of the simple version of Hotelling's rule not always hold?

13.4 Is the market price of oil an accurate measure of resource scarcity?

13.5 Define the idea of *lifetime of a resource* as a measure of resource scarcity. Why don't most economists believe it is a helpful measure?

13.6 Explain the idea behind the rebound effect in energy efficiency questions.

13.7 How do high oil prices affect how one should think about the idea of Hubbert's peak oil?

References and Additional Readings

Anderson, F. (1985). *Natural Resources in Canada* (Toronto: Methuen).

Barnett, H.J., and Morse, C. (1963). *Scarcity and Growth: The Economics of Natural Resource Scarcity* (Baltimore, MD: Johns Hopkins University Press).

Cohen, D. (2007). 'Earth audit', *New Scientist*, 194 Issue 2605: 34–7.

Devarjan, S., and Fisher, A. (1980). 'Exploration and scarcity', Working Papers in Economic Theory IP-290, University of California, Berkeley.

ENDS (1996). *The Ends Report* 263: 17–18 (Environmental Data Services Ltd).

—— (1997). *The Ends Report* 275: 43–4 (Environmental Data Services Ltd).

European Commission (1995). *Eastern Externalities of Energy*, vi: *Wind and Hydro*, Report 16525 (Brussels: EC).

Faber, M., and Proops, J. (1993). 'Natural resource rents, economic dynamics and structural change', *Ecological Economics* 8(1): 17–44.

Farzin, Y.H. (1992). 'The time path of scarcity rent is the theory of exhaustible resources', *Economic Journal* 102: 813–31.

Fisher, A.C. (1981). *Resource and Environmental Economics* (Cambridge: Cambridge University Press).

Gordon, R.B., Bertram, M., and Graedel, T.E. (2006). 'Metal stocks and sustainability', *Proceedings of the National Academy of Sciences* 103: 1209–21.

Hall, D., Cleveland, C., and Kaufman, R. (1986). *Energy and Resource Quality: The Ecology of the Economic Process* (New York: Wiley).

Hanley, N., and Nevin, C. (1999). 'Appraising renewable energy developments in remote communities: the case of the North Assynt Estate, Scotland', *Energy Policy* 27: 527–47.

——, Shogren, J.F., and White, B. (2007). *Environmental Economics: In Theory and Practice* (Basingstoke: Palgrave).

Harris, D., and Skinner, B. (1982). 'The assessment of long-term supplies of minerals', in V.K. Smith and J. Krutilla (eds.), *Explorations in Natural Resource Economics* (Baltimore, MD: Johns Hopkins University Press).

Hotelling, H. (1931). 'The economics of exhaustible resources', *Journal of Political Economy* 39: 137–75.

Hubbert, M.K. (1956). *Nuclear Energy and the Fossil Fuels*, Publication 95, Shell Development Company Exploration and Research Division.

International Energy Agency (2008). *World Energy Outlook* (OECD/IEA: Paris).

Johnson, M., Bell, F., and Bennett, J. (1980). 'Natural resource scarcity: empirical evidence and public policy', *Journal of Environmental Economics and Management* 7: 256–71.

Krautkraemer, J. (1998). 'Nonrenewable resource scarcity', *Journal of Economic Literature* 36: 2065–107.

Lasserre, P., and Ouellette, P. (1991). 'The measurement of productivity and scarcity rents: the case of asbestos in Canada', *Journal of Econometrics* 48: 287–312.

Lee, J., List, J.A., and Strazicich, J. (2006). 'Nonrenewable resource prices: deterministic or stochastic trends?' *Journal of Environmental Economics and Management* 51: 354–70.

Livernois, J. (2009). 'On the empirical significance of the Hotelling rule', *Review of Environmental Economics and Policy* 3: 22–41.

Moazzami, B., and Anderson, F. (1994). 'Modelling natural resource scarcity using the "error-correction" approach', *Canadian Journal of Economics* 27: 801–12.

Norgaard, R. (1975). 'Resource scarcity and new technology in US petroleum development', *Natural Resources Journal* 15: 265–82.

—— (1990). 'Economic indicators of resource scarcity: a critical essay', *Journal of Environmental Economics and Management* 19: 19–25.

OECD (Organisation for Economic Co-operation and Development) (2004). 'Oil price developments: drivers, economic consequences and policy responses', in *OECD Economic Outlook* No. 76 (Paris: OECD).

Pesaran, M.H. (1990). 'An econometric analysis of the exploration and extraction of oil in the U.K. Continental Shelf', *Economic Journal* 100: 367–90.

Petroleum Intelligence Weekly (2008). Vol. XLVII, No. 50, 15 December, http://www.energyintel.com/.

REAG (Renewable Energy Group) (1992). *Energy Paper 60* (London: HMSO).

Skinner, B. (1976). 'A second Iron Age?' *American Scientist* 64: 258–69.

Slade, M. (1982). 'Trends in natural resource commodity prices: an analysis of the time domain', *Journal of Environmental Economics and Management* 9: 122–37.

Smith, J.L. (2009). 'World oil: market or mayhem', *Journal of Economic Perspectives* 23: 145–64.

Tietenberg, T. (1992). *Environmental and Natural Resource Economics* (London: HarperCollins).

United Nations (2008). Commodity Trade Statistics Database, 2006, http://comtrade.un.org/pb/ (accessed 1 June 2012).

US Energy Information Administration (2007). NEMS International Energy Module (IEM), Model Documentation Report, DOE/EIA-M071.

—— (2012) *Annual Energy Outlook 2012* (Washington, DC: USEIA), http://www.eia.gov/ forecasts/aeo/pdf/0383(2012).pdf (accessed 15 November 2012).

Glossary

Adaptation An investment to reduce the severity of realized damages.

Adverse selection A problem related to the hidden type of a person or firm such that a buyer cannot distinguish the quality of a good or service.

Ambiguity Uncertainty about the probabilities of an outcome.

Ancillary benefit An additional benefit that arises from reducing fossil fuel consumption; for example, lower levels of carbon monoxide, sulphur and nitrogen oxides, and toxic trace pollutants in exhaust gases.

Autarky Where a country does not engage in international trade.

Behavioural economics The application of psychological insights into economic theory and observation.

Benefits transfer The practice of extrapolating existing information on the non-market value of goods or services.

Bid curve The use of regression analysis to determine the relationship between willingness-to-pay (WTP) measures and the factors that are thought to influence these measures.

Bid vehicle The means by which individuals pay in a hypothetical market.

Biodiversity hotpots Regions identified by Conservation International as combining high levels of biodiversity with high levels of threat to habitat.

Bioprospecting Analysing compounds derived from flora and fauna for compounds that could form the basis for new drugs.

Carbon footprint A measure that accounts for all carbon emissions generated by a nation's citizens, regardless of where the good was produced.

Carbon sink A process that destroys or absorbs greenhouse gases, such as the absorption of atmospheric carbon dioxide by trees, soils, and other types of vegetation.

Carbon tax A fee added to the price of fossil fuels according to their relative carbon content.

Characteristics Theory of Value The theory that the value of something is best explained in terms of its characteristics or attributes.

Clean development mechanism A system in which developed nations buy the carbon reductions in developing nations.

Climate change A change in the climate (global temperatures and precipitation) over time due to changes in natural process or external forcings.

Coase theorem If transaction costs are low, two disputing parties can bargain to a solution provided that a third party assigns property rights to one of the parties.

Common property A good defined by rival consumption and open or controlled access to a resource.

Comparative advantage A measure of the difference in the opportunity cost of producing a good between two countries. The existence of a comparative advantage is a prerequisite for there being a gain from trade.

Co-operative game theory This concerns the returns to forming coalitions and sharing the pay-offs.

Core In co-operative game theory: the set of pay-offs that can be agreed that will keep a coalition of players together. They must receive at least as much as part of the coalition as they do either alone or in another coalition.

Cost–benefit analysis A decision-making rule used to evaluate a number of different policy options or projects in order to determine which contributes the most to net social well-being or, equivalently, which is the most efficient in terms of its use of resources.

Critical natural capital That part of natural capital that is either essential for human survival and/or cannot be substituted for by other forms of capital.

Deforestation Kuznets curve The hypothesis that the rate of deforestation will decline when a country reaches higher levels of income.

Dominant strategy A strategy that a player can choose that is best regardless of what the other players in the game choose.

Dose–response model A measure of the economic value of the environment as an input to production by considering the impacts of pollution on market-valued outputs.

Economic efficiency Getting the most net benefits one can with the available resources.

Economic growth The change in gross national product (GNP) over a given time period—say, a year.

Economic rent The difference between resource price and the marginal cost of extraction (also called 'user rent' or 'resource rent').

Ecosystem services The valuable resources and services provided by natural ecosystems; for example, carbon sequestration, nutrient cycling, and climate regulation. Ecosystem services provide inputs into the production of some goods and services, and may also be a direct source of utility.

Environmental 'bads' Those environmental inputs for which the individual prefers less to more.

Environmental 'goods' Those environmental inputs for which the individual prefers more to less.

Environmental Kuznets curve (EKC) The idea that the relationship between income and environmental quality is an inverted U-shape; as income per capita increases, environmental impact also increases initially, until it reaches a maximum and then begins to decline.

Existence or non-use value The utility people derive from just knowing that a particular natural asset exists.

Expected utility The combination of probabilities and the utility associated with outcomes of good and bad events.

Experimental auction A method that values risk reduction using a bidding auction.

Externalities When one party imposes costs or benefits on another party without paying or receiving compensation.

Fat-tail distribution A fat tail reflects the idea that the probability of an extreme-impact event is not as rare as believed under the 'business as usual' climate scenarios.

Faustmann formula This formula gives the optimal rotation for a forest that is replanted and clear-felled at regular rotation lengths.

Flow pollution The annual rate of carbon emission.

Framing effect When people are affected by how information is presented.

Free-rider A country that does not contribute to climate policy, but that still captures all the benefits of climate protection and pays none of the costs.

Frontier model A theory of deforestation that is driven by opening up new regions to logging through investment: this contrasts with the immizerization model.

Gains from trade The hypothesis that trade raises income: it allows countries to attain more goods and services, and increases demand for environmental goods and services.

Genuine savings (GS) An indicator of sustainable development that measures the value of the net change in all forms of capital—produced, natural, human, and social—in an economy over a given period of time; a negative genuine savings value indicates that development is unsustainable.

Geochemically scarce mineral A metal held in ores (typically silicates) that requires a relatively high level of energy to extract. Such ores can be too costly to extract.

Green net national product (green NNP) A sustainable development indicator that involves correcting the national accounts to allow for environmental inputs to the economy that are unpriced by the market; for example, depreciation of natural capital and the value of changes in environmental quality that impact directly on people's utility; rising green net national product over time indicates that development is sustainable.

Gross national product (GNP) The monetary value of the aggregate output, expenditure, or incomes of a country in a given time period. Gross domestic product (GDP) is another way of measuring this aggregate output, income, or expenditure.

Hartwick rule The idea that an economy can maintain constant consumption levels over time if all rents from non-renewable resource depletion are reinvested in produced capital.

Hidden information When one person knows more about his or her actions (e.g. protection level) or type (e.g. low-cost) than the environmental regulator.

Hotelling's rule An economic theory proposed by Hotelling (1931), which predicts that, in equilibrium, the marginal profit of a non-renewable resource firm increases at the interest rate through time. Simpler versions of the model predict that the price (when costs are zero) of the non-renewable resource will increase at the interest rate.

Human development indicator A measure developed by the United Nations that uses three indicators—GDP, education levels, and life expectancy—to represent the development of a given country.

Hypothetical market bias The tendency for respondents in a stated-preference survey to overstate or understate their actual willingness to pay (WTP) for a change in environmental quality.

Immizerization model A theory of deforestation that is driven by incremental expansion of shifting agriculture driven by population growth and impoverished families striving to increase their incomes through expanding agricultural production: this contrasts with the frontier model.

Indirect benefits Environmental benefits that are measured indirectly via their role in the production process; for example, the role that wetlands play in the production of fish caught by commercial fishing.

Insurance An investment that transfers wealth from good to bad states of nature given that a bad event has been realized.

Kyoto Protocol The international environmental agreement that binds the participating countries to carbon emissions reductions below 1990 levels by 2008–12.

Loss aversion A concept from behavioural psychology claiming that people value losses more highly than equivalent gains, because they value that which they already have more than that which they could acquire.

Marginal abatement cost (MAC) The cost of decreasing emissions by an additional unit.

Market An exchange institution to create economic value through trade.

Market failure When the allocation of scarce resources achieved through markets is socially inefficient.

Maximum sustainable yield In relation to fisheries economics, this is the maximum catch that a fishery can sustain without depleting the stock.

Measure of resource scarcity The value of a unit of resource in the ground is measured as the difference between the resource price and the marginal cost of extraction. If the measure of scarcity is increasing, the resource is becoming scarcer in economic terms. Economic scarcity is distinct from geological scarcity.

Mitigation An investment to reduce the probability of damages due to carbon emissions

Moral hazard The hidden actions of a person or firm that allow them to capture benefits or reduce costs to the detriment of others.

Nash equilibrium In a gaming situation, a set of strategies, one for each player, where no player can improve his or her pay-off by switching to another strategy. In other words, this occurs when each player is playing the best response to all the other players' strategies.

Natural forest This is difficult to define, because most forests have been modified to some extent. It can be taken to refer to a forest largely made up of the endemic native species found in a region. In many cases, these forests have been modified by human intervention.

Net present value The sum of discounted benefits associated with a particular project minus the sum of discounted costs.

Non point pollution Emissions that enter water-bodies in a diffuse manner, such as through run-off from agriculture or forestry.

Non-renewable resource Any resource—for instance oil, gold and iron ore—that has a fixed stock. This contrasts with a renewable resource (such as a fishery) that grows through time by reproduction and growth.

Non-timber forest products (NTFP) This includes products taken from forest areas, such as bushmeat, nuts, berries, and rubber, that depend upon a standing forest.

Non-uniformly mixed pollutants Pollutants whose impact on water quality varies spatially.

Opportunity approach to sustainable development This requires that future generations have at least as much capital as the current generation, so that they have the opportunity to achieve the same levels of well-being as the current generation.

Opportunity cost The best alternative use forgone.

Option price The willingness to pay (WTP) to reduce the probability of a bad outcome.

Outcome approach to sustainable development This requires that utility or consumption do not decline over time.

Pigovian/green tax A price set equal to the marginal damages caused by pollution.

Plantation forest Typically, a monoculture of trees planted either for timber or for other forms of production. It is distinct from a natural forest, as it is often comprised of a non-native species, whereas natural forests are communities of species that are native or endemic to a region.

Point source pollution Emissions that enter water-bodies from a single identifiable source, such as a pipe.

Point–non-point trading An emissions trading system in which point sources of pollution and non-point sources of pollution trade emissions permits with each other.

Pollution havens hypothesis This predicts that pollution-intensive industries will relocate to developing countries as environmental regulation in developed countries is made more stringent.

Porter hypothesis A claim that environmental regulation stimulates innovation and productivity.

Preference heterogeneity The idea that people's preferences vary and thus that individuals place different values on a given good.

Preference reversal When a person is inconsistent in his or her preference rankings and the monetary evaluation of lotteries; for example, you rank lottery A higher than lottery B, but you put a higher dollar value on B than on A.

Production-function approaches Valuing non-market changes in environmental quality by estimating the implications of such changes for the output and price of a market-valued good or service.

Production possibility frontier (PPF) This gives the combinations of goods that it is possible to produce in an economy given the resources (land, labour, and capital) of that country. For instance, if there are only two goods produced—food and cloth—then the PPF tells us how much food can be produced if an amount of cloth is produced. The slope of the PPF gives us the opportunity cost of producing one more unit of a good.

Property rights The ownership of resources, and the obligations and responsibilities that go along with ownership.

Public goods Goods defined by non-rival consumption and non-excludability to access the resource.

Race-to-the-bottom hypothesis The idea that countries open to trade adopt looser environmental standards as a means of maintaining international competitiveness.

Rational choice When people make consistent choices that maximize their well-being given budget constraints.

Repeated game A situation in which a one-shot game is repeated. This may lead to a different solution to the one-shot game, especially as players gather information about the strategies of the other players.

Revealed-preference method Determining the value that individuals place on non-market environmental goods by studying their behaviour in markets for related goods; such methods include hedonic pricing and travel-cost models.

Risk The combination of probabilities and consequences of good and bad states of nature.

Risk assessment The quantitative estimation of risks to human and environmental health.

Risk perception A belief that people hold about risk and risky events.

Safe minimum standard (SMS) This identifies the minimum viable level for a natural resource, and only allows this safe minimum standard to be breached if the social opportunity cost of maintaining the standard is too high.

Safe operating space A series of threshold levels for important ecosystem processes that should not be crossed.

Self-insurance/adaptation An investment to change the severity of the realized outcomes of events.

Self-protection/mitigation An investment to change the probability of events.

Shadow project This requires any action that reduces the stock of natural capital to be offset by a physical project that replaces the natural capital loss.

Species–area curve A relationship between the area of land considered and the number of unique species found. As more land is considered in a region, then the number of extra species found tends to decline.

Stated-preference methods Direct questioning of people using surveys in order to determine their willingness to pay (WTP) or willingness to accept compensation (WTA) for a hypothetical change in environmental quality; such methods include contingent valuation and choice experiments.

Stern Review A report commissioned by the UK government to study the economics of climate change. The main conclusion was that the benefits (i.e. avoided damages) of extreme and immediate climate protection outweigh the costs.

Stock pollution The total level of accumulated carbon in the atmosphere.

Strong sustainability This requires a non-declining stock of natural capital and so assumes that natural capital cannot be directly substituted for by human, social, or produced capital.

Sustainable development Economic development that allows the current generation to meet its needs without compromising the ability of future generations also to its own needs.

Total economic value The sum of direct benefits (use + existence values) and indirect benefits.

Tradable pollution permit A market created to buy and sell the rights to emit a unit of pollution into the environment (also called marketable permits or cap-and-trade).

Trade liberalization A process by which a group of countries reduce or eliminate import quotas and tariffs.

Tragedy of the commons In the extreme version, due to Garrett Hardin, a situation in which the overuse of a common-property resource leads to resource degradation and environmental collapse. The term is also used to describe a situation in which there is an incentive for an individual firm to overexploit a resource (e.g. a fishery), leading to a Nash equilibrium in which all firms overexploit the resource.

Uniformly mixed pollutants Pollutants that have the same impact on water quality regardless of where they originate.

Use value The utility that people derive from directly making use of a natural asset.

Value of statistical life The monetary value of reducing the risks of death.

Weak sustainability This requires a non-declining total capital stock and so assumes that all forms of capital (natural, human, social, and produced) are substitutes for each other.

Willingness to accept compensation (WTA) The minimum monetary compensation that an individual would be willing to accept to forgo something good, such as an improvement in environmental quality, or to put up with something bad, such as a decrease in environmental quality.

Willingness to pay (WTP) The maximum income that an individual would be willing to give up to gain something good, such as an improvement in environmental quality, or to avoid something bad, such as a decrease in environmental quality.

Index